The Color PC

Marc D. Miller and Randy Zaucha

Hayden
Books

The Color PC

Library of Congress Catalog Number: 94-74218
ISBN: 1-56830-179-0

97 96 95   4   3   2   1

Interpretation of the printing code: the rightmost double-digit number is the year of the book's printing; the rightmost single-digit number is the number of the book's printing. For example, a printing code of 95-1 shows that the first printing of the book occurred in 1995.

Dedication

To Richard and Fiora Miller
(a.k.a. Dad and Mom)

Miss Kimberly Eckardt,
and to All Artisans of Color

Credits

Publisher
David Rogelberg

Managing Editor
Pat Gibbons

**Development
Editor**
Marta J. Partington

**Copy/Production
Editors**
Meshell Dinn
Brian Gill

**Publishing
Coordinator**
Stacy Kaplan

Designer
Fred Bower

Illustrator
Jeff Yesh

Production
Brad Chinn, Dan Caparo,
Kim Cofer, Dave Garratt,
Erika Millen, Beth Rago,
Karen Walsh, Robert Wolf

Indexer
Brad Herriman

To Our Readers

Dear Friend,

Thank you on behalf of everyone at Hayden Books for choosing *The Color PC* to enable you to learn about the exciting world of color on PCs. We think you'll enjoy the examples in this book, while getting a true understanding of the conceptual nature of color.

What you think of this book is important to our ability to better serve you in the future. If you have any comments, no matter how great or small, we'd appreciate your taking the time to send us email or a note by snail mail. Of course, we'd love to hear your book ideas.

Sincerely yours,

David Rogelberg
Publisher, Hayden Books and Adobe Press

You can reach Hayden Books at the following:

Hayden Books
201 West 103rd Street
Indianapolis, IN 46290
(800) 428-5331 voice
(800) 448-3804 fax

Email addresses:

America Online: Hayden Bks
AppleLink: hayden.books
CompuServe: 76350,3014
Internet: hayden@hayden.com

VI

Foreword

As one involved with training graphic arts professionals, I have seen intimidation and frustration on the faces of those persons seeking to understand the new tools and technology surrounding them. Yet there are few sights more rewarding than the change in people's countenances and the subsequent "ah haaaa!" when they grasp a concept that was once foreign to them.

Color reproduction is similar to mathematics because if you put the word theory after either of these words you immediately get a sour or frightened look from the person to whom you are talking. Try it. Say "mathematical theory." What comes to mind? Long equations with symbols that look like they were made from a bowl of noodles. Then try "color theory." Same complex equations with references to neutral gray compensation or limited gamut. Yuk! I can understand why people would roll their eyes and think that color theory is beyond them and best left to technicians locked away in color laboratories. Vendors offering simple solutions will often characterize color reproduction—like higher math—as too complex for the average person.

Truth is, not everyone needs to work with complex math to use a calculator, but everyone who uses a calculator better know the basic building blocks of addition, subtraction, multiplication, and division. The calculator does not understand what you want to add or subtract, but it can perform the function very fast for you. It is the same with color reproduction. If you simply want to create an image, you don't need to know the wave lengths of the colors or complex equations. But to create the colors you want, it helps to know a little about the basic building blocks of color reproduction.

The ability to perform digital color imagery is more than plugging software into your computer and pushing buttons. It involves understanding the theory behind color, how images are properly captured (or scanned), the capabilities and limitations of the processes utilized, and the final output of images. For many years these operations have been performed manually by highly-skilled craftspeople. Now the tools for performing these operations are readily accessible on the desktops of many. But the common mistake comes from believing that just because one purchases the mechanic's tools, one instantly becomes a master mechanic. Ownership of tools and technology does not make a person a master of the craft.

Few practitioners understand this better than the authors Marc and Randy. Both are craftsmen who have many years of experience in the traditional aspects of reproducing color. And, by the school of hard knocks and the fire of the production arena, they have mastered the world of digital color. We at the Graphic Arts Institute have been fortunate to have both authors teach courses at our training facility. Their practical articulation of complex and difficult concepts in the training laboratories is mirrored in the chapters of this book. I have observed them teach the beginner as well as the journeyperson in this new electronic arena, and they have received many well deserved "ah ha's" from both camps.

This book covers every important area of managing color on your computer. If you apply the principals and techniques presented, you will develop the skills necessary to maximize the capabilities of your computer system. Your careful attention to the information in this book will make the difference between "push button color" and the creation of high-quality, crafted color reproductions.

We at GAI, like most educators, emphasize the basics of the trade or craft being taught. "Learn the fundamentals!," they say. Similarly, the best approach to working with color is to bone up on the basics, rather than becoming overwhelmed by programs or the production process. By learning the basics, you can establish a foundation from which all color reproduction flows, regardless of which tool you use or the method of output that you choose. After establishing some core concepts, moving into more complicated areas won't be as difficult.

After you read even a few pages, I'm sure that you'll discover your control over digital color has increased. Although there is only *One* who is omnipresent, even I can foresee and hear the "ah haaas!" from those reading and putting into practice the information found in this book.

Stephen Whaley, Director

Graphic Arts Institute

San Francisco, CA

About the Authors

Marc D. Miller

Marc D. Miller is a digital imaging artisan. He has been in the art, printing, and prepress world for more than 15 years in what he likes to call the "imaging profession." He lectures frequently on the changing traditions of print production, color theory, and image manipulation. He emphasizes the importance of developing the instinct of craft, especially in the constantly changing world of digital imaging.

Working as a consultant for printing and prepress companies, Marc bridges the gap between digital imaging and traditional printing technology. His skills and background in photography, graphic design, and photo retouching add dimension and depth to the issues of professional printing and color reproduction. Marc concentrates on developing methods of fine art reproduction, mixing modern digital tools with traditional manual techniques. He currently works with the Arellanes Company, a traditional fine art serigraph printer, and is also a contributing writer for *International Designers Network (IDN) Magazine* based in Hong Kong.

Marc earned a degree in Commerce & Engineering from Drexel University in Philadelphia, where he concentrated on computer technology and mechanical engineering. Marc is based in San Francisco, consults abroad and is considered one of the finest retouching cooks around—when not producing digital color for his company, Creative Endeavours.

Randy Zaucha

Randy Zaucha's eight years of graphic arts schooling started in high school and continued through undergraduate school at Illinois State University and graduate school at Rochester Institute of Technology. Since college, he has accumulated 18 years in the printing trade in various positions. Randy is a journeyman color scanner operator with both time "on the bench" and positions as a color scanner trainer, demonstrator, and troubleshooter for two major scanner/pagination system manufacturers. He has more than five years of pagination and image retouching experience.

Randy also wrote and published *The Scanner Book for Color Imaging*, describing how to color-separate various types of original copy brought in for reproduction. Currently, Randy works as a freelance color consultant and gives seminars and classes on color in the field and at The Graphic Arts Institute of Northern California.

The authors can be reached at the following addresses:

Marc D. Miller
c/o Graphic Arts Institute
665 3rd Street
San Francisco, CA 94107

crtvendvrs@aol.com

Randy Zaucha
c/o Blue Monday Publishing
Box 295
2440 16th Street
San Francisco, CA 94103

randyzee@aol.com

X

Table of Contents

Acknowledgments

During the course of writing this book, we discovered that apart from its computer graphics definition, the word pixelated means "somewhat strange and mischievous or mentally unbalanced." An interesting discovery, since we spend much of our time swimming in the wonderful world of color and pixels where the term means something quite different. But many times during the course of this journey we have encountered the nongraphics definition of pixelated. Our trip was by no means undertaken alone, in fact, during our travel, we encountered many crafts people with whom we shared our mission. To those persons who helped us through those pixelated moments, we thank you. Although this is not intentional we probably may miss mentioning someone. We would like to mention specifically the following persons for aiding in our endeavour.

For their generosity, we thank all of our friends and family, including: Michael Carling; Noel Stiers; Meta Whaley; George Putkey; Edgar Guttzeit; Jill Kelly of Regalia in New Orleans, Rick Belemy of Color Services, Seattle; Tom Slick Donohue; Mo Edago, Biele Emmenberger, Diehla Henss; Ryan Miller; Ida Maddesi for all the great pasta; Scot "Scooter" Miller; Joseph "J.R." Rance, Jr.; Penny Chase of Agfa Corporation; Rebecca Field; Merril Sheilds of Octagon Graphics in San Francisco; Susan and Fred Morgan of FSI; Charly Frech; Angi Ebert; Tina Schleicher; Andrew Hathaway; Ben Barbante; Jeremy Sutton; John Ritter; Kent Manske; Hagit Cohen; Sue Culig; Corinne Okada; Jerry Bono; Leah Brouwers; Norm Leebron; Bruce Bradbury; Mark Governa; Tina Keithas; Dave Toponce; Ivor Chazan; Roger Stephenson of DuPont; Jeff Reinking; Marcus Martialé of Pixelated Productions; Ahmet Sibdialsau; Laurence Ng and Adeline Lee of *IdN Magazine*; Robert Santucci of Romar Productions; Clarence Lacy; Herb Warner and Mr. Bill Fuller; Jason Strahm, for helping with our scans; Everyone at the Digital Pond, Chris, John, Peter, Suzanne, Regan, Brett; Armando Diaz, Ron Suen and Jim Hildreth of South Park Digital; Tony Stanton at GATF; Bill Moore and Kelly Beck of Kodak; Colin Treacy of Fuji Film USA; Kevin R. McDonald of Xaos Tools; Perry Kivolowitz of Elastic Reality; Charles Cunningham of PrePress Assembly for the use of your toys; Special thanks to Lory Arellanes, Maria Schulz, and John Silletto at the Arellanes Company for the Tech reviews; and many others......

A special "thank you" goes out to Ana Guerrero, and Ned and Emily at Twisted Whisker Productions for all their support, generosity and assistance.

We would also like to extend a very special thanks to the staff and crew of the Graphic Arts Institute in San Francisco, and especially to its director Steve Whaley. Without his encouragement, faith, skill, and generosity we would not have produced this book. A simple acknowledgment is far from adequate, except to add our heartfelt thanks and appreciation.

Additionally we'd like to add a specific thanks to Marta Partington and Meshell Dinn of Hayden Books for their superior efforts in guiding us through the creation of this book. Thank you for your help.

Marc D. Miller & Randy Zaucha

San Francisco, CA

November, 1994

Photographic Credits

All images are the copyright by the photographer

XVI

Introduction

If you want to hit the mark you need to aim a
little above the target; [because] every arrow
that flies feels the pull of earth.

—Henry David Thoreau

We wrote this book with the hope that more people would realize how accessible color is to them. Ever since the digital tools hit the scene, people have been blasted with the idea that color reproduction theories are too hard to learn, and they should simply let the software take care of everything for them. Many people have felt it necessary to foster the idea that color reproduction is so complicated that it's beyond their reach.
This book attempts to dispel that perception.

With this book, we are offering a small glimpse into the world of color reproduction. We are fond of quoting the German sculptor Mo Edago who says, "Everyone is able. But not everyone is capable. Capability comes from exercise." To learn the intricacies of color reproduction you must exercise. And that exercise will strengthen your ability to work and play with color. The immediate rewards may not be readily apparent, but elevating one's self to a level where work becomes play may be reward enough.

We have tried to make the material as accessible and straightforward as possible. Remember—you don't get better at something by knowing less about it and we think you should know the following:

■ **Color theory is not beyond your grasp.**

Knowing the basics of color is the first step in controlling color reproduction. Make no mistake—learning color theory takes time to master, but it provides a more comprehensive approach when added to automatic features.

■ **Knowing the basics provides insight into all areas of digital imaging.**

Digital imaging for all its wonder and innovation still relies on the basic principals of pixels—tone and color. Sure, there are new ways to analyze and manipulate it, but the essence of color stays the same, regardless of the tools you use to create images. We believe the consistency of color is an excellent place to build a solid base of knowledge.

■ **Automation can limit your understanding of how to control color**

The best programs are those that allow you to turn off features and replace automated values with your own input. The capability to switch to manual override is a true measure of a program's power and usefulness. Remember, on *Star Trek* Scotty or LaForge always switches to manual override when the computer doesn't offer the proper solutions.

■ **The tools you use are not nearly as important as what you do with those tools.**

The future of digital imaging is not learning and relearning individual software programs, but understanding the basis of the systems that you work with. Often lost in the onslaught of technical marvels are many proven methods of image reproduction that many traditional artisans bring to the digital medium. The software tools are truly only as powerful as the experience and knowledge of the person using the software.

It is important to point out that our material by no means exhausts the discussion on image reproduction. If you use color to communicate, the more you know about color, the more you can say. We sincerely hope you enjoy your exploration and benefit during the process.

Marc Miller

Randy Zaucha

November 1994

Bibliography and Recommended Reading

The Enjoyment and Use of Color, by Walter Sargent, Dover Publications 1964, New York, NY 486-20944-X.

The Reproduction of Colour in Photography, Printing and Television.
4th ed., by H.W.G. Hunt, Fountain Press 1987, Tolworth, England, 0-88343-088-0

The Camera, the Negative and the Print, by Ansel Adams, Little, Brown & Company 1981, Boston, MA

The Permanence and Care of Color Photographs, by Henry Wilhelm, Preservation Publishing Company 1993, Grinnell, IW, 0-911515-00-3

Color Separation Techniques, by Miles F. Southworth, Graphic Arts Publishing, 2nd ed. 1981, Livonia, NY, 0-933600-00-3

Color Scanning and Imaging Systems, by Gary G. Field, Graphic Arts Technical Foundation 1990, Pittsburgh, PA, 0-88362-120-7

How to Check and Correct Color Proofs, by David Bann and John Gargan, Northern Lights Books 1990, Cincinnati, OH 0-89134-350-4

Encyclopedia of Graphics File Formats, by Murray and VanRyper, O'Reilly & Associates, Inc. 1994, Sebastopol, CA. 1-56592-058-9

The Scanner Book for Color Imaging, by Randy Zaucha, Blue Monday Publishing Company 1991, San Francisco, CA, 0-96332258-0-X

Part

I

The Basics

What Are Pixels?

"By convention there is color,
but in reality there are only
atoms and space."

Democritus,
Greek Philosopher, 460 B.C.

The question "What are pixels?" can elicit many kinds of answers. Pixels have been part of how we create images for longer than many people realize. The very word "pixel" conjures an understanding of something familiar, yet elusive. The glossary description of a pixel says that a pixel is a discrete unit or element of an entire image system. Discrete implies a unit or an element that cannot be fractionalized or broken down into smaller elements. But what does that mean and how does it apply to modern digital images? As enigmatic as a pixel may be, understanding a pixel's function is critical to your adventures with digital images.

The word *pixel* comes from the combination of two words: *picture* and *element* (not from the Latin derivative picasaurus). The first two letters of each word separated by an *x* has provided a word that has become a cornerstone of digital imagery. The *x* in the middle is actually helpful in understanding the concept of picture elements. Because pixels are located on a grid, x and y coordinates describe the location of any picture element. In other words, both an *x* and a pixel can mark a specific spot. (You sometimes hear people working in the field of video use the word "pel" rather than pixel, but "pixel" is supplanting this term.)

Every type of drawing, painting, photograph, or image uses some variation of picture elements (pixels). One of the more obvious examples is the wonderful art created using the mosaic technique and style as illustrated in Figure 1.1. If you have seen a mosaic, you may have noticed that the image is composed of tiles arranged in intricate patterns

Figure 1.1
A traditional mosaic style of art is an
obvious example of images using discrete
picture elements.

location, and color value. Regardless of how simple or complex the image system is, if you apply these criteria, you will find the rules work. Before you apply the criteria of pixels to digital images, try some simple and familiar image systems such as needlepoint (see Figure 1.2). Does needlepoint involve discrete individual units that you cannot divide? Yes, within a cloth grid each stitch is a separate element. The size of the stitches may vary, but within the cloth grid each stitch is a separate element. Each stitch occupies a hole on that cloth grid where the location of each stitch can be determined. So the second criteria is filled. The value of each stitch, even if you use only black, is the various colored threads. These three criteria work well for needlepoint, a fairly uniform and simple system. You also will find a certain uniformity with complex digital image systems. But do the three guidelines hold for something that is a complex, but not uniform, system such as photographic film?

depicting a variety of people, places, and things. What are the characteristics of a mosaic? The tiles or elements—though varied in style, size and shape—are unique individual units. Each tile or element also occupies a specific location relative to other tiles or elements and can be located using x and y coordinates. Each tile also has a color value and/or tone.

Unlike real estate, which thrives on location, location, location, a pixel or picture element is dependent on discrete individual units,

Figure 1.2
The uniform grid in needlepoint provides a
place for picture elements.

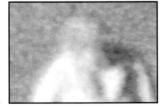

a

b

c

d

e

f

g

Figure 1.3
Even photographs
(which are
considered to be
continuous tone
images) use
pixels to create
imagery. Figures
1.3a–g show how
granular crystals
in a 35 mm
photographic
image become
visible as you
magnify the
image.

The image system of photography uses light-sensitive grains or crystals to create an image, so there *are* individual units, as you can see in Figure 1.3. The crystals are not necessarily positioned uniformly on the film nor are they uniform in size, but each crystal or grain does have its own location relative to other grains. And whether you use color or black-and-white film, each grain or crystal has a particular value. So we find that—perhaps without even realizing it—something as common as taking a picture, which presumably we all have done, uses the concept of picture elements or pixels.

Digital Pixels

When you begin to recognize the components of an image system and how to assemble images, you are in a unique position of understanding ways to manipulate these images. Your ability to create and control an image is directly proportional to understanding the system that you use to produce those images. Exploring and experimenting can expose unique aspects of an image system. But unless you discover the basic parts that make up the image system, the hit or miss exercises are as pointless as sailing the high seas without a compass or sextant. When you understand the basics, you are placed firmly in command of creating images in any manner that you want. Pixels are at the core of image manipulation regardless of whether that image system is needlepoint, painting, photography, digital imagery, or a combination of systems. No matter what system you use, understanding the relationship of picture elements to their makeup gives you greater power to create with those systems and to understand how systems interrelate on a very basic level. How do pixels relate to working with digital images? Let us explore the digital image system.

Discrete Unit

You can apply the pixel guidelines of discrete unit, location, and value to computer-based images. In digital images a picture element is indeed discrete. A pixel cannot be divided into half, quarter, or partial pixels. An individual pixel can be described by its aspect ratio. The aspect ratio of a pixel is the proportion of the horizontal edge divided by the vertical edge. The aspect ratios of all pixels used in a specific digital system are the same. You will not find a digital system that mixes pixels with different aspect ratios. Most computer systems work exclusively with square pixels, as shown in Figure 1.4. A square pixel has an aspect ratio of one.

Other computer systems, which include video, work with pixels that have other aspect ratios and, in some obscure cases, use three-sided (triangular) pixels. If you exchange images between systems that do not have the same pixel aspect ratios, you need to compensate for the difference or the image appears distorted. The most common way is to stretch an image or image's aspect ratio to match the aspect ratio of the system on which you are working. An

image's aspect ratio is the proportion of the number of horizontal pixels divided by the number of vertical pixels, as shown in Figure 1.5. The image aspect ratio is not necessarily the same as the pixel aspect ratio.

For example, if you import an image from a system that uses a pixel aspect ratio of two to one (2:1) into the square pixel environment, you will need to stretch the image's aspect ratio 200 percent horizontally to retain the proper proportions of the image. Later in this chapter we cover in greater detail how to work with pixels that have different aspect ratios.

The mathematical implications of square pixels are simple. Square pixels provide a perfect symmetry that is instinctively easy to grasp.

1300 pixels horizontal

900 pixels vertical

Figure 1.5
Image aspect ratio is the total number of horizontal pixels vs. the total number of vertical pixels.

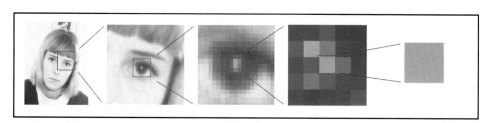

Figure 1.4
The aspect ratio of a pixel is the relationship of the width and the height.

Because each side of the pixel is equal, the nonmathematician can begin to comprehend the computations that produce the seemingly fantastic effects of digital computer graphics. Square pixels work like a jigsaw puzzle in which all the pieces fit easily with little worry about how the sides of the pieces relate. All the inner pixels are touched on four sides by another pixel. Pixels on the outer border of an image are touched on three sides, and the corner pixels are touched on two sides.

Different Types of Pixels

As mentioned earlier, some digital systems do not use square pixels. The most notable of these systems are Amigas and PCs that use Truevision video boards, and Vista color video boards that produce broadcast NTSC and PAL video. Amiga systems use pixels with aspect ratios of 1.45:1. The pixel aspect ratio for TARGA files created from the PC is 1:0.97. When you import an image file from these systems into a square pixel environment, you need to compensate for these differently proportioned pixels. These pixels are not inferior in quality to square pixels; they often are used in the video profession. The difference is corrected easily and is not a serious problem.

You may first notice that the images you bring in from these systems appear out of proportion—usually squeezed horizontally. You see this most noticeably if the image contains circular objects. A person's face or a round ball appears tall and stretched in the vertical direction. Because you have substituted differently proportioned picture elements, the distortion makes perfect sense. Because you cannot change the proportions or aspect ratio of pixels (nor would you want to), the only logical step is to stretch the image horizontally to counter the vertical distortion. This can be achieved by scaling the image in only the horizontal direction until the proportions of the image appear as they did on the system on which they were created. You can modify an image visually until you achieve the look you want. Drawing perfect circles in the image before you transfer the file to a square pixel environment is a good visual method of determining how much to stretch an image.

A more exact and direct method of stretching is taking the aspect ratio of the pixel that you are importing and increasing the image horizontally by that amount. For example, if you imported an image from an Amiga system, you would stretch or upsample the image by approximately 125 percent in the horizontal direction. Of course, if you prefer you also can downsample the image in the vertical direction to meet the required image aspect ratio. In the case of the Amiga systems, you downsample vertically 80 percent. Both methods achieve the same result in appearance, but whenever you downsample an image, you discard information that you may want to retain. Figure 1.6 illustrates the need to compensate for pixels of different aspects ratios other than 1:1.

a

b

Figure 1.6
A digital image using a pixel aspect ratio other than 1:1 (Figure a) must be stretched to be displayed properly on a system based on square pixels (Figure b).

Location

The location of a pixel is based on a centuries-old system developed by the mathematician and philosopher René Descartes. This system is known as the *Cartesian coordinate system*. Those of you who gave any thought to the usefulness of math in those tiresome high school geometry classes now have a vindicated, smiling geometry teacher. Graphics, by its very nature, is a two-dimensional system, and Cartesian coordinates aptly describe any graphic you encounter. Although some of today's computer graphics are highly complex and intricate, digital image origins are simple and basic. You don't need to become a mathematician to grasp the concepts of digital graphics because you already use the core concepts every day. The Cartesian system, as shown in Figure 1.7, consists of two axes: x

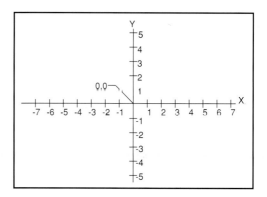

Figure 1.7
The Cartesian system is the most common coordinate system.

on the horizontal plane crossing perpendicular to y on the vertical plane. Even 3D images that display as two-dimensional use a coordinate system by adding an additional direction labeled z to indicate depth. But eventually even those 3D images are displayed on 2D systems such as monitors and print.

Each axis has a zero point. The zero point can be placed anywhere, but is most useful when placed where the x and y axes intersect. Every pixel can be identified individually using Cartesian coordinates. Figure 1.8 shows the location on a grid or map of a certain pixel with the x,y coordinates 440,98. The default origin point (x,y 0,0) for most images is the upper left-hand corner of the image.

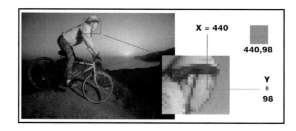

Figure 1.8
Each individual pixel has a location provided by its coordinates on the Cartesian coordinate system.

Each pixel has a unique location, and only one pixel can occupy a single set of coordinates on each grid or map of pixels. Most current software provides you with x and y coordinate information to determine the location of individual pixels.

Digital pixels exist on a grid or map commonly referred to as a *bitmap*. Often digital images that contain pixels are referred to as *bitmap images*. When retouching or altering a digital image, you may think you are actually moving pixels. But on each unique bitmap you can only reassign or modify the value of a pixel—not its location.

Changing the value of a pixel or a group of pixels to match another pixel group sometimes gives the appearance of moving those pixels. The perceived movement is very much like department store lights that seem to move— when in fact, the lights simply blink on and off, never leaving their fixed locations.

Bitmap images also are referred to as *raster* images. Raster lines are rows of pixels (see Figure 1.9). Video professionals commonly refer to digital images as raster images because video organizes images as rows of horizontal pixels and displays the image line by line.

Value/Color Resolution

Digital pixels do have a value. In fact the number of potential color choices, or the amount of potential choices per pixel, is called the *color resolution* or *color bit depth* of a pixel.

All modern digital computing is based on the *binary system*. The binary system is based on the number two. A base two system provides two choices of one or zero to indicate value. The simplest pixel has two choices: on or off; black or white; yes or no (see Figure 1.10a). A pixel with a total number of two choices is a one-bit image, or two raised to the power of one (2-1). Adding more bit (on, off) choices increases the number of potential combinations. See the chart to understand how the bit choices can be used to determine the total number of color choices (see Figure 1.10b).

The most common and established pixel value system is the 24-bit color system. Two raised to the power of 24 results in a possible total of 16.7 million color choices. In the future when discussing color reproduction, the importance of color resolution will play a critical role. For now it is enough to understand how the term color resolution or bit depth is used to describe

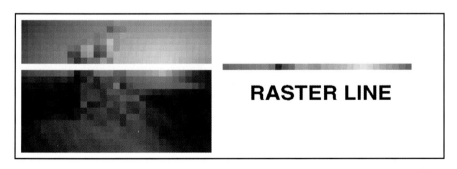

Figure 1.9
One complete horizontal line of pixels is called a raster line.

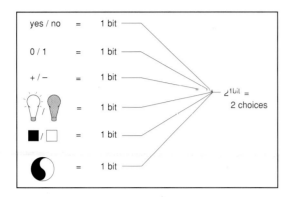

Figure 1.10a
The binary system—the basis for all modern computing—offers two choices: on or off.

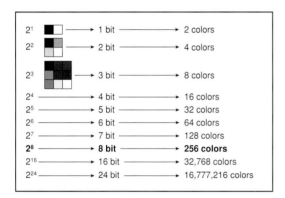

Figure 1.10b
The total number of possible colors increases exponentially as the number of bits in a color system increases.

how many potential color choices you may have in a particular picture element. (Chapter 2, "Tone and Color," will discuss color and color resolution in more detail.)

Concepts of Image Resolution

If there were a bell we could ring to get your attention, we would ring that bell the loudest and longest here. Resolution is *critical* to your understanding and work with digital images.

Understanding resolution and its relationship to digital images—and to all imagery for that matter—is central to working with and manipulating those images. You must know these concepts.

- First, the concepts are not—repeat, *not*— that complicated.

- Second, once you learn resolution concepts they will not change. That's right. Resolution may be applied differently, but the core concepts will not be updated in new revisions of some software.

- Third, *learn* it. You *do* need it, and you *will* use it.

Pixel Distribution

Now that you know what a pixel is, you need to understand how pixels are used to describe images. As mentioned earlier, pixels exist on a grid or bitmap and are components and elements of an image. The quantity or number of picture elements—better known as resolution—is critical to the detail and quality of an image. The resolution of an image equals the number of pixels per unit of measure, as illustrated in Figure 1.11. Remember that within image systems, resolution is universal. Every image system requires a certain number of picture elements spread out over a certain distance to describe an image. Resolution is a way of describing images, which are made of pixels. Without resolution, a digital image occupies no physical space.

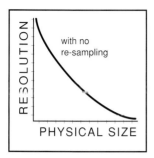

Figure 1.11
Without resolution, pixels occupy no physical space. As resolution approaches zero, the physical distance of pixels approaches infinity. As resolution approaches infinity, the physical size approaches zero.

Bitmap images are considered resolution-dependent because there is a finite number of picture elements in each individual image. How continuous an image appears depends on the number of pixels and the resolution of the image. A continuous image is one in which you cannot see the individual pixels of the system that were used to create the image. If your resolution is less than required, you will begin to notice individual pixels in the form of jagged edges, called *jaggies*. In any type of output, having visible individual picture elements is called *pixelization* (see Figure 1.12).

Resolution is the cornerstone of digital image reproduction and one of the most elusive concepts in digital imaging. When you ask someone to describe resolution and why resolution is important, you get a wide variety of answers. The reason for this variety is simple: resolution has different meanings at different stages of an image's life. Compounding the confusion is the use of problematic terminology. Regardless of the particulars, every image system uses resolution concepts.

Figure 1.12
Pixelization is when pixels are visible.

Resolution, simply stated, is an amount of something. For example, resolution can be the number of stitches in fabric, the number of grains in film, the number of colors from which to choose, the number of brush strokes, the number of bricks in a wall, or the number of pixels in a digital image, as shown in Figures 1.13a-c.

Resolution is the amount of that particular something distributed over a certain physical distance, such as the number of stitches per centimeter in a needlepoint, the number of grains per micro meter in film, and the number of brush strokes per foot.

Resolution is the amount of picture elements per constant unit of measure in an imaging system. That is the basis of resolution. We also

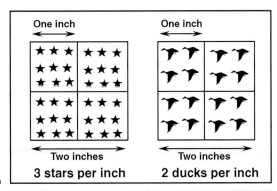

a

b

c

Figure 1.13
Resolution is the amount of something over
a specified distance such as (a)a star and
ducks per inch, (b)hands per yard, or
(c)bricks per meter.

should reinforce that we are speaking in two dimensions: horizontal and vertical, x and y. (See the following chart.)

$$\frac{\text{\# of pixels}}{\text{unit of measure}^2}$$

No matter which imaging system you use, you can describe how parts of that system are distributed to create an image. Therefore, resolution is the common element in all imaging systems that allows you to translate images from one imaging system to another.

You will notice that we use the term "image systems" when talking about pictures or images. There are many different methods or systems that you can use to create images of any kind. Resolution plays a key part in all image systems.

The following section discusses how to apply the concepts of resolution to a number of different imaging systems and how to easily translate these concepts from one system to another. The major areas that we discuss are pixels, image resolution, and output resolution.

Image Resolution

Every digital image has a certain number of pixels. How the pixels spread out over a specific distance is better known as its *resolution*. Resolution is critical to the visual quality of an image. Pixels per inch or pixels per millimeter are the most common terms. Pixel-based images are considered resolution dependent because the continuous appearance of tones and color *depends* on the resolution of an image. A continuous tone image is one in which you cannot see the individual picture elements that make up the image. We assume that the goal in most cases is to produce a continuous tone image. All reproductions of natural phenomenon are continuous to a point.

Nothing we reproduce is completely continuous. An image appears continuous because you cannot see the individual picture elements. An image in a magazine viewed at a distance of 12 inches or more seems to be without visible flaws and very continuous. Upon closer inspection you begin to see the small halftone dots that created the image and the image loses its wholly continuous appearance. Distance is a factor in determining whether an image appears to be continuous or not. Even photographs, which we all accept as continuous tone, lose their continuous feeling when seen under a magnifying glass. In a practical sense, few people view their photos under a magnifying glass, so the images retain their continuous tone feeling. This is important to understand because where and how you use your images can influence how continuous they will appear to the viewer. A perfect example of this is a roadside billboard, which is viewed at a great distance. Because of the distance, it is not necessary to have images that look perfectly continuous at a distance of one yard. (You would not gain anything by creating an image for a billboard that looked continuous at one yard.) The general rule of thumb is that if you double the viewing distance you can halve the resolution of an image and still have it appear continuous. For example, a 150 dot per inch image will appear continuous when viewed at one yard. The same image at 75 DPI viewed at two yards should appear just as continuous as the first image. Different images react differently to this effect, and the distances may vary but the concept is sound. Look at the following figures to demonstrate how the viewing distance of an image makes the image appear continuous (see Figures 1.14a-d).

High resolution in an image usually means the image will appear more continuous. However, it also depends on the distance viewed and the image size, as mentioned previously.

The examples of needlepoint and photographic film can illustrate the concept of resolution. On a needlepoint pattern that measures 10×10 inches, the resolution of the needlepoint would be equal to the number of stitches (pixels) per inch. If there were 20 stitches per inch, there would be a total of 200 stitches in each direction. The same applies to film grain. You often hear about very fine-grained film. Saying that the film is fine grained is no different than saying that the resolution of the film is high or that the number of grains (pixels) per millimeter is large. Fine-grained films are considered to be higher quality because the images appear sharper, better defined, and more continuous. If the resolution of an image is too low, the individual picture elements become visible. An enlarged photograph can appear grainy because the number of grains per inch is low. Unless you want the grain for visual effect, this graininess illustrates the concept of ineffective resolution. Effective resolution in both cases results in an image that appears to be one continuous tone and not groups of identifiable picture elements.

In fact, if you could travel to the atomic levels you would find that universal pixels are in all image systems. You could eventually break down even the finest resolution image into atoms. How continuous an image appears depends entirely on your frame of reference.

What is the required resolution of an image? That depends entirely on the method you choose to produce your image and the visual effect that you want. Don't forget that all images have some kind of resolution. Resolution is used to transport an image from one system to another. You need to determine how the resolution from one image system relates to another image system. Understanding each

Figure 1.14a
Viewing distance affects the continuous
tone appearance of an image. At an
arm's length away this image is
continuous.

Figure 1.14b
At one yard away this image looks
continuous.

Figure 1.14c
At ten feet away this image looks
continuous.

Figure 1.14d
At over twenty feet away this image
looks continuous.

imaging system's resolution requirements makes it easier to understand how to translate an image from one system to another.

Device Resolution

Because images are displayed with a variety of output systems, it is important to consider the output resolution that is available from each device. Each output device has a specific resolution that it can produce. Meeting the requirements of a device's resolution is critical to producing the highest quality image. The number of pixels you need in an image is directly proportional to the output you choose. The three most common output devices are monitors (video), halftone plotters (image-setters), and film or transparency recorders.

The higher the resolution of an image, the more continuous the image appears. Bitmap images commonly are referred to as *continuous tone images*, or CT images. When the resolution of the image matches the output device properly, you cannot see the picture elements that make up the image. The image appears as a continuous tone to the unaided eye. When pixelization occurs, you know that the number of pixels in your image does not meet the minimum number required for your output device. Images with a small number of pixels often are referred to as low-resolution or "lo-res" (pronounced like 'Pez' only with a hard "r") images. High-resolution or "high-res" images are images that contain a large number of pixels per unit of measure. Often the term high-resolution is equated with high quality. High-res does not

always mean high quality. Many other factors influence the quality of digital image reproduction (these factors are discussed in later chapters). Resolution is simply the cornerstone of all digital images.

There are two primary types of output for digital images: direct digital imaging where each pixel in an image file corresponds directly with an output imaging element; and halftone dot reproduction where a pixel or groups of pixels correspond to a dot used in printing.

In every case of reproduction, the picture elements of one system are transferred to the new system. How the resolutions of each image system relate to one another is called the sampling ratio. A certain number of pixels in one image system relates to a certain number of picture elements of another image system. With direct digital imaging, the sampling ratio is one pixel to one output dot (1:1). The most common sampling ratio of pixels to halftone dots is 2:1.

There are two major types of printing dots: fixed placement, but varied size halftone dot (*amplitude modulation*); and fixed size, but varied placement dot (*frequency modulation*), commonly called a *stochastic dot*. See Figure 1.15 for an example. Each type of output determines the required image resolution produced by that method.

You can take six simple steps to determine which kind of resolution you need for physical output. Let's discuss resolution of the two output device types.

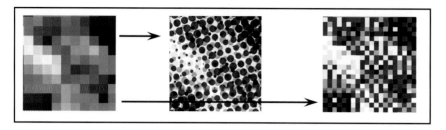

Figure 1.15
Digital image pixels relate to AM and FM printing dots.

What is EPI?

You'll notice that we use the term epi (elements per inch), rather than dpi (dots per inch), when describing the resolution of an output device. What is commonly called a 300 dpi printer really should be referred to as a 300 epi printer. The term dot has been overused when describing many types of resolution and should only be used when describing a halftone dot used for printing. Additionally, when you hear the word dot you immediately think of something round—and that is not always the case. Actually, addressability is a more precise term to use than resolution when describing output devices; but for our purposes (working with digital images), the terms are assumed to be synonymous. A typical continuous tone printer with 300 epi needs 300 pixels to produce one inch of a continuous tone image—a one-to-one relationship.

Direct Imaging

Direct imaging output is fairly straightforward. Each pixel in your image corresponds to an imaging element that places a spot of ink or light on whatever substrate on which you are working. Examples of direct imaging output are inkjet printing, transparency output, and monitor output. You may not think of your monitor as an output device, but it is exactly that. The relationship of direct output devices to a digital image is one-to-one, as illustrated in Figure 1.16. For every element per inch that can place a color spot, there needs to be a corresponding image pixel.

A monitor screen has a fixed resolution and in most cases is 72 to 80 elements per inch (epi). The very common 13-inch (diagonal measurement) color monitor has a screen resolution of 72 imaging elements per inch (epi), and a total number of display elements of 640 across and 480 down. An image that matches that number of pixels across and down displays as a continuous image without any noticeable pixels. If you simply want to view the highest quality image at the *full* size of the Apple monitor, your image need be only 72 pixels per inch. This number matches the

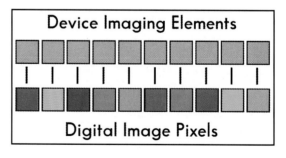

Figure 1.16
With direct pixels, imaging 10 image pixels will match with 10 imaging elements of the output device.

resolution of the monitor one to one (less than 72 ppi results in pixelization). More than 72 ppi will not improve the image because the additional pixels cannot be displayed.

When you display an image on your monitor at 100 percent or 1:1, each image pixel matches with a single display element on your monitor (see Figure 1.17a). At 200 percent or 2:1, every pixel is displayed by 2 squared imaging elements (see Figure 1.17b). At 50 percent or 1:2, every two pixels of your image matches one display element and so on (see Figure 1.17c).

Figure 1.17a
Viewing an image at 1:1.

Halftone Output

The most common reproduction of digital images is halftone dots. (Halftones are discussed in greater detail in Chapter 2, "Tone and Color," and Chapter 11, "Targeting Output".) There are two items to consider regarding image resolution when producing halftone output: the resolution of the plotter or imagesetter and the line screen the printer uses to print the image.

Each halftone dot is created by a group or a matrix of imaging elements also know as a *halftone cell* (see Figure 1.18). The imaging elements used in an imagesetter are similar to what you may find in a laser printer, except that there are more elements per inch and the elements are sharper and better defined. The quality or resolution of a halftone dot is directly related to the number of elements that the imagesetter can address to produce that dot. The more elements per inch, the more information available and, potentially, the more accurate the halftone dot. The more accurate the dot, the higher the quality of the reproduced image.

Figure 1.17b
Viewing an image at 2:1.

Figure 1.17c
Viewing an image 1:4.

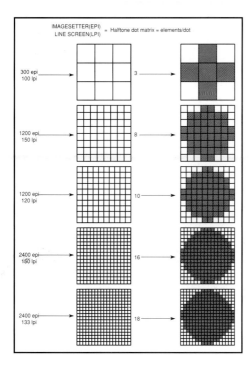

IMAGESETTER(EPI)
LINE SCREEN(LPI) = Halftone dot matrix = elements/dot

300 epi
100 lpi → 3 →

1200 epi
150 lpi → 8 →

1200 epi
120 lpi → 10 →

2400 epi
150 lpi → 16 →

2400 epi
133 lpi → 18 →

Figure 1.18
The halftone dot is created by a matrix of imaging elements called a halftone cell.

Creating a Halftone Dot

We should first discuss the term dpi. We prefer to use the term epi for output devices. The reasoning behind this is to eliminate any confusion with the elements that create halftone dots and the dots themselves. If you prefer, you can use the term dpi rather than epi.

Epi is the maximum number of individual binary spots of ink for ink jet printers, toner for laser printers, or laser light for imagesetters that an imaging device can place per inch. The spots are referred to as binary because they have only two states: on or off. The elements that create these spots are best illustrated as a grid. The grid we will use to illustrate the following information represents a 10×10 element grid. The 10 elements are spread out over 1 inch. So an

imaging device that is 10 epi means 10 linear spots can be placed per inch in the horizontal and vertical direction. Figure 1.19 shows a total of 100 elements available for on and off status.

A line screen ruling of halftone dots is sometimes mistakenly used as a way of describing digital pixel resolution. Because screen ruling actually relates to lines of halftone dots used in printing rather than digital images, you should address a line screen ruling as part of output. Too often the mixture of digital resolution and printing halftone resolution has caused confusion. For clarity's sake, digital image resolution always will be referred to as pixels per inch (ppi), and never as dots per inch (dpi). Dots per inch or lines per inch (lpi) describes the number of halftone dots or lines of halftone dots (line screen frequency) per inch. In a 133-line screen, each line contains 133 dots per inch. The terminology of dpi and lpi complements one another. The chart in Figure 1.20 describes each term.

Remember that every image system has some kind of picture element used to describe an image. Typically, high resolution produces a more continuous-looking image. When an image is moving from one image system to another, the resolution of each system is critical to achieving the highest quality image possible.

Halftone dots are the picture elements of printing. Photographic grains are the picture elements of photographs and transparencies. Screen or monitor elements are the pixels of video. When bringing an image into these systems, you must carefully consider the required resolution for each system. The special needs for each output are discussed later.

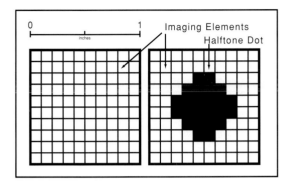

Figure 1.19
An imaginary grid helps describe how the imaging elements of an imagesetter create halftone dots.

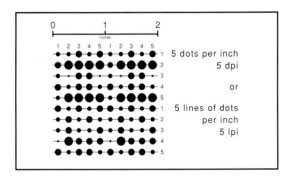

Figure 1.20
Either dpi or lpi can be used to accurately describe the number of halftone dots.

Sampling Ratio

As mentioned earlier, how the pixels of one system relate to another system is called the sampling ratio. The typical relationship of digital image pixels to halftone dots is 2:1 (see Figure 1.21). The figure shows that 2×2 pixels are used to describe one halftone dot. This is the optimum situation; using a lower amount may affect the quality of the image in some situations and using more information does not add a level of quality. Notice the details in the images shown in Figure 1.21. If you print at 150 dpi line screen, the image needs to be 300 ppi

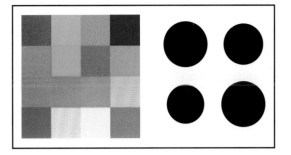

Figure 1.21
Two pixels (horizontal and vertical) relate to one halftone dot.

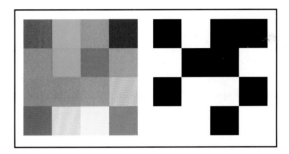

Figure 1.22
A 1:1 sampling ratio is used for frequency modulated dots, where every pixel relates to one FM dot.

(pixels per inch); a halftone line screen of 133 dpi requires a digital image of 266 ppi.

Stochastic dots or frequency modulated (FM) dots present a different solution in that the line screen (or dots per inch) is usually very high, but the sampling ratio between image pixels and dots is 1:1 (as shown in Figure 1.22) rather than a 2:1 sampling ratio for AM halftone dots. Attempts at printing stochastic screen dots run between a range of 300 to 600 dpi. The FM dot closely mimics the process of a direct digital device rather than the standard halftone dot. The image resolution needs to be equal to the line screen used. For a 200 dpi stochastic dot screen the image resolution needs to be 200 ppi. The increased detail in frequency modulated screens doesn't require increased amounts of image resolution. In fact, as you approach higher printing frequencies such as 600 dpi, you can use even less than 1:1 and go as low as 1:2 without losing detail. This depends entirely on the type of image and the amount of detail you wish to reproduce. Chapter 11 will go into more detail on how to prep your images.

Re-sampling and the Relationship to Output

It is important to stress that whenever possible you should input your image with exactly the number of pixels that you will need for proper output. But when faced with having an image of insufficient resolution for your particular output—creating new pixels (or discarding pixels) frequently can be the best solution to achieving a proper reproduction.

When the resolution of an image does not meet your established needs, you can change how the pixels are distributed; in other words, you can change the resolution. Without altering the number of pixels in your image, you can distribute them over a greater or lesser physical space. This method also will change the sampling ratio discussed earlier. Simply lowering the resolution—a quick and sometimes effective solution—will increase the size of the image but may produce jaggies that are unacceptable (depending on the details of the image). It is important to remember that size is relative to your resolution (see Figures 1.23a and 1.23b).

Another method you can use to get your desired amount of resolution is to change the number

Figure 1.23a
An image 450 pixels by 450 pixels with a resolution of 300 ppi reproduces at a physical size of 1.5 x 1.5 inches.

Figure 1.23b
The same image with a resolution of 150 pixels per inch reproduces at a physical size of 3 x 3 inches.

of pixels in an image, and correspondingly its resolution, by increasing or decreasing the total number of pixels. Scaling, sampling, re-sampling, upsampling, downsampling, and "resing"-up (or down) all are common terms used for increasing or decreasing the number of pixels in an image and, accordingly, its resolution to meet reproduction requirements.

When changing the resolution of an image by re-sampling, you either add or subtract pixels from the bitmap of an image, as shown in Figure 1.24.

Subtracting or scaling down an image is an easy process. You simply decide what your effective resolution should be and throw away the picture elements that you don't need. If you have matched the required resolution for your output device properly, you should have an image that appears continuous regardless of how many pixels you discard. You do not gain quality by using more pixels than required by your output method. Using more pixels than you need also contributes to increasing the size of the file.

Sampling up or down places stress on some images that may hinder the level of quality you want to achieve. There are two primary methods used in downsampling (discarding pixels) or upsampling (creating new pixels) a digital image: replication and interpolation.

Replication and Interpolation

If you have an image at the incorrect resolution for your desired output, your first option should always be rescanning the image. If scanning your image again is not an option, the next best solution is re-sampling. Whether you re-sample up to increase the total number of pixels, or down to decrease the number of pixels, there are two methods to achieve your desired resolution: replication and interpolation. The concept of re-sampling or creating new picture elements is often lumped under the moniker of interpolation. This labeling is misleading and incorrect.

Replication literally replicates or duplicates existing pixels when upsampling. If you have one red pixel, replication simply creates another red pixel group equal in value to the original. Although this duplication does increase the resolution of the image, it does not appreciably affect how continuous an image appears. In fact, when you replicate images, you may see the effects of pixelization (see Figure 1.25).

Fine detail reproduction may suffer when using replication, but replication is very useful when you are working with flat solid colors or images that do not contain critical tones like flesh tones and blends. Replicating pixels is also extremely quick to process. If your results do not require a high-quality, continuous tone,

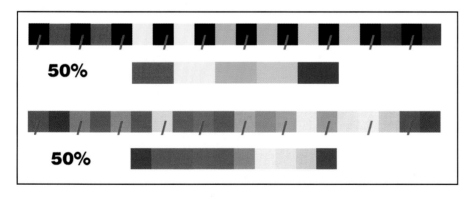

Figure 1.24
Downsampling an image by 50 percent discards every other pixel.

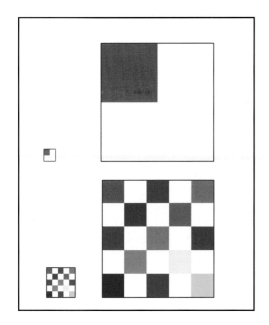

Figure 1.25
2 x 2 pixels and 5 x 5 pixels replicated
by 400 percent result in 8 x 8 pixels and
20 x 20 pixels.

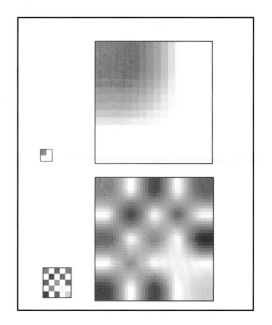

Figure 1.26a
Bilinear interpolation of 2 x 2 pixels
and 5 x 5 pixels by 400 percent results in
an averaged 8 x 8 pixels and 20 x 20
pixels.

replication can be an extremely useful way to meet the resolution requirements of your chosen output.

Interpolation is a more complicated method of creating new picture elements. Interpolation, rather than simply duplicating existing pixels, considers the individual pixel and also the surrounding pixels in determining values of new pixels. In a basic sense, interpolation averages existing pixels to create new pixels.

There are two types of interpolation: linear and bicubic. Linear and bicubic interpolation refer to the types of mathematical algorithms used to determine the value of the new pixels. *Linear* interpolation is faster to process, but *bicubic* is considered higher quality. In most cases, the gain in quality is much better than the sacrifice of processing speed (see Figures 1.26a and 1.26b).

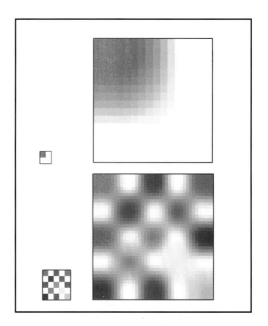

Figure 1.26b
Bicubic interpolation uses a slightly more
sophisticated process to average pixels
compared to bilinear interpolation.

Increasing resolution by interpolating picture elements typically yields a more continuous tone image than replicating. Two important issues are associated with interpolation: the processing time to interpolate pixels is much longer than with replication, and excessive interpolation results in an image that appears very soft and out of focus. Later, we discuss methods in image retouching that compensate for this softness, but there is no substitute for having your image at the proper resolution without interpolation or replication. You should recognize that digital scaling is not a complete panacea for correcting images that do not have the correct resolution. Interpolating pixels should be done sparingly and with special consideration as to the desired quality of image output.

If scaling is used properly, the results can be exceptional and extremely effective. There are guidelines you should consider when scaling a bitmap image by either replication or interpolation. In general, replication is most useful if you have straight vertical or horizontal lines. And as mentioned previously, it's more successful to replicate flat, single-colored areas. Diagonal lines, circles, or curves accentuate the jagged edges when replicated. Interpolation with its averaging process is most useful when you are scaling curves and diagonal lines because the averaging process tends to soften and smooth out the edges. Smoothing out edges too much is not always desirable and may create an out-of-focus look. When you are working with blends of color and tone, interpolation is a great benefit. Images with graduated color blends of tone and organic images, such as clouds, are perfect examples of the type of image that can be scaled as much as you like with interpolation. With no edges to consider, you get a

softening effect from interpolation that actually can add to the overall effectiveness of an image.

There are situations (as the physical output size of the image increases and/or the device resolution (epi) increases) when a combination of interpolation and replication are beneficial. After you have interpolated an image as much as possible, you can continue increasing the number of pixels using replication without increasing the softness that accompanies interpolation. There are even special instances when images can benefit from both replication and interpolation. You can perform a step-re-sampling by alternating replication and interpolation and scaling an image in small increments until the desired effect is achieved. This is a rare circumstance and involves substantial trial and error when all other methods of re-sampling have not worked.

When re-sampling an image, you should scale to a whole, round number when possible. If you need to scale something 190 percent, you can scale by 200 percent and then either discard pixels or adjust the resolution to meet your requirements. The reason is simple mathematics. When you give the software program easy-to-digest figures, the software creates new pixels with a degree of uniformity. If you need to re-sample to a specific number, avoid percentages with decimal points.

Recall that digital bitmap is very uniform and scaling an image by 50, 150, 200, or 400 percent is easier than scaling by more complex numbers. It is good to reiterate that these are only guidelines and not rules. Obviously, there are times when you need to scale an image a specific amount and you should be aware of the available options. Only you can decide which methods to use and how appropriately they meet your needs.

Downsampling

Downsampling is important because it is typically preferable to have more pixels than you need for a digital image and to discard the extras. When you use replication while down-sampling, you are simply discarding the percentage of pixels that you do not need. So if you reduce an image by 50 percent you will discard every other pixel. This quick and easy method may sometimes result in strange patterns because the pixels you have thrown away are no longer there to help create the detail within an image.

If you use interpolation to downsample your image by 50 percent, not only are you discarding every other pixel, but an averaging of the remaining pixels helps smooth out any alarming patterns that may be produced. Typically, any image with several horizontal and/or vertical lines may result in an undesirable

pattern occurring, as illustrated in Figure 1.27b. Even with interpolation, there are some patterns like venetian blinds or plaid clothing that should not be downsampled. In most cases of downsampling you use interpolation.

UpSampling

Whenever you create new pixels by scaling an image, pixels that already existed in the bitmap image are used as references. The new pixels that are created are based on these existing pixels. Mathematical algorithms are used to create these new picture elements. Every piece of software uses similar algorithms, but each piece is unique in deciding how to achieve higher resolution. Most professional programs have acceptable sampling algorithms.

Interpolation does produce a softer image, so the less upsampling you do to an image, the better. Chapter 10, "Filters," discusses using

Figure 1.27a
The original image.

Figure 1.27b
Downsampling may create undesirable patterns in an image.

sharpen filters to help alleviate the out-of-focus appearance associated with interpolation.

There is no substitute for having your image at the proper resolution without resorting to any up- or downsampling. With few exceptions, scaling is not a solution without some cost in quality. Scaling images that do not have the correct resolution should be done sparingly with special consideration to the desired quality of your output.

Adding pixels or upsampling an image to increase an image's resolution is an involved matter. Although most software handles this process very well, you need to understand the implications of creating new pixels and the different methods available (see Figure 1.28).

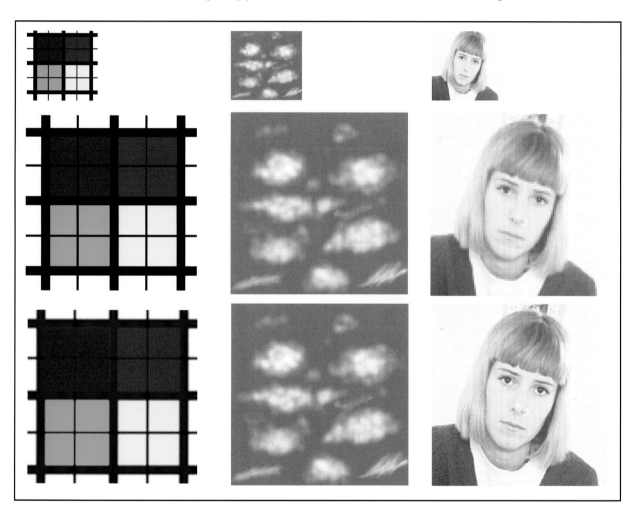

Figure 1.28
The images illustrate the results of replication and interpolation with horizontal and vertical lines, organic tones, and blends such as clouds and fleshtones.

Checklist

If you use the following steps you can eliminate most of the problems regarding the proper resolution of your digital images.

1. Determine the final physical size of the image that you wish to reproduce. If you do not know what your final size will be, then always defer to the maximum possible size. For example, if you are creating an image for a magazine cover, you know that the maximum size of your output will be the physical size of the magazine. Let's use 8 inches × 10 inches.

2. Determine the resolution of your direct output device or the line screen of the halftone screen you plan to use. Again, if you are not sure what the line screen will be, defer to the maximum possible line screen. Let's use 150 dpi line screen.

3. Identify the sampling ratio of your output device, which means the relationship of image pixels to either halftone dots or direct imaging elements. Because we are using halftone dots, the ratio is 2 image pixels per 1 halftone dot, or 2:1.

4. Multiplying step 2 by step 3 gives you your resolution: 150 dpi x (2 pixels per one halftone dot) equals 300 pixels per inch (ppi).

5. Multiplying the physical size (step 1) by the resolution (step 4) will give you how many total pixels (width and height) that you will need. This information is useful for scanning your image to the proper number of pixels, especially if the physical size of your original is different from your final output size.

Eight inches x 300 ppi equals 2400 pixels, and 10 inches x 300 ppi equals 3000 pixels. You can stop here if you are creating an image from scratch.

6. To determine the scanning resolution required, take the total number of pixels and divide that number by the physical size of your original image. This will give you the resolution that you need to scan your original image. For example, if your original is a 4 inch × 5 inch transparency, then 2400 pixels divided by 4 inches and 3000 pixels divided by 5 inches equals 600 ppi—which is the resolution that you should scan your original, with your scanner set at 100 percent. Remember that the physical proportion of the original and final output should be the same.

7. If your scanner allows magnification, then simply divide the resolution you get from step number 6, in this case 600 ppi, and divide by your desired resolution of 300 ppi to get an enlargement of 200 percent. A 4 × 5 inch original enlarged by 200 percent gives you a final image of 8 × 10 inches. Enter into the scanner a resolution of 300 ppi with a 200 percent enlargement. The result in pixels is exactly the same as 600 ppi at 100 percent, only the terms are different.

8.   You should always keep some relationships close at hand:

Physical Size (length and width) × Resolution = Total Pixels (length and width)

Total Pixels divided by Size = Resolution

Total Pixels divided by Resolution = Size

Some people may still find the process confusing. However, if you follow these steps each time, you will discover that the process will become second nature and you won't even need to use this guide.

Final Word

You must first grasp what a pixel is in order to understand resolution. The word pixel comes from a combination of two words: picture and element. Every kind of image, whether a drawing, painting, or photograph, uses some variation of picture elements or pixels.

A pixel must meet three criteria. First, a pixel is a discrete individual unit and cannot be divided into fractional parts.

Second, each pixel has a location. The location of a pixel can be determined by the centuries-old Cartesian coordinate system and has a specific location that can be identified by x & y coordinates.

Third, a pixel has value. The value of a pixel is based on the color data that the pixel contains.

Regardless of how simple or elaborate the image system, you will find the rules work.

Some basic guidelines to follow, which depend on the image, are: try to scan at the resolution you want to use; try not to upsample more than 200 percent; try to upsample and downsample in even increments if possible (i.e. 25, 50, 150, 200, 400 percent); keep an original file from which you do all sampling and do not sample and re-sample an image over and over. If you don't get the size you want on the first try, go to the original image and sample from it.

Tone and Color

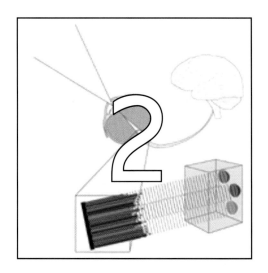

"Color is one of the two
principles of art — the
other being form."

Leonardo da Vinci,
15th Century Painter

Tone and color are inextricably part of our daily life. Tone provides shape and definition, while color makes things easier to see. Color provides the eye with the means to hold onto an object. Colors provide the mind with easy access to those things that are familiar and a method to organize what is seen. Color helps us identify things. Tone helps us define things. Before you begin to evaluate color and its intricacies you should first become familiar with tone and how it shapes the way you see.

Tone

Shape is created by tone. Without tone, color can provide no shape or definition to an object. Tone has few of the visual limitations of color. Black-and-white photography, television, and newspapers that rely exclusively on tone do quite well when reproducing images. Without color, tone still can carry the most important aspects of an image to the viewer. Without tone, color images lack the shape characteristics necessary to complete the image. Tone can be described as one numeric value. Color requires a much more complex system.

The analysis of all images begins with tone. Before we can discuss the intricacies of color, you must establish a firm understanding of tone. Tone, quite literally, is the structure that holds an image together. Without tone an image would collapse into meaningless mush.

The terms used to evaluate an image and describe tone are varied but very specific.

- *Lightness* is the tendency of the object's surface to be illuminated. White has a lighter quality than black, as in the statement, "it is light outside; or, it is dark (not light) outside."

- *Brightness* is a measurable amount of light reflected from an object with different types of lighting.

- *Value* is a specific measure of brightness of a given object or image.

- *Tone* is subjective—not specifically measurable—and relative to the other values contained in an image. Tone and value are often combined to describe an image or object.

- *Key* describes whether an image has mostly bright values (high key) or dark values (low key) or normal with neither light nor dark values dominating.

- *Halftones* reproduce the illusion of tone by using an arrangement of patterns using two values, typically white and black. A gray tint created by halftones is actually a combination of black dots and white paper.

Dynamic Range

The human ability to see tone is described as the *dynamic range*, sometimes called the tonal range. Human visual perception from bright sunlight to dark shadow conditions is approximately six orders of magnitude or 10 to the 6th power. Normally, we cannot see the entire visual tonal range at a given time because different lighting conditions reduce visibility of different areas of the scale. Color perceptions are also dependent on visual and environmental conditions (as you will read later).

The greater the dynamic range of an imaging system, the more tone and tonal steps available to the images. Dynamic range is often used as a relative measure from one imaging system to another. For example, the dynamic range that can be photographed is approximately 10 to the 3rd or 4th power, and the printed page is approximately 10 to the 2.3 to 2.5 range. The greater the tonal range, the more tone the system can reproduce and the better the images will appear. Nothing comes close to matching the total range of the human visual system.

Image reproduction from one imaging system to another typically reduces or compresses the tone and the dynamic range of the original image. Tonal compression describes image reproductions that have fewer value steps or tonal steps than the range available in the previous system. A compressed tonal range will look fine if not compressed too far and if all the tones in the image stay, for the most part, relative to one another. Because reproduction systems are relative, the entire tonal range of a particular image being reproduced can appear acceptable. The tone and color produced by television are not that precise in relation to natural phenomena. Judged by itself, the tone used in television resolves itself to create a very believable image.

Tonal compression literally means that you are losing values of tone. In the places where you lose the values, the tone impacts the reproduction. If the darker areas are compressed, there are fewer levels of tone to create details in the dark areas of the image. This may not be a problem if there is not much important information in the dark areas. However, if there are details that you wish to keep in the dark areas, you may want to compress the tonal range in the lighter areas. If there is detail in the lighter areas that you don't want to lose, you must make a decision. If you compress equally along the tonal range, you may sacrifice some detail in every area. Do you begin to see the pattern? The ideal would be to transfer all the tone; the reality is that some tones cannot make the trip to the new imaging system. There is a constant balancing act when it comes to reproducing tone. Figure 2.1 illustrates the concept of tone compression between image systems.

Value is a term used to describe the amount of light or dark in an image. The untrained eye or novice easily can recognize about five steps in value from white to black when presented separately. With a little training and practice, you can recognize twice as many value steps and place them in their appropriate positions on a scale from the lightest to the darkest value. You can distinguish even more steps if they are arranged in order. A firm grasp of the five basic values helps to identify and define the intermediate steps when using a larger scale.

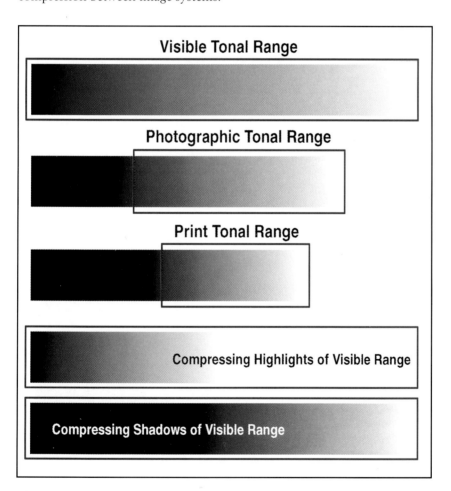

Figure 2.1
The red boxes indicate how the range of tone from nature, photographic film, and print relate to one another.

The most basic scale of five values is a white and a black, with a gray of mid-value in between. There is a value placed between the middle value and white and between the middle value and black for a total of five tones. This gives you a scale of white, light gray, middle gray, dark gray, and black (see Figure 2.2). These steps are commonly referred to as the *highlight point* (where tone begins), first one-quarter tone, midtone, three-quarter tone, and *shadow point* (where tone ends). If you are completely familiar with the scale of white to black, then it is easier to identify corresponding values when adjusting an image during production. You can see how this can help your future exploration of tone and color adjustments.

The next most useful scale, shown in Figure 2.3, is the 14-step scale because it encompasses

readily visible steps with a good range of tone. *Grayscales* are a generic term for these steps of tone. Grayscales play an important role in relating and transferring the tone of one imaging system to another. You will find various types of grayscales used throughout a reproduction process. Grayscales are used to ensure predictable tone reproduction. Calibrating one image system to another relies heavily on how the grayscale from each image system relates to one another. The specific numeric value of each tone in a grayscale also provides a quantifiable method to relate tone from each image system. For example, the 20 percent tonal value measured from one image system should still measure 20 percent on a new image system. If the measurement is off, adjustments may need to be made during the reproduction process to ensure a more accurate tonal reproduction.

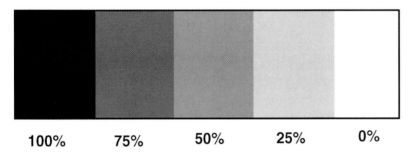

100%   75%   50%   25%   0%

Figure 2.2
The unfamiliar eye can easily distinguish the order of five grays from white to black.

100% 95% 90% 80% 70% 60% 50% 40% 30% 20% 10% 5% 3% 0%

Figure 2.3
The 14 step grayscale is used extensively to ensure reliable reproduction visually and numerically from one image system to another.

Measuring Tone—Density Dmax Dmin

Two measurements are useful in evaluating the tone of an image: how dense is the tone, and how does this value relate to other values within the image. The most important tool in measuring tone is the densitometer, which is used for calibration and determining a system's consistency. All tones have density, which is the ability to stop or absorb light. With a densitometer, you can measure the lightest gray (usually white) and then make this gray the staring point or zero-density unit. In this way you can also measure how grays relate to one another in an image. You are able to measure and get a specific value of any gray. The specific numbers or values are not as important as the relationship of the tone within the image.

After setting the zero point (known as "zeroing out") of the densitometer, you can then measure any value of gray. The densitometer will assign a number on a scale that runs from zero to six (which is supposed to be the blackest black). Measurements rarely hit six, and most density measurements range from 0 to 3.8. Photographic transparencies seldom reach 3.4

and print material rarely reaches 2.0. A pure carbon black is theoretically a density of 4.0. The dynamic range is judged partially by the minimum and maximum density the system can produce. The minimum density possible in a particular medium is called the Dmin and the maximum density the Dmax. Photographic media is most often measured in terms of Dmin and Dmax. You will find the reproduction of photographs relies on the measurements of density to play an important role in translating tonal information from the photographic-to-print imaging systems as illustrated in Figure 2.4.

A typical densitometer (shown in Figure 2.5) measures how much light passes through or is reflected from a tone. The reported value can be in either density units in a logarithmic fashion, positive or negative dot percents, or other specialty modes. In order to create high quality imagery, fixing the proper measurements for tones is a regular and necessary procedure. Remember that without proper tone, the hues of color cannot create the shape needed in an image. Images starting with poor tone lack the structure to create a pleasing reproduction, regardless of what you do with color.

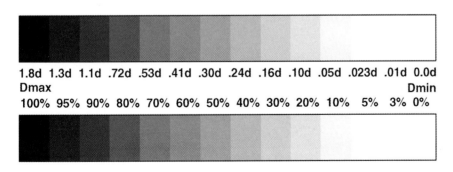

1.8d	1.3d	1.1d	.72d	.53d	.41d	.30d	.24d	.16d	.10d	.05d	.023d	.01d	0.0d
Dmax													**Dmin**
100%	95%	90%	80%	70%	60%	50%	40%	30%	20%	10%	5%	3%	0%

Figure 2.4
The density range for photographic film is greater than the density range of printed material as the Dmax numbers indicate.

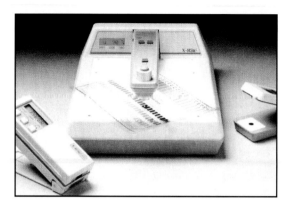

Figure 2.5
The densitometer is used to measure
density values of tones and to assign
numeric values.

The Tonal Curve

The working language of graphics is the curve. A curve provides an elegant, straightforward, and precise representation of tonal information. It cannot be emphasized enough that all important adjustments to an image can be made using a curve. Learn how to use a curve well, and you will have complete control over an image. To work efficiently with people correcting tone, you must understand the use of numerical information and graphics information in the form of a curve. Numerical tables complement the curve. Tables used with curves provide precision when making changes. Tables usually show before and after values at specific reference points. Specific methods of using curves and tables will be discussed in Chapter 6. Figures 2.6a and b show how curves and tables reflect the visual change of tone in an image.

Light Energy

Color is light energy. Light energy exists in the form of waves and particles that vibrate with different degrees of rapidity. Waves exhibit different lengths or frequencies measured in nanometers, which are one billionth (10^{-9}) of a meter. The wavelength of light determines how the light wave is perceived as color. The range of light you can see with your unaided eye, known as the visual spectrum, is 400 to 700 nanometers (nm) (see Figure 2.7). Light-wave lengths above 700nm are infrared energies. Lengths below 400nm are ultraviolet energies, X rays, and gamma rays. This range of color is your starting point for understanding color.

You can remember the spectrum of visible colors by using the anagram of red, orange, yellow, green, blue, indigo, violet—better known as our friend Roy G. Biv. The most dominant or primary colors are red, green, and blue—the capital letters in Roy's name.

Color gamut, or simply gamut, is a frequently used term in color reproduction, meaning a range of color. Gamut literally means the total range of possibilities as in the statement "run the gamut." All perceived color can be interpreted using the visible spectrum. As you will read, our biological gamut of color is largely based on a red, green, and blue color gamut. This physiological interpretation offers the primary reason that colors on a computer monitor or television are combinations of red,

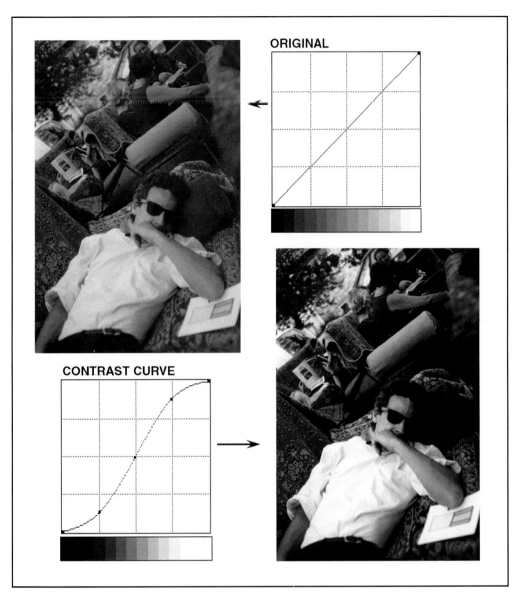

Figure 2.6a
The straight 45 degree curve in the upper right indicates a steady state where the original tonal values equal the corrected values of the image in the upper left. The "S" shaped curve in the lower right communicates a contrast change in the tonal values of the image where the dark areas are darker and the light areas are lighter.

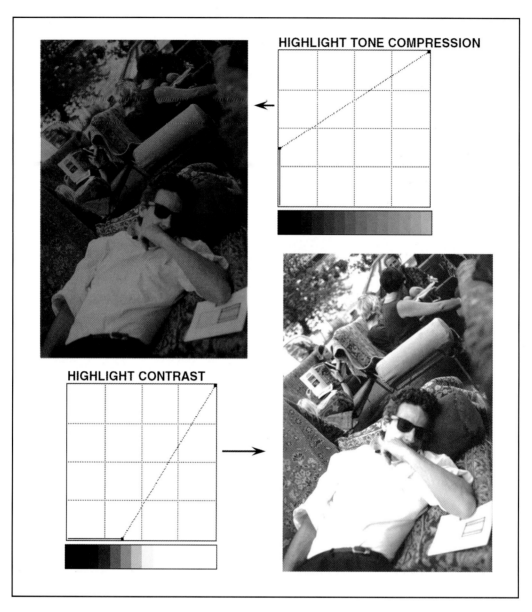

Figure 2.6b
The top image is described as being flat while the associated curve also is
visually becoming flat as the tonal values are compressed towards the middle
tones. The bottom image and curve communicate that both the light and dark tonal
values are being compressed linearly resulting in a smaller tonal range.

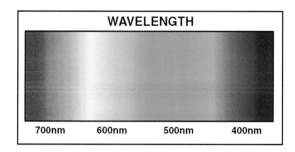

WAVELENGTH

700nm   600nm   500nm   400nm

Figure 2.7
The visual spectrum of color which lies
between the infra-red and the ultra-violet
can be easily remember by using the
anagram of Roy G. Biv.

green, and blue. It makes sense that the reproduction of color would have a basis in the RGB color system, similar to human perception.

Unfortunately, color cannot be sliced into digestible sections easily. You need to understand that color, in nature, exists in overlapping, almost fluid, waves that freely mix with one another. The colors red, green, and blue are not sliced perfectly into three parts but contain portions of one another mixed together. There is a transition from one color to another, and opinions vary regarding where one color begins and another ends. The general range of red, green, and blue are: red areas, 580nm and greater; green areas, 580-490nm; and blue areas, less than 490nm. There are areas of transition from one color to another, such as blue-green (480-510nm), yellow-green (550-570nm), and yellow-orange (570-630nm). How these transitional areas are perceived contributes to the differences of color perception from person to person.

Color Perception Influences

People perceive colors in many different ways. There are three important influences in the way a person perceives color: physiological, psychological, and environmental.

Physiological Influences

You perceive the differences in light wave energy (color) through your dual optical receptors—better known as your eyes. The structure of your eyes determines how you perceive color. Light enters through the pupil. Just in back of the pupil is the lens which focuses light on a membrane in the back of the eye called the retina. The retina is made up of optic nerves which transmit light sensations to the brain (see Figure 2.8). The word retina literally means net. The retinas in your eyes contain approximately 137 million of these optical nerve fibers or cells. The two types of light-sensitive cells are known as rods and cones. About 130 million optical fibers are rods and the other 7 million are cones. The cones are shaped slightly like a bowling pin, and the rods are shaped as if you had stretched out a cone. They are microscopic in size and these millions of rods and cones exist on the retina, which is a little more than one inch in diameter.

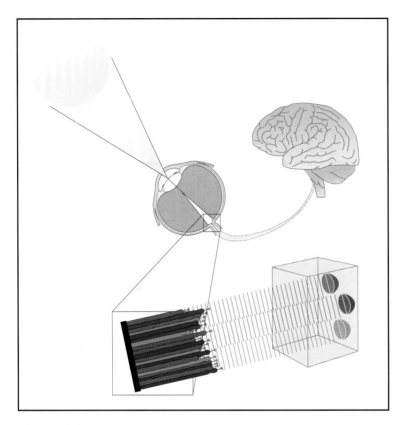

Figure 2.8
Rods and cones in the retina are sensitive to light energy
which is perceived as color by the brain.

The rods and cones contain chemical substances that are specially tuned to changes in light. Cones transmit the hues of color or the length of a light wave, and rods transmit the value, strength, and relative brightness of a light wave. Without cones, a person would only see in black and white tones. Rods do not transmit color information. Rods are spread throughout the retina while cones are concentrated and bunched mostly in the center. This grouping explains why colors are best seen directly ahead. Our peripheral vision does not perceive color very well. Wave a colored card at the side of someone looking straight ahead. They will be

able to see the movement, but the color will not be as apparent if you were to wave the same card directly in front of the person.

There are three types of color-sensitive cones. Cones are most receptive to the wavelengths of red, green, and blue light energy. The cones do not necessarily contain only red, green, or blue absorbing chemicals. Each type of cone is most sensitive to one band of red, green, or blue light energy, but it is also receptive to the wavelengths of the other two colors. Light reaching the cones triggers an electrical signal that is sent to the brain, processed, and then interpreted as a portion of the visual spectrum.

Color blindness is the result of chemical imbalances in the cones of the retina. These differences can be slight or dramatic. Color blindness is found predominately in males. About one man in twenty and one woman in two hundred are more or less blind to red or green or both. Almost no one is blind to yellow, blues, and violet. Color blindness can be classified into three major types: most common red-green deficient, less common blue-yellow deficient, and extremely rare chromatic color blindness where no color is perceived. Genetically, every person exhibits slight variations of light-wave sensitivity. Physical differences in cones help explain why two people can look at the same object and perceive different quantifiable color values.

Psychological Influences of Color

Awareness of personal preferences to certain colors helps you understand the emotional effects of your color selection. The psychology of color is one of the most inexact sciences but also one of the most powerful. Colors are also associated with emotions and can influence your subconscience. Although the specific reasons for this association are debatable, everyone is familiar with the related effects of color on emotions. Colors such as red or orange elicit a sense of speed or quickness, that tend to excite or give lively feelings, and may be considered warm or hot. Cool colors such as blue and violet produce feelings of calm or soothing cool and shade. Dark greens, browns, and beige are typically considered nurturing colors.

Psychological influences are difficult to categorize but the influence can be just as great as physical and environmental influences. How we personally feel about colors we can only know ourselves. There are groups of colors that send messages to a person when they see those colors. Some colors seem more familiar and comfortable while other colors are exactly the opposite. Even animals and insects appear to have marked preferences for certain colors. Or, at least their reactions are influenced by changes in color. Colors affect the emotions—a like or dislike for a particular color can influence how we see that color. A classification of colors and their associated emotions is difficult to create. Our response to color is linked with associations to experiences and cultural influences.

Overall, a preference of blue over all other colors seems to be fairly general, red a distant second, green third with violet, and then orange and yellow. All this being highly subjective, there are certain metaphors and archetypes linked with specific colors: white is associated with purity, innocence, divinity, and conversely blankness and emptiness. Black, the opposite of white and conflicting with light, indicates mourning, darkness, or strength—restful, compared to the agitation of white. Yellow, the lightest of colors, symbolizes the light of the sun. Gold symbolizes a kingly, noble metal, divine love, or enlightenment. Yellow can also signify deceit or treason, as used in "a yellow streak." Red, the most emotion-filled color, denotes love, energy, valor, fire and, in a bad sense, cruelty, wrath, and also sin. Blues elicit truth, wisdom, loyalty, and love—like red—only a cooler fire. Green, like blue, can mean truth and also growth, life and hope, and, in a bad way, green indicates jealousy.

color and viewing abnormalities. Improper convergence and alignment of the electron beams also contribute to color and viewing distortions.

Prototype display screens that bundle tiny light-emitting diodes (LEDs) are being developed. LED systems, similar in concept to displays in laptop computers, are beginning to reach the same color quality achieved by CRT monitors. Although many quality issues still must be resolved and wide spread implementation is far off, the physical savings of flat LED displays makes them a promising innovation to professional color imaging.

Convergence

How close the red, green, and blue electro-magnetic waves meet onscreen indicates the quality of display convergence. Perfect convergence or registration keeps halos of color from appearing. A halo is an unwanted border of color outlining the desired color. Lack of convergence, which is most noticeable around edges of black type, contributes to a fuzzy, out-of-focus look. The focusing system in a CRT display literally must force the electron beams to come together, or converge. This task is difficult because the electrons have different charges and tend to repel one another. The overall sharpness and clarity of an image suffers when there is lack of proper focusing or registration (see Figure 2.10).

The focusing system converges the electron source to a point on the screen. Not all points on the screen are an equal distance from the focusing lens. The best convergence occurs at the center of a screen. As you travel to the corners and edges, a less-focused image appears. This distortion occurs because the edges of the

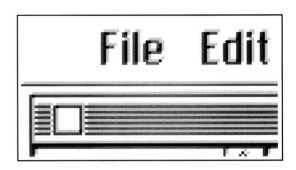

Figure 2.10
An example of poor convergence.

screen are not the same distance from the source as the center of the screen and therefore are not in perfect focus. High-precision quality displays diminish this problem by changing the methods of focusing. Creating screens with extremely curved surfaces compromises quality but alleviates the problem. All screens are curved to a certain extent. Convergence is one reason that large-screened monitors are so long. The further the focusing lens is positioned from the screen, the less dramatically the screen needs to be curved.

Gamma

Every monitor has a certain associated bright-ness called *gamma*. Gamma is the slope or gradient of a line representing the brightness of a monitor. A gamma of 1.0 indicates a slope of 45 degrees, a gamma of 2.0 indicates a slope of 63 degrees, and so on. Having monitors set to the same gamma amount helps establish a consistency from screen to screen.

Most image programs enable you to adjust the gamma of the monitor, which typically is set from a value of 1.0 to 1.8 for computer graphics and 2.2 for video (see Figures 2.11a-f). When the gamma is set, the white and black points stay anchored and the line or curve bows out. You

Figure 2.11a-f
The original printed image (a) and corresponding monitor gammas of 1.0(b), 1.4(c), 1.8(d), 2.0(e), and 2.2(f).

may have your own preferences, but you need to keep a consistent gamma value set on your monitor. Changing the gamma changes the display of information but not the actual information. Although you may change your monitor gamma to make the image appear brighter, the actual digital information does not change. When you are judging images on various monitors, keeping the gamma constant ensures a certain level of consistence. Making your monitor too bright is not always advisable. Although the image looks vibrant on the screen, you may be creating biases that are unrealistic when you reproduce the image in print or on film. Consult with whoever produces your color reproductions and try to match the gamma settings of their monitors.

A popular software tool is called Gamma, by Knoll Software, which enables you to adjust the gamma of a monitor. Remember that changing the appearance of the image on the monitor does not change the file's image information. Therefore, changing the gamma of the monitor does not change the way the image reproduces. But changing the gamma is a useful way of adjusting the displayed image to match the output.

Transmissive and Reflective

A monitor is a special source of projected light energy. Most color reproduction is in the form of either transmissive or reflected light. Transmissive color passes light energy from a particular source through an image to reach the observer. The dye and pigments filter light waves to produce the color. Anything you can see light through is transmissive in nature. Examples include stained glass windows and

common film transparencies (see Figure 2.12a and b). Reflective color is light energy whose light waves are bounced back or reflected to the viewer. The inks and dyes associated with reflective color absorb or reflect waves of color. Printing is the most familiar form of reflected light energy (see Figure 2.12c).

Images and objects can only transmit or reflect light waves that exist in the light that falls upon them. Images do not create the colors that they exhibit. The colors perceived from a transmissive or reflective image depend on two things: the wavelengths present in the source and the wave lengths that are eventually received by a viewer. Look at a red stained glass window. The red glass only allows the red light waves to pass. The viewer then sees red glass. Sunlight, which has a full spectrum of light, sends out all colors. If a blue light were shined through the red glass you would perceive no color because the blue light wave cannot pass to the observer.

If a printed image is illuminated with a white light, which contains all the visible colors (i.e. 5000 K), then the imagery shows off those colors in that image. If an image is illuminated with only red light, then the image will only reflect the areas that contain some amount of red. If you shine an orange light then only the areas that contain orange will be reflected back to the viewer. The source of the light is as important to the perception of color as the object that you are viewing.

Transmissive image substrates are generally better than reflective substrates because the light rays pass directly through the material from their source, while in printed material the rays are bounced back in a diffused and scattered way. Also, any reflection taking place from a transmissive image is bounced back to

Figure 2.12a
A stained glass window is a perfect example of a transmissive substrate.

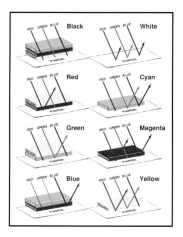

Figure 2.12b
Transmissive substrates filter light energy to produce color.

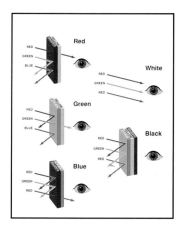

Figure 2.12c
Reflective substrates bounce light energy to produce color.

the source of light and not to the observer. There is no appreciable amount of white mixed into a transmissive image but a reflective image is diluted by the surface reflection of white, which mixes with the pigments of the image. This is a partial explanation as to why transparencies and monitors seem more pure and vibrant than many printed images.

You can have physical differences in color due to the reproduction methods and color gamut limitations of the type of output selected. The difference in the types of ink sets used from one printer to another is an example of how the physical reproduction of color can vary. The absorption and reflective properties of inks and dyes play a major role in determining how an image is seen when reproduced. We will address these particular issues in later chapters.

Surrounding Color

Besides the actual reproduction method used, the physical arrangement and lighting of color has dramatic effects. Dimly lit rooms and fluorescent or incandescent lights all contribute to the way a color or colors are perceived. Viewing color in proper or consistent lighting conditions also is important.

Because colors influence other colors, the best way to judge a color is to surround it or isolate it with a neutral color—white, gray, or black. Because there is no color to influence or to create a bias, you can assess the color accurately. Surrounding color does influence the perception of color as shown in Figure 2.13.

Viewing two colors simultaneously influences their appearance. For example, if a yellow and a blue card are placed beside each other, the

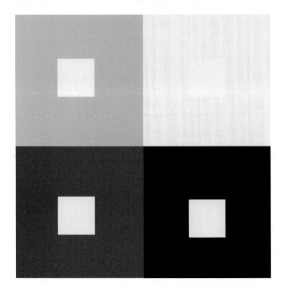

Figure 2.13
The yellow squares may appear different but in each case the surrounding color influences the perception of the same yellow color.

Figure 2.14a
The yellow and blue both look more intense when placed together than when viewed separately.

Figure 2.14b
The warm advancing red color has more visual impact than the cool receding blue.

yellow card appears more yellow and the blue card seems more blue than if the cards are moved apart or viewed separately (see Figure 2.14a).

Any featured color can be further intensified by using a complementary surround color. If a featured red area is surrounded by blue, the red has much more psychological impact than if it is surrounded by white or a warm color. This is because blue is a counterpart or complement to the color red. The surrounding blue intensifies and supports the appearance of the red in Figure 2.14b.

Green also is a complementary color to red. If you are so inclined, you may want to perform an experiment with color. Spend an entire day in a red-lit room, eating red food, while wearing red clothes. After being completely saturated with red, step onto a lush green lawn. The greens will appear incredibly intense. This

intensity, which might not last as long as the time you spent in the room, is partly a result of the green and blue cone receptors having little or no stimulation for an extended period. Although you may not work all the time in a red room, you may want to be aware of how surrounding colors in your environment can affect your perceptions of color.

Forgiving Brain

Regardless of any real or imagined biases that may exist, our own visual system is very forgiving. Because your brain retains a memory about color information, even if you see a color that is not exactly correct, your visual system will compensate for any deficiencies by retrieving color information from memory. Unless you have something to compare colors to, isolated colors easily are enhanced by your memory bank of colors. A perfect example is television. When you watch persons on the screen, you accept that the color of their flesh is accurate. Unless the color changes radically—perhaps to a green—or a live person stands near the television for comparison, you accept the color on the screen as representative. You actually add to that color from your past experiences.

The environment in which you live and work definitely affects how you perceive color. Whether you believe it or not, you also have your own established dispositions regarding color. You have colors that stimulate you in different ways, and you naturally have favorite colors. Because you have personal color preferences, you tend to skew any judgments of color reproduction toward your own preferences. Your personal bias is a strong influence on color reproduction. Although not quantifiable, your personal color biases contribute to problems with color reproduction. Awareness of any possible bias is a step toward compensating for that particular bias.

Basic Color Space

A color space is a method of organizing color. In a digital color system, each pixel is described by combining the primary colors of red, green, and blue (RGB). Red, green, and blue take advantage of the triple nature of color. White light, as you know, is a combination of all colors in the spectrum. The visual spectrum can be divided into three parts called a tri-chromatic color system. The primary tri-chromatic color system is red, green, and blue and combines to create most of the visible spectrum. It may be more accurate to divide the color spectrum into more than three parts, but the complexity of such a system does not justify the minimal gains in color range. Tri-chromatic color systems, of which RGB is a member, are the minimum color systems that produces the largest color range. Tri-chromatic color is a universally accepted process of producing color, whether in photography, television, printing, or digital computer graphics. This commonality links all modern image systems. The big display screens at major sports stadiums also use triples of RGB. From a distance, the image has many different hues. But when you get close to the screen, you see only the individual RGB bulbs.

Because our eyes receive information within a red, green, and blue system, it is possible to create close to all visible color by using an RGB based display system. Remember every created color system uses your eyes as the starting point. Complex color systems can be reproduced and interpreted by using current inks and pigments, but each color system exhibits limitations in trying to meet the standards your eyes have established (illustrated in Figure 2.15). Because of the limited color gamut (color range) of phosphors on a monitor, or pigments in a transparency, or ink on paper, you need to consider and compensate for deficiencies in each color reproduction process. An understanding of how color and color reproduction involve constant ebbs and flows is critical to your ability to use color effectively and grasp the craft of color reproduction.

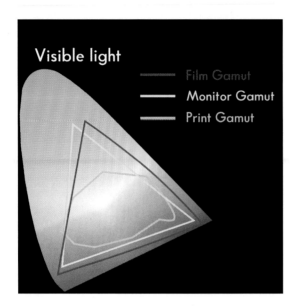

Figure 2.15
The color gamut of nature, monitors,
transparencies, and print image systems.

For color reproduction, tri-chromatic methods cannot achieve correct color reproduction of all colors. The problem cannot be avoided, but you can compensate for it by using special techniques. Remember this when you are trying to match colors from different color systems. Trying to match all the image's colors can be a fool's folly. There is no way to perfectly match everything, especially when you consider you are starting with limited colors and all the complex influences present. When trying to get one system to match another, you must realize that no systems can match all the colors we see with our eyes. It is not necessary to produce all colors to create pleasing and representative color images.

The Additive Principle of Red, Green, and Blue

Red, green, and blue are called additive primary colors because when light from each of these colors is projected on one another, the result is all wavelengths of visible light, or white light (see Figure 2.16). Because white is all colors, all you need to produce any color is the ability to vary the proportions of red, green, and blue independently. You can experiment with the variations of RGB color by using image programs. You'll find that all reproduced color starts from an interpretation of the primary RGB color space. The default color of RGB is black.

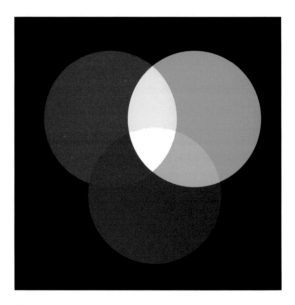

Figure 2.16
Red, green, and blue are additive primary
colors. When mixed at their maximums they
produce white.

The Subtractive Principle of Cyan, Magenta, and Yellow

In an additive color space, all color (white) is produced by mixing the primary colors of red, green, and blue. Subtractive color produces white (all color) by the total absence of the secondary colors of cyan, magenta, and yellow (CMY) (see Figure 2.17). Blending the maximums of cyan, magenta, and yellow produces black. Although at first glance subtractive color seems very different from additive color, the two are directly inverse. The default color of CMY is white.

Figure 2.18 shows that combining any two additive primary colors makes a subtractive secondary color. Combining any two subtractive secondary colors creates an additive primary

color because the addition of red, green, and blue cancels producing white light. The third color excluded from these pairings is called the complementary color.

additive colors	subtractive colors	complementary colors
R+G = Y	Y+M = R	R:C
R+B = M	Y+C = G	G:M
G+B = C	C+M = B	B:Y

Subtractive color is used in reflective displays such as photography and printing. Combining varying intensities of cyan, magenta, and yellow dyes produces a wide range of colors. All you need to create a subtractive color reproduction is the ability to control the concentration of CMY dyes on film, transparency, or paper. This theory works well in controlled situations, but the practice of subtractive color reproduction is complicated. In photography, cyan, magenta, and yellow dyes are used without other colors to achieve the desired color reproduction. In printing, an additional color, black, is necessary to compensate for ink deficiencies. (The letter *K* indicates black to avoid confusing *B* with the color blue.) Impurities in the inks and dyes may absorb color when the color should be reflected to the viewer. This absorption creates darker areas in a color reproduction that are undesirable. Theory rarely lives up to its billing. Cyan, magenta, and yellow printing inks when added 100 percent should produce a pure black, but instead create a muddy brown. The creation of an artificial independent black helps achieve a true black. The use of four colors presents special concerns that are addressed in the chapters dealing with four-color printing.

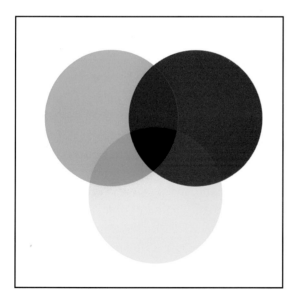

Figure 2.17
Cyan, magenta, and yellow are subtractive secondary colors. When mixed at their maximums they produce black.

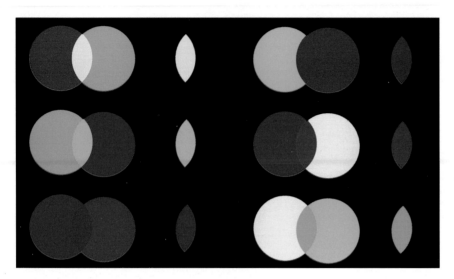

Figure 2.18
Mixing two primary colors produces a secondary color. Mixing two
secondary colors produces a primary color.

A major disadvantage to additive color such as RGB is that reproducing color with RGB requires some kind of special device or projection to display the colors. Subtractive color does not need any special device such as a monitor to be viewed, but subtractive color does have reproduction difficulties, as mentioned, that need to be addressed.

This relationship is especially important when color separation results are being analyzed because subtractive colors normally are used as printing ink colors, while the source of the image is from an additive color system.

Hue, Saturation, and Value (HSV)

Any color and tone can be described by analyzing it in regard to three criteria: hue, saturation, and value (HSV).

Hue is the type of color being described, such as red, cyan, brown, and orange. The number of hues you can distinguish under ideal lighting

conditions may be as high as 500. When looking at printing inks and monitors, the number of hues you can distinguish is determined by the properties of the pigments and phosphors that make the colors.

Saturation is the strength of a color or the amount of hue. For example, fire-engine red is more saturated than brick red. When you use printing inks, the maximum amount of saturation you can produce is printing a solid (100 percent) film of ink on the paper or substrate. Saturation also can describe the purity of a color. If saturation is at 100 percent, the color is considered pure, having no gray or neutral component (equal amounts of RGB or CMY). The lower the saturation, the closer the color is to gray or black. Zero or no saturation is a gray tone or black.

Value is the amount of relative brightness of the color, usually expressed as light or dark. Brightness is the degree of illumination in an area. As a color's value increases toward 100 percent, the color becomes whiter, and at 100 percent it becomes a white. Conversely, as a color's value drops to zero, this color becomes black. At a value of 50 percent, halfway between white and black, you have a color in balance tending toward neither black nor white. The color appears the most vibrant at this point.

The hue, saturation, value color model is shown in Figure 2.19.

You often hear HSV called HSB because value and brightness are similar. You may notice that on sunny days colors tend to be washed out because the value of color is very high and is tending toward white. One of the best times to view color is during an overcast day when the daylight value is not as direct and bright. Take a walk after a rainstorm during the day and notice how vibrant many colors appear. Furthermore, during the evening's starlight and moonlight, the colors in objects seem to disappear. At night the value is very low or tending toward black.

Based on the previously defined terms, a description of a bright, heavily saturated orange color is easy to understand and "see" without

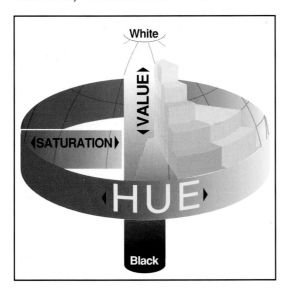

Figure 2.19
The HSV color model.

visually observing the color. Being able to understand a color verbally is useful when you discuss possible color adjustments with someone at a different location. Although we do not recommend that you rely exclusively on this method, HSV is another useful tool in communicating and understanding color.

Classifying Colors and Tone

Hues which approach red, and tones which contain red, are almost universally considered warm colors while colors that tend toward blue are considered cool (see Figures 2.20a and b). Green and violet contain elements of both warmth and coolness. In the color circle they stand as dividers between the cool and warm colors.

Some colors, mostly in the warmer range, appear to a viewer to advance while cool colors tend to retreat. One explanation is that warm colors are frequently those of light while cooler colors are used as shadow tones. So red on blue would tend to place the red in the foreground and recede the blue into the background.

Certain colors define patterns more clearly. Experiments have indicated that for normal eyes yellow light has more defining power than most any other light of equal brightness. This is the reason that some street lamps (sodium based) and fog lights on cars are yellowish. Long distance target shooters sometimes use amber glasses to bring out the detail of a distant target. White on a green field is very easy to read from great distances which is one of the reasons road signs contain those colors. But, black on yellow seems to be the strongest foreground background combination (as shown in Figure 2.21).

Figure 2.20a
Examples of cool receding colors.

Figure 2.20b
Examples of warm advancing colors.

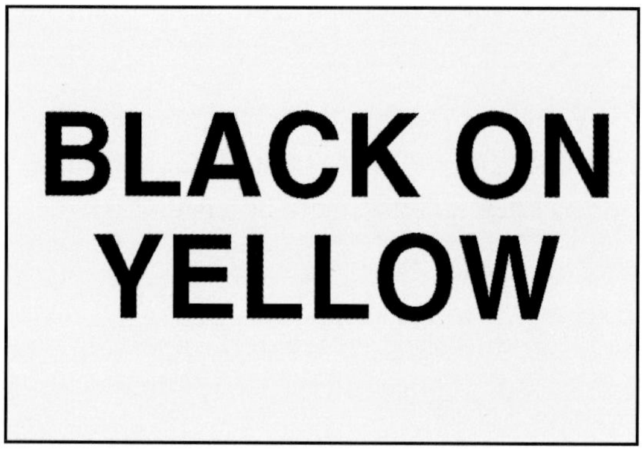

BLACK ON YELLOW

Figure 2.21
A yellow field defines black type very well.

Neutrality

Neutrality or neutrals represent equal values of perceived red, green, and blue. Neutrality means that no single color has more influence than another. If the red, green, and blue values are equal, they effectively cancel each other out. Neutral colors also are known as grays and literally contain no color or color bias. Gray

colors are equally perceived values of RGB between white and black. White represents the maximum perceived value of RGB and the minimum gray; and black, the maximum gray, represents the total absence of the light waves of red, green, and blue.

It is easier to identify and recognize a given value in neutral grays than in colors because the stimulation that colors produce on our eyes is likely to deceive us. If we display a yellow, a blue, and a red of the same values on a grayscale monitor, the result would be three identical grays alike in value. However, if you place that same yellow, blue, and red on a color monitor, the untrained eye is likely to perceive the blue as the darker tone, the yellow as the lightest, and the red somewhere in-between (see Figure 2.22). If you become thoroughly familiar with a scale of neutrals from white to black, you will become more adept in recognizing tones in neutrals and colors.

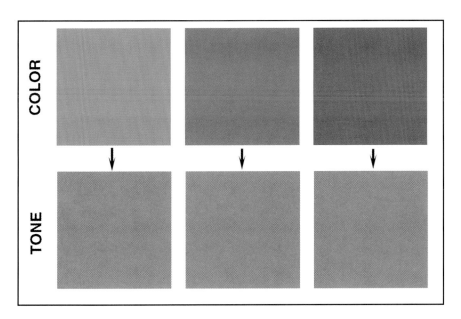

Figure 2.22
The colors may appear to have different tonal values but in fact
are all the same tonal value.

Digital Values of Color

The value of a digital pixel is based on the number of bits of information the pixel contains. The number of bits of information is also known as bit resolution or color resolution.

The binary code that is the basis of all modern computing is the method used to ascribe value to a pixel. The simplest pixel has two choices: on or off; yes or no; black or white. The total number of choices is two raised to the power of one. The two is the base number system, and one is the exponent and indicator of the number of bits of color value per pixel. A pixel with two raised to the power of one is a one-bit pixel, and the image described by a map of these one-bit pixels is called a one-bit image. A bit of information is the binary choice of zero or one, on or off, as mentioned. Adding more bit

(on, off) choices to a system increases the number of potential combinations. The chart in Figure 2.23 illustrates how the choices of pixel values increase as you increase the number of bits (on, off choices) per pixel.

The most common and established digital pixel value system is the 24-bit color system. As Figure 2.23 shows, 2 raised to the power of 24 results in a total possible choice of 16,777,216 colors—a few more than your crayon box offers. In fact, the human eye cannot distinguish the subtle variations of many of the millions of colors. Although 24-bit color does not encompass the entire range of color we can see with our unaided eyes, it comes close.

The bits indicate the number of color values a system can produce. For each 8 bits, 256 levels of electric signals are sent out by the electron guns. For photo-realistic images, a minimum of 24-bit color is required. Twenty-four-bit color

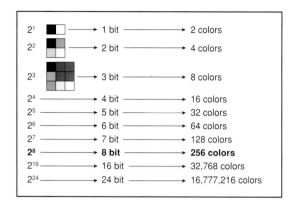

2^1	▇▢	→ 1 bit	→ 2 colors
2^2		→ 2 bit	→ 4 colors
2^3		→ 3 bit	→ 8 colors
2^4		→ 4 bit	→ 16 colors
2^5		→ 5 bit	→ 32 colors
2^6		→ 6 bit	→ 64 colors
2^7		→ 7 bit	→ 128 colors
2^8		→ **8 bit**	→ **256 colors**
2^{16}		→ 16 bit	→ 32,768 colors
2^{24}		→ 24 bit	→ 16,777,216 colors

Figure 2.23
The total number of color choices
increases as the color bit depth
increases.

gives 8 bits of information for each of the red, green, and blue guns. In 32-bit color, the additional 8 bits of information may exist for an alpha channel or a mask channel. The mask channel does not display color but is used when compositing images together. These channels need the 8 bits to store the mask information. CMYK color uses 32-bit color, 8 bits being distributed to each of the four colors.

Each red, green, and blue color shares equally the total 24 bits (on, off choices), so each has a value range of 2 raised to the power of 8, resulting in 256 levels or choices for each color of red, green, and blue. Every pixel in a 24-bit image has a separate value of red, green, and blue combined to establish a final composite value of color (see Figure 2.24a). You can adjust one, two, or all three color values of a pixel to create a new pixel value, which you can do when color-correcting images in the RGB color space. The total number of unique color combinations is 16.7 million, as mentioned previously.

When you work with printing colors, a 32-bit color system applies. In printing, each picture element is described by a combination of cyan, magenta, yellow, and black (CMYK). Although including a fourth channel to a tri-chromatic system seems to defeat the purpose of minimizing the number of color channels, you will discover that the addition of a black channel is necessary to compensate for deficiencies in printing inks. Because the printing process does not have the same range of color possibilities as

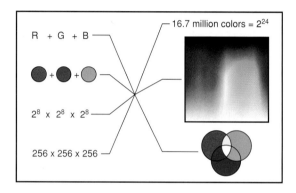

Figure 2.24a
In a 24-bit color system, red, green, and
blue each have 8 bits of color
information.

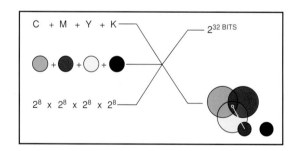

Figure 2.24b
In a 32-bit color system, cyan, magenta,
yellow and black each have 8 bits of color
information.

digital pixels, you cannot deduce that the total range of color for print is 4,294,967,296 colors. We discuss the range of print colors later. For now, you should understand that the black channel produces an additional 8-bit system for a total of 32 bits, as shown in Figure 2.24b.

Expanded Bit Depth

As color systems become more sophisticated, the concept of 36- and 48-bit color is becoming more popular. These systems distribute 12 bits of information—or 4,096 levels per red, green, and blue. Although this number makes the file size quite large, the increased color information is invaluable in many film-recording environments. The images are manipulated in a 36- or 48-bit environment and then converted to 24- or 32-bit by taking the best 8 bits of color, determined by algorithm in the program software.

Many scanners are now able to work with 30-, 36-, or even 48-bit color software and then determine which 8 bits will be used in the 24-bit color system. This is often referred to as "best 8 scanning" since we cannot work with the total number of bits scanned. You occasionally may hear of high-end scanners that scan "best eight." These scanners can scan 12 bits of color information and then discard the 4 bits the program decides are not needed as illustrated in Figure 2.25. Although this technology perhaps is far off for most retouching work, you should be aware of the eventual expansion into this area. In a 36- or 48-bit system, all the bits do not necessarily need to be used for color information. Multiple alpha and mask channels are extremely useful, especially for layering multiple images, typically done in video. Moving to 36

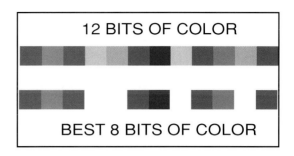

Figure 2.25
A 12-bit per channel scanner typically has software to determine the best 8 bits of information in the raw scan to create a 24-bit image.

bit is an option that some people are choosing to use in order to compensate for deficiencies related to the translation process to CMY from RGB colors.

Video Boards

Photo-realism greatly depends on the amount of color available in your color system. To display color information on a monitor, you need a video board to translate the digital values into electric signals that send electrons to the screen.

When you are working with color photographs, 24-bit color displays are a necessity. You may work with 24-bit images using only an 8-bit display, but it is extremely difficult to "see" the full range of the color necessary to produce realistic images. Because 24-bit color contains more than 16 million color possibilities and 8-bit display shows only 256 of these colors, there is a huge difference in colors seen. Any cost savings you achieve by using an 8-bit video board do not justify the loss in color displayed.

A 24-bit color image requires an enormous amount of processing. Many video boards offer QuickDraw accelerators that help speed up processing time. In addition, many video boards now incorporate direct video input. Therefore, you can input video images directly into your image processing programs.

Variations of Color Reproduction

Understanding that color systems are not perfect helps your ability to deal with the inevitable variations in all color reproductions. As mentioned previously, many variations exist in color reproduction methods. Color reproduction is fluid and may differ from one process to another. Even matching color from the same reproduction method is difficult. Different printing shops offer various and different results. Even matching color from one monitor to another monitor is difficult. Color matching from one color system to another is troublesome because the only element you can rely on is your own experience and knowledge. Several manufacturers have established standards for color matching. Each has its own bias and benefits. Establishing your own consistent environment ensures that your color accuracy is kept dependable and predictable.

Eliminating the variables, or at least anticipating variable effects, is what the craft of color reproduction is all about. For example, the red in a tomato typically reflects to your eyes the following portions of the visible spectrum: 50 percent of red, 30 percent of orange, 20 percent of yellow, 15 percent of yellow-green, 10 percent of green, 10 percent of blue-green, 5 percent of blue, and 5 percent of violet. Imagine how complex a color system would be if you needed to consider all these variables!

Checklist

To work effectively with color reproduction, you should be thoroughly familiar with:

- The difference in tones from light to dark.

- How density is used to measure tone.

- The use of tone to create shape in an scene.

- The basic principles and relationships of additive and subtractive color.

- Communicate color to others with the terms hue, saturation, and brightness.

- How curves are used to describe and adjust tone.

- The subtle and not-so-subtle influences of physiology, environment, and psychology on color perception.

Final Word

You must understand that your color perception is more than qualitative logical percentages and values. Physical, environmental, and emotional responses to color contribute to the explanation of why judgments of color from one person to another can be different.

An awareness of the factors that influence color perception provides an insight into the complexities of color. No person sees color exactly the same as another person. There are many factors that influence the way color is perceived. This is not to preclude someone from working with color. Quite the contrary—the more you know about the processes that allow color to be used and perceived, the better you can understand how to control and use color information whether visual, numerically, or both.

Scanning

"Know then thyself;
pressure not God to scan."

Alexander Pope

Images used in most Macintosh image programs must first be converted into digital pixels. Special devices called *scanners* are used to convert images into pixels. Scanners link physical scenes or images to digital computer systems by converting an image into binary information. Scanners only provide a representative sampling of a scene or image. The more samples of a scene or image taken, the more representative the digital image is when compared to the original image, and the more accurate any further reproduction of the image will be. This digital information can then be used in manipulation software for eventual transfer and output to a variety of other image systems such as film, print, and video.

But what is a scanner? And why is it important to understand the function of scanning? To understand the computer scanner it may be helpful to revisit our most familiar scanning device. The simplest, most sophisticated scanner is the eye.

Light energy reaches our eye by passing through a lens which focuses the light onto sensors called rods and cones clustered on our retina. The retina then sends an electrical signal to appropriate parts of the brain where the information is organized into image information. If you use your own physical sensors as a foundation, understanding how digital scanners function is very straightforward.

Scan, Scan...
Give Me Scan!

A scanner is a device that converts scenes and images into digital information. The scanner literally slices a scene into equal parts that are referred to as picture elements or pixels. The number of parts or pixels varies depending on how many samples are taken of the scene or image. The number of samples a scanner can make depends on the number of sensors available in a scanner and the scan pitch. The scan pitch is the speed at which the hardware moves across the image. The more samples taken from a scene, the more accurate the digital version of the image or scene. The more samples the scanner makes, the more pixels there are; the more pixels, the higher the potential image resolution. Figures 3.1a-d illustrate the process that a scanner performs to convert an image to digital information.

Each sample the scanner "sees" may contain many values and colors. The scanner can see a dynamic range of colors, called the *color resolution* or *bit depth*. It is the job of the scanner hardware and software to designate one individual color or value per sample. One color is selected from the range of RGB color resolution available with the scanner. The one color value is then assigned to one unique pixel. Using a systematic pattern, the scanner continues to analyze the scene until the entire designated scene has been sampled (viewed by the scanner). Then the samples are converted into picture elements and temporarily stored.

To determine their final color value, the stored pixels created by the samples are then analyzed further by digital software. The range of color or bit depth used by a scanner may be more than a software program needs to create and manipulate digital images. The scanner software matches the best range of color from its samples to the best range of color used by the image software. The scanner literally discards color information to create the best possible range of color for each individual picture element. The

Figure 3.1a
The original image.

Figure 3.1b
The lines represent the slices a scanner makes to analyze an image, often called scan lines.

Figure 3.1c
A representation of the resulting digital information captured by a scanner.

Figure 3.1d
A representation of digital information prepared for print.

pixels are then arranged in a digital file and either stored for later retrieval or transferred to image manipulation software for eventual physical output.

To better understand how various scanners work, try performing a simple experiment. Hold a coarse mesh screen (like a fence or chicken wire) at arm's length in front of you. Look through the screen with both eyes open and try not to move your head. Report to a friend the color you see through the first hole. If there is more than one color seen within the hole, make your best guess at the predominate color and try to mix the colors to create one unique color. Move down to the next hole and repeat this process until you become exhausted and cross-eyed, or until you begin to understand that a scanner is doing the same exact thing only much faster and with smaller samples (holes). Renaissance painters used a similar method for painting landscapes. They looked through a screen that divided a scene; they painted each section separately until the entire scene was reproduced exactly to scale. Digital scanning is simply a variation of a very old process. If you refer back to these concepts while working with a scanner, you will find that many complex functions are not so complex (see Figures 3.2a and b).

Types of Scanners

The two main types of scanners are *PhotoMultiplier Drum* scanners and *CCD scanners*. Each type of scanner has pluses and minuses associated with its use. Depending on the type of scanner you use, samples can be taken in a number of ways. There are three primary criteria used to discuss how a scanner is judged: the

Figure 3.2a
An original scene before scanning.

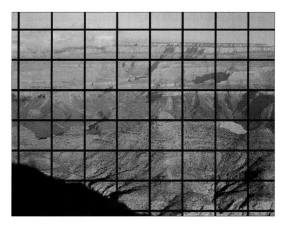

Figure 3.2b
An illustration of how a scanner or a painter divides an image into parts for easier analysis.

optical resolution, the dynamic range, and what kind of imagery can be scanned. Other considerations include speed, cost, and ease of use.

Optical Resolution

The *optical resolution* of a scanner is the maximum number of sensor or sample elements available per inch or millimeter. Resolution is an amount of something per unit of measure. When referring to scanning, that "something" is either the sampling elements or the scanning sensors per inch. We prefer to use the term scanning elements per inch (epi) to avoid confusion using the term dot, but if you prefer, you may exchange the term epi with dpi.

A scanner can only make as many real samples as its optical resolution provides. The higher the optical resolution, the more sensors are available to the scanner. As more samples are made, more picture elements are created and potentially the resolution of the digital file is increased.

There is a method called resolution interpolation where the scanner takes the pixels of an image and resamples the pixels to the desired image resolution. Interpolation is only a partial solution since the interpolation creates new pixels from exiting pixels and does not provide additional picture information from the original image source. If any resampling needs to be done, you should resample in an image manipulation program after the scanner has made the greatest amount of samples possible.

Flatbed scanners often are referred to as 300 by 600 epi; the 300 is the optical resolution and the 600 is the maximum scan pitch. The *scan pitch* is the speed that the scanner moves across the image and the amount of image information the scanner can focus onto the sensors (see Figure 3.3). You can think of scan pitch as how thin a slice of an image the scanner can cut. A 300 epi scanner can have a maximum of 1/300th inch focused onto each sensor. If the scanner moves half the speed or distance of the normal 300 epi speed, the scanner can focus double the amount of information onto the sensor or a maximum of 1/600th inch. The effective optical resolution is doubled to 600 epi, but only in one direction. The other direction must be interpolated to match the 600 epi resolution.

Remember that resolution is an amount of something. With scanners, the amount (resolution) refers to samples. Interpolation does not create any new samples. When judging a scanner's resolution, the most important number is the optical resolution. But higher optical resolution is not necessarily indicative of the scanner's performance.

One of the more important considerations when using a scanner is the amount of detail a scanner can see. A scanner's optical resolution is not necessarily indicative of its functional resolution. The true or functional resolution of a scanner is the actual amount of detail a scanner captures. Using a simple resolution tester is a good way to judge how well a scanner resolves details, as illustrated in Figure 3.4. Resolution problems are easier to spot in black-and-white line art.

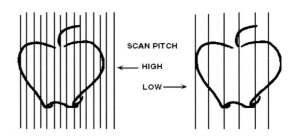

Figure 3.3
The illustration shows that more slices indicates higher scan pitch.

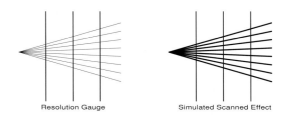

Figure 3.4
A resolution tester. As the lines converge to a point, a scanner has more difficulty reproducing the fine lines and details.

Dynamic Range

Dynamic range describes the total range of visible tone. Dynamic range is used as a relative measure from one imaging system to another. For example, the dynamic range that can be photographed is approximately 10 to the 3rd power, and the printed page is approximately 10 to the 2.0 to 2.3 range. The greater the dynamic range, the more tone the system can reproduce and the more pleasing the images will look relative to our ability to perceive tone. The human visual system's tonal perception outperforms any type of reproduction method.

The dynamic range is described also as the *density range*. Density is the capability of material to absorb or stop light. As density increases, the amount of light reflected or transmitted decreases. The total density range is described by the minimum density (Dmin) and the maximum density (Dmax). Knowing how the tonal range of an image is described by Dmin and Dmax helps relate the reproduction of those images with whatever medium you want.

The density values used are logarithmic. The exponents of the general descriptions above are density values. Specific density ranges for every material vary, but there are some general ranges for the most popular materials.

Theoretically, a carbon black has the highest material density of 4.0 and is considered the maximum Dmax possible. Transparency material can range anywhere from 3.0 to 3.6 Dmax. Most commercial 35mm slides rarely exceed 3.0, and only the higher quality 4" × 5" and 8" × 10" transparencies reach a Dmax of 3.4 to 3.6. Reflective photographic prints, such as cibachrome or fujichrome prints, have a Dmax range of 2.0 to 2.8. Printed material Dmax depends entirely on the type of paper and inks used. Newsprint has a Dmax near 1.7 and smooth-coated paper can go as high as 2.0. As you can see, the Dmax of an imaging system can give you insight into the range of tone possible within that system. You can understand that the Dmax of newsprint cannot be expected to fully reproduce the dynamic range of a 35mm slide with a Dmax of 3.0. But the Dmax of each system provides an excellent starting point from which to relate the systems to each other, as illustrated in Figure 3.5.

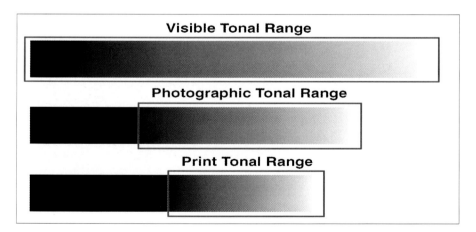

Figure 3.5
The red boxes illustrate the range of reproducible tones for each image system.

Scanners also are measured by the dynamic range that they can capture. A scanner should at least be able to reach the Dmax of the material and a little beyond to make sure all the shadow tone detail is captured, as illustrated in Figure 3.6a. Since most commercial photography does not go beyond a Dmax of 3.0, a scanner needs to reach at least a dynamic range of 3.4 to capture an acceptable range of tone. The highest quality scanners have a dynamic range of 3.8; this range sufficiently captures the darkest tones and details of high quality transparencies. If a scanner has a dynamic range that can only see a Dmax of 2.0, then it is not well suited to reproduce the darker tones of transparencies and is only appropriate for lower range prints, as illustrated in Figure 3.6b.

If your scanner doesn't capture the fine tonal detail in an image, the details cannot be created in the software. Basically, if your scanner doesn't see or sample detail, then no amount of image manipulation can bring detail back. Color can be adjusted and corrected. Loss of fine detail cannot be corrected so easily. In addition to optical resolution, the dynamic range of a scanner is an important factor in handling image detail and color fidelity. The range of detail and color a scanner can see is directly related to the quality of output you will get from the digital file. The dynamic range of a scanner is directly related to the total amount of color bits the scanner can see. Because the human eye sees the most detail from highlight to midtones, scanner manufacturers minimize deficiencies in dynamic range by sacrificing detail in the shadow end.

Bit depth

The color resolution or *bit depth* available from the scanner's sensors is related to the dynamic range of a scanner. Many scanners are now able to work with 30-, 36-, and even 48-bits of color information. This provides each color of red, green, or blue with either 10-, 12-, or 16-bits and a tonal range of 1024, 4096, or 65,536 steps. The color software within the scanner then determines which 8 bits or 256 tonal steps per red, green, and blue will be used in the commonly used 24-bit color system.

You may hear of high-end scanners that scan "best 8," often referred to as "best 8 scanning"

Figure 3.6a
A scanner with a high dynamic range will hold important detail in the shadows.

Figure 3.6b
A scanner with a low dynamic range will lose shadow detail.

because the scanner's software determined which best 8 bits used by the image system that it will transfer to pixels. These scanners can scan between 10- and 16-bits of color information for each red, green, and blue color channel and then discard the 2 to 8 bits the program decides are not needed.

Scanning at a greater bit depth helps ensure a greater range of tone and color being sampled and potentially a greater degree of accuracy in the resulting digital file. Simply scanning more bits does not guarantee a better scan. The software used to determine which bits to keep and which to discard plays a large role in determining the level of quality the scanner can achieve. Some programs now allow a greater degree of control in choosing which area of the bit depth to keep and which to discard (see Figure 3.7).

Substrate

Scanners can scan two types of material: *transmissive* or *reflective*. Transmissive scanners pass light through the image to the sensors.

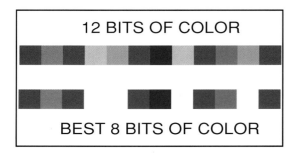

12 BITS OF COLOR

BEST 8 BITS OF COLOR

Figure 3.7
Choosing the best bits of color means that some pixels won't be making the trip to 24-bit digital image land.

A reflective scanner bounces light off the original to the scanner sensors. Each substrate has special concerns to be addressed when scanning. Some scanners scan only one substrate; others scan both substrates.

Because a scanner makes reproductions of whatever it analyzes, items that are scanned are called *originals*, *original copy*, or just *copy*. Color copy that is transmissive (through which light can pass) is called a *transparency*, or *chrome*. Thirty-five-millimeter slides are examples of chromes. Any copy that is not transmissive is reflective. Reflective copy is scanned by using light reflected off the copy into the analyzing optics and sensors of the scanner. Color prints commonly are called *C prints*, and drawings and paintings are called *art*.

Drum Scanners

The *drum scanner*, or rotary drum scanner, is appropriately named because it uses Plexiglas cylinders, called *drums*, to hold the copy being scanned (see Figure 3.8).

Figure 3.8
A modern color drum scanner.

Characteristics of Drum Scanners

Since the 1970s, drum scanners have been producing the bulk of all color separations used in the printing industry. Previously, separations were made by photographic methods. With the advent of digital imaging systems in 1979, the scanner also became a digital input device that converted photographic images into bitmapped pixels.

Drum scanners are designed specifically to sample flexible photographic images into RGB and CMYK color spaces. Hardware configurations come in single, all-in-one unit models and in modular form composed of two or three sections. Early models were analog machines with dozens of knobs and buttons; the latest drum scanners are digital with keyboard numeric control.

Drum scanners can be designed to perform two functions: input and output. Some scanners are used only as input devices, whereas others can separate and expose the separations directly to predetermined positions on film for page assembly purposes. These functions can occur simultaneously, whether the output is to film or to a digital storage device. Input involves the sampling (scanning) of an original image. The analyzing section of the machine handles the input. Output to film is accomplished by imaging photographic film; the exposing section of the scanner handles the output.

Anything flexible enough to be wrapped around the drum scanner's input cylinder can be scanned, provided it is within the cylinder's size dimensions, is of uniform thickness, and is not more than an inch thick. Items that are not flexible need to be converted to a flexible medium such as a color print or a transparency, which are the most commonly supplied image formats.

The drum scanner analyzes the copy being scanned by passing a beam of light through transmissive subjects (transparencies, slides) or reflecting off of opaque subjects (color prints, artwork). The light source must emit the complete visible spectrum of light so that all the possible colors of the original subject are transmitted to the scanner. The analyzing light source also should be of steady, stable illuminance. The most typical kinds of light sources are xenon and quartz halogen bulbs.

Sampling speeds of 30 seconds per inch are typical—making up to 50 samples per millimeter or 2,540 samples per inch. Optics and drive mechanisms meet strict manufacturing tolerances to ensure consistent sizing and image quality.

For transmissive subjects, the analyzing light can be focused into a tiny beam as small as .02mm. The beam passes through the Plexiglas cylinder and the transparency mounted on it. When the cylinder makes one complete rotation, the beam has sampled a vertical slice of the image. This scanned piece of image is called a *scan line*, which is a unit of information for the drum scanner, as illustrated in Figure 3.9. The amount of data in a scan line depends on the scanner's available resolution and the requested image resolution.

Reflective subjects must have the analyzing light reflected off their surfaces. Usually, this light is beamed onto the copy from multiple directions using fiber optics to give an even illuminance of the reflective original.

As the scan progresses, the cylinder continues to revolve, and the analyzing beam travels across

to produce higher quality images of superior tone and detail. (This information was referenced from Gary G. Field's *Color Scanning and Imaging Systems*.)

There are single-pass and three-pass scanners. A one-pass scanner scans copy one time, flashing red, green, and blue light as it moves across the copy. The three-pass scanner goes over the copy three times, each pass filtering the red, next the green, and then the blue on the third and final pass over the copy (see Figure 3.11).

The actual hardware is compact because of the CCD linear array size and because there is no need for a special exposing section. The small dimension of CCD units has inspired the term *desktop* scanner because the entire unit can fit on a desktop.

Flatbed CCD scanners are strictly input devices and all signals from them are digital. The CCD image file contains only RGB data. Conversion to CMYK values is performed on a workstation as a separate function included with the scanner's software or using different programs designed for RGB to CMYK translations. These translations from RGB to CMYK color space should be calibrated for the color characteristics of the CMYK system. (See "Special Concerns for Color Separation" in Chapter 15.)

Linear CCD Scanner Array

A linear CCD array is a row of sensors that scans one line of pixel information at a time. Either the copy moves across the focusing lens and light or the light and mirror move as the copy stays stationary. For many transparency scanners, the template holding the original copy slowly moves across the light source, and the color information is bounced off mirrors through a lens to the CCD linear array. As samples are taken, the information is transferred and stored temporarily in a buffer. The number of pixels desired determines the number of samples taken. A stable, even light source is necessary for illuminating the original copy held in the flatbed template. Xenon or quartz halogen bulbs normally are used for light sources.

In single pass scanners, copy is scanned three times: one pass each for red, green, and blue information. Color data from the scans can be stored temporarily in a small, one-image buffer housed in the scanner until it can be transferred to a workstation. The buffer on a scanner frees your computer for other processing and permits you to retrieve your image at your convenience. Many other CCD scanners transfer file information to the workstation during scanning and tie up the workstation during the scanning process as illustrated in Figure 3.12.

Area Array CCD Scanner

An area array contains sensor elements placed in a matrix that capture an entire image in one or three exposures without moving the sensors or copy. Area arrays are faster but more expensive than linear areas. Also, the largest area arrays have smaller resolution capabilities than the highest resolution linear arrays. The exposure time of a linear array can be close to four minutes while an area array can be exposed in less than a second. The commercial PhotoCD scanning system uses area arrays to provide a quick production of a large amount of images (see Figure 3.13). Digital cameras have either linear or area arrays.

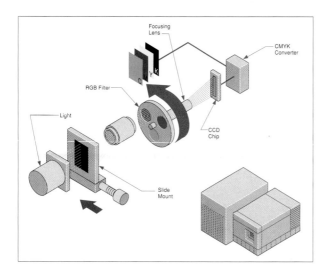

Figure 3.11
A three-pass linear CCD
scanner.

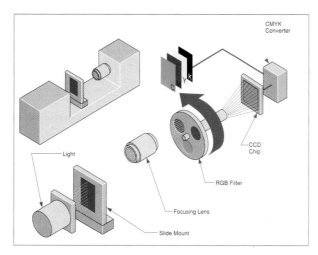

Figure 3.12
Single-Pass CCD linear
scanner.

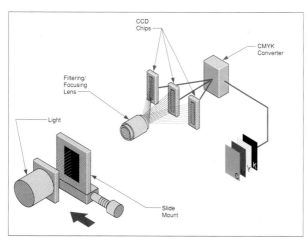

Figure 3.13
Three-exposure CCD Area
Array scanner.

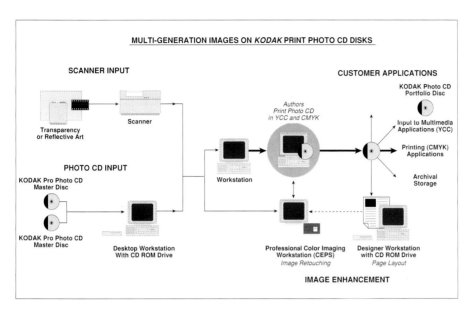

Figure 3.14
The production path of PhotoCD image scanning.

PhotoCD Scans

The PhotoCD system marketed by Kodak is not so much a scanning method as it is a scanning system. The PhotoCD system provides a convenient and inexpensive method of scanning and storing negatives and positive film to compact discs.

Up to 100 digital files are compressed and stored in a proprietary Kodak YCC file format. The PhotoCD authoring system scans images with an area array scanner. The scanned RGB information is converted into the YCC color space. The Y represents the luminance or grayscale values of the image and the C values are the color chrominance values. Designed initially for display on televisions, the YCC color space is similar to the way television broadcast color is

transmitted. The YCC is easy to convert to display on television monitors, but introduces some problems when converting to CMYK.

The YCC format makes it convenient to compress the values to fit more images on the CD-ROM disc. Since the luminance is the most important part of the human visual system, the PhotoCD system compresses the chrominance data to achieve file saving.

There are two PhotoCD systems: the standard, which allows only 35mm size film to be scanned, and the ProPhotoCD, which provides scanning of film up to 4 by 5 inches. The standard system provides five different resolutions up to 2,048 by 3,072 pixels. The Pro version provides seven resolutions up to 6,144 by 4,096 pixels. The entire PhotoCD system is outlined in Figure 3.14.

Digital Cameras

Digital cameras are fast becoming a new method of digitizing scenes. Rather than using film (including exposure, processing, and scanning), the digital camera allows immediate introduction of a scene into a digital workstation. There are many reasons to believe that digital cameras will become common in the future. For now there are several issues about the effectiveness of digital cameras that need to be addressed: resolution, dynamic range limitations, cost, and convenience. The two types of digital cameras are linear and area array CCDs.

The linear cameras have an obvious disadvantage because the scene must be focused onto the arrays one scan line at a time. This means that the exposure times could reach up to seven minutes depending on the resolution required. The long exposure means that still images are the only realistic elements that can reliably be photographed. The long exposure is not a problem for product or catalog shots, but to illuminate the scene you need to use a constant source of "hot," color corrected light. The amount of heat generated by the constant illumination can be problematic to the sensitive computer circuitry if it is not vented properly.

Linear array cameras are much less expensive to produce, and the resolution they can achieve is much greater than the typical area array. The largest commercially viable area array camera is 2,048 by 2,048 elements, and the linear array cameras can produce images upwards of 7,000 by 6,000 pixels. The area array cameras can use the fast strobe light to make exposures, but even the area arrays suffer a significant heat build-up if not properly cooled.

There are several low resolution area array cameras capturing 640 by 480 pixels. Several photojournalists are using a Nikon camera that uses existing lenses and captures 1,524 by 1,012 pixels. The sampling is done using a single two-second or less exposure, similar to a photo graphic camera. Image data is recorded on a reusable magnetic floppy disk at a fixed resolution, or a half resolution that doubles during the digitizing stage. Half resolution (field mode) doubles the number of frames you can store on one disk. Of course, image quality and sharpness is reduced because there is less information using half resolution. Using a frame grabber, the disk is placed in a still video player. The individual frames from the camera's disk can be stored digitally as standard file formats (such as PICT and TIFF).

Video sources are analogous to the digital camera. Video cameras capture images onto analog tape. A video capture board isolates individual frames and transfers them to a workstation. The resolution of images from video sources is typically around 512 by 486 pixels. You should consider the final use of the image when you are using video images for reproduction to mediums other than video. Video does not carry the color fidelity and resolution required for many print applications, but multimedia presentations work well with video source images.

Digital cameras are sure to become a more common fixture in image reproduction (see Figure 3.15). Because the photography and scanning operations are eliminated, you can enjoy significant time and cost savings. But film still provides a level of quality, flexibility, cost, and speed that will be difficult to match. Both

Figure 3.15
An image captured by a digital camera.

film and digital cameras will have areas where one excels over the other. The trick, as with any new technology, is to find the areas where it is most suited.

Comparing Drum and CCD Scanners

Two areas in which drum and flatbed scanners differ the most are speed and cost. An 8" × 10" final size scan from a 4" × 5" original averages only two minutes on a drum scanner versus at least an hour using a CCD device. The CCD method takes much longer because three steps are required to get to film: the scanning (three passes to get RGB), translating of the CMYK files from the RGB data using software, and the imaging of the film on an image setter. CCD scanners may be slower than their powerful rotary drum counterparts, but the CCD scanners

can deliver excellent reproduction quality for a price much less than the typical drum scanner.

Training on a CCD scanner usually is accomplished in a day because the machines are simple to operate, but color theory and press condition knowledge still should be a part of the operator's skills.

Scanner Resolution

As mentioned in Chapter 1, device resolution pertains to the number of image elements per unit of measure. Scanners are categorized by their input resolutions, described as samples or elements per inch (epi) or elements per millimeter (epmm). (DPI is incorrectly used to describe scanner input resolution.) Typical CCD scanner arrays can range from 2,048 to 4,096 total elements; therefore, files created by CCD scanners are limited by the fixed number of elements.

Image pixel resolution is adjusted by focusing the array with lenses over a small or large physical copy size. For example, a 2,048-element array focused over the width of a 4" × 5" copy produces more sampling per inch than if focused over the width of an 8" × 10" piece of copy. You should consider this difference when comparing scanners described as 300 to 600 epi. This designation means the scanner can produce input samples from 300 to 600 samples or pixels per inch of copy. But as the copy size increases, the relative image resolution decreases because the sampling of the fixed CCD elements are spread over a greater distance.

In comparison, high-end drum scanners can achieve sampling rates of up to 2,540 epi and are limited only by the precision and quality of the optics used to produce the digital scan, not by fixed elements. The more samples you scan from an image, the more image pixels you produce and the more accurate the digital reproduction. It is important to remember that the maximum amount of samples needed is proportional to the resolution of your output device. Inputting more data than your output device can handle is called oversampling.

As previously mentioned, the amount of digital information input to the color system should be compatible with the amount of information needed at the output stage. Too little information results in a poor-quality image, and too much data wastes storage space and needlessly increases processing time.

Sizing With Scanners

Another basic difference between high-end and low-end desktop scanners is the method used to determine output image size and resolution. Most drum scanners can size original images to a wide range of magnifications and reductions, typically 16–3,000 percent. Resolution is automatically set according to selected screen ruling (LPI), or selected by hardwired settings in the scanner, or selected using a desired resolution value entered by the operator.

Desktop CCD scanners typically scan at only 100 percent. Sizing is accomplished either by re-sampling the total amount of pixels or by limiting the number of sensors used during the scanning process. The scanner always scans at 100 percent; it is fixed to specific sampling resolutions due to the number of elements in the CCD array. The specific sampling resolutions are usually even increments of the maximum scanning resolution. If a scanner has a

maximum of 300 sampling elements per inch, then available resolutions would be 200, 150, 100, 75, 50, and so on. Any other sampling rates will involve sampling the image up or down after the scan.

Regardless of the type of scanner you use, you must take a sufficient number of samples of the original image to produce a digital image with enough pixels to satisfy the output resolution requirements. To determine which file resolution to ask the scanner for, you must use math to make some final determinations.

1. Determine the final physical size of the image that you want to reproduce. If you do not know what your final size will be, then you should always defer to the maximum possible size. Let's use 8"x10".

2. Determine the resolution of your direct output device or the line screen of the halftone screen that you plan to use. Again, if you are not sure which line screen will be used, then you should defer to the maximum possible line screen. Let's use a 150 dpi line screen.

3. Identify the sampling ratio of your output device—the relationship of image pixels to either halftone dots or direct imaging elements. Because we are using halftone dots, the ratio is two image pixels per one halftone dot or 2:1.

4. Multiplying step 2 by step 3 gives you your resolution: 150 dpi × (two pixels per one halftone dot) equals 300 pixels per inch (ppi).

5. Multiplying the physical size (step 1) by the resolution (step 4) will give you the total pixel width and height that you will need. This information is useful for scanning your image to the proper number of pixels, especially if the physical size of your original is different from your final output size.

6. To determine the required scanning resolution, take the total number of pixels and divide that by the physical size of your original. This will give you the resolution that you need to scan your original image. For example, if your original is a 4" × 5" transparency, 2,400 pixels divided by 4" and 3,000 pixels divided by 5" equals 600 ppi. Therefore, you should scan your original at 600 ppi resolution (with your scanner set at 100 percent). Remember that the physical proportion of the original and final output should be the same.

You also should recognize that the same 4" × 5" original scanned for 2,400 by 3,000 pixels can be scanned a variety of ways depending on the controls available on the scanner. For example, 600 ppi at 100 percent is the same as scanning an image at 300 ppi at 200 percent. The total result of pixels is the same. Figure 3.16 illustrates this concept.

Be sure that your image size ratio does not exceed the range of 30-600 percent for transparent originals. If so, you may want to consider having the scan done on a high end scanner for better results. With reflective originals, try not to enlarge more than 200 percent. Reflective originals, such as C prints, degrade rapidly in quality after being enlarged more than two times. (For best results, start with originals 4" × 5" or larger.)

If the scanner operator enters an odd magnification that is not a simple division of 300, the scanner arrives at the correct pixel count by upsampling or downsampling by software. For example, a 144 percent enlargement of an image at 300 ppi would first be scanned at 300 ppi and upsampled 44 percent, or scanned at 600 ppi and downsampled 72 percent automatically by the scanner.

As mentioned in Chapter 1, any interpolation of the image during the reproduction process may cause degradation of the image. Therefore, scanning at 300 ppi or 600 ppi will yield direct pixel imaging from the scanner without using image degrading interpolation. Unfortunately, for most scanning some interpolating will be needed to achieve proper final image size. There are two choices available to adjust size using postscan interpolation: internal scanning software and external software programs. We recommend testing scan images with fine detail at odd sizes and at various reductions and enlargements using each software. Then use the one that gives you the best reproduction.

When sending away images to be scanned, it is important to be aware of the fundamental differences between sizing and nonsizing scanners. Be sure to give the final resolution needed (in ppi or in total pixels), as well as the percent magnification or reduction required for each subject being reproduced. Never request scans by file size only.

Scanned 100% @ 150 ppi
Physical size 50% of orig.

**ORIGINAL SIZE
2 by 1.5 inches
ALL IMAGES
OUTPUT @ 300 PPI**

Scanned 100%
@ 300 ppi
100% of orig.

**Scanned 100% @ 408 ppi
Physical size 166% of orig.**

**Scanned 100% @ 600 ppi
Physical size 200% of orig.**

SIZING WITH RESOLUTION ADJUSTMENTS

Figure 3.16

Checklist

1. Whenever submitting scans to be done off-site, be sure to include both the magnification (or reduction) percentage and resolution in pixels (total or ppi). Inquire about the types of scanners available and their capabilities. Be sure that your images not only end up at the correct physical size but also at the correct number of total pixels.

2. Before scanning, thoroughly clean all images of dust and dirt. Notice if the dirt is on the image or in it. Transparencies can hold dirt inside the emulsion layers; dirt and dust is often transferred to the image in a photographic print. Dirt and scratches that cannot be physically removed should be electronically edited out.

3. Carefully analyze each image to be scanned for color reproduction characteristics such as image quality (proper exposure and graininess) and reproduction aim points such as highlight/shadow points and special colors (see Chapter 14).

4. Make sure that your scanner has solid footing. Outside vibrations during the scan will reduce quality.

5. Post-analyze the scan to see if you matched the prescan analysis.

6. Retouch any unwanted specs and spots.

Final Word

The scanning step can be considered the most important step in the entire reproduction process because if you don't capture all the original image data to begin with, you can't retrieve it later on. Original image data not brought in by the scan cannot be replaced by replication or interpolation because the computer cannot imagine what was missed. If all the critical data of the original does not come in the front end, it cannot appear at the back end.

We cannot emphasize enough the importance of a good quality original. Although the reality of everyday production precludes having perfect originals every time, you should always choose the best possible image to scan.

Operating a scanner involves many steps that must be performed in a specific sequence. Training usually takes two to three weeks. Working in a high-speed production scanner shop requires experienced craftspeople to produce the highest possible quality and quantity. Scanner operation, color theory, photography, and press conditions are all considerations a journeyman operator will make while scanning.

Color scanning is a craft done with the goal of obtaining the best reproduction of the subjects being sampled. As with any craft, attention to detail and knowledge of the entire reproduction process will yield the best results.

Image
Rendering

"Imagination is more
important than knowledge."
Albert Einstein

Not long ago, the definition of graphics was very specific. Physical representations of images and graphics created with traditional methods were easy to recognize. Not only could you see or touch a painting, photograph, ink, or pencil drawing, but you could also easily recognize and identify it as a graphic. Now with the emergence of computers, the definition of graphics has been expanded to include any digital data that is intended to be output to some kind of visual and/or physical form. Think of digital data as virtual output. The intention of physical output has been equated to actual output. The data is not yet output, but it has all the required instructions that describe an image or graphic.

The traditional method of judging a graphic is no longer sufficient in the modern world. Computer graphics basically represent a potential for a graphic. When digital data is interpreted into some kind of physical display—such as paper, film, or a monitor—it is a graphic in the purest sense of the word. Although a file contains graphic information, it has only the potential for graphic display. At some point, all digital data must be interpreted into visual information or picture elements for us to see it as a graphic or image. Strings of binary information do not reach our eyes as a panoramic scene (as illustrated in Figure 4.1a) until they are translated (see Figure 4.1b). A graphic in binary code contains the information needed to create visual output. Literally, binary image information represents the potential for visual information, but digital information is not physically visible.

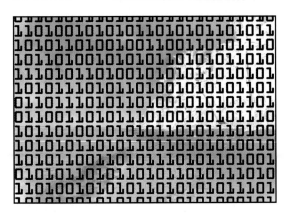

Figure 4.1a
The zeroes and ones of binary code cannot be seen as images until they are interpreted and rendered to physical output.

Figure 4.1b
The actual image after being interpreted.

Input is the conversion of physical visual information into digital data. Output is the conversion of digital data into visual information. The digital production process also includes scanning and rendering. Scanning is the term used to convert physical visual information into digital data. Rendering is the term used to convert digital data into physical visual information.

What goes in must come out. For digital data to come out as something you can recognize, you must interpret or render the data into visual stimulation. You should become intimately familiar with the term render. At some point, all computer graphics must be rendered to be seen. No exceptions.

You may find it helpful to know some of the synonyms for the word *render*. To grasp the relationship of rendering to digital output, you can use the words *make, assign, provide, show, translate,* and *interpret* in place of render. For example, you can say "Digital data is rendered into visual output." Well, some of the words may need some verb tense changes, but you get the idea. You must assign the data to some visual form.

At points during the production process, digital data must be converted into picture elements for display. Regardless of the output that you have planned for your digital information or how the imagery is manipulated, humans recognize the patterns of imagery as something familiar. We must at some point have that image created into picture elements. We cannot "see" an image with a string of math. Our eyes are made up of individual receptors that sense light reflection. Math does not reflect light into the eyes. This may seem like a trivial distinction, but acknowledging the abstract nature of digital data provides a greater insight into the creation and manipulation of digital images. Digital imagery can be created with many methods, but there is always a translation to pixel-based information when the images are finally output.

Bitmap & Vectors

All computer graphics can be placed into two main categories of image creation: bitmap and vector. A bitmap image uses picture elements or pixels. (The word raster is often used instead of bitmap, but it means the same thing.) Vector data is a way of creating shapes and lines using points and mathematical formulas to connect those points.

The term *graphic* is often associated with vector, and the term *image* is usually associated with bitmap. Graphics, as we know them, are shapes and lines that are created by vector data. Images are associated with photos or scenes that are created by bitmaps. Although the terms are interchangeable, vector graphics and bitmap images help define which kind of data is being used and how it is created.

Bitmaps

Pixels are arranged on a grid called a bitmap. This grid or map contains individual picture elements in a pattern representing the scene to be displayed. The variety of values for each pixel is defined by the color-bit depth. Corresponding imaging elements on an output device create an image when the bitmap pixel information is rendered to the device. A bitmap image is *resolution dependent* because the digital data being rendered into an image depends on the number of pixels and how the pixels are distributed over a physical distance. For a more in-depth discussion of bitmaps and pixels review Chapter 1, "What are Pixels?."

Vectors

Vectors are a series of points using mathematical formulas to connect the points. Unlike pixels, which are discrete individual units, vector points are not discrete. A bitmap image contains pixels at a fixed location described by x and y coordinates. A point in a vector language such as Postscript describes a place of transition in the formula that is used to create lines and shapes. Vectors are primarily used for line drawing. Files that contain vector data sometimes are referred to as linework files. A simple shape such as a circle can be described as $x^2 + y^2 = r^2$ as shown in Figure 4.2.

Points in a vector graphic have a location but no area until the points are rendered to a visual output device. Without a specific area to describe, vector data is easily altered and resized without any resolution considerations or loss of quality. Due to the lack of resolution considerations, vectors are considered resolution independent.

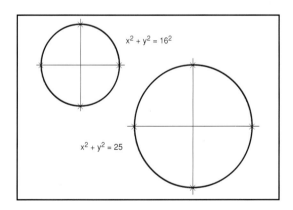

Figure 4.2
A circle with a radius of 4 is easily scaled to a radius of 5 without loss in quality by simply changing the values in the formula for a circle.

Resolution independent means that regardless of output size, the vector information stays the same. You easily can resize or scale vector graphics without losing quality before rendering the data to visual output. The quality of vector graphics is not dependent on the digital information, but on the quality of the output device to which the information is being rendered. Vector data is rendered at the resolution of the output device. Bitmap images are resolution dependent because the size of the physical output depends on the resolution of the image, and the quality is compromised if the image is resized or altered excessively.

As vector graphics become more complex, so do the formulas or languages that describe them. The most common vector-based language is PostScript. PostScript is popular in typography because type is changed and altered frequently. Type is a common vector-based element that is often scaled to many different sizes while retaining its quality whether the type is as small as 8 points, or as large as 300 points. You can resize and change any vector graphic freely without loss of relative quality as shown in Figure 4.3. With this flexibility in mind, why would you use anything but vectors to create images? As you will read, vectors do not provide a complete solution to image creation.

The quality of output from vector data is typically high, but it depends greatly on the resolution of the output device. The lines and curves are sharp, well-defined, and continuous if they are output to a high resolution device. Simple lines and shapes are relatively easy to describe using vector data. Vector data also contain specific attributes of lines and shapes such as line thickness, fill area, and color.

Vectors easily can describe simple spot color, but describing complex color with vectors is neither simple nor effective.

Vector Color

Vectors and the shapes they describe are extremely pliable. Transition steps between different shapes are easily produced. In this process, often called "in-betweening" or "tweening," two or more objects can metamorphose into a sequence of intermediate steps from one object to another (shown in Figure 4.4). Blends of color can be created using a tweening process. The blends created with vectors are complex and can be complicated to output.

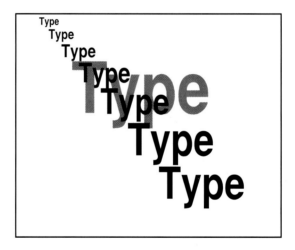

Figure 4.3
Type is the most common use of vector graphics because of the need for high quality and easy resizing.

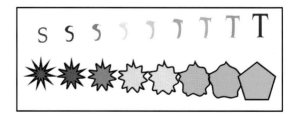

Figure 4.4
Vector shapes and objects are easily tweened.

Using vectors to define more elaborate color, such as continuous color tones or blends, has disadvantages. The complexity of the formulas to create color is so great that the file sizes become large and often are completely unmanageable. The amount of data required for complex color also increases the time it takes to process and render to output. Colors used in vector graphics typically are limited to spot colors and simple blends. Steps or banding can be seen in many blends created with vectors (see Figures 4.5a-c).

The complexity of color makes vectors a poor choice for dealing with photographic images. The bitmap is better equipped to handle and produce vignettes and blends of colors because a bitmap simulates how you actually see the world and images. Vectors deal best with outlines and shapes; bitmaps deal best with colors and blends. An ideal solution is to bring the two together. Most image programs now enable you to render vectors into a bitmap so that you can take advantage of a bitmap's superior handling of color.

Rendering & RIP

Because every image you see is made of picture elements, at some point, all digital data—whether vectors or bitmaps—must be rendered into pixels. All images you see have pixels as their base. Rendering, or translating digital data into physical output, is the most important part of realizing the images you create. The term RIP (*raster image processing*) is casually bandied about when digital files are output to printers and imagesetters. Basically, RIP and render mean the same thing: translating digital image data into physical visual images and graphics (see Figure 4.6).

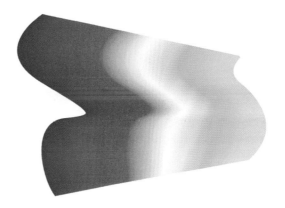

Figure 4.5a
Shaped blends can be created with vectors.

Figure 4.5b
A bitmap-only processed blend.

Figure 4.5c
A vector processed blend can have banding problems.

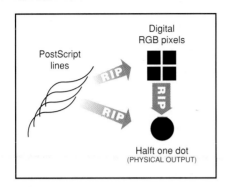

Figure 4.6
Vector data can take different paths when rendered to physical output.

Raster Image Processing

Contrary to the feelings of many persons who have waited long hours for their printed output, RIP does not stand for "rest in peace." The term RIP or RIPing is used to indicate the conversion of digital information into physical output. Each horizontal line of a bitmap's pixel information can be referred to as a scan line or a raster line. Raster images are images with lines of pixels and RIP is the name used to indicate the processing of those images. As mentioned earlier, you can interchange the term RIP and render because they have the same meaning. We prefer the term render because it is more precise as to what is actually happening to digital data. But RIP has such a significant place in digital vernacular, you may need to use both terms.

The simplest output devices translate only one raster line (see Figure 4.7) at a time and then output that line to film, paper, or a monitor. A more effective method would be to have an entire image analyzed at one time and have a processor convert all the necessary information into visual output. This method of converting digital information into output is called raster image processing (RIP). The words that you are

Figure 4.7
A complete horizontal line of pixels is called a raster line.

now reading are a result of raster image processing. Created on a word processor, the digital data was translated into physical output. Monitors are another example of the result of raster image processing. Any image you see on your screen is digital information translated into light for you to view.

Awareness of the translating function of RIP helps you understand the importance of preparing digital data correctly. If a foreign word is spoken incorrectly, the translation of the word will not be correct. The same is true for digital data; if the data is not correct to begin with, the RIP function will not correct the data.

The processing of digital data to printed output often requires the image processor to know and understand the details of the output device. *Printer Page Descriptions*, or PPDs, are specific files that contain important information about the output device in order to connect an image application with the output device. If you consider PostScript to be the primary language, PPDs are the dialects that an output device understands. Without a PPD, the output device may not interpret and output the file properly. Most output device and image applications outline which PPDs are needed to correctly RIP and output the digital data.

RIP is actually a program that can reside in one of two locations. First, and most common, is the hardware RIP. A hardware RIP is a computer attached to an output device with the singular purpose of translating digital image data for output. Image data is sent from a workstation to the computer that is attached to the output device. The hardware RIP program has one function: to interpret the image data and give raw on/off instructions to the output device. The RIPing process is complex and much of the output device's rating is based on the image processing speed. The speed of the interpreter or RIP is a big factor in the efficiency of the entire reproduction process. Because of the dedicated computer, hardware RIPs are typically faster than software RIPs.

A software RIP performs many of the same functions as a hardware RIP. The software RIP is usually located at a workstation that is not necessarily dedicated only to the RIP function. The software RIP still interprets the digital data into information that is required for the output device to function properly. The main disadvantage to a software RIP is that the workstation may not be configured to perform at speeds equal to a dedicated hardware RIP. Software RIPs also are hindered because they usually require a large amount of free hard disk space. The hard disk storage is necessary because all of the digital data that is processed must be saved before it is sent to the output device.

Regardless of these inconveniences, software RIPs are gaining favor for a variety of reasons. The biggest advantage with software RIPs is that they can be easily upgraded. When a new feature or faster software is developed, a software RIP can be installed like any new version of software. Unlike a hardware RIP which may require replacement of physical parts to the dedicated computer, the software RIP is simply loaded on the required workstation. Since the software RIP works with existing hardware, you have no additional expense in buying or maintaining separate hardware.

Although it may be problematic for software RIPs to save the processed digital data before sending it to the output device, there is a potential advantage. The saved processed image data can be available for additional alterations and manipulations. Whether you use a software or hardware RIP, the function is primarily the same—to interpret digital image data into physical output.

Bitmap Direct Image Rendering

This is a good place to emphasize that all digital data that we see must be rendered to visual output. The most straightforward way is direct image rendering. Each bitmap pixel matches with an output imaging element. The best example of direct image rendering is a monitor.

Monitors, like all output devices, have a fixed number of imaging elements. The optimum way to output to a direct imaging device like a monitor is to match bitmap pixels to imaging elements one to one. Any more pixels than the number of imaging elements available will not display (see Figure 4.8). Any fewer pixels means the physical size of the image displayed will not fill the entire monitor.

A typical direct imaging color printer (often called a continuous tone printer) has 300 imaging elements per inch (epi). This means that 300 pixels in a bitmap image are output at a physical size of one inch. A bitmap image 1200 pixels across and 1500 pixels down and a

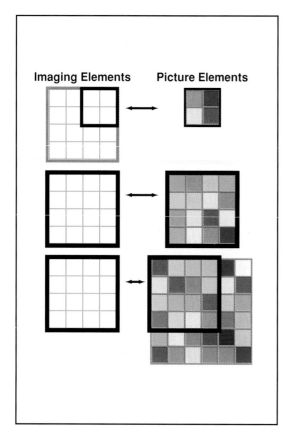

Imaging Elements   **Picture Elements**

Figure 4.8
The picture elements of a digital image
match directly with the imaging elements
of a direct imaging device like a monitor.

Figures 4.9a-b
Continuous appearance when pixels match
one to one with direct imaging output.
Pixelization occurs when the number of
pixels is less than the device's full
capability.

resolution of 300 pixels per inch (ppi) results in
a physical output size from a 300 epi printer of
4" × 5". If the physical size needs to be greater,
then the number of pixels will need to be
increased or the resolution will have to be
adjusted. If the resolution is changed to 100 ppi,
each pixel will occupy 3 imaging elements
across and 3 imaging elements down. As a
result, the continuous quality of the image will
not be high (see Figures 4.9a and b).

Bitmap Halftone Rendering

The relationship of bitmap pixels to imaging
elements of direct image output devices is very
different than to halftone output. Halftone
output relies on the resolution of the bitmap

image as well as the resolution of the output device. The way in which bitmap pixels relate to halftone dots is just as important as the way in which the resolution of the output device impacts the quality of halftone dots. The resolution of output devices is also discussed in Chapter 1.

Pixels to Halftones

To understand the rendering of bitmap pixels to halftone dots, you should begin with one basic assumption: in most cases the optimum relationship of pixels to halftone dots is two to one (2:1). Since we are working in two dimensions, 22 pixels per 1 halftone dot—the combined value of the pixels relates to the value of the single halftone dot.

Halftone Dots

Laser printers, imagesetters, and printing presses only print solid areas of a color. These printing devices cannot produce shades of gray. To create an illusion of tone, the imaging element of the output devices are used to create solid dots called *halftones*. A group of equal-sized solid halftone dots placed on a fixed grid creates the illusion of tone commonly referred to as *screen tints*. The halftone dot creates the illusion of differing amounts of tone by varying the physical size of the dots. The larger the dot, the darker the tone—the smaller the dots, the lighter the tone. Figure 4.10 shows screens that create gray from 10 to 95 percent.

Halftone dots are fixed on an imaginary grid, as shown in Figure 4.11. On this grid there are a fixed number of halftone dots per inch. Each

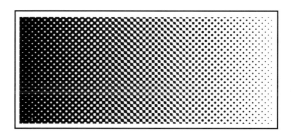

Figure 4.10
Halftone dots are used to create visual tones.

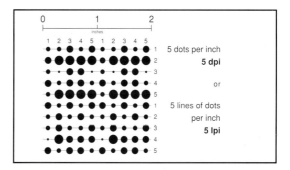

Figure 4.11
The lines of halftone dots per inch (lpi) describes line screen resolution for print output.

halftone dot changes its value by changing its size. Halftone dots are considered amplitude modulation dots because in a given image the size or amplitude changes, but the number or frequency of halftone dots does not change. The number of halftone dots per inch (dpi) is the resolution of the halftone dots that create tone.

If you can imagine lines running through the middle of each halftone dot, you would find that the distance between each line is identical to the distance between each halftone dot. This is consistent with the imaginary grid on which halftone dots are placed. The lines are used to describe the resolution of halftone dots as *line* screen or *lines per inch* (lpi). The term *screen* relates to traditional nondigital methods of creating halftones with a physical halftone screen.

The higher the line screen is, the more dots per inch you have. The lpi or dpi relates to the overall quality of the tone produced with the dots. To fit more dots per inch requires a smaller and finer dot. A smaller halftone dot is less visible to the eye. The finer the dot is, the more continuous an image using halftone dots may appear, as illustrated in Figures 4.12a-d.

The individual halftone dots are created using the imaging elements in the output device. In the grid of halftone dots, each dot sits in an individual cell. If you look at the individual cells, you will find that each cell consists of the imaging elements available in the output device. The number of imaging elements per inch (epi) available in an output device is called the *device resolution*. The higher the device resolution (epi) is, the more elements are available to create a halftone dot.

To determine the number of imaging elements available to create a halftone dot, you must take into consideration the lpi or line screen of the halftone dots used and the epi or resolution of the output device. Consider a line screen of 100 lpi that is output from an imagesetter with a resolution of 1200 epi. (Remember that you are always working with two dimensions.) Every inch contains 100 dots and every inch contains 1200 imaging elements. Each dot is then created by a cell that contains 12 by 12 imaging elements. A 12 by 12 cell is a total of 144 on/off imaging elements. The 12 by 12 cell can

potentially create 144 different halftone dots and therefore simulate 144 levels of gray.

To illustrate graphically how a halftone dot is created, let's work with a smaller number of imaging elements. If you print with a halftone line screen of 20 lpi and you have an imagesetter that is 80 epi, each halftone dot will be created from a cell of 4 by 4 imaging elements. This cell provides 16 levels of gray, as illustrated in Figure 4.13a. If you take the same imagesetter and instead want a line screen of 40 lpi, each halftone dot will be created from a cell of 2 by 2 imaging elements and will provide 4 levels of gray, as shown in Figure 4.13b.

High quality digital imaging is based on 256 levels of gray or 8 bits of tonal information. In order to create 256 different halftone dots, you need a minimum-sized halftone cell of 16 by 16 imaging elements. It is easy to translate the tone from 256 digital values to 256 halftone values since it is a one-to-one relationship.

Although few printing presses can accurately print 256 different halftone dots, having 256 different halftones provides a greater degree of accuracy as well as a direct translation from 8-bit digital tonal values. Figure 4.13c illustrates how the resolution of the output device and the halftone line screen determine the size of the halftone cell available. Note that a very common 2400 epi imagesetter uses a 16 by 16 image element cell to create a halftone dot for a 150 line screen, the most popular line screen used in commercial printing.

Another key ingredient to creating tone with halftone dots is the angle of the rows of dots.

Figure 4.12a
Image with 65 lpi.

Figure 4.12b
Image with 85 lpi.

Figure 4.12c
Image with 120 lpi.

Figure 4.12d
Image with 133 lpi.

The halftone dots are most visible when at a 0 degree angle and least visible when rotated to 45 degrees where the dots seem to visually mesh together. The eye is very sensitive to uniform patterns, and placing halftone dots at angles helps disrupt the uniform rows of dots. Figures 4.14a-c show how the angle of halftone dots affects how smooth the tone appears.

The imaging elements of the output device do not rotate to create angled halftone dots. The imaginary cells of imaging elements rotate to accommodate the creation of angled halftone dots. The intricacies of halftone screening and angles are beyond the scope of this book, but you should be aware of the basic issues surrounding the creation and structure of halftone dots.

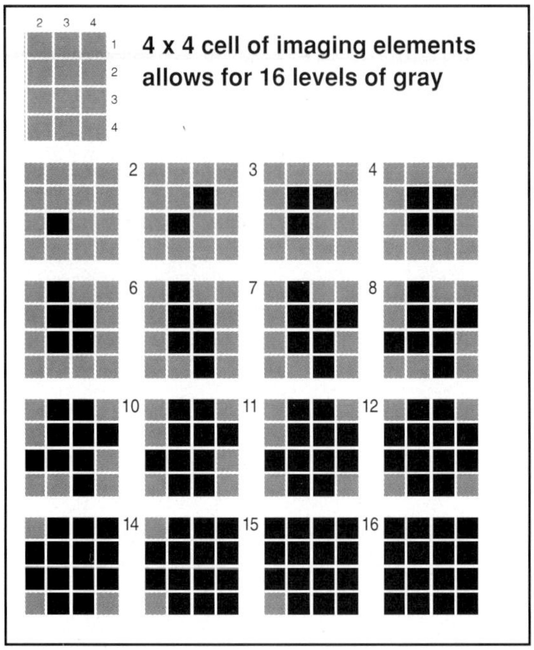

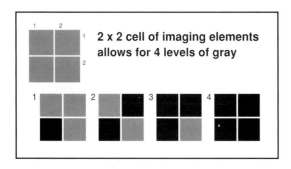

Figure 4.13a
A halftone cell of 4 by 4 imaging elements provides for 16 different halftone dots and 16 levels of gray.

Figure 4.13b
A halftone cell of 2 by 2 imaging elements provides for 4 different halftone dots and 4 levels of gray.

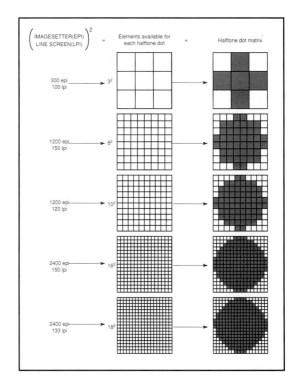

Figure 4.13c
The number of imaging elements available for each halftone cell is determined by dividing the output device resolution (epi) by the number of halftone dots per inch (lpi).

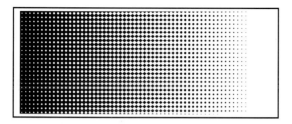

Figure 4.14a
Halftone dots at an angle of 0 degrees.

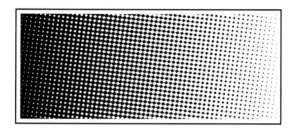

Figure 4.14b
Halftone dots at an angle of 8 degrees.

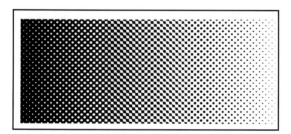

Figure 4.14c
Halftone dots at an angle of 45 degrees.

Frequency Modulated Dots

Frequency modulated dots (FM) or fixed-sized random dots are another method of creating printed tone. These dots are often referred to as *stochastic dots*. Stochastic comes from a Greek word meaning random. FM dots create different tones by regulating the number or frequency of dots, not by varying the size of dots, as is done with more traditional amplitude-modulated (AM) halftone dots.

Describing halftone dots as either FM or AM is similar to the difference between FM and AM radio broadcasting. The AM radio signal is like the AM halftone dot because distance between two radio waves or AM dots is always the same. The amplitude or size of the wave or dot varies. With FM radio waves or printing dots, the frequency or distance from wave to wave or dot to dot varies while the amiplitude, or size, stays the same.

In AM dot printing, the larger the dot, the greater the value of the tone, and the smaller the dot, the lighter the values of the tone. In FM dot printing, you print more dots to create darker tones, and you print fewer dots to create lighter tones. Figures 4.15a-d illustrate the differences between AM and FM dots.

The relationship of bitmap pixels to FM dots is one to one. Typically, FM dots are printed at very high dot frequency, starting at 300 dpi and reaching upwards of 600 dpi. Because there are not fixed rows of dots with FM dots, the term lpi does not apply and the term dpi is appropriately used to describe the total number of dots per inch.

Like AM halftone dots, FM dots are created using the imaging elements of the output device. The cells are of fixed size and are either turned completely on or off. The cells are most efficient when the number of dots per inch of FM dots divides evenly into the device resolution. For example, an output device of 1200 epi outputting a dot frequency of 300 dpi creates an FM cell of 4 by 4 imaging elements. But that same 1200 epi device outputting a dot frequency of 350 does not result in an even number of imaging elements for each cell. This may lessen the quality of the dots since they may not all be of a fixed size.

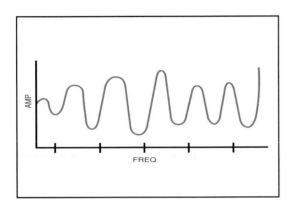

Figure 4.15a
An amplitude modulated (AM) wave.

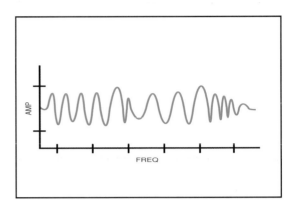

Figure 4.15b
A frequency modulated (FM) wave.

Figure 4.15c
An amplitude modulated (AM) halftone dot image.

Figure 4.15d
A frequency modulated (FM) stochastic dot image.

If you use the same example as the halftone dots above and use a device of 80 epi and a dot frequency of 20 dpi, you get that same 4 by 4 cell of imaging elements. If you try a dot frequency of 30 dpi, the cell of image is approximately 2.67 by 2.67, as illustrated in Figure 4.16.

The previous sections show how imaging elements can be used to produce the tonal values of a bitmap image. The same imaging elements can be used to reproduce the lines and shapes of vector graphics.

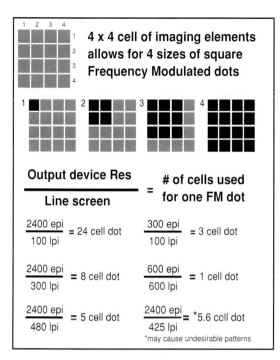

4 x 4 cell of imaging elements allows for 4 sizes of square Frequency Modulated dots

$$\frac{\text{Output device Res}}{\text{Line screen}} = \frac{\text{\# of cells used}}{\text{for one FM dot}}$$

$$\frac{2400\ \text{epi}}{100\ \text{lpi}} = 24\ \text{cell dot} \qquad \frac{300\ \text{epi}}{100\ \text{lpi}} = 3\ \text{cell dot}$$

$$\frac{2400\ \text{epi}}{300\ \text{lpi}} = 8\ \text{cell dot} \qquad \frac{600\ \text{epi}}{600\ \text{lpi}} = 1\ \text{cell dot}$$

$$\frac{2400\ \text{epi}}{480\ \text{lpi}} = 5\ \text{cell dot} \qquad \frac{2400\ \text{epi}}{425\ \text{lpi}} = {}^{*}5.6\ \text{coll dot}$$

*may cause undesirable patterns

Figure 4.16
The most uniform FM dots are created when using an output device whose resolution is evenly divisible by the dpi used.

Rendering Vector Graphics

Vectors describe a shape or a line in relative terms. A line described as six points thick and two inches long turns on the number of output imaging elements necessary to produce a line six points thick and two inches long. Unlike bitmaps which relate pixels to imaging elements (directly or to halftone dots), vector data simply ask for a certain size and area. The output device produces the lines and shapes requested by turning on the number of imaging elements needed to execute the instructions. You won't find a direct relationship between vector data and imaging elements; you'll find only a set of instructions to render the vector data to a certain size.

As mentioned previously, all output devices have a fixed number of imaging elements. The imaging element of an output device is easily looked at as a grid. Each square in the grid has the potential to be an on or off choice. A bitmap image's pixels correspond to imaging elements. A vector graphic sends an instruction to an output device. If you could hear a conversation between a digital data and an output device, you might hear something like this from a bitmap image: "This pixel at these coordinates corresponds to an imaging element on your output device at these coordinates. Turn that element on." A vector graphic's conversation with an output device might be: "Turn on the number of imaging elements that produce a line six points wide and two inches long." The real conversations would obviously contain much more information and be much more engaging, but the concepts are sound, as illustrated in Figure 4.17.

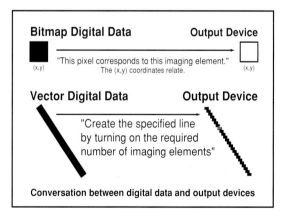

Bitmap Digital Data   **Output Device**

"This pixel corresponds to this imaging element."
The (x,y) coordinates relate.

(x,y)   (x,y)

Vector Digital Data   **Output Device**

"Create the specified line by turning on the required number of imaging elements"

Conversation between digital data and output devices

Figure 4.17
What you might hear if you could listen to a conversation between images and output devices.

All types of output, as noted in Chapter 1, are some form of bitmap imagery. No matter how smooth an image may appear, it still is composed of individual parts or picture elements. Digital vectors do not have these individual bits of information—only points and math connecting those points. But, when you output vector information to physical display, the data must be interpreted into a bitmap of picture elements. To display vectors the data must be rendered directly to the output device's imaging elements and/or to halftone dots.

Although we could discuss this indefinitely, the best way to understand the rendering process of vector data to output is to show a visual representation of the process (see Figure 4.18).

When vector data include values of tone and color, halftone dots are used. The halftone dots are created by cells of imaging elements as discussed earlier. In order to achieve the smooth edges associated with vector graphics, the halftone dots are often sliced or divided where necessary to keep the edge of the graphic as visually smooth as possible, as illustrated in Figure 4.19.

The higher the resolution of the output device, the smoother the lines and edges of vector data will appear. Laser printers between 300 and 600 epi are sufficient for most situations, as illustrated in Figure 4.20. A device resolution of 1200 epi is the minimum required for professional typography and line drawings used for reproduction. If halftones are to be produced along with vectors, then a device resolution of 2400 epi is required.

Vector Rendering to Bitmap

Rather than going directly to an output device, there are advantages to converting vector data to bitmap data. The graphic can be manipulated after being converted to a bitmap by using a variety of tools found in retouching programs such as Adobe Photoshop. Bitmap images are typically faster to output because there are fewer computations made compared to vector output.

Blends or vignettes of color created by vectors are the best candidates for rendering into a bitmap image. Due to the complexity of color, rendering vector-created blends into a bitmap improves quality and increases the speed of output. Vector blends can typically have a problem with banding or sharp tonal steps in the color. The disadvantages of converting vector data to bitmap information include the standard problems associated with bitmaps: resolution dependence, which may cause a loss of quality when resizing an image; and the lack of line and shape editing capabilities. Depending on your output needs, rendering vector data to a bitmap is a useful option.

Photoshop enables many PostScript graphics to be directly imported to a pixel-based bitmap. The RIP or rendering process of converting PostScript vectors into a bitmap must answer two questions: at what bitmap image resolution is the data rendered and are the edges of vector data rendered with alias or anti-alias edges.

First, you must determine at what pixel resolution the objects should be rendered. Because objects are resolution independent, there is no restriction on the amount of resolution you can have. (Base your decision on the guidelines

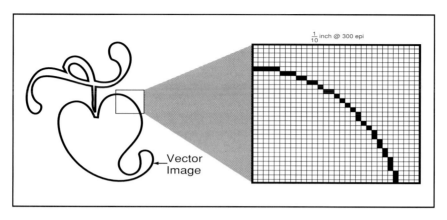

Figure 4.18
When vectors are output, the digital data turns on the required
number of imaging elements of the output device.

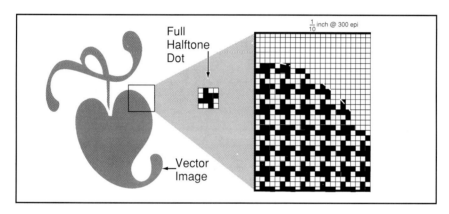

Figure 4.19
Full halftone dots are divided to create the smooth edge in a
vector image. Note that imaging elements cannot be split. They are
either on or off.

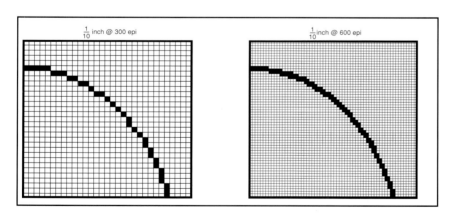

Figure 4.20
As the resolution of the output device increases so does the
smoothness and quality of vector lines.

outlined in Chapter 1.) Remember, the higher the resolution is, the larger the file size and the longer the rendering time from object to bitmap.

Your next choice involves whether you want alias or anti-alias rendering. *Alias* edges are hard edges and *anti-alias* edges are softer averaged edges. Chapter 7 discusses in greater detail the difference between alias and anti-alias edges. Alias rendering will process much more quickly than anti-alias rendering. In most cases, especially with blends of color and curved edges, you will want anti-alias rendering because of the averaging that takes place; however, there are some notable exceptions. When you work with images of a very high resolution (above 300 ppi), PostScript outlines and type may look better with a sharper aliased edge. Without high resolution, though, the edges may look pixelized and ragged, and then the softer anti-aliased edges should be used (see Figures 4.21a and b).

Straight horizontal and vertical lines do not benefit from soft anti-aliasing; they look better with aliased rendering. See the comparison of the two types of edges in Figures 4.22a-f. Flat-colored objects with few curved edges also are candidates for the quicker processing speed of rendering alias edges. Anti-alias rendering is always used for type in video displays, because type and edges on video are more visually pleasing with soft edges.

Resolution Independence

There is now a movement within the graphics community to convert complex color and imagery into formulas. Describing complex color as formulas would allow bitmap images to be manipulated as if they were as resolution independent as vector graphics, while retaining all the color and complexity of images. Converting bitmaps into formulas is not a trivial or simple task. The first program to attempt to offer this function is the software application Live Picture. Although Live Picture is the first in the marketplace, there will no doubt be a long line of products to attempt similar conversion and control of digital imagery. The increase in raw processing power has opened the door for greater advances in the manipulation of images.

Figure 4.21a
Type with alias rendered edges.

Figure 4.21b
Type with anti-alias rendered edges.

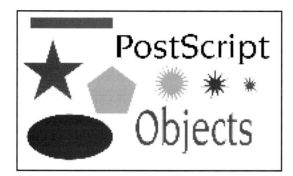

Figure 4.22a
Vectors converted to a low resolution
bitmap.

Figure 4.22b
Vectors converted to a high resolution
bitmap.

Figure 4.22c
Aliased rendered edges can look sharp if
produced at a high resolution.

Figure 4.22d
Anti-aliased rendered edges provide a
smooth appearance.

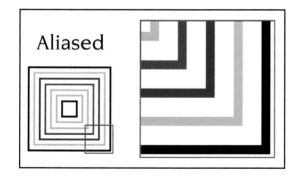

Figure 4.22e
Horizontal and vertical lines are best
rendered with aliased edges.

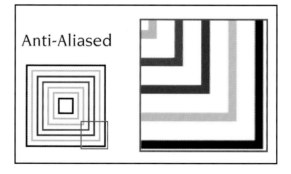

Figure 4.22f
Anti-aliased rendering of horizontal and
vertical edges can appear out of focus.

Chapter 9, which discusses manipulating images, also talks about Live Picture.

Bitmap images readily describe complex color and scenes with pixels. The discrete nature of pixels allows bitmap images to be conveniently modified. Bitmap images are rendered easily to halftone dot output. Conversely, bitmap images do not scale very well. Enlarging a bitmap image, adding pixels, reducing an image, or discarding pixels can compromise the quality of an image.

Vector-based drawing programs, such as Aldus Freehand and Adobe Illustrator, are important tools in a creative environment. Vectors can easily create lines and geometric shapes, and are easily scaled and resized. Vector drawing also enables you to create intermediate steps between two or more groups of shapes to create blends and stylized graphics. Conversely, vector data does not describe complex images, such as photographs, very well. Also, the quality and speed of the output from vector data depends on the attributes of the rendering software and the resolution of the output device.

Whether or not you use vector languages such as PostScript in your drawing environment, you still should know the best ways to reproduce these objects. By linking objects created in a PostScript outline environment into a pixel bitmap environment, you can expand your creative and production capabilities. Even if you work solely in a bitmap environment, you should understand the many capabilities that vector graphics give you.

All display imagery is based on pixels. Bitmap images and vector graphics are not visible until they are ripped or rendered into a pixel-based output. RIP stands for Raster Image Processing. Raster is just another synonym for bitmap or pixel-based imagery. The RIPing process can be thought of as the conversion of abstract digital image information into concrete displayed images. No imagery is visible without picture elements, whether it is rendering to a monitor or printer.

Final Word

Type, logos, graphs, and diagrams are usually graphics with sharp edges and no continuous tones. These graphics are reproduced best as vectors.

Photos, color paintings, color wash, and shaded areas are pixel-based images with continuous tones. These images are reproduced best using bitmaps and output methods such as direct pixel imaging and halftones.

Be sure that you always know the resolution of your output device. To determine the number of imaging elements available to create a halftone cell, divide the resolution of the output device by the line screen of the halftone dots used (see Figure 4.23). The optimum halftone dot is made from a cell of at least 16 by 16 imaging elements.

You can render vector blends and curved lines using anti-aliasing for optimum quality. You should render type anti-alias when displaying on monitors, and render type alias when using high resolution output such as transparencies.

$$\frac{\text{Imagesetter Resolution (epi)}}{\text{Line Screen (lpi)}} = \frac{\text{Halftone}}{\text{Cell Matrix}}$$

$$\frac{2400 \text{ epi}}{150 \text{ lpi}} = 16 \times 16$$

Figure 4.23
A formula to determine the quality of your halftone dots.

Because the PostScript objects need to be converted first to raster information and then to halftone dots, the RIP process of converting pixel-based, bitmap color images to halftone dots is generally faster than the process of converting PostScript-based color images into halftone dots. Also, there are output devices such as film recorders that image pixels directly and do not have any PostScript RIPing capabilities.

Digital
File
Storage

"I am myself and what is around
me, and if I do not save it,
it shall not save me."

José Ortega y Gasset

It is important to understand the options that you have when storing a digital image. A graphic image is stored as binary information called a *file*. Digital files organize and store the pixel information of an image. These files are stored on physical devices called *hard drives* or *disks*. In photography, the photographic grains are held in a film emulsion mounted on an acetate base. Image storage necessitates choosing the proper storage method. Just as the type of film used affects the final visual outcome, so can the type of digital files and storage medium affect the final production of your images.

Real Potential

Digital image and graphic data only represent the potential for output to a physical display. Many people fail to grasp that the files stored on a hard disk only store the information that is used to produce a graphic or image onto various media. The files are not the actual graphics or images, but they are the instructions used to create the visual information. This graphic or image data needs to eventually be interpreted or rendered to physical copy. Hard copy output such as ink on paper or light from a monitor is the actual graphic or image. This is an important, albeit esoteric, distinction.

Files are to images as blueprints are to buildings. It is fairly obvious that a blueprint contains instructions on how to construct a building. No one would ever mistake the plans for the actual building. Files are blueprints for images and graphics. Until an output device uses the digital information and constructs the image, the files are simply the raw plans for a visual image.

Storing digital data in appropriate file formats provides an important link between creation and production. When the digital information is prepared properly, the entire work flow progresses much more efficiently. Production artists who work with digital files must instinctively understand that the production of graphic images is not complete until the output meets the desired specifications. Too often, many artists working with the computer are content to accept the results they see on a screen without considering the next logical step in the production of an image (unless, of course the screen is your final destination). The oft spoken goal of "what you see is what you get" (WYSIWYG), probably should be altered to "... what you have in your hand and is approved by your client is what you need, regardless of what you see on the screen." Too often people are surprised by the results their digital files produce. The idea that digital data is somehow flawless ignores the many variables present during all production processes. The digital information is a part of a very intricate planning process. Even when you are only in the planning stages of production, you should be aware of all the conceivable steps involved. Following the life of an image to its ultimate conclusion

before you begin the actual production is a developed skill. This abstract thought process is difficult to achieve, and it is the biggest hurdle any person needs to overcome when working in digital image production.

Data and Files

Two primary types of digital graphics (bitmap and vector data) were discussed in Chapter 4. Bitmap data describes pixel information arranged on a grid. The numerical data in a bitmap file corresponds to physical pixels on an output device, such as a plotter or monitor. The numeric data is not a visible image until it has been rendered to some type of output.

Vector data typically describes lines and shapes. Specific points and numeric formulas connect those points, creating various images. Like bitmaps, the actual numerical data represents physical information that is visible only when rendered to an output device.

In addition to bitmap and vector data formats, there is a *metafile data format* that stores bitmap and vector information together in one file. As graphic artists work more with both bitmap and vector imagery, metafiles are becoming a common necessity. Photoshop currently saves path information; Illustrator and Freehand also enable bitmap information to be placed with vector graphics; and other programs are implementing some type of graphic mixture to meet the needs of graphic artists working with vectors and bitmaps.

Simple streams of pixel information are written sequentially. From left to right, top to bottom, each pixel is written into a raster file. Raster is a term often used in conjunction with bitmap images. A raster line is a complete horizontal line of pixel information. A monitor displays pixels as raster lines scanning these lines of pixel information across the screen from top to bottom. You often hear the term raster image intermingled with the term bitmap image; for the most part, they are the same. Writing each pixel individually is an effective, predictable, and simple method, but the corresponding file is large. Unlike vector images, which store file information as formulas for connecting points, raster images save each picture element as an individual piece of information on a bitmap.

File Structure

The typical file has four parts: a header, a palette, the data, and a footer (see Figure 5.1). Actually, there are several other parts that can be included in a file, but these four are common to most files that deal with graphics and images. Without getting into precise details about each specific part, it is helpful to understand the basic structure of files.

The header of a file contains information to identify itself. The header is like a name tag: "Hi My Name is TIFF." Imagine all the files on your hard drive with these name tags or headers identifying themselves to applications. It's like a big convention where every file can be recognized by its name tag or header. Specific information regarding the total number of pixels (in addition to the structure, compression, and version of the file) is also included in the header. The header gives the computer important information about how the information is to be stored. The most common problem facing the cross-platform interchange of files is lack of recognition of the information contained in the header. Applications must first

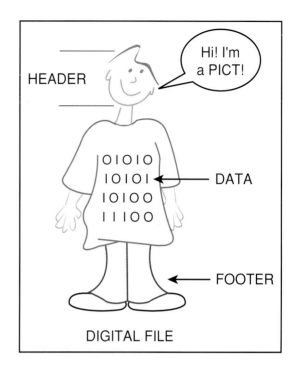

Figure 5.1
The basic parts of a file.

understand what kind of data the file contains and how the data is organized before it can interpret the data.

The palette portion of a file contains the pertinent information regarding the colors used in a file. Color maps or look-up tables, along with color bit depth, are a sample of the kind of color information that is placed in the palette. Many files include the palette information along with the header.

The heart of the file structure is the actual data that describes the images or graphics. The arrangement of the data is usually very straightforward. The simplest arrangement of the data is in rows or raster lines of data.

The footer is usually at the end of the graphic information and is where new information about the file format is added. This is to ensure that any program applications reading the data will be compatible to older versions of the file format. Yes, file formats, like programs, undergo revisions to accommodate new features and new types of data.

File Formats

Choosing a digital file format directly relates to what you want to do with an image and where you wish to transport it (your output device). When you store a set of images for future use, the color quality and your storage capabilities are deciding factors in choosing file formats. The need to save vector and bitmap information also will determine which file formats you use. Most imaging programs accept many file formats. Each program usually has an internal format that stores any special features found only in that particular program. Every application also saves files in common formats, so images can be exchanged freely among different programs.

The amount of color information stored on a file is the same as the bit depth of the pixels used in the image (see Figure 5.2). In the case of an RGB color image, the information is stored as binary numbers that indicate the value of each red, green, and blue component or channel. You can think of an image and the corresponding file as a collection of channels. In the case of a 24-bit RGB image, the red channel uses 8 bits, or 256 steps, to describe the red values contained in the pixels, the blue channel uses 8 bits for all the blue information, and the green channel uses 8 bits for all the green information. A 32-bit CMYK file follows this same pattern, except there are four channels that describe the cyan, magenta, yellow, and black information.

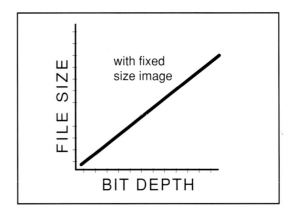

Figure 5.2
The bit-depth is the number of color choices available to a system, and it impacts the size of a file.

Most retouching programs also contain alpha channels, or mask layers. These additional 8-bit channels are not used to describe the color of an image, but contain important information that is used for masking and compositing of images. (Chapter 9, "Collage and Retouching Techniques," discusses channels further.)

As mentioned in previous chapters, an image with 24-bit depth pixels is considered a 24-bit image, and the file containing this image is called a 24-bit file. An image with 8-bit pixels is stored as an 8-bit file, and so on. You usually can save a lower color information file into a higher one, but not the reverse. For example, you can store or save an 8-bit image in a 24-bit file format, but you cannot save a 24-bit image into an 8-bit format without losing color information. Depending on your needs, the loss of color information may be negligible.

The amount of color information has an impact on the size of the file. Obviously, the more bits of information that you have in any system, the more space you will need to store that information.

One of the new clichés of the '90s is the statement, "I need more memory." As you begin to work more and more with color images, you will become intimately familiar with this statement. As they say, it comes with the territory.

The amount of storage space required for your images can be computed easily. Simply multiply the number of horizontal pixels by the number of vertical pixels. That calculation gives you the total number of pixels in the bitmap image. You then multiply that number by the number of total channels contained in the image: four for 32-bit images, three for 24-bit images, and one for 8-bit images. The resulting number is close to the total size of a file—conveyed in bits of information. Header information may slightly increase the final size of the file. The following formulas show how easily you can compute the size of a file by entering the variable information.

pxs wide × # pxs high × 4   =
    file size of a 32-bit image in bytes

pxs wide × # pxs high × 3   =
    file size of a 24-bit image in bytes

pxs wide × # pxs high × 1   =
    file size of an 8-bit image in bytes

One bit of information is one binary number. Storage mediums are measured in size by bytes, kilobytes (K), megabytes (MB), and gigabytes

(GB). One byte is equal to 8 bits of information. One kilobyte is 1,024 bytes; one megabyte is 1,024 kilobytes; one gigabyte is 1,024 megabytes. These sizes can be rounded off for easier negotiability. The following equations give the specifics of how the bits and bytes work. It is easy to find out how much space you may need for a given image and then plan accordingly to meet those storage needs. Different file formats deal with ways of making the file sizes smaller, but this formula always gives you the near-maximum storage space a particular file requires.

File Compression

Consider a topic that is always one of the hottest issues discussed in the world of digital images: file compression. Trying to fit more into less has been the goal of nearly every traveler since Marco Polo had his camel sit on his trunk so that he could take home all his goodies. The digital traveler is no different. Compression removes redundant data and then codes the remaining data with fewer instructions to take up less disk space. An example of compression is using fewer words to convey the same meaning. Compression algorithms code data to reduce redundant information without losing the integrity of the data. There is no specific compression file format. In other words, file

8 bits	=	1 byte		
1,024 bytes	=	1 kilobyte (KB)	=	1,048,576 bits
1,024 kilobytes	=	1 megabyte (MB)	=	1,073,741,824 bits
1,024 megabytes	=	1 gigabyte (GB)	=	1,099,511,627,776 bits
1,024 gigabytes	=	1 tetrabyte (TB)	=	1,125,899,906,842,624 bits

formats can have compression built into them, but a compression algorithm is not a file format.

The idea of compacting or compressing a digital file to save storage space is nothing new. In fact, many of the file formats listed later in this chapter have some method of arranging the data to make the file as small as possible. Compression has a way of making the files as small as possible while retaining the integrity of the images and graphics. The size of a file impacts greatly on the speed of transfer from one system to another. So the smaller, compressed images transfer faster and easier over electronic data networks. In addition, the amount of storage necessary for archiving them is lowered substantially. Compression can play a pivotal role in image management and distribution.

In a bitmap image file, the bitmap data is only partially compressed—the header is left alone. Because vector files are algorithms, they are already compressed, in a sense. Any additional compression used on vector files is performed on the header information and may have little effect on the overall size of the file.

Lossy and Loss-less Compression

Compression algorithms, or schemes, can be classified as one of two types: loss-less or lossy. The two names describe exactly how the compression works. Loss-less compression schemes retain all the pixel information no matter how many times you compress and decompress the file. Lossy compression schemes throw away and lose pixel information from the original image. Consider frozen orange juice or instant coffee. Simply add water and you return to what you had before. But it isn't that simple. Just as the coffee and orange juice don't taste exactly as they would if they were made fresh, a lossy compressed file loses something evident when the file is reconstituted or decompressed. In many cases, it meets our needs—but at times, there is no substitute for the real thing.

In practical usage, lossy compressed images may not reveal any imperfections—but lossy compression is not without a sacrifice. The more you compress using lossy compression schemes, the more the quality and integrity of the image diminishes. You should always be aware that lossy compression carries a cost in quality that you may or may not want to pay.

Loss-less Compression

The majority of compression is loss-less. Loss-less compression, sometimes called nondestructive compression, does not compromise the quality of an image to attain a savings in file size. Although the space savings may not be as substantial as with some lossy compression schemes, loss-less compression guarantees that you retain the information of your original image. Most imaging applications contain file formatting instructions that perform some degree of loss-less compression. Other than the image program itself, there are programs specifically designed to compress all types of digital files. Some commonly used loss-less compression programs are PKZIP, StuffIt, DiskDoubler, and CompactPro. File compression takes time, but these programs compress files and save space enough to warrant their use, especially when transferring or archiving images.

Run-Length Encoding

Run-length encoding (RLE) is a method of utilizing repeated patterns in a bitmap image to squeeze pixel information into smaller files. RLE works by providing a count and a value of a pixel. The count refers to the number of times the pixel's value should be repeated. Imagine traveling from pixel to pixel on a raster line. When runs of the same color are encountered, run-length encoding writes to the file the number of pixels and the corresponding value. If an image has blocks of color, rather than wasting space by calling out the value of each of the pixels, RLE creates what can be considered packets of information. RLE is a loss-less compression scheme and involves no image degradation because it does not destroy information; it only catalogs the pixel information differently.

The pixels of each packet have the same value and are adjacent to one another. Figure 5.3 illustrates the concept of RLE. The more similar or larger areas of solid color there are in an image, the smaller its total file size.

An image with a solid white background is a perfect example of an image that benefits greatly from RLE. An image with complex color blends and shifts does not benefit as well from RLE. The two example images in Figures 5.4 and 5.5 have the same number of total pixels, but their file sizes differ greatly because of the relative color complexity on the image with the larger file size. RLE usually deals with the separate channels of color information for each

Figure 5.4
A scene with a variety of tone does not compress very much with RLE.

Figure 5.5
A file with flat areas of tone compresses easily and is much smaller when it is not compressed.

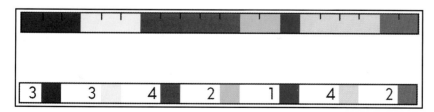

Figure 5.3
Run-length encoding groups similar pixels together.

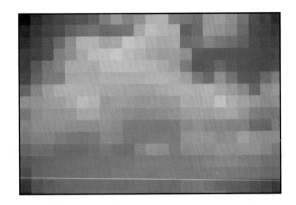

Figure 5.6
Starting from the top going left to right, adjacent pixels of the same value are grouped together for RLE compression.

pixel, but RLE also works with multiple channels, incorporating and coding the values together with the color channels. There are many other ingenious methods of nondestructive file compression; and although discussing them all would be intriguing, it is sufficient to simply be aware of the basic concepts behind saving digital pixel information (see Figure 5.6).

LZW Compression

One of the most common loss-less compression algorithms is the Lempel-Ziv-Welch (LZW) compression scheme. LZW compression is found in the TIFF and GIF file formats and is a standard in PostScript Level 2. More sophisticated than most RLE compression schemes, LZW compression employs a substitution algorithm. The algorithm collects patterns of data found in an uncompressed file and stores these patterns into smaller but equivalent patterns of data. Like RLE compression images with complex colors, blends and noise (and

therefore more patterns) do not compress as well as images with few complex colors.

You may want to note that any LZW or RLE compressed image will not benefit from any additional third-party compression programs like PKZIP, StuffIt, CompactPro, or DiskDoubler. If you plan to use these compression programs, do not compress your images inside the image's application because the third-party compression program will not compress the file any further.

Lossy Compression

Lossy sometimes is called destructive compression. But lossy sounds better because that name implies it simply loses something without eliminating it, when in fact, lossy does just that. Trying to store a high-resolution 24-bit color image on a floppy diskette is as cumbersome as trying to carry a heavy 24-volume set of books in your pocket. Although digital systems may not seem physically large, the size comparisons between files that contain detailed color information and files that use lossy compression are accurate.

JPEG Compression

The Joint Photographic Expert Group (JPEG, pronounced as "jay peg") developed a standard for compressing bitmap images using a lossy compression scheme. Unfortunately, there are a variety of interpretations of this standard. However, the basic premise of JPEG is used throughout the various interpretations. There are many implementations of JPEG and not all are compatible with each other. JPEG is not a file format, it is a method of lossy compression.

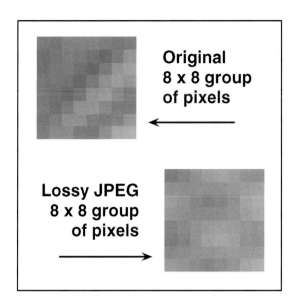

Figure 5.7a
An 8 by 8 group of pixels is the basis of JPEG compression.

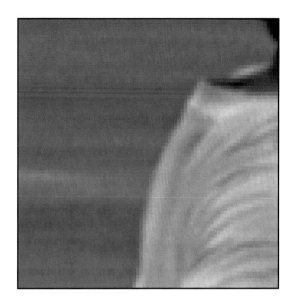

Figure 5.7b
A magnified, uncompressed group of pixel values.

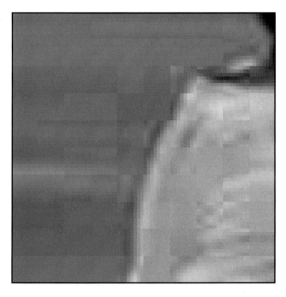

Figure 5.7c
The same group of pixels compressed using JPEG. Note the 8 by 8 pixel squares.

Predictable patterns, as you have seen, partly explain how pixel information is compressed using RLE or LZW compression. JPEG compression simply creates predictable patterns by altering the existing data into manageable patterns. The JPEG compression scheme sections an image into 8×8 pixel areas. It uses an algorithm called *Discrete Cosine Transform* (DCT) to average these 8×8 pixel blocks or cells into manageable and predictable patterns. The predictability of these patterns makes it easier to save or encode the image file in a very small amount of storage space (see Figures 5.7a-c).

JPEG compression enables you to decide by how much of a factor you want to compress an image. You specify the compression rate by a Q (quality) factor usually between 1 and 100. The smaller the number, the more compression will occur and the lower the quality. A factor of 100 produces the best quality compression, but the largest file. The best Q factor setting depends entirely on the content of the image you are compressing and the level of quality you require. The trick in JPEG compression is to find the largest amount of compression with the greatest level of quality. The numbers do not relate directly to the amount of storage space saved, but simply indicate the factor of compression occurring. A setting between 80 and 100 is recommended to keep the integrity and quality of an image used in a printing environment. For less critical output such as video, you can use a setting as low as 20.

The compression is to be used only at the factor chosen during the first compression of a particular image. You can compress a file, decompress it, and then compress it at the same factor as much as you like. But if you compress an already compressed file using a higher ratio of compression, the quality deteriorates more rapidly than if you had chosen the higher ratio to begin with. You can compress and recompress a file using different Q factors, but remember your frozen orange juice. If you were to continually hydrate and rehydrate the mix, back and forth, you eventually would end up with pale-colored water with no flavor or texture.

To find the best mix of quality and compression using JPEG, start with a quality factor setting of 80. If you see any visible defects in your chosen output, increase the value and resave the file. If the quality is acceptable, decrease the quality setting until the image quality is just acceptable. This will provide you with a settings range that you can choose from based on your needs.

There is a cost of quality and speed when you compress something with a lossy scheme. You should use lossy compression schemes only after completing all necessary retouching of the image. And software implementation of JPEG compression and decompression can take an extraordinary amount of time. Specifically dedicated hardware chips added to the circuit boards of your computer can compress images much faster than software alone. If you plan to use compression frequently, you may want to invest in such a chip. The chips only take seconds or minutes to implement the compression and decompression schemes. Many multimedia video boards now include such a chip to increase the performance of creating and editing video sequences.

Lossy types of compression can be a useful way of optimizing your available storage space, but remember: if you don't need compression, don't use it. This is especially true for finely detailed, high-quality print images. You will find that storage media are making tremendous advances in their capacities to save larger amounts of digital information. The lossy compression routines, for the most part, are geared toward sending digital information over phone lines and networks. These little packages can be sent quickly and efficiently and then expanded at the destination point. Video, for which the quality level is not as critical as with print, is a medium that takes best advantage of the file savings that lossy compression affords. Even so, regardless of the medium you choose for output, it is important to be aware of the benefits and corresponding costs in regard to lossy compression. Make your choices accordingly.

Figure 5.8a
An original image with no JPEG
compression.

Figure 5.8b
Lossy compression with good quality.

Figure 5.8c
Lossy compression with medium quality.

Figure 5.8d
Lossy compression with low quality.

If you have ample backup devices and minimal network transfer needs, there is no reason to JPEG compress an image if all you plan to do is archive the image.

Retouching a JPEG image can be problematic because the 8 × 8 cell can interfere with the transition from one area of pixels to another. Also, after any retouching, the JPEG cells must be recompressed, which may degrade the image further. Filters have an especially nasty way of showing off the imperfections of a JPEG file, and flat areas of color do not compress as well as more complex areas of color. You only want to use a lossy compression scheme like JPEG after all the image manipulation and color correction has been completed. Be sure to keep an original version of the image if additional corrections are anticipated.

The images in Figures 5.8a-d show examples of files that have used the JPEG Lossy compression scheme.

File Formats

A file format is a way of arranging data to suit specific purposes. Many different file types or formats are used with many programs and computers. Though it may seem logical to have one common format for digital files, different file formats offer different options that can be useful depending on what you plan to do with the files. Each format is like a different language.

File types or formats are like memoranda in the United Nations. The information being delivered must go to someone who can interpret it. For example, the memorandum meant for the

French ambassador should go to the French embassy. If the French memorandum went to the Chinese embassy, it would be useless without someone there to interpret French. Digital files are the same; they must go where the file format can be interpreted properly. Regardless of which format you use, be sure to anticipate whether someone other than yourself will need to use the file and match that person's format preferences as well. The most common formats that are used are discussed in the following sections.

There are too many to mention all of them. The formats mentioned in this chapter represent the most common file formats used in image production. Several other formats can be read from various programs. The specific image applications dictate which types of files can be imported. The most useful programs can import a variety of file formats. Many of these formats are very narrow in their scope and may be of limited use in a professional full-color environment.

You also should note that there are a number of retouching systems that do not support any of these formats. When this is the case, you can use a RAW format within Photoshop. This file format is a generic format of raw pixel information and no header information. When using any type of raw format, you always should know the total number of pixels, resolution, and bit depth of the image—without this information, reading raw data can be problematic.

TIFF

The Tagged Image File Format (TIFF) is the most commonly used bitmap format, and it is one of the most flexible formats. This format, introduced by Aldus Corporation in 1986, is used extensively on many systems, including Macintosh, DOS, UNIX, and Windows. Because you can save the file in an IBM PC format, you can pass the files from system to system with relative ease. Because TIFF is so flexible and used by many different programs, there are some differences in how individual programs implement and create TIFF files. For example, with Photoshop, TIFF files can save up to sixteen 8-bit channels of data. Other programs cannot read the extra channels.

Most programs enable you to save a TIFF file with or without any program-specific options to allow easier portability among different platforms and applications. Many programs are moving toward a more standard interpretation of the TIFF format. However, you should be aware that images saved in different versions of TIFF may not work with some programs. Even so, most programs today accept the 5.0 and 6.0 version of the TIFF file format.

TIFF files are accepted by a wide variety of page layout programs, which makes it an excellent cross-platform and cross-program file format.

The Tagged Image File Format also takes advantage of LZW compression. This compression, developed by the team of Lempel, Ziv, and Welch (LZW), results in a smaller file size. It is important to recognize, however, that not all page layout and composition programs can read LZW compressed files. If you are ever in doubt, do not use the LZW compression option. Always be aware of where you plan to transport your images because that will affect your decision on how to prepare your TIFF files. There is also a JPEG implementation of TIFF, but the results

have been so unreliable that it is not recommended that you use any TIFF JPEG options.

TIFF/IT

There are many graphics professionals who want proprietary image systems like Scitex, Crosfield, and others to work with software developers in implementing the reading and writing of a new version of TIFF 6.0, called IT8.8 or TIFF/IT. It is an ANSI and ISO approved standard file format that provides for an exchangeable standard data format for use across a variety of systems and devices.

Many people are trying to encourage the use of this format, which would read and write the TIFF/IT file format directly onto different tape drives and optical disks that are connected directly to proprietary and desktop image systems. TIFF/IT would also provide for the transmission of files more easily between different systems over high-speed telecommunication networks. The format may also provide the ability to read, write, and edit text and images regardless of the applications used. The likelihood of this version of TIFF being implemented is debatable.

PICT

PICT is Apple Computer's internal format that is intended as a standard format for images in the Macintosh environment. Nearly every paint program on the Macintosh reads and writes to the PICT format. This compatibility enables you to exchange files freely between different Macintosh programs. Because of a PICT file's complexity, PICT is seldom supported by other platforms.

The PICT format originally was a one-bit-per-pixel format for MacPaint files. It later was modified to include up to 32 bits per pixel of color information. Sometimes you hear color PICT files referred to as PICT2 files. But it generally is accepted that when you refer to a PICT file, you mean the PICT format that allows color information. The PICT format always saves four channels and the default resolution is always 72 ppi. The PICT format is commonly used by video producers because most monitor resolution is 72 epi, and the additional channel, or alpha channel, is accessed for a variety of masking and special effects options.

PICT is a metafile format that can be used to contain object data. For example, if QuickTime is installed on your system, the PICT format can access the JPEG compression scheme contained in QuickTime. PICT is used almost exclusively for video and multimedia projects, but word processing programs and some layout programs will accept PICT file information. Figure 5.9 shows the options for saving a PICT file.

EPSF

The metafile Encapsulated PostScript file (EPSF) format was designed primarily to store vector graphic information that is used in the PostScript language. EPSF is a subset of the Adobe created PostScript Language, which is used as a page description language. The EPSF format is used to save bitmap graphics and vector graphics, or a combination of the two. When it is used to save bitmap image data, the EPS format is often inefficient in exporting files to page layout programs because of its lack of a loss-less

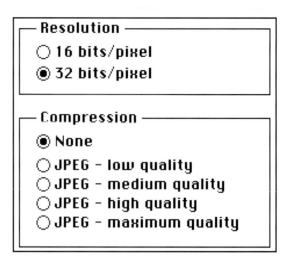

Figure 5.9
PICT file options.

compression scheme. The file size is usually bigger than other standard file formats used for page layout programs.

The file format was originally developed by Altsys to be used in object-oriented PostScript graphics. You can save an EPS file as one composite file of RGB or CMYK images for output directly to color PostScript printers. You also can save a full 32-bit separated CMYK file as a five-file Digital Color Separations (DCS) EPS file.

The DCS EPS format saves the color separation information in a separate file for each of the four process colors. The fifth file is a low-resolution PICT image—known as a PICT preview—that is used as a proxy for placement into a page layout program. The four other files are linked to this proxy; they must always follow it wherever the PICT preview is saved. The diagram in Figure 5.10 illustrates this concept.

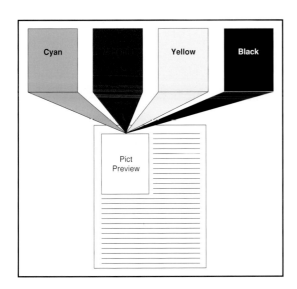

Figure 5.10
The five files of EPS format.

Most page layout and graphic programs now accept TIFF files (the most notable exception being Adobe Illustrator), so the need for EPS files is not as great. But PostScript Level 2 should add some important features including device independent color, data compression, and step and repeat capabilities, which will make it a more attractive option for page layout placement. EPS files should be used primarily at the final stages of production in order to save storage space.

Often people will ask what the difference is between EPS and EPSF files. The answer is: there is none. The shortening of the name has more to do with its use on DOS-based systems in which a three-letter prefix is used to indicate the type of file.

GIF

GIF is the file format that choosy mothers choose. This file format is not very useful in professional image production, but it's worth mentioning, even if it's just to get people wondering how to say the name. Developed by CompuServe, this file format only saves files with a maximum of 256 colors (8 bit). Because it uses an LZW compression scheme, it is a popular format for exchange over modems.

The biggest debate regarding this well-established file format is not how it works—but how the name is pronounced. It is hilarious to hear people debating whether GIF is said with a soft "g" or a hard "g". We prefer to pronounce it "guyf" with a long "i". But we can't decide whether or not to use the hard or soft "g". ;)

TARGA

The TARGA or TGA format was designed for, and is a standard for, programs using the Truevison, TARGA, and Vista video boards. Primarily used in the PC world, this format is useful if you plan to transport your images into professional video systems. The TGA format uses an RLE compression scheme and can save up to 32 bits per pixel. TGA was designed for and is usually dependent on Truevision-based hardware and video cards, but this is not always the case. The file usually can be transferred easily from one system to another.

Many programs enable you to save and read an image in the TGA file format. However, when you transport TGA files to other systems, you should remember that the filename must have a maximum of eight letters in the name, plus a ".tga" suffix. An appropriate filename would be "thecolor.tga." When reading files from PC systems, be aware that there are several types of TARGA file formats, each of which has special considerations. You should refer to the system where the file was created to be certain.

IFF

The Interchange File Format is used almost exclusively with Amiga systems. This 24-bit format uses an RLE compression scheme and is used primarily with video production. The Amiga is used in conjunction with the NewTek Video Toaster, an inexpensive professional video system.

PhotoCD

The PhotoCD is not so much a file format as it is a CD-ROM storage system. This is a proprietary format that Kodak has decided not to make public (see Chapter 3, "Scanning"). The PhotoCD systems save the files into two formats: the proprietary Kodak format and PICT. There are five resolutions subsampled from the largest size (128 pxs by 192 pxs) to the maximum (2048 by 3072). See Figure 5.11. The Pro PhotoCD maximum pixel size is 6144 × 4096 pixels.

The Kodak file format uses a YCC format, which is based on the CIE L*a*b* color space. L*a*b* is a device-independent color space that, theoretically, contains all colors within human perception.

MPEG

The Motion Picture Experts group has developed the MPEG (pronounced "em peg") specification to store sound and digital video information. Although not a file format per se, the primary use for MPEG is the storage of audio and video data in a single file for use in Macintosh and Windows multimedia systems. Though the name is similar to JPEG, and the

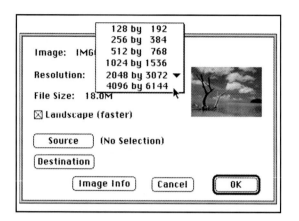

Figure 5.11
The size options available in the standard PhotoCD.

development groups originally started together, MPEG is a completely different implementation of similar technology; the two are not directly related. The most current version is MPEG-2.

QuickTime

QuickTime is the method used by Apple to store digital audio and video data for both the Macintosh and Windows platforms. Similar in concept to MPEG, QuickTime also offers a variety of compression methods, including JPEG, to compress single-frame images. The PICT format makes use of QuickTime to implement JPEG compression when saving to PICT format files.

Windows Paint Bitmap

BMP is the native format for Microsoft Paint. Initially a one-bit format, BMP now saves files up to 24 bits per pixel. Used primarily on a variety of PC platforms, BMP is used for data exchange and storage. BMP provides an RLE compression scheme and is considered a very stable format. Unfortunately, it has little use in page layout or production operations.

Photoshop

Adobe Photoshop now has three major internal formats 2.0, 2.5, and 3.0, with each number corresponding to the version of Photoshop. These metafile formats are considered native to Photoshop and are the default format used in Photoshop. You can save the Photoshop format in a number of different color spaces from one to 32 bits. In addition to the 24 bits of color information, this format can save single or multiple 8-bit alpha channels for various image compositing purposes. The 2.0 version of Photoshop is a simple format that has no compression associated with the files. Photoshop 2.5 introduced the capability to save up to sixteen 8-bit channels of information, and it also includes a loss-less RLE compression routine.

The 3.0 version enables you to save up to 99 object layers and twenty-four 8-bit channels. Remember that every independent layer and channel that you save increases the file size.

In most cases, you cannot use this format in a page layout program. Although many programs support the 2.0 and 2.5 versions, if you plan to use the image in other retouching programs, save the file in one of the previously mentioned file formats. The Photoshop 2.0 and 2.5 formats also can be read directly by the Scitex Visionary and VIP II system—a dedicated prepress system—but the Scitex CT format mentioned later in this chapter is preferable.

RIFF

The Raster Image File Format is the default format of Fractal Design's Painter & ColorStudio program. The RIFF metafile format also saves multiple layers or objects. This image file format works with 32 bits of information, and includes options for compressing the file to save storage space. In most cases, you would not use the RIFF format in a page layout program. RIFF is extremely useful in conjunction with Painter because it saves space. Because few programs have included support for the RIFF format, if you plan to use an image in other programs, you should save the image in one of the more common formats.

Scitex CT (Continuous Tone) & LW (Linework)

This image file format is used to export 32-bit CMYK or grayscale images into a format that the Scitex prepress workstation can read. Saving files into this format is a useful way of connecting open architecture workstations like PCs or Macs to a dedicated prepress system like Scitex. Many separators with Scitex systems have an extension to their workstations called Visionary, now known as VIP II. This extension links a computer to a Scitex system and enables the free exchange of files from one system to another, as long as they are saved in the Scitex CT format. Previously, if a separator did not have the VIP extension, you still had the option of exporting the Scitex CT file to a nine-track tape drive system attached to your computer. The tape was then read by tape drives used by all Scitex systems. The nine-track tape is not used frequently because now most Scitex systems have direct links to various desktop storage devices.

The Scitex Linework file is a bitmap of rendered vector information. Unlike PostScript, which uses the output device to interpret and render the vector information, Scitex renders vector information into a separate file format. The LW and CT are combined at the time of output. There are software utilities available that enable you to read and write out to Scitex Linework files through a program such as Photoshop.

Crosfield CT (Continuous Tone)

Like the Scitex CT, the Crosfield CT format enables you to export files that can be read directly by the Crosfield workstations. The same options apply, except that the dedicated system that Crosfield uses to link the desktop is called StudioLink.

Storage Media

Each type of image storage media has its pros and cons. A transparency is perfect for viewing an image without any special device, such as a computer. But try sending a transparency to several locations over a phone line in order to meet a one hour deadline. Waving a magnetic field around a transparency won't do much, but you can say *goodbye* to any bits and bytes saved on your magnetic hard drive. Fire and heat seem to have the same detrimental effect on nearly all image storage systems, so keep the blow torch a good distance away. Regardless of how you store your images, you should be aware of the various issues regarding image storage.

Digital storage offers many advantages over traditional mediums, but many issues still need to be resolved. While the rush to digitize the world continues unabated, it is important to recognize the limitations of storing those digital images. We can get a pretty good idea how long different types of physical media, such as photographic film, will hold up over time. But there is yet to be a definitive study on the care and permanence of digital storage media. One reason is that the storage media seems to become obsolete before it wears out. But with changing technology comes a discussion as to whether or not the stored images are worth the trouble of transferring to another medium. Walk into any digital prepress shop that has been around since the '80s, and you will see large 9-track tapes clogging most of the available storage space. Most prepress houses archive jobs for clients for one to three years, unless the client requests special storage. After three years, those tapes are typically erased, recycled, and used again. Many images and graphics used in a commercial venture may not warrant special storage beyond a week, but the attitude toward long-term storage is changing to include a more archival view of data. Most people assume digital storage to be at least as reliable—if not more reliable—than more traditional media. Whether this view is accurate or not is a matter of debate. What is clear is that special care must be taken, even with digital data, to protect the integrity of the stored information.

Regardless of the debate over the long-term durability of digital media—will the storage devices themselves become antiquated before the digital information has a chance to deteriorate? Fifty or even 20 years from now if people say they have SyQuest, will anyone be able to retrieve the files or even know they are? Will librarians of the future, eager to view images from the last decade of the 20th century, spend most of their time begging museum curators to let them use the CD-ROM drive on display in the "Computers of the Past" wing? Only time will tell if most digital storage media will even need to outlive their inevitable obsolescence.

There are a variety of methods you can use to store digital files. Reliability, cost, speed, convenience, and compatibility are the most common reference points used to compare storage devices. Reliability is the most critical of digital storage device factors.

Hard Drives

Hard drive is the generic term used for magnetic-based storage devices used on most computers. Most of the large hard drives are fixed inside a computer and they store operating systems, applications, fonts, utilities, and data files for jobs in progress. The typical hard drive used in digital image production is at least 1 gigabyte and typically 2 gigabytes. There are hard drives that are larger than 2GB, but most of the current operating systems only accommodate the partition of 2GBs. A partition is a way of dividing a single hard drive into separate hard drives. Though not physically separate, the operating system of the computer acts as if each partition is a separate hard drive. As operating systems evolve, partitions greater that 2GB will be possible, and larger drives will become more common.

In order to properly maintain digital data on a hard disk, it is helpful to understand how data is stored on a disk. Data is written to a hard drive in concentric circles called tracks. Each track is divided into equal segments called *sectors*. The tracks and sectors are established during the formatting of the drive. A sector stores 512 bytes of data. A grouping of sectors is called a *block*. The block is the smallest area of the hard drive that can be used to store data. The typical block contains 8 sectors or 4096 bytes (4 K). Files that are larger than 4 K, which is nearly all images files, are distributed among the required number of blocks.

The directory (also called a file allocation table) is a record of the files (and their location on the drive) and the unused space on the drive. The directory is needed for the computer to quickly locate and retrieve files from the hard drive. Files are saved to blocks on an empty hard drive, and are written contiguously from wherever the last file has left off. As files are deleted from the hard drive, the blocks become available for other file data. As files are added and deleted over time, clusters of available blocks are scattered all over the hard drive.

At a certain point, a file to be placed on the drive will find that there are not enough continuous blocks to store the data intact. When this happens, the file data is split into fragments and stored on the first available blocks. The file fragments are stored in nonsequential blocks throughout the hard drive. As more files become fragmented, more time is needed to search and access data than if the files were saved in contiguous blocks.

Optimization

Fragmented hard drives and files are more prone to failure and potential data loss. A frequent and useful process is to defragment the files on your disk or optimize the hard drive. Defragmenting your files simply seeks out all files that are stored nonsequentially and literally reattaches and stores them as sequential data. Though defragmenting your files will help improve the reliability of the individual files, it does nothing to improve the performance and overall reliability of the hard drive.

Optimizing rewrites all the files and stores them all sequentially on the hard drive for quicker and easier access. Optimization also creates the largest free contiguous space available to read and write data. Most image programs need the hard drive as a storage area for temporary working files. The typical image program requires three to four times the image file size in free hard drive space. For example, a 10 megabyte file requires 30 to 40 megabytes free on the hard drive to work efficiently.

If the empty space on the hard drive is not contiguous, the program must work harder to find empty areas to store the often large temporary files. The additional time taken to read and write the temporary files to and from the hard drive may slow your production down considerably. The more adding and deleting of data to and from a hard drive, the more often defragmenting and optimization may be necessary.

Preventive care for your hard drive will help ensure long reliable service. Most optimization programs provide an analysis of the hard drive so that any potential disk problems can be identified and corrected before they become an even bigger problem.

Maintaining your hard drive should include a daily or at least weekly ritual of defragmenting and/or optimizing your hard drive. After

archiving, between shifts, or during lunch or after work are excellent times to run any defragmenting or optimizing program.

Though rare, power interruption during optimization can cause the loss of data, and precautions should be made to safeguard any important data. Before you optimize or defragment any hard drive you should be sure all data has been backed up on another drive. This ensures that any problems that may occur during optimization will not result in the permanent loss of data.

A fragmented hard drive is like a messy kitchen. If things are thrown all over, it is very difficult to work effectively. But if the kitchen is clean and the tools and ingredients are organized, you can work very fast and effective with no problem. Like cleaning your kitchen, optimizing your hard drive makes it a much friendlier place to work. Don't let anyone tell you that optimizing your hard drive is not necessary. You simply have to take the proper precautions to ensure the optimum level of efficiency for your tools.

RAID

A RAID is a grouping of multiple storage devices. RAID (redundant array of inexpensive devices) systems group hard drives together to create faster data reading and writing over multiple systems. Data is written or striped across two or more drives, which improves performance by reducing the seek and access and increasing transfer rates. A fast, single hard drive may be able to transfer data at 3 to 5 megabytes per second, but an array of two similar drives can achieve transfer rates up to 7 megabytes a second.

The RAID achieves the increase in speed basically because the data is redundant and can be accessed simultaneously over the multiple drives. A RAID system is also desirable because of the parity or error corrections built into the systems, which helps secure data and allows for easy data recovery if one drive goes down.

There are many different types of RAID systems available from many different companies. There are six to ten different setups, or levels, of RAID drives depending on whom you talk to. The three basic types are: Level 0, called disk striping, reads and writes data on multiple disks very fast with no parity. Level 1, called disk mirroring, includes parity checking but none of the speed performance of level 0. Because it provides for the protection of data, it is a popular choice for file servers. Level 2 is like a combination of Level's 0 and 1 but the improved performance is not great. Level 3 has at least one drive dedicated to parity and the remaining drives are setup as an array for increased speed performance typically needed for video transfers. The remaining RAID levels are mostly variations and combinations of the previous levels with different amounts of data security and speed performance.

The combinations of speed and data security make RAID a low cost and effective method of storage and transfer of digital data.

Removable Hard Drives

Removable magnetic hard drives are a common and popular method of moving data from one system to another. The most common manufacturers of magnetic, removable hard drives are SyQuest and Bernoulli. These removable hard drives differ from their larger counterparts in that they are quickly removable, and can be sent to different locations. Removable drives are typically not as fast to read and write as fixed hard drives, so it is not advisable to work directly from the removable hard drive. It is best to transfer files from the removable drive to the main hard drive to perform any work. The storage capability of removable devices vary from 44 megabytes to 1.3 gigabytes.

CD-ROM

Hard disk drives and floppy disks store data magnetically, while a CD-ROM (Compact Disc-Read Only Memory) stores up to 600M of information optically. A laser etches information onto a thin layer of aluminum, which is covered by a poly-carbonate plastic. The laser creates either a pit or a land on the surface of the reflective aluminum. The pits and lands reflect different amounts of light to a photo light detector, which interprets the light as either 0s or 1s of binary data.

Data on a CD-ROM is arranged more densely than on magnetic drives by a magnitude of almost 150. Unlike magnetic drives, which store information in concentric data tracks, CD-ROMs store data on a single track that spirals outward from the center of the disc. A CD-ROM rotates its disc at variable rates, while disks with concentric tracks spin at a constant speed. The disc spins slower to read data from the outer portion of the disc and faster near the center.

With a CD-ROM, you cannot alter or erase data on the disc. The CD-ROM is considered a WORM drive that enables you to Write data Once and Read data Many times. The speed at which data is read and transferred is not as fast as some magnetic drives. However, because of its low-cost video and multimedia storage capabilities, producers see the CD-ROM as an excellent distribution medium for digital data.

Magneto Optical

Magneto optical disks combine the read and write capabilities of magnetic hard drives and the densely packed data capability of CD-ROM discs. The metal alloy used in CD-ROMs and magneto optical discs are resistant to magnetic charges, which makes them less susceptible to magnetic field problems. Only when the alloy is heated by a laser does the material become available to influences from magnetic fields. Unfortunately, the magnetic resistance of the alloy requires two passes by the read/write head to complete the writing of data. This greatly reduces the performance and speed of the drive. Nonetheless, magneto optical drives are assumed to provide a greater long-term stability than many magnetic-based media.

Shuttles

Hard drive shuttles are examples of combining the flexibility of removable disk drives and the speed and storage capability of fixed magnetic hard drives. Shuttles are primarily used within a high-capacity production environment. Shuttles are simply a high-capacity hard drive attached to a workstation through an adapter called a shuttle bay. Each workstation has at least one fixed hard drive and shuttle bay. When large amounts of information need to be transferred to another workstation, the shuttle hard drive is removed and placed into the bay of the required workstation. This eliminates the need for any additional transfer to a fixed hard drive because

the shuttle drive has similar speed and performance capabilities. Although it is not intended for long-term storage, the shuttle contains all the information required for one or several projects. When the projects have been completed, the shuttle drive can then be used for the next project.

DAT Tape

DAT (Digital Audio tapes), which were thought to be the next big thing for the music industry, are actually more popular with people archiving information and making backups of digital image data. The DAT tapes are four millimeters (4mm) wide, have two lengths available (60 or 90 meters), and are able to store at least 2 GB (up to 8 GB) of information, depending on the formatting. DAT tapes are slow compared to hard drives, but because they are used primarily for archival purposes, this is rarely a problem. DAT tapes are also a low cost, highly effective way of moving large projects from one location to another. Some DAT tape drives use a hardware-based compression scheme to reduce the amount of tape used. You should be aware that unless you use the same exact type and model drive, this information will more than likely not be usable on other DAT drives. When shuttling information to an unknown drive, it is best to turn off any hardware compression before making the backup. DAT tapes provide a reliable method of archiving projects and data over a long period of time. Though susceptible to magnetic field influence, if stored properly, the data should be stable and highly reliable. Because of the relatively low cost of DAT tapes, it is typical to make more than one backup of important information for additional reliability.

Exacbyte tapes are similar to DAT tapes in function, but are physically different. Exacbyte tapes are eight millimeters (8mm) wide and also are used by portable video recorders. They have similar functions and attributes as the DAT tape. Exacbyte tapes are used mostly by digital video producers because the capability of reading and writing video information directly to tape is extremely important.

Archives

Archiving information should be done on a fairly regular basis to ensure that the most recent data has been saved. Archiving stores digital information that you may need later. Archiving is intended for long-term storage requiring storage media that can hold large quantities of data. The short-term benefit to archiving is that you free up valuable high-speed hard disk space for new information. Backing up data at least once a week ensures that if the main storage system fails there will be a backup of important working files.

Future Storage

Ten years ago, a 3.5-inch diskette held only 400K of digital information. Now, in the same amount of physical space, a 3.5-inch disk can hold at least 256 MB, an increase of more than 600 percent. Eventually, the physical and mechanical limitations of the spinning drive will make way for faster, more compact storage devices. The moving parts of drives have improved, and access and transfer times have increased. But spinning disks do have their limitations in the physical world. Waiting for a

disk to spin to the appropriate spot may only take a second, but with devices that are measured in milliseconds, that second could seem like days.

The future of digital storage will eventually move to nonmechanical devices. Solid state holographic crystalline chips will be the eventual evolution of data processing and storage. Solid state chips will become the favored storage medium for two reasons: chip stability and speed-of-light accessibility.

Imagine a hard drive in the palm of your hand that has no moving parts to slow it down. Many issues will need to be addressed to bring the cost, performance, and reliability to an acceptable level, but this is the next logical avenue to explore. Imagine walking or running with a music chip in your pocket, listening to the latest hipster, and you have instant access to any portion of the music. Small versions of this already exist for answering machines. It is only a matter of time before similar chips will become the answer to digital image storage. Simple adapters to the chips would help avoid any obsolescence problem.

The CPU ROMs placed in every computer are already working examples of how applications and data can be stored on a chip. Ultimately, you will carry programs on these chips and plug them directly into any workstation. There are many implications of read/write chips, and their implementation is not as far off as people expect. As soon as mass manufacturing costs drop, it will become the storage media of choice. Archival storage may still require even more inexpensive systems like DAT tape. But, for distribution, daily work, and short-range storage, solid state is the eventual place the industry will go.

Checklist

In a production environment, files have three purposes. The first purpose involves working with and processing image and graphic information. This requires fixed, high-speed hard drives to provide the greatest performance. The second involves delivering the files to other locations. Transfer can be performed using a removable hard drive or by sending information over telecommunication lines. Compression plays a role in making digital data more transportable. The third involves long-term storage or archiving of digital image and graphic data. Choosing file formats that fit all of these purposes is important to the overall efficiency of production.

■ Choose a file format that meets the requirements throughout the production process. Make sure that everyone involved in the process has the capability to read the file format. Service centers may prefer one file format over another; your service center will let you know which it prefers. Be sure the service center clearly explains which options, if any, should be attached with the data files.

■ Compress files only when necessary. Use a loss-less compression scheme to ensure the integrity of the data. Use a third-party compression utility only if the file format is not already compressed. Use a lossy compression scheme like JPEG sparingly and with an awareness of quality loss. Compress a JPEG file only after all color and image adjustments are complete. Always retain the original file if you anticipate the need to make additional corrections. Using this procedure ensures that you will have the greatest amount of color information with which to work. Never work on an original image without a backup copy. Accidents do happen.

■ When buying removable storage devices, discuss your options with those persons with whom you plan on doing the most business; try to match their storage capabilities.

■ Archive images and projects often. Always archive original image data before doing any compression. Be sure to choose an archival system that allows large amounts of data to be stored reliably. Save important images on a variety of backup systems and save copies at remote locations for an even greater degree of safety.

■ All storage media should be stored in stable temperature environments no greater than 72° F (24° C). Keep all media away from any magnetic fields. Magnetic field sources include: monitors, speakers, headphones, watches, and magnets. Remember, the reliability of digital storage devices is still in question—so no precaution is considered too great.

Final Word

Of all file types available, the TIFF format is the most widely used and the most flexible. TIFF is such a popular format that most service and production centers prefer to have files in this format.

Working with digital color images means working with extremely large files. The storage devices that hold these files are as varied as the formats you can save them in. The debate continues over which methods work best for long-term storage. Digital storage has not been around long enough to accurately judge the long-term effects on the information stored. This is why very important images always seem to find a home, not only in several digital media, but also as some more predictable, physical form such as film transparency. Some general conclusions can be drawn from certain digital media, but the truth is that no one really knows how long most digital storage devices will retain the integrity of their information.

Because hard drives are not very portable, removable hard drives are popular solutions for transporting large amounts of data. Another popular storage and transfer medium is the DAT tape, a cheap and inexpensive method to archive and store information.

Optical devices are popular for multimedia because CD-ROMs have the storage capacity required for images that are used in interactive video programs. Until recently, optical drives, which are based on the same technology as music CDs, could only read information. Magneto optical drives now offer write capabilities. There are also authoring systems that enable archiving to CD-ROMs, but they are only write-once systems.

Compression of images and graphic data is useful using either a loss-less or lossy compression scheme. Loss-less retains all the original data before compression. Lossy alters data to achieve higher amounts of storage saving. You should always be aware of your quality standards and transfer needs when making any decisions regarding data compression.

Color Space and Curves

"I try to apply colors like
words that shape poems, like
notes that shape music."

Joan Miró, Painter

People use spoken and written languages to organize and communicate ideas through words. There are also languages used to organize and communicate color. The languages of color are called *color spaces*. A color space is used to organize and quantify color values in order to easily and reliably communicate those values. Simply put, a color space communicates the values of color from person to person or image system to image system.

Just as a variety of languages are spoken in the world, many different color spaces are used to communicate color. If you concentrate on the idea that a color space is a language, you will discover parallels between language and color space that make it easier to understand how color is communicated. You'll notice dialects, or variations of how a basic color space is used, just as there are dialects in languages. The more you work with a color space, the easier it is to articulate your color ideas. To help with the concepts in this chapter, you may want to review Chapter 2 in which the properties of color are discussed.

Color Communication

What is your favorite color? Blue... no? Red? It's a tough question and, depending on the reproduction quests you embark upon, can even be hazardous to your visual pleasure. An even tougher question is how do you communicate your favorite color so that someone can understand and reproduce it? Should you communicate color with poetic descriptions or with precise scientific physical measurements? Describing color is an inexact and fluid exercise, and the reality is that both subjective and objective descriptions are needed to accurately communicate the sensations of color. General visual descriptions do not provide the level of precision needed to reproduce color accurately or reliably. And numbers alone cannot capture the nuances of color in an ocean sunset. The distinction between artist and scientist becomes blurred because each discipline contributes to the communication and appreciation of color.

Before you consider the digital methods of controlling color systems, you must accept the fact that color is not perceived the same way by everyone and people seldom use the same language to communicate the colors that they do see. Each color is perceived differently both physically and psychologically. As an individual, you have your own personal preferences. However, when you venture outside your personal domain and talk to other people, the language used to communicate color is often imprecise. For example, you can try describing to someone over the phone which shade of red you need to match. Terms like apple, brick, and fire-engine red are all used to describe different shades of red. These may be very descriptive and provide a feeling for the type of red desired, but give few clues as to how to create and match the color.

Personal Preferences

When talking about color, people usually use personal visual experiences as a reference, for example: green grass, blue sky, and lemon yellow are all subjective descriptions of color. Imaging systems, such as a computer or a printing press, require quantifiable numbers and percentages to describe color. Describing the above colors numerically in the CMY color space yields: 100% cyan and 80% yellow, 60% cyan and 25% magenta and 5% cyan, and 15% magenta and 95% yellow respectively. Numeric descriptions not only provide precision but serve as a reference point from which to judge, compare, and adjust color. With numeric information, if someone says, "that lemon is too bright," you can adjust specific values to more appropriate values. Without the specific values, "too bright" can mean many different things to different people.

The problems in color reproduction occur when translating from the subjective description to objective values.

Translations

The essence of color reproduction involves effectively translating color values from one image system or color space to another system or color space. Just as translations from one spoken language to another do not encompass all the subtleties of each language, neither do translations between color spaces and image systems encompass all the color values of each color space. If you do not grasp the basic fact that you cannot interpret all color perfectly in every type of reproduction process, you will always be disappointed with the results or reproduction.

Describing complex scenes where colors blend into other colors is a combination of subjective and objective interpretation. The subjective description of color is the fluid and exciting part of working with color that comes only with the day-to-day experience of working with color. There is no other way to develop a proficiency at recognizing colors except by practice. Any mastery of color reproduction must include both a visual and numerical comprehension of color. Each method provides support to any visual description and communication of color.

Before trying to communicate color, graphic artists should agree on color descriptions that are mutually understandable. Deciding which color space to use is a part of establishing standards of communication. All persons involved in the color production process should be able to understand how to reproduce the colors requested. It makes no sense to work with a color system whose values you do not understand or cannot reproduce.

Color spaces are used to help quantify the objective aspects of color communication. By using numerical data, persons and computers can begin to speak the same color language. Learning how numeric values relate to color requires repetition in order to master the process. Combined with subjective descriptions, numeric data is the most accurate method of communicating color values.

Color Spaces

In order to work effectively with color, you must grasp how color is organized and which tools are used to manipulate color. Color spaces are models used to organize visual color. The primary color production systems—printing press, film transparency, and monitors—all require different but related color spaces to reproduce color.

Each color space is a different language. Translation between color languages is just as important as translation between spoken languages. Like spoken languages, color translations do not always communicate all the subtleties from one system to another. A bad reproduction is like a bad translation. If the color is translated properly, the visual message of color is communicated accurately.

The variety of color spaces are mostly complementary to one another. Most new color spaces are attempts to create an all-encompassing range of color, independent of the type of device or kind of color reproduction. The most common and widely used color space is CIE L*a*b*. CIE L*a*b* conceptually contains all the values of visible color, which theoretically makes it an ideal candidate to translate from one system to another. You can think of CIE L*a*b* as an interpreter that knows all languages.

The three major types of reproduction use two color spaces, RGB or CMY, to physically produce color. Professional color reproduction relies on the capability to understand and communicate with RGB and CMY values. All other color spaces are secondary and at some point must be translated into either RGB or CMY for output. Color spaces such as HSV and HSB are subjective descriptions used to communicate color values. Before we discuss any other color space, let's first take a look at RGB and CMY.

Production Color: RGB and CMY

Printing, transparencies, and monitors are the three primary types of image and color reproduction. Printing complex images requires using CMY inks to create reflective color. Transparencies use CMY dyes exposed by RGB light to create transmissive color. Monitors use

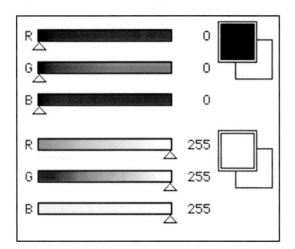

Figure 6.1a
No RGB value creates black; maximum RGB
creates white.

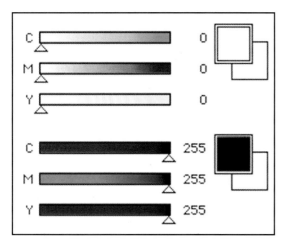

Figure 6.1b
No CMY value creates white; maximum CMY
creates black.

light-sensitive phosphors excited by photons vibrating at wavelengths corresponding to RGB to create luminous color. Red, Green, and Blue (RGB), and Cyan, Magenta, and Yellow (CMY) are the backbone of all complex color reproduction. The relationship between RGB and CMY color is something to know intimately if you plan to work with color.

Red, green, and blue are considered primary additive colors because you must project full values of red, green, and blue to create white. Cyan, magenta, and yellow are considered secondary subtractive colors and produce white by the total absence of color. If you are printing on white paper, you create white by subtracting all the color from the paper. If you want to create black with RGB, you turn all the colors off; to create black with CMY, you turn all the colors on (see Figures 6.1a and b).

RGB

The most familiar color space used by graphic artists using computers is Red, Green, and Blue (RGB). RGB color is the most popular because of its similarity to our physical ability to view color. The cone receptors in our eyes are most sensitive to one of the three colors—but not necessarily exclusive to just one color. RGB is used by all monitor displays to show color and by scanners to input color. The visual spectrum of colors is split into three channels by wavelengths, called primary additive colors. There are shades of yellow that are difficult to describe using RGB, but the 24-bit color systems of most digital systems are sufficient to describe most of the colors perceived by the human eye.

In a 24-bit system, each channel of color contains 8 bits of information with a range of 0 to 255. RGB is a difficult way to communicate color because giving values of 45 Red, 137 Green, and 193 Blue means little to most people (see Figure 6.2). It is also difficult to use RGB values to shift from one shade of color to another, for example from an aqua to a light blue. Also, color matching systems like Pantone, Trumatch, and Toyo are not easily broken down

132

Chapter 6

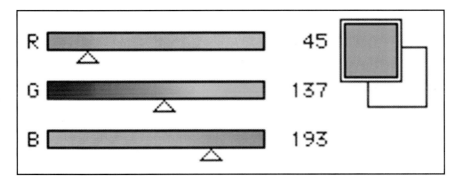

Figure 6.2
RGB values do not easily communicate the visual appearance of color.

into RGB units. However, most color editing programs do provide a link to RGB. Programs like Adobe Photoshop use the RGB color space as the primary environment to work with digital images. These programs enable conversion either directly from RGB to other color spaces or via CIE L*a*b*.

All input scanning is produced by light passing through RGB filters to sensors. Monitors are based on the RGB system. Printed material cannot use RGB alone to create a wide variety of colors. If anyone says that he is printing with only RGB ink, ask him how he creates the color yellow. RGB is not device independent and needs to be converted into other color spaces before being output to various printers. A more appropriate color space for printed material is cyan, magenta, and yellow.

CMY

The subtractive color space of cyan, magenta, and yellow is used in reflective displays, such as photography and printing. Pure CMY values are directly inverse to RGB. The CMY colors are referred to as secondary colors because CMY does not directly match our visual sensors, as do the primary RGB colors. Each channel of CMY

in a digital 24-bit system is described in units of 0–255; 8 bits of binary data for each color of cyan, magenta, and yellow. The colors approach white as each value of CMY nears 0, and the colors approach black as values approach the maximum of 255.

Unfortunately, it is only in the digital realm where the CMY color space is pure enough to be the exact inverse of RGB. When physical CMY inks and dyes are used to produce reflective or transmissive color, the range of values drops considerably. Impurities in inks and dyes cause the reflected light to be trapped or diffused, resulting in incomplete color information reaching our eyes. Rather than measuring tone and color as distinct 0 to 255 levels, CMY inks are measured in percentages from 0–100, as shown in Figure 6.3.

All you need to create a subtractive color reproduction is the ability to control the concentration of CMY dyes on film, transparency, or paper. Combining varying intensities of cyan, magenta, and yellow dyes does produce a wide range of colors. CMY does have advantages, although the range of color is not as large as RGB. Producing color with RGB requires some kind of special device or projection to

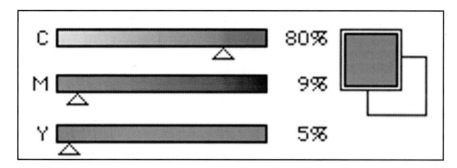

Figure 6.3
The CMY values of color communicate easier than RGB colors.

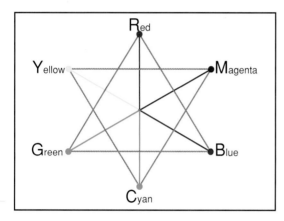

Figure 6.4
A color triangle illustrates the relationship of RGB to CMY.

display the colors. The subtractive color space of CMY does not need any special device, such as a monitor or projector, to be viewed.

The relationship between RGB and CMY is especially important to grasp when color separation results are being analyzed. Their inverse relationship, though not perfect, provides insight on how to relate additive RGB color to the subtractive CMY color all the way through the production process. A visual representation of the connection helps clarify their relationship in Figure 6.4.

CIE Color Spaces

The Centre Internationale d'Eclairage (CIE) is an international organization that first established specifications for measuring color in 1931. These specifications are internationally accepted color standards for colorimetric measurements. There are three major CIE color models: x*y*z*, L*u*v*, and L*a*b*. The CIE x*y*z* was developed in 1931. In 1978, CIE established two approximately uniform color spaces to serve as new standards: CIE L*a*b* and CIE L*u*v*.

CIE defines color as a combination of numbers from three axes—x, y, and z, and both L*a*b* and L*u*v* were derived from CIE x*y*z*. The intent was to create a more accurate and uniform reference of visual perception. It is impossible to tell from CIE x*y*z* numeric information how similar two colors are, but L*a*b* and L*u*v* are more capable in this regard. CIE-based color spaces have a luminosity channel and two chrominance or color channels (see Figures 6.5a and b).

CIE L*u*v* is primarily used with displays of color on monitors. The "L" refers to Luminance, and the "u" and "v" relate to chrominance. CIE L*a*b* is most popular with color print

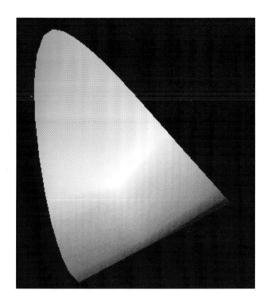

Figure 6.5a
The CIE x*y*z* color space was developed
in 1931.

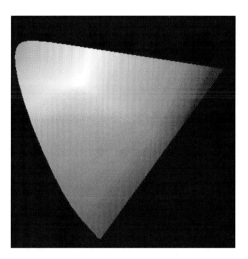

Figure 6.5b
The CIE L*a*b* color space was developed
in 1978.

reproduction. As in the L*u*v* space, "L" refers to Luminance and the "a" and "b" refer to chrominancies that are closer to human perceptions than L*u*v*. The "a" component ranges from green to magenta, and "b" ranges from blue to yellow.

CIE color models define color values mathematically and are considered device independent. CIE colors should not vary with different output devices that are properly calibrated. Most attempts at developing device-independent color management solutions center around the CIE theory and the CIE L*a*b* color space. The CIE L*a*b* color space is the most popular vehicle to communicate from one color system to another. CIE L*a*b is used in many software programs to characterize and translate color values because L*a*b* encompasses and includes both RGB and CMY color spaces.

CIE L*a*b* color may work as a scientific numeric description of color, but it is a poor

choice when communicating color between people. CIE color is simply a vehicle that carries color values from system to system.

Try explaining to a printer that you want the luminance cut back or to increase the *a chrominance value, and you'll be speaking a language that sounds like gibberish. You must understand that CIE color is a theoretical color system and there is no way to produce color using CIE values alone. At some point, the color values must be translated into either RGB or CMY color in order to be displayed.

Adobe uses CIE L*a*b* as a recommended color mode when moving images between systems and when printing to Postscript Level 2 printers. The YCC color space used by the Kodak PhotoCD system is based primarily on the CIE L*a*b* color space. This means that the YCC space is theoretically device-independent as well as supported by Postscript Level 2.

AeQ Meta RGB

There is still some debate as to the effectiveness of CIE L*a*b color. Although the CIE L*a*b* color space is used widely by most vendors of desktop publishing, there are those who believe that CIE L*a*b* is ill-suited for the desktop. Most notable is E.M. Granger, a well-known color theorist Ph.D., who has stated in recent papers that CIE L*a*b* is not uniform, not well-matched to human visual dynamics, and computationally inconvenient. Granger continues to state that because CIE is based on a complex cube root math system, it's difficult to map the color using desktop devices that rely heavily on more basic linear equations.

He further argues that you essentially lose colors—most notably in the shadows and highlights—when you render a CIE L*a*b* color image to a desktop publishing device. The drive toward using 36- and 48-bit color systems is an attempt to compensate for the deficiencies of translating the cubic relationship of L*a*b*. The 24-bit color systems, he believes, are more than sufficient to reproduce most visible color. Granger concludes by offering a solution based on a natural model of human vision called Guth's ATD space. He believes that Guth's ATD system models human vision better than CIE L*a*b* or CIE L*u*v*.

Appearance-equivalence systems, as they are better known, refer to a system that concentrates on matching an image during the reproduction process rather than modeling it on human vision. The system reproduces color accurately by duplicating the reflective properties of the original. Put another way, the color source acts independently from the restraint on it by using a complex arithmetic system such as

CIE L*a*b*. Light Source, Inc., of Larkspur has developed a color management system incorporating these ideas called AeQ Meta RGB .

Appearance-based systems are fairly easy to understand. When using a standard colorimeter measuring device, differences between one color and another can be measured by CIE coordinates—but, visually, you can perceive no difference. While the CIE space attempts to correct for measured differences, an appearance-based system concerns itself with matching the human perception of the color. Although appearance-based systems are not perfect, they are better attuned to how individual viewers see an image.

The emergence of ATD-based color spaces heralds future innovations of appearance-based, device-independent color systems. The innovation of the AeQ color space appears to be an ideal candidate for a standard graphic arts color space. The AeQ color space meets important criteria: device independence, linked easily to existing CIE spaces, based on simple linear math and includes virtually all printable colors. More will be written about this color space in the future as it eventually emerges as one of the standards used for desktop reproduction of images.

Hue, Saturation, and Value

For artists and designers, the HSV color space offers a friendly, familiar interface for easily adjusting color that is based on the visual physical mixtures of paint (see Figure 6.6). Traditionally, painters create various colors by adding white, black, and gray paint to pure pigments. The digital components of the HSV

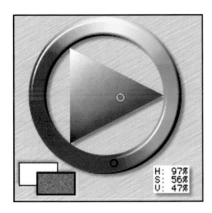

Figure 6.6
Color from the program Painter is chosen using HSV.

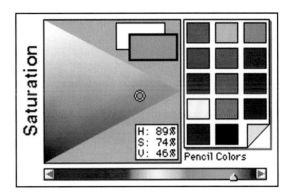

Figure 6.7
When changing only the values and saturation of a color, the hue stays the same.

color space do not mix together to create color, but vary certain properties of a color to mimic the physical mixing of paint.

Hue is the dominant wavelength chosen from the visible spectrum such as red, orange, violet, and so forth. The units for hue range from 0-360 degrees. *Saturation*, which is often referred to as *chroma*, is the strength or purity of color (also referred as the amount of white in a color). A saturation of 0% is white and a saturation at 100% contains no white and results in a pure pigment. *Value* is the brightness or the amount of black in a color. A color with no value (0%) is solid black. Value also is used when describing tone and tonal ranges that contain no hue or color.

The HSV model of color space is a linear system that changes as the visual color results change. Specific colors are communicated mainly by hue degrees with color strength determined by saturation/brightness values. Grays are not affected by hue and are composed by varying the brightness of a saturation of zero.

Adjusting the hue component in the HSV system is the same as selecting a color from the visible spectrum such as red, orange, yellow, green, blue, or violet. After the dominant color or wavelength of light is selected, the strength and purity of the color can be modified using the saturation and value components. The S and V components control the amount of white and black mixed into the particular hue that you selected. If a hue comes up on the strong or intense side, it can be subdued by adding white (reducing saturation) or by reducing black (increasing value or brightness). Conversely, if a hue is perceived as too weak, it can be strengthened by decreasing white (increasing saturation) or increasing black (decreasing brightness), as illustrated in Figure 6.7.

Similar to HSV color space are the HSB and HSL models for color appearance. With the HSB model, the value component is replaced by a brightness component. With the HSL model, the value component is replaced by a luminance component. Compared to the value modifier, brightness is described as being less linear and represents color more like the human eye does. HSB color manipulations are similar in nature to the way artists mix paint, but they are not practical for specifying colors for print.

Based on the RGB color space, HSL, HSB, and HSV color spaces are not device independent and require a conversion to other color spaces before being output to various printers. They are mainly used in the design stage of the color reproduction chain of events. Using the previously defined terms, a description of a bright, heavily saturated violet color is easy to understand and "see" without visually observing the color. Being able to understand a color verbally is useful when you discuss possible color adjustments with someone at a different location. Although you cannot rely exclusively on this method, HSV is another useful tool in communicating and understanding color.

Specialty Color

The color space used to communicate color depends primarily on the type of output required. Color description like Pantone, Toyo, and Trumatch systems use specific numerical color mixes and work easily when you are working with noncomplex scenes, such as flat areas of spot color. These color matching systems are cumbersome and difficult to use in complex scenes like photographic images.

A Pantone book contains a full spectrum of colors, each numbered with mixtures of Pantone inks that compose that particular color. Colors are communicated using Pantone numbers. To create a specific color, the printer follows an ink mixing formula (using specially formulated Pantone inks) to make that color on the press.

Pantone also offers CMYK equivalents for its special colors. Unfortunately, the CMYK space can only reproduce about half of the colors available from Pantone. The printer must be certain that the CMYK values will produce the equivalent color using process inks.

Trumatch uses standard process ink percentages to describe the variety of colors possible from CMYK percentages. All the colors in the Trumatch system are printable with CMYK inks. The different hues are organized for easy movement from one tint to another. Printers sometime produce similar books showing how the different percentage of CMYK inks produce specific color. Investing in such a book is worthwhile and makes communicating color much easier.

The Color Triangle

If you are going to produce color, you should understand the relationship of RGB to CMY. Few people know how to think in RGB or CMY terms. Therefore, it is helpful to use a simple diagram to assist in any color correction using either RGB or CMY color spaces. The diagram is easily drawn on notebooks, scratch paper, or tabletops.

Although at first glance the additive primary colors of RGB and the subtractive secondary colors of CMY seem very different, they are the direct inverse of one another. Combining any two additive primary colors makes a subtractive secondary color. Combining any two subtractive secondary colors creates an additive primary color. The third color excluded from these pairings is called the *tertiary* or *complementary*

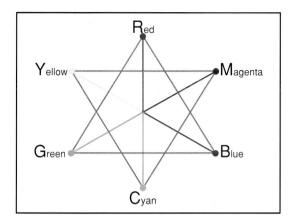

Figure 6.8
The color triangle is very useful when working with RGB and CMY colors.

color. The easiest way to illustrate this concept is by using a color triangle (see Figure 6.8).

Press operators, print buyers, and retouchers all are familiar with this triangle. The corners of one triangle are RGB, and the corners of an inverted triangle are CMY. Although most programs enable you to correct only with RGB, it is useful to have the option to correct in the pure CMY as well.

The triangle works in this way: two corners of a triangle added together produce the color between those two corners. For example, the yellow corner added with the magenta corner produces red, which is between those two corners. The color that does not contribute to the color red is directly opposite the red, which is cyan and is referred to as the complementary color. If you want a print image to be more red, you can do two things: add yellow and magenta or reduce cyan. In general, it is a good idea to remove color and see if that meets your need before you add color. Complementary colors contribute to the shape and tone of an image. You must take care not to completely eliminate

complementary colors or your image may lose detail and look flat.

The remainder of the triangle works the same way. If you would like to decrease the amount of yellow in an image, you simply can decrease the yellow. You can achieve the same correction by decreasing the red and green (which make up yellow), or you can add blue, which is the complementary color to yellow.

Table 6.1 RGB and CMY relationships

additive colors	subtractive colors	complementary colors
R+G = Y	Y+M = R	R:C
R+B = M	Y+C = G	G:M
G+B = C	C+M = B	B:Y

You will notice that the triangle mimics the round hue color picker found in most color programs (shown in Figure 6.9). You can see the triangle relationship in the color program and identify where colors like orange and purple are created. There are some printers attempting to compensate for the lack of vibrant colors used in standard printing by adding additional colors. The additional print colors created—sometimes referred to high-fidelity or hi-fi color—still come from the basic color space of RGB and CMY. No matter which type of color reproduction you perform, you will be better served knowing the basics and using a color triangle.

Even though the triangle does not take into consideration the additional black ink used in CMYK, this correction tool is always a useful

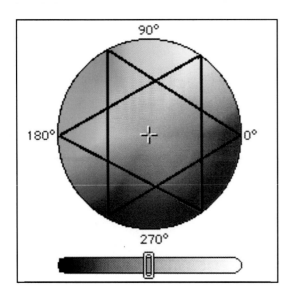

Figure 6.9
A round hue color picker matches the color
triangle.

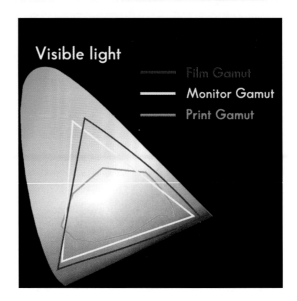

Figure 6.10
An illustration of color gamuts.

guide. If you are speaking to a printer about increasing the saturation of the blues, you will find it more precise to simply ask for an increase of cyan and/or magenta or a decrease of yellow. This information gives the printer a better idea of the type of blue you want. If you understand and use this simple triangle relationship, you have the basic building blocks to make any color correction you desire. Everything else that is discussed in this book revolves around the relationships described by the color triangle. Even if you never go beyond this point, you will find the triangle tool useful when communicating color adjustments to all artisans involved in color reproduction.

Converting from RGB to CMY (K)

Changing from the RGB color gamut (total range) of monitor displays to the CMYK color

gamut of print can be a tricky and very fluid process. In theory, you should be able to simply invert RGB values to get CMY values. Unfortunately, theory doesn't always live up to expectations. Printing inks are not perfect and contain impurities. These impurities prevent the RGB gamut from being completely reproduced with cyan, magenta, and yellow inks. That means it is almost impossible to match RGB colors produced on a monitor exactly to those produced in print. All colors produced in RGB do not necessarily exist in the inks and dyes of CMY. Figure 6.10 graphically represents the relationship of monitor displays to print.

Each component of CMY subtracts a primary wavelength of light from the visible spectrum. Practically all complex printed photographic color images are based on the mixture of cyan, magenta, yellow, and black pigments. Black is added to increase contrast and compensate for the inability of the CMY dyes to create a true black. If you print 100% for each CMY, the result will be a muddy, warm brown. Unlike RGB where equal amounts of each color create gray, the impurities in the CMY dyes require unequal amounts of cyan, magenta, and yellow (see Figure 6.11). Generally, more cyan and equal amounts of magenta and yellow create a neutral gray. Chapter 13 discusses gray balance using CMY pigments.

Ultimately, digital images that are to be printed must enter the CMYK color space. Almost every software program has some kind of RGB to CMYK conversion process. Each is unique and may provide different controls and different results since there are infinite ways to translate RGB to CMYK. CMYK is not considered device independent because various output devices with different ink sets require different combinations of CMYK to make similar colors.

The better programs allow you to see the numeric values of color in an image before you convert to CMYK using an onscreen densitometer (see Figure 6.12). This prediction allows you

to make color adjustments in the larger RGB space before any conversion and then make any fine-tuning corrections when you're in the CMYK color space.

After you convert an RGB file into CMYK, you should never convert back to RGB. The color gamut of CMYK is smaller than RGB and converting CMYK to RGB will not bring back the original RGB information. You should always retain the original RGB file if you anticipate the need to make additional corrections.

Adding special colors to enhance the finite gamut of CMYK has usually been confined to spot-colored areas. Spot color is a flat, toneless area of specific color. The emergence of new printing technology—most notably stochastic or frequency-modulated screening—has peaked a new interest of adding special colors to tonal areas of an image to achieve a richer range of tone and color. There has been much discussion about so-called high-fidelity color or hi-fi color (see Figure 6.13). Any extra color is added in addition to (not instead of) CMYK. A solid knowledge of CMYK is imperative for any color reproduction.

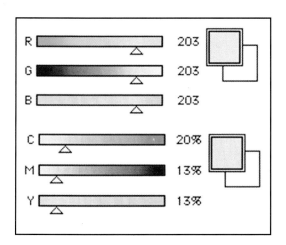

Figure 6.11
Equal amounts of RGB on monitors produce gray, while unequal amounts of CMY produce gray in print.

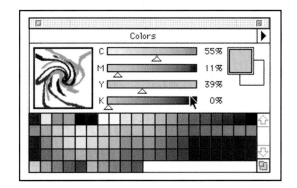

Figure 6.12
The onscreen densitometer is an important color tool.

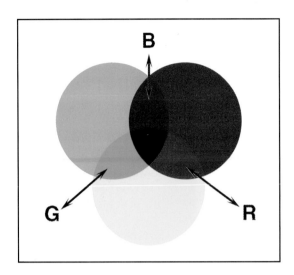

Figure 6.13
Hi-Fi color is a method that replaces the red, green, and blue produced by CMY inks with individual red, green, and blue inks.

Color Reproduction

Color reproduction is the process of imitating the sensations of color and tone from one image system into another image system. Most color reproduction is an attempt to match our physical environment, which is the most comprehensive and basic image system.

The practical reality of color reproduction is that each color system introduces variables which must be anticipated in order to achieve a pleasing reproduction of color. Assorted environmental issues like the types of dye or ink and viewing conditions, combined with efficiency issues like cost and speed, hinder reproduction. Every reproduction process fails at some time to translate sometimes trivial, sometimes important, details of original color.

There are many variables that influence color reproduction. The most practical objective is to produce a consistent and predictable range of color from the system you intend to use. In order to master color reproduction, you must understand which battles are worth fighting and which battles are best left unfought. In other words, you must know what you can control and accept what you cannot control.

Knowledge, skill, and experience are the most powerful allies in your campaign to reproduce color.

Color Management

Color management is the generic term for controlling the color reproduction process to ensure a certain level of predictability and quality. Color management systems are an attempt to map images created with a variety of color spaces to one common color space that is used by a variety of devices. This is known as *device-independent color*. The theory is that no matter which device you output to—monitor or printer—the colors should visually match.

At the core of color management is the device profile. The device profile is a manufacturer-supplied calibration of input and output devices. *Calibration* is a combination of visual and numeric evaluations judged against established standards.

A tendency in color reproduction today is to have generic software perform much of the device calibration required. There is an underlying belief that only the manufacturers of color management systems can provide a reliable source of color matching and that the average person should not be burdened with the process.

Proprietary color management systems are not the only avenues in which you can achieve reliable color reproduction. The developers of CMS systems must follow the same procedures available to any person wishing to calibrate an imaging device. Even if you do decide to rely on an outside color management system, it is useful to understand how these systems work in case you want to expand and explore other possibilities.

Another method is to match the display monitor to your final output device using special calibration software. Of course, there are several pitfalls to relying on the accuracy of a so-called calibrated monitor, especially if you have a coworker who thinks it's time to spin the brightness and contrast knobs for his viewing pleasure. No matter how you slice it, you are judging two vastly different types of color reproduction. The monitor is luminous color and the printed page is reflected color. They are different.

Color management solutions are extremely useful for those persons who need to communicate with remote locations. CMS provides a link from the original to the final reproduced image. Ideally, the color of the images being used will remain the same throughout the reproduction process from start to finish, and offer a consistent result as long as everyone involved uses the same matching system.

CMS solutions rely on a concept called device-independent color. The color from the scanner to the monitor to various output devices should all match and visually relate to one another. Most systems use the CIE L*a*b* color space to move color from one system to another. Using device profiles, the CMS is responsible for organizing and translating the color values to ensure accurate color reproduction.

Each of these CMS systems must keep abreast of the differences in ink sets and colorants of the various output devices and map to them. This matching is difficult because pigments can vary a little or a lot even with the same device. Color management systems attempt to calibrate to your specific device by using standard images as a reference from which visual adjustments can be made. The colors in these images should match from device to device when the system is properly set up.

Device-Independent Color

In an attempt to classify all colors, many manufacturers of color applications have put forward the concept of device-independent color. The theory behind device independence is that regardless of the path reproduction takes, the colors will remain visually the same on every device used. This concept is attractive to those not familiar with color reproduction techniques.

Various interpretations of the CIE color spaces are used in a number of proprietary color management programs that provide a link from original to final reproduced image. Ideally, the color of the images being used will remain the same throughout the reproduction process from start to finish. The features employed to translate this color uniformity are device profiles.

Most of the information about device-independent color has been confusing because of statements like "...print all the colors available on the monitor" or "...perfect color matching from any output device" or words to that effect. What much of the promotional material neglects to include is that many of these color systems are not perfect and that all devices and types of reproduction have limitations.

There is no such thing as a perfect color matching. Device independence provides a method of relating color from one system to another in some uniform fashion. It does not necessarily match colors from each system. A green on a monitor is still going to look more vibrant than a printed green. The device profiles are supposed to take into consideration the limitation of each device and provide the best possible reproduction of color.

Color management manufacturers must provide a profile for each device that you use. Scanners, monitors, and printers of every make and model have a profile that describes the intricacies present in the devices. Scanning profiles also may have options for the different types of media that you may scan. Slides and transparencies require different profiles than prints and drawings do. Output printers also have different profiles for the variety of papers or ink sets that are used to print images. Just as you keep a constant watch over software upgrades, you should keep profiles up to date because they may change as system software and hardware is modified.

Device Profiles and Calibration

A profile is a brief sketch describing someone or something's significant features. In color management, a device profile describes the typical or standard operating condition of a scanner, printer, or other device. The profile establishes a standard from which you can judge whether the device is working properly.

System calibration is the linking of reproduction devices in an entire system. How the devices relate and transfer information to one another is just as important as profiling each individual device. Profiles supervise stability; calibration connects all the devices together. Profiling and calibrating will result in a more predictable and consistent color system.

Calibration can be as simple as visually comparing output to a standard, or as complex as measuring dot percentages at key points on a standard test image. When a production environment is calibrated properly, an image should look very similar at each stage of the production process, but not necessarily exact. For example, if an input device says the tone is 10%, a properly calibrated system should output close to a 10% tone.

Prepackaged solutions do not always provide the greatest amount of flexibility. The better color management systems allow profiles to be adjusted if a supplied standard does not meet expectations. Whether you buy profiles or produce your own, calibration and device profiling is an ongoing operation whose level of quality is directly related to the amount of time you put into the process (see Figure 6.14).

Custom Tools

Many new color management systems require a hands-on approach, which requires you to take the measurements to ensure greater reliability. The idea that users know their environment best is at the center of the thinking for at least two companies in particular: Light Source

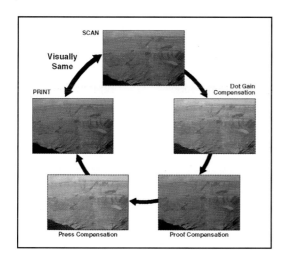

Figure 6.14
The relationship of calibration and
profiles in a color management system.

Computer Images of Larkspur, California and Fidelity Software Imaging (FSI) of Columbus, Georgia. Both of these companies offer solutions to color reproduction from two seemingly different, but similar approaches. Both require more user involvement to establish the production process.

Light Source offers a complete system based on a 32-band color measurement instrument called the ColorTron. This digital device is marketed as an all-in-one densitometer, colorimeter, and spectro-photometer that is able to measure the color from any source. The concept is that all color can be communicated through measurement. If you can measure the color, then you can specify numerically the precise colors you would like to see. Software then organizes and relates the color from original to digital display and from proof to final output. This extremely comprehensive process requires the user to be involved and to take appropriate color measurements throughout the process. By providing the measurements, the colors theoretically stay consistent throughout the production process—regardless of the type of output.

Kolorist by FSI was developed by printer Fred Morgan. Primarily for the print industry, Kolorist uses density readings from the actual inks used to establish a precise link from computer to final output. The calibration of actual printed material to create color separation tables results in a greater degree of accuracy and consistency. Any kind of printed output is possible to calibrate to this system, but FSI does not believe in attempting to calibrate the monitor because of too many inherent problems with monitor technology. Software controls allow the user to identify and compensate for areas of the image that are not printable based on the measurements taken. The solution is very compact, and the controls allow all professional levels to take advantage of this measurement approach.

Whether either of these particular products establishes itself as a primary solution is irrelevant. What is more important is that the view of color production has shifted from a fully automated solution to one that combines automation with control and input from the user. This combined approach is a more comprehensive solution and one that more software manufactures should take heed of.

Onscreen Densitometers

In every imaging program, you choose colors by picking them from a color palette. Most palettes have a mixing area in which to mix colors. The color palettes also are used to indicate the specific values of color. The palette uses color values of 0 to 255 or percentages of 0 to 100. When working with CMYK values, you use only percentages because they directly relate to the halftone dot percentages during output. The palette indicator is always an excellent reference point to numerically check the result of a correction.

Most programs provide a specific window from which to take value readings. The value readings should correspond to the values you will receive from physical output measured by a densitometer (see Figure 6.15). The digital onscreen densitometer, as the window is called, shows the values before correction and the values with correction. The densitometer is a good check to make sure that you have accomplished what you intended during the color correction. You always should double and triple check your values and never assume that what you see onscreen is what you actually have—especially if you want specific color values.

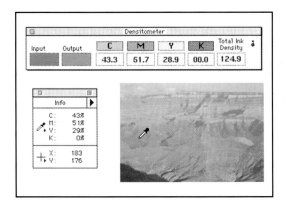

Figure 6.15
An onscreen densitometer is your link to reality.

Color Corrections

The majority of all image manipulations are color and tone adjustments. Color correction is usually the first and, oftentimes, the only image processing performed on an image. Image processing is a generic term used to refer to any type of procedure that is used to alter an image. Color corrections are performed for two reasons: first, to prepare the color information for a specific type of reproduction; and, second, color corrections are performed to create visual effects not present in the original image.

In most color reproduction processes, adjustments are necessary to ensure proper reproduction of color. As mentioned earlier, converting from RGB to CMYK is not an exact process. The conversion process takes a toll on the accuracy of the color reproduced. Fine-tuning of color may be needed after conversion to ensure the best possible reproduction. For example, a digital file output to a film recorder needs a different color correction than files destined for output to a color laser printer. For many color files destined for offset printing, color corrections are necessarily based on the type of paper or type of inks and dyes used during the printing process.

Many manufacturers present various types of color matching standards. Whichever form these matching systems may take, at some point they all involve color correction or adjustment to meet the needs of the output device being used. In color management systems, color and tone corrections are used to achieve the calibrations necessary to meet the output requirements of devices outlined by their profiles. Figures 6.16a and b illustrate why a correction is often needed before output.

The second most common use for color correction is to adjust the color in an image in order to create a desired visual effect. These visual effects vary from subtle to extreme—from helping an image look more real to making the image look more unreal. Color corrections are often necessary to reproduce memory colors like those found in natural settings such as blue skies, green grass, and flesh tones.

Other visual corrections include removing color biases or color casts in an image. A *color* cast is an unnatural or unwanted bias of one color. A greenish face has an obvious color cast of green. Color corrections can compensate for this unnatural bias by eliminating a portion of the color that causes the cast (see Figure 6.17).

Completely changing an original color to a new color is another visual way of color correcting an image. For example, you may want to change the color of a sweater from green to red or give a

Figure 6.17
Removing green from an image reduces the green cast.

person with brown eyes, blue eyes. These are specific color corrections and are called *localized corrections,* and they normally do not involve the entire image. More common is the *global correction*, which involves the entire image.

The best color corrections are the ones that you do not notice. You also can use color corrections

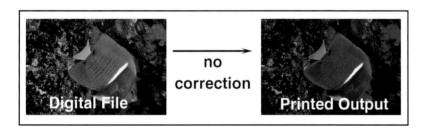

Figure 6.16a
A process without correction before output.

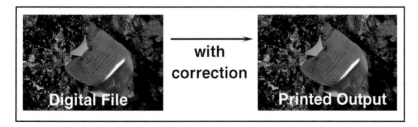

Figure 6.16b
A process with correction before output.

to create extreme visual effects. Color corrections such as posterizing, solarizing, and arbitrary mapping represent only a few. These color adjustments rarely contribute to the realism of an image—but offer unique visual effects that, If used appropriately, produce stunning results (see Figures 16.18a-f).

Color corrections in most image retouching programs usually can be accessed using three methods: sliders, curves, and tables. Sliders are a quick and easy way to access color corrections, but curves are a more comprehensive and flexible method. A program that links both methods offers the greatest flexibility. Tables are used to indicate specific numerical changes in color and tone. Tables are a useful complement to curves and sliders.

Basic Color Correction Guidelines

Regardless of whether you use sliders or curves or both, when performing a color correction you should be aware that sometimes more is less. The more color adjustment you make to the original image, the less the image retains its original color values. In most cases, this change is fine because you are performing the color correction for a reason. But you always should limit your color correction as much as possible. If you scan an image properly, no color correction may be necessary.

No correction means that you can spend more time on other issues regarding the image. In general, when large color corrections are made, maintaining a strong tonal range and detail in the image can be difficult. Often, detailed parts of an image are sacrificed to create the proper

Figure 6.18a
Original image.

Figure 6.18b
Contrast correction.

Figure 6.18c
Equalize correction.

Figure 6.18d
Posterize correction.

Figure 6.18e
Saturation correction.

Figure 6.18f
Solarize correction.

color. This loss may not be a problem in some cases, but no image processing is without some sacrifice. If color correction is performed properly, the benefits far outweigh the sacrifices. But we cannot emphasize enough: garbage in equals garbage out. Start with a high-quality image, and you'll have more options. Start with a low-quality image, and you'll have fewer options.

Preparing Images for Color Corrections

There is no substitute for a quality original. Do not become so reliant on your software program that you routinely accept low-quality originals. By using good source material, you have more options and flexibility than when you use originals that contain color casts, scratches, and exposure problems. Although it is true that many color corrections can be accomplished easily, you should always be less inclined to stretch the boundaries of what is considered good source material.

Your first concern should be to maintain a good tonal range. Although color provides the punch in most images, tone provides the structure. Special attention should be paid first to tone and then to color. The dynamic range of an image is only as good as the tonal range in the original. The quality of a scanned image will determine how much of the original's tonal range should be brought to the correction stage. Dramatic corrections may impact negatively on the range of tone in your image. To view how you are adjusting the tone of an image, you may want to include a grayscale to see how the tone is changed while making color adjustments (see Figures 6.19a-b).

If images lack detail, you cannot create detail with color corrections. Although color corrections may help the appearance of an image, you cannot create something that is not there. Only if you are willing to painstakingly paint details into an image will you get new detail. If color corrections eliminate detail from an image, you cannot retrieve the detail later with other corrections. Once it's gone—it's gone. (See Figures 6.20a-b.)

Global and Local Corrections

Most color corrections are performed on an entire image and are global corrections. Isolating part of an image and applying a desired adjustment to specific areas of an image is a localized correction and it requires protecting portions of the image from the color adjustment.

After an isolated area is color corrected, artifacts may remain that indicate that an image correction was made. The artifacts are usually sharp jumps from one color value or tone to another tone. Ragged, pixelized edges are a common result of color correcting a specific area. Too much adjustment and too little consideration about how well the correction will match the entire image may give your corrected image an unnatural look. Always consider how the entire image will look if you correct only one area. If a localized correction is absolutely needed, any ragged pixels can be smoothed and blended with the rest of the image to try and achieve a better overall feel to the image (see Figures 16.21a-c).

Figure 6.19a
Placing a grayscale in an image before correction helps you see the tonal changes made during any correction.

Figure 6.19b
An image with grayscale shows tonal change.

Figure 6.20a
Highlight detail present in an image must be corrected carefully.

Figure 6.20b
Too much correction in an image may eliminate important highlight details that cannot be retrieved.

Color Space and Curves

Figure 6.21a
The uncorrected image.

Figure 6.21b
A global color correction
affects the entire image.

Figure 6.21c
A localized color
correction affects only the
sky of the image.

Color Correction Tools

There are a variety of tools used to adjust the values of tone and color in a digital image. The most useful tools are curves, tables, and sliders. Each tool provides a different approach to adjusting color and tone.

Curves are the primary language used by graphic artists to indicate tone and color changes. Curves are a precise, fluid, and extremely flexible way of correcting color. Curves are graphic representations of tone. When used in conjunction with numeric tables and sliders, curves are the basic tool that you can use to manipulate and alter the values of an image.

Tables are a numeric collection of tone and color values. There are two parts to a table. The first part has numbers that indicate the values before any adjustment. The second part

contains numbers that relate to the corrected values. Tables are precise adjustment tools and can easily affect very specific areas of an image.

Sliders are very basic tools. Each slider has a specific function of tone and color adjustment. Sliders are not very flexible but they are straightforward, easy-to-use color adjustment tools.

Curves & Tables

There is a chicken and egg relationship between curves and tables. Information from tables is used to plot curves, while information from curves is used to create tables. Which comes first depends are your perspective, but you should understand the symbiotic relationship curves and tables share.

Tables and curves both show before and after information about an image correction. The before and after data in a table is represented by numbers, while in a curve the before and after data is represented as a line. The before and after data is also called original and corrected data and is used as the x and y coordinates in a curve.

A table shows change in an image by a difference in the original and corrected data. A table with no difference in the original and corrected data means that no change has occurred. Figures 6.22a-b show tables and how they indicate change.

The data from the table is plotted on an x and y axis to create a curve. The visual change in a curve off the 45 degree straight line indicates change in the image (see Figures 6.24a-b).

The curve can be altered further and the resulting changes in the data will create a new table (see Figures 6.24 a-b).

The tables and curves above relate to the visual changes in the images in Figures 6.25a-c.

Whether you use a table to create a curve or use a curve to create a table, you are still describing the before and after conditions of color corrections. Both tools accomplish the same thing in different and complementary ways.

0	25	50	75	100
0	25	50	75	100

Figure 6.22a
A table indicating no corrections.

0	25	50	75	100
0	10	50	90	100

Figure 6.22b
A table whose values indicate a tone change.

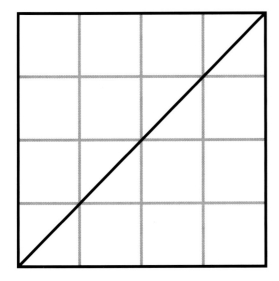

Figure 6.23a
Curve from above table in Figure 6.22a.

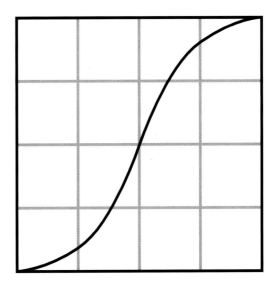

Figure 6.23b
Curve from above table in Figure 6.22b.

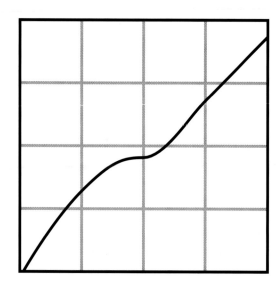

Figure 6.24a
Curve from Figure 6.23b altered further.

Parts of a Curve

A *color curve* is a visual description of all tone and color in an image from the absolute minimum to maximum. Any color and tone adjustment that you make to an image can be represented or controlled by a color curve. Curves are a link to understanding color and tone corrections. As the shape of a curve is altered, the values and appearance of image change.

Tonal curves show before and after information. To show change in an image, you plot the original (input) tonal range versus the final (output) tonal range. The resulting curve indicates the difference between the original image and the altered image.

The x-axis represents the input or original color. The y-axis represents the output or corrected color. When the curve is at a 45-degree angle, the x and y values are equal and so are the input

0	25	50	75	100
-2	35	45	65	90

Figure 6.24b
A new table is created from the curve in Figure 6.24a.

and output values. The image indicates a steady state in which no changes are indicated.

The slope is the ratio between the value of x- and y-coordinates on the curve. A slope of one means the curve is at a 45-degree angle. The slope of the curve is also called the *gamma*, and the specific slope of any point along the curve is called the *point-gamma*. Gamma usually refers to contrast adjustments in the middle part of the curve. (You read about gamma in Chapter 2 as a description of the brightness of a monitor. The gamma of a monitor also is represented visually by a curve.)

Images divide their tone information into four parts, known as *quarter tones*. The first quarter tone is highlights. *Highlights* are the whitest or brightest parts of an image. Highlights range from the endpoint of minimum tone to the first 25% of tone value.

The second and third quarter tones found in the center of the curve make up the midtones. The *midtones* of an image are areas of color and tone between the darkest and lightest areas.

The fourth quarter tones are *shadows*, and they range from 75% value of a color to maximum 100%. These terms often are used in color correction. You should become familiar with the concept of quarter tones to describe a color image. If a client asks you to lighten the

Figure 6.25a
The image has no corrections as is,
indi-cated by the table in Figure
6.22a and the curve in 6.23a.

Figure 6.25b
The image reflects the changes as
indicated in the table in 6.22b and
the corresponding curve in 6.23b.

Figure 6.25c
The image reflects the changes
indicated in the curve in 6.24a
and the corresponding table in 6.24b.

shadows, your client wants the area of the fourth quarter tone adjusted. Chapters 14, 15, and 16 go into greater detail about how images are analyzed and adjusted using quarter tones.

There are many types of curves, but two types are common in the printing industry (see Figure 6.26). One type of curve matches photographic density versus dot percentages. This curve shows how tone from the photograph is converted into printing dot percentages.

The second and most commonly used curve is dot percentage versus dot percentage. This curve allows a comparison of halftone dots, which also provides systems calibration, dot gain analysis, and color and tone adjustments (see Figures 6.27a-b).

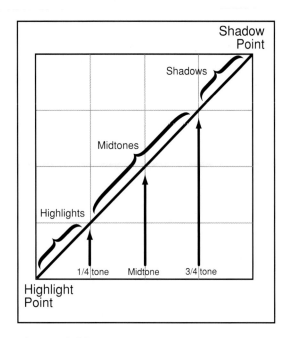

Figure 6.26
The main parts of a curve.

Numeric Tables

Numeric tables are used in conjunction with curves to provide a way to indicate change verbally and in quantifiable terms. The x and y coordinates are laid out numerically and correspond to curves. If you develop your skill with both tables and curves, you can increase your efficiency and accuracy when communicating and performing color and tone adjustments.

The more steps in a table, the more accurate the control is. Tables can be created into few or many data points depending on the amount of control you wish to have.

Tables are critical in order to achieve precise calibration of image systems. A densitometer is used to measure exact tones produced from an

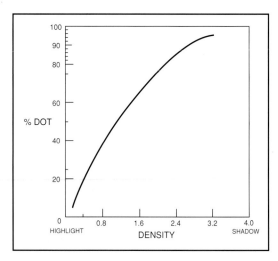

Figure 6.27a
Density vs. dot percentage curves indicates how tone densities from originals are transferred to dot percentages.

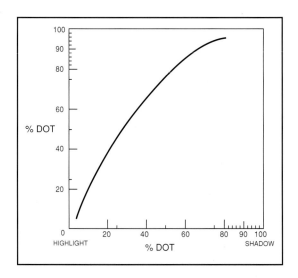

Figure 6.27b
Dot percentage vs. dot percentage curves are used to analyze how dots react to compensate from dot gain, system calibration, or color and tone corrections.

Gray Balance

	5	10	15	20	25	30	40	50	60	70	80	85	90	95	100
C															
M	3	6	9	13	17	21	29	37	46	57	71	76	82	87	92
Y	3	5	9	13	17	21	29	37	46	57	71	76	82	87	92
K	5	10	15	20	25	30	40	50	60	70	80	85	90	95	100

Figure 6.28
A 14-point table used for gray balance adjustments.

output device. These readings are placed in tables and create the shape of the curve that can be used to adjust an image before output. The 14-point tonal control is shown in Figure 6.28.

Many programs have a feature called a transfer function that allows you to compensate for the differences between reading digital values and the actual values of the printed output. The transfer function is a curve connected to a table and ensures that the data you have in your image is what you get upon output. Almost every imaging program and imagesetter has some variation of this function.

Sliders

Sliders also are used to make color adjustments. Sliders are accessed differently than curves, but the resulting corrections are the same. The linear representations of a slider give quick access to a specific tonal adjustment. If you first understand color corrections using curves, using sliders is easy. If you learn only to use sliders, grasping curve correction methods is more difficult. It is important to see how useful both sliders and curves can be. Figures 6.29a-c show examples of popular slider correction methods and their corresponding curve shapes. Knowing how to use the information sliders provide—with the precision of curves—increases your

control over an image and gives you more options to pursue. The best programs are those that link curves and sliders together to allow both to be used at the same time.

Two examples showing how standard fixed sliders limit control are contrast and posterize. If you simply rely on a standard posterize effect, you will be able to create only basic effects. But by knowing that posterize is a flat curve with steps, you will find that there are many more effects possible when using a curve (as shown in Figures 6.30a-b).

Contrast is a common adjustment in which a curve provides more control. A contrast slider is very uniform and adjusts the highlight and shadow quarter tones equally. With a curve, you can adjust the quarter tones individually to suit the particulars of the image. All in all, the more you know about curves, the more control you will have over adjustments with your images.

RGB Corrections

All images in a digital system start in RGB color. Before converting any RGB image into other color spaces for output, you should know how to make corrections before any conversions take place.

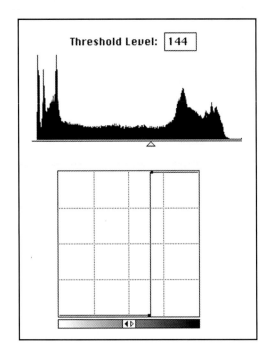

Figure 6.29a
A straight vertical line in a curve is
the same as a threshold slider.

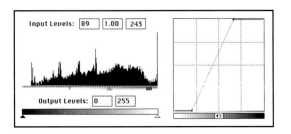

Figure 6.29b
The levels slider is the same as moving
the end points of a curve and/or the
midtone point.

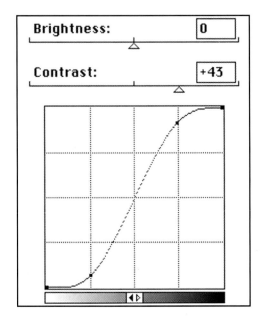

Figure 6.29c
A contrast slider is shaped like an 'S' in
a curve.

Those people who immediately convert to CMYK for print do not take advantage of the larger RGB color space and may lose important tone and color information. You may not be able to make all corrections in RGB, but you will get a better conversion when moving into CMYK. Any additional corrections made in CMYK will be easier to make, more effective, and less time consuming.

Chapters 14, 15, and 16 discuss the methods of analyzing an RGB image based on the predicted CMYK values found on an onscreen densitometer. All images for print must be converted from RGB to CMYK whether performed by a scanner or on a workstation.

CMYK Corrections

Color curves are constantly used in professional settings—especially with CMYK images. The values used on a CMYK curve are solely percentages, whereas RGB curves use either levels from 0 to 255 or percentages. The percentages used by the CMYK curve correspond to halftone dots used for print output.

There are individuals who believe print corrections should only be made in CMYK. We believe that using multiple masks and combining color channels to achieve color corrections is counterproductive when simple global curve movements in RGB will accomplish the same results. Figures 6.31a-c illustrate the concept of correcting RGB before any conversion to CMYK.

Additional corrections can be made to fine tune the image tone and color in CMYK. As you will read in later chapters, there are specific techniques used to alter CMYK images. The curve plays an important role in accessing these corrections.

Figure 6.30a
The original image before posterization.

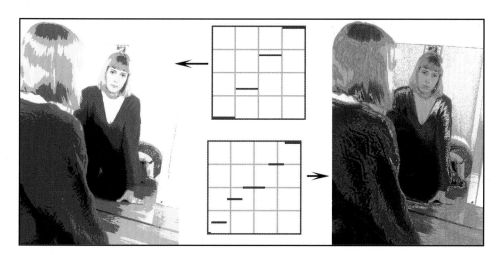

Figure 6.30b
A standard posterize effect on the left and customized effect using curves on the right.

Figure 6.31a
A typical looking image (simulated) from a desktop scanner before conversion to CMYK.

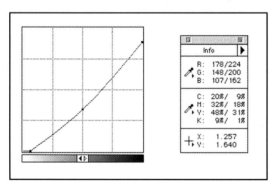

Figure 6.31b
Correcting in RGB before conversion utilizes the larger RGB color space.

Figure 6.31c
Result of the correction yields an image of normal tone range when converted to CMYK.

Checklist

These steps illustrate how a calibration works:

- Print the grayscale image on your output device.

- Use a densitometer to measure the percentage of dot printed.

- Record the values and the difference between the predicted and actual percentages.

- Printed values can then be used to create a curve that is applied to the image before output.

Figure 6.32
A grayscale is a barometer of tonal change.

Chapter 6

Final Word

Working with light and color is not an exact science. Remember that everyone sees color differently. This is because the colors we see with our eyes are influenced first by our physical abilities to perceive these light waves, and secondly by our psychological or personal feelings toward them. Also, it is important to understand that conversions from one color space to another are not perfect. Errors are inherent in the conversion process, and the amount of error varies among each particular system.

A color space describes in quantifiable, orderly, and visual terms the colors that you see and reproduce. Often the arithmetic equations used to describe these color spaces are long strings of numbers and symbols that hold little significance for the average user. The jury is still out on which color spaces are the best for a particular situation and device.

You should know how RGB and CMY relate to one another if your final output is to print, know the basics of CMYK, and know how the various outputs relate to one another in your visual frame of reference. If you are working with color design techniques, HSV or HSB may be more effective in achieving the psychological changes desired while developing your work. Engineers, scientists, and many programmers may prefer the exactness of CIE numbered colors, but CIE has little significance to the physical production of color. The best piece of advice is to know the color space that you use as well as you can.

Start with quality originals and perform color corrections only when necessary. You should perform one correction at a time, rather than multiple corrections.

To paraphrase an old saying: "You can match color for all of the people some of the time. You can match color for some of the people ALL of the time. But you can't match color for ALL of the people ALL of the time." Automated, perfect, and reliable color matching is not here yet. And there is much discussion as to what level it will ever reach. The truth is that because we all see color differently, it is very difficult to get color to match for all people all of the time. The hype surrounding "perfect" color matching often clouds the realities of color reproduction. Don't starve while looking for the perfect apple in an apple orchard.

Part

II

Image Manipulation

Basic
Tools and
Functions

"Ultimately, mankind is
superior to any mechanical device."

James T. Kirk, Fictional Character

A tool used in digital retouching and painting is a device within an application program that creates or manipulates the values of picture elements. Blur tools blur an image; paint tools paint an image. A tool may have various options and may perform many tasks, but in general, tools have specific functions. In image programs and applications, each tool has a unique icon associated with its function (see Figure 7.1).

Typically, the tools are placed in a toolbox (see Figure 7.2) similar to your own toolbox containing wrenches and screwdrivers, but more organized (if your toolbox is anything like ours). Each tool usually has several variations from its basic function that makes the tool more adaptable and customized. We will not discuss individual tools in every program

Figure 7.1
The icons of digital tools typically refer to the function of the tool.

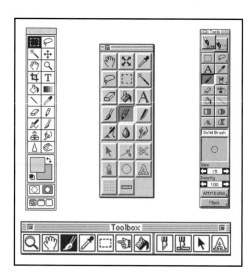

Figure 7.2
Some common toolboxes.

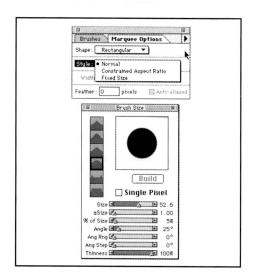

Figure 7.3
Programs like Photoshop, Painter, and others place tool options on floating windows which can be left open while you work with an image.

because that would take an enormous amount of time. But many common tools are available in nearly every program. It is important to recognize the similarity that each tool has from program to program, especially since you may need to work with a variety of programs to perform certain tasks.

In this chapter you will find a basic introduction to particular tools that will lead to your own experimentation. Keep in mind that you are the user of the tools, not the other way around. The techniques and material described here are by no means the only ones that are effective. Not only are you encouraged to experiment, but you will find that experimentation is necessary to become accustomed to the tools that you are using. You will discover many effective variations that you can customize for your specific purposes. Our intention is to simply outline the various manipulations and encourage you to reach your destination by whatever method you deem appropriate.

Digital tools can be broken into three categories: paint or draw tools, selection tools, and viewing tools. When navigating different programs, you can access many additional options contained in each tool in different ways. The following six suggestions may help in finding tool options. Some of a program's options are documented in the manual; some are undocumented. The undocumented ones are called Easter eggs. An Easter egg is an undocumented feature placed by programmers into a program to encourage exploration of the program.

- Double-clicking an icon is standard for bringing up many different options, most of them good.

- You're looking for options; the Option key held down while double-clicking or choosing a menu item may give you some options.

- The Command key is a favorite for toggling between choices on tools.

- The Control key is a seldom-used, but fast-growing toggling choice for many programmers.

- Combining any of the previous keys, Command, Option, and Control, with the Shift key is always a fun and fruitful exercise.

- The sixth and most boring suggestion is to actually read the manual. Hey, why not? It's there for a reason, and you may find some very interesting information.

Paint and Image Programs

Paint programs differ from image programs. Paint programs concentrate primarily on the creation of images, whereas *image programs* concentrate primarily on processing images from paint programs or scanned originals. In a pure sense, paint programs and image programs are the same; a scanned original is digital information used by all programs. But most paint programs do not have complete facilities to process images for color reproduction. As features from both types of programs are incorporated into each other, the distinction between paint programs and image programs will blur (see Figure 7.3).

The Blank Canvas

Tools used to create or alter color values of pixels into lines, curves, and shapes are considered paint tools. When you start with a white blank page in an image program, you may think there are no pixels, but in fact all the pixels are present. The pixels are simply white. When you

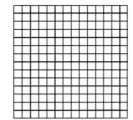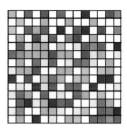

Figure 7.4
A blank digital canvas is simply pixels waiting to be changed to different values.

draw in a digital environment, you are reassigning the color values of the existing pixels, even though you may feel as though you are placing new pixels on the page. Michelangelo believed his sculptures existed in the blocks of stone before he began working. All he needed to do was take away the bits of stone that didn't belong. In a blank digital image file, your images already exist; you simply must turn on or off pixels to reveal those images (see Figure 7.4).

The Color Palette

The *color palette* in all digital programs is the source of your color options. Dipping your brush into a pan of light is an accurate way of describing how you choose digital paint colors for a drawing tool from a color palette. Like a traditional paint palette, this electronic palette enables you to mix colors (see Figure 7.5). The mixing palette introduces the first level of improvisation available to the digital artist.

The color palette on most programs enables you to choose colors in two ways: by using sliders to numerically adjust the color values or by visually picking a color from a palette. The colors are chosen from the primary values of red, green, and blue (RGB); cyan, magenta, yellow (CMY); hue, saturation, value (HSV); or hue, saturation, brightness (HSB). In each case

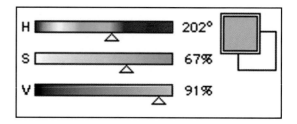

Figure 7.6
Hue, Saturation, and Value adjustments are excellent ways to choose colors.

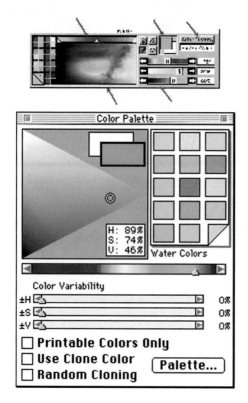

Figure 7.5
The color palette is the place that image programs provide for choosing color.

the color is formed and has a basis in the red, green, and blue color space. You also can select color from an area that has a range of color premixed for you. Most programs also enable you to mix your own color as you would using a real painter's palette. This flexibility in a program gives you a freer sense of determining the colors that you want to use in your image.

Paint tools simulate the action of real paint brushes without the smell and mess. Imagine 16.7 million tubes of colored paint and a cat who likes to wander. Paw prints would be an understatement. A useful method of choosing color is adjusting the hue, saturation, and value of an image (see Figure 7.6). For artists and designers, the HSV color space offers a friendly and familiar interface. HSV adjusts color

visually, based on the physical nature of paint mixing. Traditionally, painters create various colors by adding white, black, and gray paint to pure pigments. The digital components of the HSV color space do not mix together to create color. Instead, they vary certain properties of color which mimic the physical mixing of paint.

Many artists are overwhelmed and distracted by the shear number of color choices that digital systems provide. A useful approach is to limit your primary palette of color to no more than 16 colors including black. Like a traditional painter, any subsequent variations can be made by mixing these colors using the mixing palette. Mixing base colors also will provide you with a better insight into the complementary values of the colors that you use.

The HSV model of color space is a linear system that changes as the visual color results change. Specific colors are communicated mainly by hue degrees with color strength determined by saturation/brightness values. Grays are not affected by hue and are composed by varying the brightness of a saturation of zero.

Adjusting the hue component in the HSV system is like selecting a color from the visible spectrum such as red, orange, yellow, green, blue, or violet. After the dominant color or wavelength of light is selected, the strength and purity of the color can be modified as desired using the saturation and value components. The S and V components control the amount of white and black mixed into the particular hue selected. So if a hue comes up on the strong or intense side, it can be subdued by adding white (reducing saturation) or by reducing black (increasing value or brightness). Conversely, if a hue is perceived as too weak, it can be strengthened by decreasing white (increasing saturation) or increasing black (decreasing brightness).

Changing the display controls on your monitor does not change the real values of the actual digital file. The color palette is your link to the reality of the color values that you use. Regardless of how the image is displayed on your screen, you can check and base your choices on the values indicated on your palette. If you rely solely on what you see on the monitor, you risk reproducing your image incorrectly (see Figure 7.7).

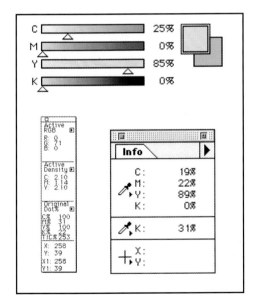

Figure 7.7
Always check the onscreen densitometer to verify the values of your color choices.

A perfect example of monitor dependency was illustrated a long time ago when a client who needed slide output brought in a job. After we took his file and produced the slide, the client remarked that the colors were wrong. "That is not supposed to be red; it's supposed to be green," he said. Displaying the image on our computer revealed that the slide produced exactly what was in the digital file. The client suggested that we had altered the file somehow. We showed how this was not possible, but we could not come up with an alternative solution to the radical color shift.

We suggested that the client return to his system and display the file he had given us. When the client called back, he said the file was displaying exactly as he thought it should. When we looked closer at the color shift, we realized that the colors red and green were being exchanged. We asked the client to check the cable link from the video board to the monitor. That turned out to be the problem. The red cable was plugged into the green port and the green cable into the red port. Swapping cables had exchanged the red and green channels of the monitor, and the colors of the image that the client thought he was creating were not actually there. We repaired the image by swapping the red and green channels during output processing to produce an accurate slide.

Although this example is extreme and is not likely to happen with newer systems, it does illustrate the difference between the digital information and the monitor display. From that day on, the client always made sure to check the values of his displayed colors with the values indicated on his palette.

Alias and Anti-Alias Drawing

The biggest drawback in bitmap images is how pixels actually work within a bitmap to create continuous lines and curves. The resolution of an image and the total number of pixels determine how smooth or continuous drawing lines in a bitmap may be. The result of drawing in a low-resolution bitmap commonly is called stair stepping or jaggies, as mentioned in Chapter 1, "What are Pixels?" Everyday experiences always are an excellent reference point for understanding the implications of anti-aliasing.

When you see people and objects, you perceive a physical depth to them. You see depth and not simply a flat surface for several reasons. First, by virtue of using two eyes from two reference points, you can see stereoscopicly, adding to the perception of depth. Another important reason is that light bends around objects. No matter how three-dimensional objects are lit, a shadow is cast along the edges of the objects. This edge shadow is not a solid dark shadow. In fact, from the lit area of an object to the edge of the darkest shadow there is a transition or blend of light to dark. Simple and immediate white-to-black transitions do not exist in nature (see Figures 7.8a-b). There is always a gray area that introduces the lightest area to the darkest area. This phenomenon is studied in geometric or optical physics and is based on defraction principles. These principles are applied to the concept of anti-aliasing.

Any discussion regarding draw tools and how draw tools make marks must start with an understanding of the concepts of *alias* and *anti-alias* drawing.

The definition of alias is something against something else. If you look at the color edge of aliasing, you see that the color is directly against what it is laid on. Anti-aliasing opposes the "againstness." Being opposed to aliasing (anti-aliasing) means creating a transition, a merging,

Figure 7.8a
Even though the shadow on the building looks sharp, the edge is soft.

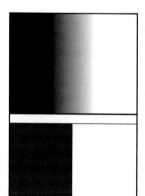

Figure 7.8b
All edges have an area of transition from dark to light. Sharp immediate transitions of dark to light do not exist in nature.

or a blurring of borders. The colors may have their own location or space, but they are linked by a common blurred border that they both share. You often hear anti-aliasing spoken of as blurring an edge, softening an edge, or blending an edge. Depending on how you use anti-aliasing, all of these are part of the description but not the complete picture.

Edges are considered to be places of clearly identifiable transition—borders separating one color area from another color area. By averaging the values of pixels along an edge, you can create a smooth transition from one color to another. This transition mimics what you see in nature—the bend of light around an edge. Anti-aliasing is necessary because of the way we see. Blurring an edge simply is not enough. If you average the pixels at an edge too much, the edge becomes out of focus and unnaturally blurred. If you do not blur the edge enough, you do not gain the pleasing visual advantage of a natural look. Figure 7.9 shows a good example of how aliasing and anti-aliasing appear.

Anti-aliasing uses algorithms to produce the averaging. Most paint tools have anti-aliasing built into them. In the brush or draw tools, anti-aliasing usually is uniformly distributed. When vector objects, such as type, are introduced into the bitmap, the anti-aliasing is more specific.

Anti-aliasing is necessary for creating pleasing type in a bitmap image. You can see in the example that along the curved edges of color the averaging is more than it is along straight portions (see Figures 7.10a-b). Anti-aliasing directly considers the shape and direction of the edges in the image. When you render postscript objects such as type into a bitmap, sophisticated algorithms determine the amount of anti-aliasing the edges need.

The processing time required to perform the calculations of soft edges can slow the use of drawing tools using anti-aliased edges. The cost of higher quality is slower processing speed. Anti-aliasing usually is worth the cost in speed. Increasing the processing power of your computer with special accelerators is suggested if you plan extensive use of anti-alias drawing tools. Figures 7.11a-c show examples of aliasing and anti-aliasing edges used in drawing.

Figure 7.10a
Anti-aliased rendered type.

Figure 7.10b
Aliased rendered type.

Figure 7.9
The edges of the oval shapes show aliased and anti-aliased edges.

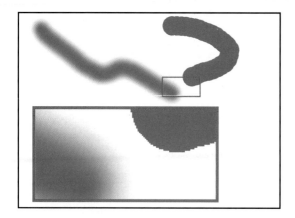

Figure 7.11a
The strokes show a moderate anti-aliased
edge vs. an aliased edge.

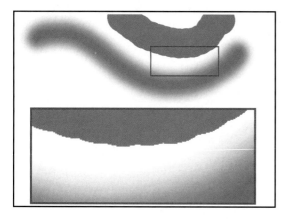

Figure 7.11b
A substantial anti-aliased edge vs. an
aliased edge.

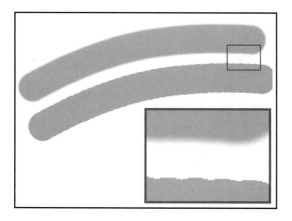

Figure 7.11c
A slight anti-aliased edge vs. an aliased
edge.

Drawing and Painting Tools

In every case of digital painting, experimentation is the key to understanding the many uses of the tools. As you use the digital image programs more, the drawing and painting tools' creative possibilities will become more familiar to you. References to traditional tools such as paintbrush and airbrush are used only as convenient slang to communicate the concept of the draw tool. But digital drawing and painting tools do not act exactly like traditional paintbrushes or pens and pencils. Linking the description of digital tools to traditional tools ultimately limits the ability to describe digital drawing tools accurately and effectively.

Drawing tools are better described as aliased or anti-aliased. The anti-aliased drawing tools are described by the amount of anti-aliasing produced and the patterns or marks the tools create.

Pencils

Drawing tools called pencils give you a flat, aliased, jagged-edged mark. Using pencils is an excellent way to draw large amounts of flat color into one area. Because pencils do not use anti-aliasing algorithms, drawing on the screen is extremely quick.

Pencil tools are one of the few drawing tools that draw in near *real time*. The standard of real time is the time it takes to draw with a real physical pencil.

Real time on a computer means that the motion you make with your mouse or pen immediately transfers to the screen with little or no waiting time. The amount of processing speed and RAM your computer has will directly impact how close you come to real-time drawing. The speed at which you move your mouse also contributes to how close you come to real-time drawing. When you hear someone speak of drawing *near* real time, that means the amount of time between making your stroke and seeing the mark on the screen is small.

Scribbling is the benchmark by which all computer drawing is measured. Scribbling is not a quantifiable figure, but when you can scribble as fast as you do with a lead pencil without waiting for the marks to appear on the screen, you have reached real-time digital drawing. Pencil tools come closer to scribbling than any other draw tool (see Figure 7.12). Achieving real-time drawing for all drawing tools is an ongoing goal for many developers. Real time is a buzzword that describes the actual experience of using the tools and measuring the performance by your own standards.

Figure 7.12
Real pencil scribbling vs. digital pencil scribbling.

The pencil, despite the aliased edge, makes marks quickly and often produces the effect of a real pencil. You can make your marks with a pencil and later apply a blurring effect to soften the hard edges. You can achieve the softening using either a blur tool or a filter, which is discussed later. The pencil tool is used for flat fills of color. It acts like a very big paintbrush that you might use to cover a wall. When you are not concerned about intricate areas such as molding, you can cover the area with flat color. There are also options with all drawing tools that allow you to paint with opacity to lay the color more subtly on the image. The color can be made to affect only areas of color lighter than the chosen color, darker than the chosen color as well as affecting only the hue, saturation or values of the colors being painted over (see Figure 07.13c).

If you need to get rid of the background of an image, you can use a pencil tool to quickly scratch out the main areas while leaving the more detailed areas for finer drawing tools. Most programs provide for drawing straight lines. Using the pencil tool to draw perfect horizontal or vertical lines avoids the problem of anti-aliasing. In fact, for horizontal and vertical lines, using an aliased tool such as a pencil is preferable because the lines are crisp and clean. The horizontal and vertical lines of anti-aliased tools leave an averaged soft edge that gives an undesirable out-of-focus effect. You also can use the pencil tools to trim ragged edges of an image horizontally and vertically to give crisp, clean cuts to an edge. The pencil tools are simple but effective drawing tools (see Figures 7.13a-c).

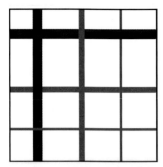

Figure 7.13a
Drawing
horizontal and
vertical lines is
done effectively
with a pencil.

Figure 7.13b
Cropping away
parts of an image
works well with a
pencil.

Figure 7.13c
From left to right, the flat color is
added as a solid to values darker
than the chosen color, to values lighter
than the color, to only the hue component
of the image, and as a simple coloriza-
tion of the image.

Brush Tools

Paint tools generally come in two types: paint-brushes and airbrushes (see Figures 7.14a-b). Usually, the two tools act very similarly, with two exceptions. Both tools have soft anti-aliased edges, but the airbrush typically is much softer. And because the airbrush has more of an anti-aliased edge to compute, the airbrush is slower than a paintbrush tool.

Both a paintbrush and an airbrush tool have the option to adjust the opacity of the color being painted. Opacity usually is indicated from 0 to 100 percent. The value of 0 percent is com-pletely transparent; 100 percent is completely opaque. Opacity is a very useful option that helps the airbrush mimic the action of a real airbrush. In most programs you have the option of keeping the opacity of the chosen color constant or allowing the opacity to build with repeated passes over the same area. A traditional airbrush artist sprays paint on a page gradually and with each stroke adds color until the desired opacity is reached. By gradually laying down color, the artist has control over the shading and depth of the strokes. You can achieve the same effect by setting the opacity control of a brush tool 50 percent or lower (see Figure 7.15). Even if a program does not enable the building of opacity, straight opacity is a useful way of achieving subtle color effects where harsh, flat color otherwise would be a distraction.

Because the brush tools have anti-aliased edges, the brushes are excellent for editing an image with a soft edge around it. The anti-aliased nature of brush tools also is extremely useful when you are creating soft-edged masks (see Chapter 9, "Retouching and Collaging Images"). Because the brush tool marks are complex, the speed and real-time drawing of the brush is not very good. You may need to adjust your drawing style away from a scribbling motion to keep on an even pace with the speed of the computer.

Figure 7.14a
Paintbrush marks typically have a slight
to moderate amount of anti-aliasing.

Figure 7.14b
Airbrush marks usually have a dramatic
amount of anti-aliasing.

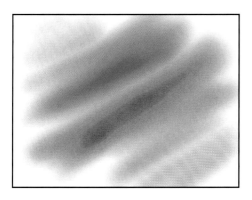

Figure 7.15
A digital airbrush, like a real airbrush,
can regulate opacity by layering color.

Even with the lack of speed, the brush tools are at the core of all image creation on digital image programs, and they are extremely flexible and useful. As the processing speed of the computer increases, the real-time speed of the brush also increases. Each image program has variations on how it implements brush tools. How versatile an anti-aliased brush is in a program is one indication of the overall versatility of the program.

Pressure Sensitivity

Drawing with a bar of soap is not considered natural. Drawing with a mouse is similar to using soap. A mouse is not a good drawing tool because the actual movement and the claw hold of the mouse are painfully unnatural for drawing. Also, there are limited resources for changing the thickness of the marks you make while drawing on the fly. Pressure-sensitive pens offer a more familiar and realistic way to draw. When you use a special pen and a table, the physical action of creating pressure enables you to vary your marks in many ways. Pressure-sensitive pens are the most significant tool for digital artists and retouchers to arrive on the scene in many years. Wacom was the first to introduce these pens; many companies now offer pressure-sensitive styluses for use in many programs. Most of the tablets use a Wacom emulator to achieve the action of pressure. In short, the tablet sends and receives digital signals, which translate into variable strokes and marks (see Figure 7.16). Pressure pen functions are divided into four types: pressure radius, pressure opacity, pressure blends, and combinations of all three.

Figure 7.16
The pressure sensitive tablet provides a pen stylist to create a more familiar drawing environment.

Figure 7.17
Changing the radius of your marks with a pressure-sensitive pen stylus.

Pressure Radius

The amount of pressure a pen applies to the tablet can alter the radius of the marks made on the digital image. The harder you press, the fatter the line becomes. This effect corresponds with what you would expect with a real paintbrush. Because the pen information is digital, you also can reverse your usual thinking—so that when you press harder, the result is a thinner line, and when you press lightly, it results in a thicker line radius (see Figure 7.17). This variation opens many avenues not available in a traditional drawing environment. Also, it is impossible to match the simple mark made by a pressure pen with a mouse.

Pressure Opacity

The amount of pressure that you apply with a pressure pen regulates how dark or how light a mark appears. You regulate the opacity of a pen in the same manner as the radius. The harder you press, the darker the mark appears (see Figure 7.18). As mentioned before, you can reverse this process and make the harder pressure result in a lighter, less opaque line.

Figure 7.18
Changing the opacity of your marks with pressure.

Pressure Blends

Many programs enable you to describe a blend of color by having the pressure of the pen regulate the position of the marks on the blend. In Figure 7.19, the blend has been defined from red to blue. As the pressure increases, the mark becomes more blue, and as the pressure decreases, the mark color changes to red.

Combinations

Mixing the techniques from all three pressure effects creates many interesting marks. By combining radius, opacity, and blends in different ways, you can create marks that

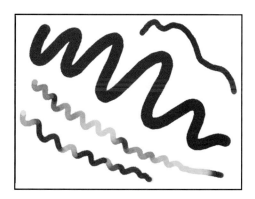

Figure 7.19
Changing the color blend of your marks
with pressure.

Figure 7.20a
Simulating
charcoal marks.

Figure 7.20b
Simulating pastel
marks.

Figure 7.20c
Simulating
watercolor
marks.

Figure 7.20d
Simulating oil
marks.

Figure 7.20e
Simulating
pencil marks.

simulate many traditional methods. Figures 7.20a-e show examples of effects you can get with pressure sensitivity.

These effects are by no means the only types of marks you can create. But there is no way to create any of these marks without a pressure-sensitive stylus using digital media. At first, you may find working with a tablet unusual. But just as you learned to use a mouse, you can learn to use a tablet; in fact, using a tablet becomes more natural and often preferable. The features of this tool are especially attractive, but not limited, to artists.

Programs like Painter, Pixel Paint, and others offer an incredible variety of marks and effects using pressure-sensitive drawing tools. Combined with simulated paper textures, the images that the digital canvas can yield seem limitless.

Eyedropper

The eyedropper or syringe enables you to pick up color from your image without having to go to the color palette. In this way you can be assured of having an exact color match because you choose the color directly from the image. Most programs enable you to access the

eyedropper while using a drawing tool by holding down either the Option key or the Command key. This method of choosing a color is extremely convenient because you do not need to stop drawing to change your color.

The eyedropper usually has the option of picking up either the value of the individual

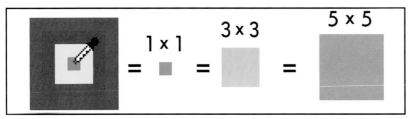

Figure 7.21
Three methods of picking color with an eyedropper are: point sample; 3 x 3; and 5 x 5 average.

pixel it touches or the average value of a group of pixels. This sampling method is a convenient way of getting the overall color value in an area of an image. But for precise pixel-by-pixel retouching, you often need to sample the value of the pixels individually (see Figure 7.21).

Softening and Blurring Tools

Usually, the icon for blur is in the shape of a raindrop. The blur tool averages pixels that it touches to create a softening effect. This effect is extremely useful when you are trying to get rid of unwanted jagged edges when compositing different images together. Softening an edge sometimes is called feathering an edge (see Figure 7.22). Blurring should be used sparingly because too much blurring along even a jagged edge may create an undesirable soft halo effect, defeating the purpose of hiding jagged edges in the first place.

A great way to understand how the blur tools work is to pass over the same area repeatedly and see what blurring does to a single group of pixels. Figure 7.23 illustrates that with enough blurring, all the pixels eventually become the same value, devoid of any texture or depth. In areas such as flesh tones, variable tone is a

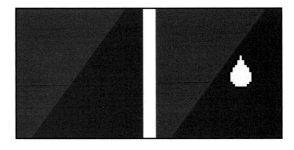

Figure 7.22
Blurring an edge creates a softening effect.

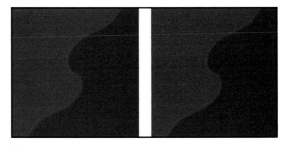

Figure 7.23
A straight line blur on an edge is easier to detect (left) than a blur applied irregularly (right).

critical part of the image, and texture is needed for a more realistic look. A good method to try when using a blur tool is not to follow a specific pattern. Instead of placing even strokes on the same area over and over, use an irregular, spotty method. Use the unevenness of an image to hide the retouching. Patterns in digital images are easy to identify; it is useful to stay away from predictability as much as possible to lend a more realistic flavor to an image.

Sharpening Tools

Sharpening tools, usually combined with the blurring tool, increase the contrast of the pixels you touch, effectively increasing the difference between those pixels (see Figure 7.24). Because it is most useful near edges of color, the sharpening tool is of little production use in flat areas of color tone or blends of color. In fact, in these tone areas, you should avoid the sharpening tool. As with the blur tool, making repeated passes over the same area gives you an excellent indication of how the sharpening tool works. Again, as with all tools, avoiding predictable drawing patterns adds to a realistic look of an image. If you need an area sharpened, use a slightly irregular method rather than simple back-and-forth strokes. Remember that you always can reuse a tool. Resist the temptation to simply jump to the effect you need; start slowly and then build up to the point where you achieve the desired effect. With time and experience, you may be able to simply make the stroke you need and move on. A slower method may take more time, but the final result will be more appealing overall.

Figure 7.24
Sharpening an edge increases the contrast between colors.

Cloning Tools

Clone tools enable you to take the values of actual pixel groups from one area of the same image (or from a different image) and paint those pixels in another location on the bitmap. Remember, even though it may look as if you are moving the pixels, you simply are reassigning the pixels that you paint with the values of pixels from another area. Programs such as ColorStudio incorporate the clone feature with existing drawing tools. Some of these programs, such as Photoshop, have separate tools specifically for the clone feature, called rubber stamp tools. The clone tools take a sample of the entire image. You choose the origin or source point for a clone tool. When you draw the first stroke, you begin literally to redraw starting with the source point you have chosen. Clone is the most significant tool to use when retouching images because you can repair, alter, or create images based on existing textures and color. You can measure the power of computer retouching programs by the versatility of the clone feature contained in the program.

There are three important variations of clone tools: clone align, clone nonalign, and clone revert. Clone align enables you to choose a source point (see Figures 7.25a-c) and, regardless of the number of times you stop drawing to judge how the image looks, clone align picks up where you left off without leaving any seams or interruptions in the image. Clone align is extremely useful in copying a large part of an image when you must pause frequently to judge the progress of the image creation.

Figure 7.25a
Original image.

Figure 7.25b
The source of the clone is
indicated by a cross.

Figure 7.25c
Clone align allows you to
stop and continue drawing
many times to complete the
cloning of the image.

Figure 7.25d
Clone nonalign returns to
the source point each time
you stop painting.

Figure 7.25e
Clone revert can clean any
marks that you don't want.

Figure 7.25f
Clone revert acts like a
true eraser and reveals the
original image.

Unlike clone align, clone nonalign returns to the original source point each time you stop drawing (see Figure 7.25d). This enables you to create multiple copies of the same area if you desire.

Clone revert enables you to revert or paint back to the saved version of an image. Clone revert truly acts like an eraser because you can paint back to whatever you started from without having to reopen the image and start over. Clone revert is an excellent and important creative and production tool (see Figure 7.25f).

Erasers

Erasers simply paint back to the background color of the image (see Figure 7.26). Most eraser tools have an aliased edge but many programs offer anti-aliased edges as well. The eraser in many programs also has an option of painting or erasing any changes back to the originally saved image. Most programs, including Photoshop and ColorStudio, use clone revert tools to perform this paint-back erasing function *with* soft anti-aliased edges. Any of the drawing tools can perform the job of an eraser by simply choosing the background color and painting with that color value.

Figure 7.26
The eraser is typically used to eliminate large amounts of imagery very quickly.

Line and Shape Tools

In some programs you can create anti-aliased shapes directly on the bitmap. Circle, polygon, and line tools sometimes are useful ways of creating bitmap objects. If the edges of shapes are not anti-aliased, their use is limited (see Figure 7.27). Bitmap shapes and lines are not easily enlarged or scaled without losing a degree of quality. Creating lines and shapes with vector-based object programs such as Freehand, Illustrator, and Shapes (ColorStudio) is much more effective and flexible. You then can convert the object into a pixel bitmap for further manipulation.

Smear, Smudge, and Stretch Tools

Various drawing tools in digital programs allow for unique creative effects. Smear, smudge, and stretch are close variations of one another, and each program can intermix the terms to describe

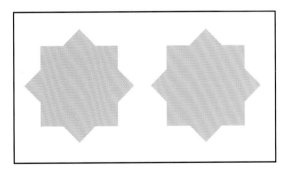

Figure 7.27
An alias shape and an anti-aliased shape.

the same effect. Smearing is an option in most programs that spreads the color of one area into another. The effect is like dragging your finger through a charcoal drawing or wet paint. If you ever have drawn with a lead pencil or charcoal, you know how useful taking your finger to blend and soften harsh areas can be. In fact, the icon most often used for this effect is a finger. A smudge tool acts in the same way as a smear tool but usually with a greater amount of color mixing. Stretch tools, sometimes called pull, take a portion of an image and pull that portion, creating an elastic stretch effect not unlike Silly Putty. Stretch tools usually do not mix colors like the smear or smudge tools; they keep the colors and texture intact. Stretching part of an image into another also is an excellent way of touching up areas of an image because you closely match textures. Figure 7.28 shows how smear, smudge, and stretch appear.

Drawing Tool Sizes

All drawing tools have variable drawing or pen tip sizes. Pen or drawing tips are measured in pixels and are defined from very fine tips (one to ten pixels) to very wide tips (50 or more pixels). (See Figure 7.29). The size of your pen tip directly relates to the speed at which you can

draw. The larger the tip, the more computer computation is required and the less quickly you can draw.

With larger tips, you can use a spacing feature that enables you to determine how far apart each deposit of color lands. If you make a single 20-pixel mark, you need only another 20-pixel mark spaced 10 to 20 pixels apart from the first to achieve a continuous line. Spacing helps relieve the amount of figuring necessary for a drawing to work and results in faster drawing times. The spacing, by placing spots of color at regular intervals, also works well for design effects (see Figure 7.30).

You can create and define your own custom drawing tips in most programs. The ability to custom create the tip of your drawing tool is useful for design and production techniques. A custom tip also can mimic traditional paintbrushes by determining how the color is dispersed (see Figure 7.31).

Specific variations on these tools are available in many different programs. These variations include the capability to define a particular pattern and then use a tool to paint that pattern repeatedly. Some variations also enable you to paint with graduated shades and paint on only specific ranges of color.

Figure 7.28
The effects of smear, smudge, and stretch.

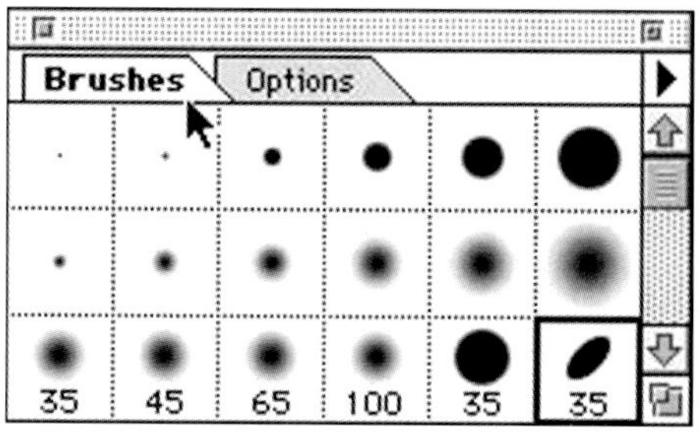

Figure 7.29
Various pen tips.

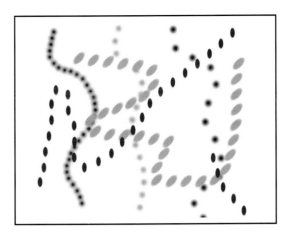

Figure 7.30
Spacing a 20-pixel brush by 10 pixels, by
20 pixels, and by 30 pixels.

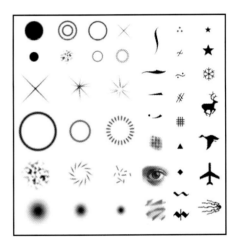

Figure 7.31
A few of the custom tips created in
Photoshop.

Fill Tools

Fill tools, also called paint bucket tools, enable
you to fill designated areas with flat or graduated color blends. Instead of using a drawing
tool, you can use a fill tool as a quick way to
pour and place color. Most digital image
programs enable you to control the specific
areas in which the fill tool pours the color by
protecting selected areas. See the discussion of
selection tools in the next section.

Besides providing flat color, the fill tools allow
graduated blends of color. You usually create
graduated color by choosing two colors and
creating linear, circular, radial, or (with three
colors) triangular blends (see Figures 7.32a-c).
These blends can be extremely useful for
creating new backgrounds. Besides some of the
fantastic rainbow-type colors, blends in nature
also can be simulated. Sunsets and blue sky are
typical examples. Except for the sky and some
unique tropical flowers and shadows, uniform
blends or vignetting tones do not exist in
nature. That is why many uniform, digitally-
created blends seem a little unrealistic. When
using blends, you should be aware that the
more colors you use, the more unnatural the
blend may appear.

The most common exception to blends in
nature is blue sky. The blue color in a sky
becomes less saturated (more washed out) near
the horizon. To create a realistic blue sky in the
background of an image, be sure to use a fill
tool to create a blend from a saturated blue in
the upper sky to a less saturated blue near the
horizon.

Selection Tools

Selection tools are critical to any image program. By isolating chosen pixels, the selection

Figure 7.32a
Linear blend.

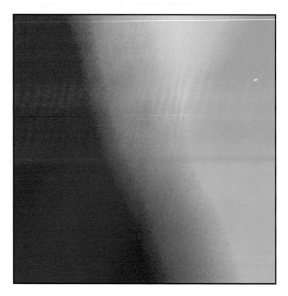

Figure 7.32b
Triangular blend.

Figure 7.32c
Radial blend.

tool enables you to modify or protect areas of an image without affecting other elements of the image. Selected areas of an image can be cut and copied and then pasted into a different image or in a different location within the same image.

When a selected part of an image is cut or copied, the cut or copied piece is placed into a clipboard. The clipboard is a buffer area used by image programs to hold pixel information. You can apply or paste any pixel information in the clipboard into any chosen image. The clipboard acts like a holding area for pixels chosen by selection tools while you decide where those pixels should be placed. When you paste pixel information of an image from the clipboard into another image, that pasted group of pixels is called a floating selection. A pasted image is called floating because you can move that group of pixels without affecting the image beneath the selection. Dropping a floating selection literally bonds the floating pixel information directly to the position on the base image's bitmap (see Figure 7.33).

There are four variations of the selection tool: rectangular, oval, lasso, and automatic selections. The rectangular selection creates square or rectangular selection regions. The oval selection

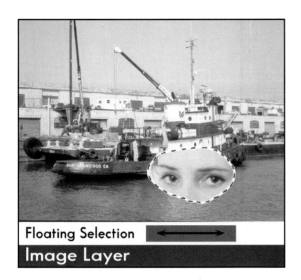

Figure 7.33
Floating selection top view and side view.

Figure 7.34
Selections created by rectangle, oval,
lasso, automatic, and combinations of
all four.

Figure 7.35
The selected area is the only area
in which painting is allowed.

creates circular or oval selections. The lasso selection enables you to freely select areas and pixel groups. Automatic or magic wand selections select pixel groups based on a chosen value range of color. You can mix these selection methods to create irregular selected regions by adding or subtracting from a selection. You also can alter the paths of a selection to expand, contract, or create borders by designated pixel amounts (see Figure 7.34).

A selection area can act as a mask. A mask is used to either protect or modify a specific area. We further discuss masks in Chapter 9. Figure 7.35 shows how a selected area is used to limit where a drawing tool can paint.

Selections also are used to crop unwanted portions of an image. Some programs, such as Photoshop, have a separate cropping tool that crops or clips away unwanted portions of your image. You also can save the paths of selections for use later. Some selections may take a great deal of time to create, and saving these selections at intervals while creating a selection ensures that your work is not lost.

Viewing Tools

Similar to viewing tools, zoom tools enable you to see an image at different levels. Like a magnifying glass, this tool enables you to zoom into an area of fine detail, fix something, and then zoom back to see the overall image. Traditional artists are familiar with the process of working with their noses inches from their drawing boards to make sure the finest detail is captured, and then holding the page an arm's length away to see whether they achieved the desired effect. The zoom tool does just that, but on a much bigger scale. The capability to see and adjust individual pixels in an image is vital to the detailed effects you may need to create. Changing the eye color of a person is a typical, fine-detail job, which requires individual pixel work that only a zoom tool can provide as shown in Figure 7.36. It is useful to work in a magnified area and at the same time to see an overall view of an image.

Pan tools enable you to quickly move to a different part of an image without having to use the zoom tool. A hand is usually the icon used to indicate a pan tool. Panning is useful when you are working with an image magnified to the individual pixels. By using the pan tool you need not stop working at that magnification; you only move the image to the area that you need, as illustrated in Figure 7.37).

Many types of video boards include both the zoom tools and the pan tools. Hardware-implemented zoom and pan tools are much faster than software-controlled zoom and pan. Using a video board with this capability makes retouching digital images faster.

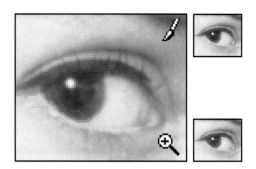

Figure 7.36
Retouching an eye is easier with the image magnified.

Figure 7.37
Panning moves the image like moving paper on a table.

Final Word

With any craft, the better you know your tools, the better you will become at that craft. You will find your own preferences and effective combinations of tools. Always be aware of the available tools because you never know when a tool you seldom use may meet your needs for a special effect.

Many programs give you the opportunity to save versions of a particular technique. But you also may want to keep a list of your favorites. Try to change one variable at a time to discover the result instead of changing many variables simultaneously. A step-by-step method helps you understand what the variables are doing to the mark you are making.

The undo function is a wonderful and useful option that enables you to revert and undo marks or strokes that you just made. In a strict production environment, undo is necessary for seeing the before and after of image processing. But in a creative setting, undo causes many users to get bogged down. You may get bogged down because you tend to think about a mark as though that mark will make or break the entire image. If you make a mark and then undo to try the mark again, this process becomes a catch-22. As time passes, if you eventually become satisfied with a mark, you already have broken whatever rhythm you needed to be creative. Unfortunately, the wonder of the computer, in cases like this, has undermined the fluid expressive nature of creating images.

If you are not sure you like the mark, save a version of the file before the mark was made and move on. You may surprise yourself and realize that the fluid nature of image creating is more important than trying to make everything perfect on the first pass. Don't get caught up in a loop of undo, undo, and undo because you never will reach completion, or if you do you will never be satisfied.

Most programs give you the option of turning off undo. This may sound a little scary at first, but try it. You'll save disk space while undo is off, and you always can go back to the original. Working straight through is a good way to examine how you are drawing and is much better than lamenting over each stroke, which interferes with your creative flow.

With advances in computer technology, digital painting will change constantly, as will your techniques for using the computer to create marks. Don't be afraid to venture into unknown territory. The computer is a tool that is under your guidance and control, not the other way around.

Dynamic
Effects

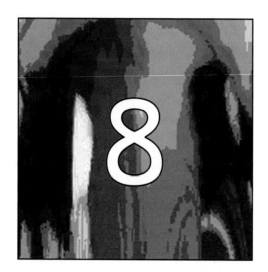

"Convenience breeds apathy; just
as iron rusts, so does inaction
sap the vigors of the mind."

Leonardo da Vinci

Rotating, scaling, skewing, stretching, and flipping are called *dynamic effects*. You can perform dynamic effects on the entire image or on selected areas within the image. With nearly all dynamic effects, sampling up or down must occur because actual pixels do not rotate or stretch. The illusion of dynamic effects is accomplished by reassigning the values of pixels. In a bitmap image the pixels themselves do not move. By creating new values, the pixels visually achieve their distortion effects. In most cases sampling is required to change the values of pixels. Sampling uses either interpolation or replication to produce new values. Interpolation averages existing pixels to new pixels; replication simply duplicates the values of existing pixels. You can review the effects of interpolation and replication in Chapter 1, "What Are Pixels?"

Rotating

Rotation seems like a natural process. Taking a piece of paper and turning it is quick and easy. Rotating bitmap digital images is a far more complex and lengthy process because of the sampling needed to produce the effect of turning an image. The pixels used on most computers are square and they are displayed square. Displaying square pixels at an angle is only possible if you find someone to hoist your monitor and hold it at an angle for you. But to digitally rotate an image even by a small amount, the program must achieve this rotation by sampling and creating new pixel information (see Figures 8.1a-f).

For most dynamic effects, including rotation, you should use interpolation for sampling, although sampling by replication accelerates the process. Sampling takes processing time, so dynamic effects take processing time. Programs and computer processors often are judged by the speed at which they rotate an image. You can review the difference between replication and interpolation in Chapter 1 if you are unsure about which method you should use.

Rotating for Output

The two types of image orientation are landscape (head left or right) and portrait (head up). Landscape orientation occurs when the longer edge is the horizontal edge. Portrait orientation occurs when the vertical edge is the longer edge and the top of the image is up (see Figures 8.2a and b). Most output devices are set for portrait printing. If a printer receives information from a landscape-oriented image, the printer must turn the image to match the method of output. You will find that rotating an image page into a

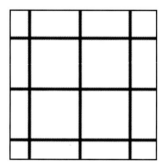

Figure 8.1a
Horizontal and vertical lines when rotated must have sampling to create the effect of rotation.

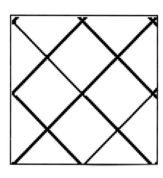

Figure 8.1b
The horizontal and vertical lines rotated by 45 degrees.

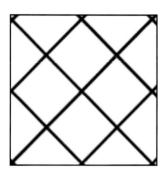

Figure 8.1c
The horizontal and vertical lines rotated 45 degrees using interpolation.

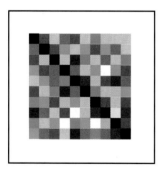

Figure 8.1d
Sampling is also required to rotate images. A magnified view of pixels before rotation.

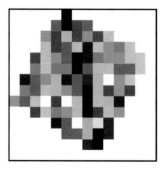

Figure 8.1e
The pixels after rotating the image 30 degrees using replication as the resampling method.

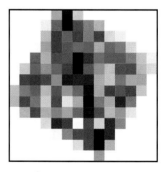

Figure 8.1f
The pixels of Figure "d" after rotating the image 30 degrees using interpolation as the resampling method.

Figure 8.2a
An image in a portrait orientation.

Figure 8.2b
An image in a landscape orientation.

Flipping

No sampling need occur if you are rotating an image by 90-degree increments or flipping an image. Because you are rotating the square pixels from the edge of one side of a pixel to the next edge, there is no reason for any type of sampling. If a sampling is performed for 90-degree rotations or for flipping, the image is adding unnecessary pixel values and you are waiting for processing that is not necessary.

Flipping an image creates a mirror of the image or selected area. Programs can flip either horizontally or vertically as shown in Figures 8.3a-c. As mentioned, flipping an image should not introduce any type of sampling. But if your program must sample, choose replication over interpolation because of the time-saving factor.

portrait layout before printing decreases the amount of time needed to process and output the image. The reason for the speed increase is that the computer has more processing speed than most output devices. Rather than making the printer perform the work of rotating, you should rotate the image while it is still on your workstation. In general, you always should prepare the image to meet the method in which the output device prints before sending the image to the output device.

Figure 8.3a
The original
orientation of the
image places the woman
outside the cafe.
Notice how you can read
the name of the cafe.

Figure 8.3b
Flipping the image
horizontally creates
the illusion that the
woman is inside the
cafe.

Figure 8.3c
Flipping the image
vertically may create
the impression that the
espresso is too strong.

Figure 8.4a
Original image.

Scaling

Scaling an image or a selected area means that
you are re-sizing the area by creating new pixels
through sampling. If only a portion of the
image is to be scaled, you cannot scale larger
than the bitmap of the base image or you may
lose part of the scaled portion. Usually, you

Figure 8.4b
An image whose size has changed by the
same percentage in the width and height
(scaled proportionally). This example is
sized at 125 percent.

Figure 8.4c
An image whose width and height are
changed with different percentages is not
scaled proportionally. This example is
sized at 125 percent in the height and 200
percent in the width.

have two options when you scale something.
You can scale proportionally or non proportionally. Proportionally means that you maintain
the ratio between the height and width during
re-sizing. The symmetry between the horizontal
and the vertical measurements stays the same
when you scale proportionally (see Figures 8.4a
and b).

Nonproportional scaling means that any resizing that you perform can stretch either the
width or the height without any relationship to
each other. You can stretch an image solely in
the vertical or solely in the horizontal direction
or a combination of the two. The effect of this
nonproportional scaling usually results in
distortion of either the horizontal or the vertical
direction. Distortion can be seen easily in
objects that should be perfectly round but are
stretched flat or tall as illustrated in Figures 8.4c
and d.

Figure 8.4d
This nonproportional scaling is 200
percent in height and 100 percent in
width.

Scaling is useful if you need to create the effect of elements that are supposed to be in relative sizes compared to one another. A person standing next to a building is a perfect example. The person detracts from the realism of the image if the person is three or four stories tall compared to the building. Scaling either the building up or the person down keeps the proper balance between the two elements in an image as shown in Figures 8.5a and b.

Distortion

Distortion of images provides an avenue for artists to create effects that go far beyond the basic rotate and scale. Distortion allows you to literally twist and shape images like putty. You will find that the processing time may limit the number of distortion variations with which you can experiment.

Because distortion effects usually take an enormous amount of computer processing time, we recommend that you work with a low-resolution version of your image. Experiment with the effects you want before applying the effects to a high-res file. Although you will not be able to use the low-resolution information, the time you save allows you to experiment with many more options than if you work only with the high-res file.

Figure 8.5a
Elements scaled improperly may distract the viewer.

Figure 8.5b
Scaling properly helps produce a feeling of realism.

Figure 8.6a
An unaltered
original image.

Figure 8.6b
Horizontal skewing
of an image.

Figure 8.7b
Envelope distortion
provides for
several points from
which distortion of
an image can be
made.

Figure 8.7a
Simple distortion
allows only the
corners of a
selection to be
altered.

Figure 8.6c
Vertical skewing of
an image.

Skewing

Slanting an image only on the horizontal or only on the vertical axis is called *skewing*. You can think of skewing as italicizing an image. Skew tilts the image to an angle. You can use skewing to create a sense of perspective or to better fit an image into a scene. Skewing often is used to simulate shadows, as illustrated in Figures 8.6a-c.

Distortion Envelopes

Some programs now offer the capability to distort an image using a number of control points rather than the typical four-cornered approach. A simple distortion uses the four corners of a selected image. An envelope is a more complex and intricate method of distorting an image (see Figures 8.7a and b).

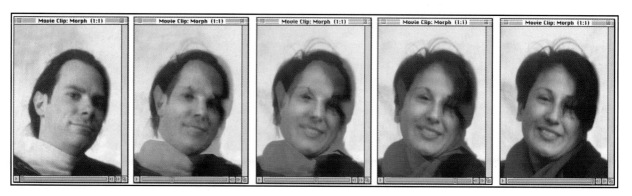

Figure 8.8a
Morphing blends images by distorting images into each other using Elastic Reality.

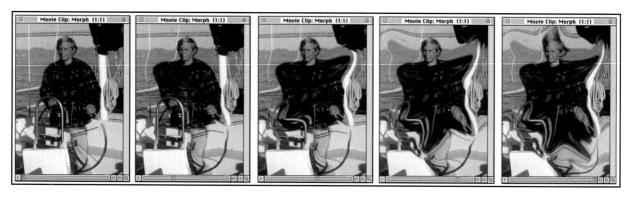

Figure 8.8b
Images become like plastic using morphing programs like Elastic Reality.

Morphing

Morphing also makes use of a type of envelope distortion. *Morphing* is a way of creating transition from one image into another (see Figures 8.8a and b). Although it's usually used in video production, you also can use the morphing technique to create unique distortions of still images. Morph by Gryphon Software, Elastic Reality by Elastic Reality Inc., Metaflo by The Valis Group, and Digital Morph by HSC software are only a few examples of desktop distortion and morphing programs.

Figure 8.9a
Original image.

Although programs enable you to distort a selection to simulate a sense of perspective, the effect is limited because there is no information in the image to actually create the real perspective of an object. Still, using distortion to create perspective can be an extremely effective way of helping the parts of an image give the impression of depth. By using distortion, you can pinch pixels inward along an edge and distort the image to create a perspective effect (see Figures 8.9a and b).

Figure 8.9b
Perspective distortion applied to elements in the image.

Final Word

Producing a quick sketch or rough draft usually is necessary to help formulate ideas. More traditional methods of hand layout and retouching always have required well thought out plans and experimentation to produce the best possible solution for a particular job.

Working on a computer should not change this important process of creating a plan of action. If you have established a blueprint of how to assemble your concept, you will waste less production time waiting for an image to be processed.

You could spend an hour waiting for an effect to be completed, only to find that the result is less than desirable. Usually, this disappointment occurs when you do not have the luxury of additional time to try something different. A low-resolution version of your image provides the quick-sketch environment that you need to plan your project.

Many programs now provide a preview window before you apply any effect. The dynamic effects are applied to a screen version of the areas selected. This process enables you to experiment quickly with many different options. Then, after all your decisions on scaling, rotation, and skewing are made, you can begin the processing of the high-res information. The program will perform all the complicated computations required to achieve the desired effects. Although you still need to wait for processing, the time spent on experimenting with different effects is greatly reduced because you do not have to wait for every individual rotation or scaling to process.

Experimentation also helps you avoid constantly applying distortion to a group of values that will impact negatively with multiple re-samplings. If you are trying to create realistic effects, you should tryto distort an image as little as possible whenever feasible.

Even with the advent of programs that allow large files to be manipulated, smaller files will always be quicker to process and will provide you with an instant thumbnail so that you can approach and plan the full production of your images in the most efficient manner possible.

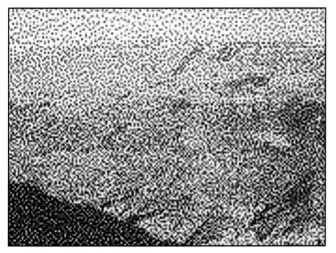

FM dots can create interesting effects at
different resolutions. 50 dpi

FM dots at 100 dpi.

FM dots at 200 dpi.

FM dots at 300 dpi.

FM dots at 400 dpi.

Original 150 lpi AM dot image.

Dynamic Effects

Masks and
Retouching

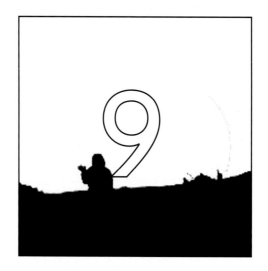

"Essentially you cannot improve
upon something you cannot do
or understand."

Mo Edago, 20th Century
non-Euclidean Sculptor

At the core of all image manipulation is the merging and collaging of images into one cohesive image. Everyone is familiar with cutting pictures from a magazine and pasting them together to create a new scene. Image programs use so many different techniques to produce collaged images that it is impossible to mention all these variations, but the consistent thread through all methods is the use of masks to create composite images.

In traditional layout, the simplest process involves cutting an image and then pasting it directly onto the layout board. For more elaborate collaging areas where specific areas of the image are to be protected, a material called *Rubylith* is used. The Rubylith material acts as a protector or mask for a chosen area. A mask indicates where spot color is to be laid onto an image, or it protects an area that is not supposed to be altered.

Digital masks work in the same way as Rubylith. By designating an area, you can protect, or leave unprotected, specific areas for altering color or collaging images.

Retouching is a manual editing process which attempts to improve the reproduction quality of an image. Retouching can involve removing blemishes or dirt from an image, correcting and adjusting colors, as well as repairing physical damage present in the original image.

Cut, Copy, Paste

If you are familiar with word processing programs, you are familiar with the options of cut, copy, and paste. Image programs use these options in much the same manner as word processing programs.

Cut and copy options take a selected area of pixels and place that pixel image information into a buffer called the clipboard. A *buffer* is an area in which you place and store pixel information while working with an image or a group of images. The most common name given to a buffer area is called the *clipboard.* As the name implies, the clipboard is like the traditional hand layout area where you keep an image until you decide where you want to place that image. The cut option removes the selected pixels and leaves behind a blank space. The copy option simply duplicates the pixel information of the selected area but leaves the original area untouched. The paste option takes whatever is in the clipboard and places it into the image.

When pixel information resides in the clipboard, you can paste the pixel information to any location on any image—even an entirely different image from where the pixels were cut or copied. Pasting the image data from the clipboard onto the image puts that pixel information above the image—literally floating in a different layer above the image area. This floating action enables you to move the pasted pixel information freely without altering the image underneath. Similar to taking a clipping from a magazine and experimenting with different positions, you easily can move a

floating selection (see Figures 9.1a-c). After you have chosen the proper position for the selection, drop the selection into the image. Dropping or deselecting a floating selection into an image locks the floating pixels directly onto the pixels underneath. You cannot move that group of pixels after you have dropped the floating selection. Many programs offer several pasting variations that allow adjustment of the floating image's transparency to create subtle collaging effects. Transparency of the floating image is controlled while the pixels still are floating—not after the selection has been dropped or placed into the image (see Figures 9.2a and b).

Figure 9.1a
You can move the floating selection without affecting any part of the image underneath.

Figure 9.1b
The floating selection is active until dropped.

Figure 9.1c
When it is dropped, the pasted image can no longer be edited.

Figure 9.2a
Transparency is adjusted while the selection is floating.

Figure 9.2b
After the floating selection is dropped, the transparency cannot be adjusted.

The resolution of the floating selection matches the resolution of the base bitmap image. For example, if you paste an image that is 300 pixels wide by 200 pixels high into another bitmap image, the values of the floating selection will match the same number of pixels in the base bitmap image. If the resolution of an image is 100 ppi and you paste that image into a bitmap that is 300 ppi, the resolution of the floating selection and base image is still 300 ppi (see Figures 9.3a-c). You cannot mix different resolutions; there are no exceptions. You can scale the floating selection to increase the number of pixels and therefore the physical size; this requires upsampling to increase the total number of pixels.

Remember that you are not moving the pixels of the base, nor are you covering them up when you drop a floating selection. When you drop a floating selection you are simply re-assigning the value of the pixels in the base image. After you have dropped the floating selection, the values are now part of the base image—although now it appears that you have placed new pixels in the image. Dropping a floating section is like placing glue on a picture and pasting it down. Try to pick it up and you take what is underneath along with it.

Because the clipboard actually is holding image information, the operating speed of your program may diminish slightly. To help alleviate this problem, after you are finished using large images in the clipboard, simply make a small selection of pixels and copy that information into the clipboard. The clipboard can hold only one image at a time, so the smaller copy resides in the clipboard and eliminates any potential speed compromises.

Figure 9.3a
An image with 300 pixels across by 200 pixels down.

Figure 9.3b
An image with a resolution of 300 ppi.

Figure 9.3c
When Figure 'a' is placed together with Figure 'b,' Figure 'a' matches the resolution of Figure 'b', yet the physical size is different.

Image programs such as Photoshop have three of their own buffers within RAM (if available) or on the hard drive. These additional buffers are used to hold the working image information, the transformation image information, and any undo information. To work optimally with an image you need at least three times the file's size in RAM or at least that amount of memory on the hard drive. Accessing the hard drive will slow down processing as the program can only go as fast as the read and write capability of the drive. Solid state RAM is always a faster place to process digital data.

Objects and Layers

Objects or layers, as they are called, provide the option of having multiple floating selections active all at the same time over a base bitmap image (see Figure 9.4a). Until the final rendering of the image, the floating selections can stay floating even after you close and save the image. Since the layers are always floating until dropped, you can return to the image at any time and move, replace, or delete any image in a layer without disturbing the integrity of the base image as shown in Figure 9.4b. This allows for numerous position changes of elements in an image. Layers can also contain independent channel and mask features because each object layer is actually an independent image file. This layering concept may be familiar to you if you use vector drawing programs like Illustrator and Freehand.

You should be aware that adding an object or layer of bitmap imagery will increase the file size. As you add more information, the application must keep track of all the data and may

Figure 9.4a
Objects, or layers, provide multiple floating selections.

Figure 9.4b
You can move objects or layers without affecting the base image until they are dropped.

begin to slow or perform sluggishly. Always try to keep the amount of information within the capabilities of your system, otherwise performance and efficiency will suffer.

Masks

Masks are used to identify specific areas of an image that you want to protect or alter. Masks are often used to perform color corrections in

Figure 9.5a
A selection is indicated by the dashed line.

Figure 9.5b
Only the selected pixels can be affected. The pixels not chosen are protected from alterations.

specific colors of an image, but are most commonly related to the collaging of images.

The simplest mask uses the selection tools to define a pixel area of the bitmap image. Having an area selected indicates that any alteration (such as painting or color correction) is performed only in the selected area. The selected area protects or masks any other area (see Figures 9.5a and b). Different image programs implement masks in different ways, but the function and the results remain the same.

Why Use Masks?

Why do you need a mask? Why not just place the image you need exactly on top of the image that you are creating? The key word is *exactly*. It is difficult to merge exactly what you want onto another image. Although some masks take time and are intricate, you can be assured that the

results are going to be accurate and are not going to need large amounts of touching up. Plus, the advantage that anti-aliased edges provides is not obtainable by any other method. The examples in Figures 9.9a-d show the relative ease of merging two elements using masks.

The quality of your collaging is directly proportional to the masks that you create. If you are careful and spend time with the edges of a mask, the results will be reflected in the form of the seamless merging of image elements. If you do not take care during this mask making, the realism of the final image suffers. As always, the best masking and collaging examples are the ones in which you do not notice that there has been any editing or collaging done to the image.

Figure 9.6a
Masks are great when you are on vacation
and the weather won't cooperate. Simply
stand in the appropriate spot and wave.

Figure 9.6b
Mask of the foggy background.

Figure 9.6c
The new background to replace the fogged-
in Grand Canyon.

Figure 9.6d
New image with new background that proves
you were really there.

Selection Masks

The four most common types of selecting tools
are the Rectangular, Oval, Lasso, and Automatic
selections. The Rectangular selection tool creates
square or rectangular selection regions; the Oval
selection tool creates circular or oval selections;
and the Lasso selection tool enables you to
freely select areas and pixel groups. Automatic
or magic wand selection tools select pixel
groups based on a chosen value range of color.
All of these selection tools can be used together
to create irregular selected regions as illustrated
in Figure 9.7.

When you are working with complex image
areas, making a selection mask is usually time
consuming. Rather than trying to make a
selection perfect in one pass, you should select
the general area you want and then subtract or
add from the area you need selected. Usually, a
combination of selection tools is critical to
produce an accurate selection mask.

Some people think that the automatic selection
tool is the only tool they require. The automatic
selection tool is an excellent method of selecting a range of color values, but this method is

Figure 9.7
Selections of any shape or size can be
created by using various selections
tools.

Figure 9.8a
A typical process used to achieve a
desired selection.

Figure 9.8b
Adding and subtracting from a selection.

Figure 9.8c
The final selection.

not perfect. Unless you have an area of color values that is vastly different from other adjacent values, a selection that is automatically chosen usually requires some kind of refinement and alterations. The automatic selection tool provides an excellent starting point from which you can make further adjustments to create your final selection (see Figures 9.8a-c).

Saving Selections

During the course of creating a selection, you should save your selection periodically because a simple click of the mouse outside the selected area deselects that area, and you lose the selection. Also, by saving a selection you can retrieve the selection for use at any time during your retouching work.

Saving a selection basically involves saving a mask. Most programs have separate areas called alpha channels for saving mask information. Many selection masks are difficult to reproduce, so saving the information in a separate layer or channel ensures that you need not again define an area or areas to protect. A channel containing a selection mask often is referred to as a mask layer. This layer does not affect the RGB composite color of an image. Instead, this channel layer holds the selection information for later use. The mask layer is an 8-bit channel and contains up to 256 levels of grayscale information. Each time you add a mask layer to an image, you effectively increase the file size by one-third the size of the color image. A mask channel's grayscale information can be fully edited with any of the tools used on the color image (see Figure 9.9).

Many programs also enable you simply to save the outline of a selection as a path. Saving a selection to a path and not to a mask channel eliminates the problem of increased file size

Figure 9.9
The selection from Figure 9.8 saved as a mask.

because saving a path requires very little memory. Still, as you read further, you will see that mask channels are a useful part of merging images together.

Mask Channels

In addition to the channels which carry color information, most programs have mask channels. When you are implementing mask channels, the black area in the channel indicates full protection and the white area indicates no protection. When you paste an image from the clipboard as a floating selection, the areas that have white in the mask channel allow the floating image to show through completely; the areas of black protect the base image from the floating selection (see Figure 9.10a). You can also reverse this convention so that white is full protection and black is no protection, as shown in Figure 9.10b.

Figure 9.10a
The effect of the mask seen in Figure 9.9
on a floating selection where black is
full protection and white is no
protection.

Figure 9.10b
The effect of a mask can be reversed so
that white is full protection and black is
no protection.

Density Masks

Recall that basic masks either protect an image area or they do not. Black typically indicates full protection and white no protection. Density masks allow degrees of protection between the no protection of white and the full protection of black. A gray value in a mask protects an image depending on the value of that gray. A 50 percent value in a mask channel means that the mask is not fully protecting the image but is allowing 50 percent of any change to occur. The density mask is a useful method to regulate the effects of collaging to create transparency.

When the mask contains areas of gray, then a percentage of the image shows through depending on how close the gray value is to white or black. For example, a 30 percent gray protects only 30 percent of the image while 70 percent

gray in a mask channel protects 70 percent of the image. The gray blend in Figure 9.11a acts as a density mask. When the floating selection is over the areas closer to white, less of the image is seen; and when the floating selection is closer to areas of black, more of the image is seen (see Figures 9.11b and c). Gray in the mask channel creates a transparent effect in the floating image.

Density masks are also the basis for selective color corrections. Specific areas of tone and color can be identified to allow precise adjustments in only those areas designated—for example, correcting the amount of cyan in red colors. Where the various tones of yellow and magenta channels overprint to create red is the only place the cyan will be allowed by the mask to make color adjustments.

Anti-aliased Masks

Having gray values in the mask channel is an important advantage of digital masking. The soft edges of anti-aliasing create a sense of optical and visual realism that are important for collaging. Accurate, soft-edged masks are nearly impossible to make by using the traditional Rubylith or photographic methods of mask

creation. The benefits of anti-aliasing are clear. Masks using anti-aliasing on the edges are typically more effective than masks that do not use the anti-aliasing provided by 256 levels of gray channels. The examples in Figures 9.12a and b and 9.13a and b indicate the differences involving images merged with and without anti-aliased masks.

Figure 9.11a
A mask with a blend of gray.

Figure 9.11b
When the image is floating over areas where the mask is dark, less of the floating image is seen.

Uses of Anti-aliased Masks

Most programs that use masks enable you to "see" through the mask so that you can base the creation of the mask on the original image. The capability to create a mask based on the original image is vital. Without this opportunity, you lack any of the subtle control necessary to use masks effectively. A perfect example where anti-aliased density masking is needed would be masking out hair.

Figure 9.11c
When the image is floating over areas where the mask is light, more of the floating image is seen.

Masking out frizzy hair is always a very difficult process because the light, thin lines of hair typically are not solid colors but are a mixture of the background and hair colors. Careful examination of the edge of the hair usually shows that any mask created there must be a

Figure 9.12a
An aliased edge mask.

Figure 9.12b
Blue background merged into image with
aliased mask.

Figure 9.13a
An anti-aliased edge mask.

Figure 9.13b
Blue background merged into image with
anti-aliased mask.

soft gray and must never have solid white or black areas for these individual hairs. If you disregard the frizzy hair altogether, the result often is an unnatural "cut out" look (see Figures 9.14a and b). Making intricate density masks can be a painstaking operation, and shortcuts usually are regretted. Although creating some of these masks requires a lot of time, you must decide how much time the image requires to reach the desired quality.

Obviously, the more masking you perform, the better you become. The best way to attack masking of any kind is to make a quick, general mask, and then edit specific areas in the mask channel. Each refining step moves you closer to your goal of an acceptable mask (see Figure 9.15).

Figure 9.14a
Poor masking around hair.

Color Corrections with Density Masks

Density masks also can be used to make specific color adjustments. By creating a mask based on color channels that overlap, you can isolate specific ranges of colors. Remember that the density of a mask will determine how much of an effect any image processing will have on that area of the image. For example, in Figure 9.16a, a density mask created as a blend regulates the amount of effect a filter will have. A filter applied to the images in Figures 9.16b and c has more effect in the lighter areas of the mask and less effect in the darker areas of the mask. The density mask in Figure 9.16a literally dilutes the strength of the filter.

The diluting effect of a density mask works with any image process, including color adjustments. For example, if you want to correct the green colors in a CMYK image you can simply change any CMYK value only in areas where there is green. Where the various tones of cyan and yellow channels overprint to create green, it creates a density mask (see Figures 9.17a and b). This is the only place any values of CMYK will be allowed by the mask to make color adjustments. The resulting mask channel affects green colors only, and other colors in the image will not be affected (see Figures 9.18a and b).

Figure 9.14b
Good masking around hair.

Figure 9.15
The progression of general mask to finished mask. The mask is edited and refined at each stage to produce a final mask that is used in the composite.

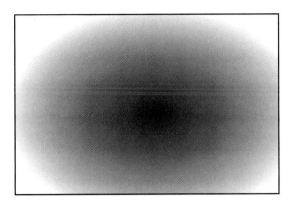

Figure 9.16a
A mask created from a blend of gray.

Figure 9.16b
The filter has more effect in the areas
where the mask is less dense.

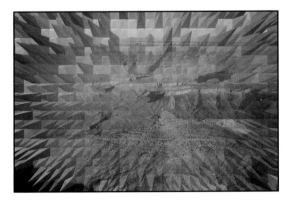

Figure 9.16c
Using filters through density masks is one
method of creating unique effects.

Many programs have specific functions to permit selective color corrections. These selection color options perform the same function of creating a density mask without actually having to go to the trouble of creating a density mask. Regardless, it is useful to understand the process of density masks because you may want to isolate colored areas or apply filters in specific areas of color.

Density masks also are useful in creating touch plates or spot colors. Touch plates are tonal areas where a specific color, other than the standard CMYK, is added to enhance the image.

The basic premise behind seven-color printing or hi-fi color is touch plates. The touch plates are created by intersecting pairs of the CMY colors. For example, the area where C and M overprint is a blue touch plate; the C and Y overprint is a green touch plate; and the Y and the M intersection is a red touch plate (see Figures 9.19a-f). Multiple combinations of different percentages of CMY can create other colored touch plates beyond the red, green, and blue. The actual production of touch plates must take into consideration many issues, including subtracting appropriate amounts of CMY color replaced by touch plates. Density masks are an important part of collaging and color correction and are well worth the effort to understand and use.

Partial File Editing

Quick editing is a feature of Photoshop that is implemented in different ways by other programs (see Figure 9.20). Quick editing has become a generic term for dividing up a large bitmap into smaller files. Faster editing is possible because of the smaller file size. When only a small area of a large image file needs to be worked on, it is much faster to divide the file into smaller parts and only read the part that you need to change. You should avoid performing any color adjustments when the files are divided because the sections will not match properly.

Figure 9.17a
The cyan and yellow channels are the dominant colors used to create green.

Figure 9.17b
The areas where only cyan and yellow channels overprint each other with little or no magentA and black create the density mask used to correct only the green colors in the image.

Figure 9.18a
The original image before corrections.

Figure 9.18b
Only the greens have been altered by using the density mask in Figure 9.17.

Figure 9.19a
The original CMYK image.

Figure 9.19b
A red touch plate.

Figure 9.19c
A green touch plate.

Figure 9.19d
A blue touch plate.

Figure 9.19e
The three touch plates of red, green, and
blue are simulated together.

Figure 9.19f
A simulated effect of red, green, and blue
touch plates.

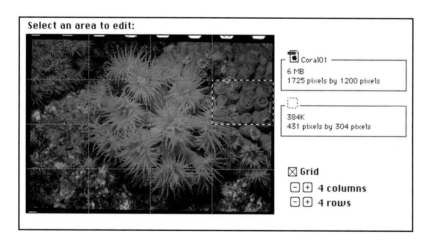

Figure 9.20
Quick Editing in Photoshop enables you to
divide the image into smaller files for
faster editing.

Retouching for Repair

Retouching an image is an acquired skill. Like
just about everything else, the more you do it,
the better you get. Retouching literally covers

everything you can possibly do to an image. Since discussing infinity is beyond the scope of this book, it is probably more helpful to discuss how to approach a retouching project for some kind of photographic repair. Repair is the most prevalent use of retouching—even if it is simply to eliminate a speck of dust from a scanned image.

When handed a transparency or photograph that may need retouching, your first question should be, "What is the final result supposed to be?" When you establish the goals of the retouching, you can then prepare a plan of action. After you determine the final requirements of the image, you may discover a simple crop can reduce the amount of work necessary to repair the image (see Figures 9.21a and b). If you simply dive into a project, you may find that you have spent time on areas that will never be in the final image. The following images are courtesy of HAGIT COHEN and Copyright 1994.

Prepare the image for scanning. You will find many old photographs and transparencies are too fragile to wrap around a drum scanner; therefore, a flat mount CCD scanner should be used. Be very careful when cleaning the original photograph! Photographic materials, especially transparencies, use dyes placed into a gelatin base. Over an extended period of time, dirt and dust sitting on an image will actually sink and melt into the photographic material. If you rub too hard, you may take off more than just dust and dirt. Excessive cleaning will also take off substantial amounts of film emulsion and imagery. Like pulling on a loose thread on a sweater, you may discover that the entire sweater will unravel. Rubbing too hard may literally rub away the image. Older photos should be cleaned primarily with compressed air. Any dirt should be retouched out during the digital image stage.

After you have established which areas of the image are important to work on, draw a sketch or print a copy (see Figure 9.22). The sketch will provide a blueprint from which you can keep track and plan your work. Chapter 12 discusses the methods of scanning preparation.

Take a look at the digital image on your monitor. We have assumed that you have scanned everything at the proper resolution. You should prioritize the retouching you will do. Identify

Figure 9.21a
The image to be edited before cropping.

Figure 9.21b
Cropping reduces file size and eliminates any extra retouching work.

the areas that will need the most attention: large tears, holes, and large amounts of dirt. Save the big areas of retouching until last. There are two reasons for this. First, it is easy to become overwhelmed with repair and retouching. Saving the most visible problems until the end gives you an opportunity to work with the image. As you view portions of the image, you get a good feel of the texture and nuances that will ultimately make your repairs more believable. Second and more substantially, the best source of repair material comes from the image itself. You should first take care of the small dirt and dust specks because those areas may become source material for the larger repairs. You don't want to double your work by repairing a tear with dirty source material. You will just have to repair it again later.

Cleaning dirt and dust is fairly straightforward. Cloning brushes are the primary tools used in retouching repair. The clone align setting allows for quick cleaning of small specks (see Figure 9.23). You need to choose the smallest brush size that will cover the specks when you are cleaning them. Because you need to match the

surrounding area, choose the closest clone source that is at least twice as far as the size of the brush. Often a large brush tip will overlap into the clone source and create an unpleasant pattern (see Figure 9.24). Whenever you retouch, you want to be as unobtrusive as possible. You should try to keep the original integrity of the image and avoid major surgery.

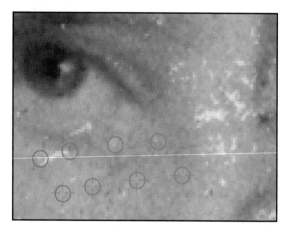

Figure 9.23
Clone align used with a small brush is useful for quick cleaning of dust and specks. The open circles indicate the brush size and the crossed circles indicate the clone source.

Figure 9.22
A simple sketch or b/w output is a useful guide to track the areas of the image that you are working on.

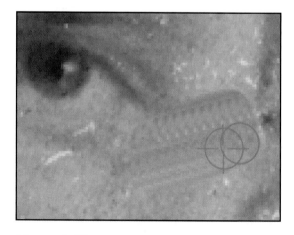

Figure 9.24
If your clone brush is too large and the clone source is set too close, a step-over pattern may result.

To view the image, you should zoom at least 1:1 so that all the image pixels are displayed. Zoom in as close as you can in order to see the dust and no further. The more image you can see when you work the better. If you magnify too closely you may lose perspective of how the repair should be done. Magnification level is also a matter of taste, so work with a view you feel most comfortable with and don't feel that you have to stay at one magnification. Zoom in and out as needed but, after working at high magnifications, always take the time to inspect the overall image to make sure the repair is achieving the effect you desire.

Work in a defined pattern (see Figure 9.25). For example, start in the upper left and clean everything displayed before you scroll to the next area of the image. Like mowing a lawn, you want to make sure that you cover the entire image. A meticulous approach will ensure that the entire image is seen and any problems are addressed. If you bounce around the image, you are likely to miss something.

After dust and dirt have been eliminated, move on to scratches. You also can address and repair the scratches while you are cleaning the dust. A typical method used to clean a scratch is to draw a straight line with the clone align tool from one end of the scratch to the other. This direct approach may work well in flat areas of color, but it works poorly in complex pattern areas.

You should repair a scratch by using a zipper pattern. Although it is much more time intensive, you should establish a new clone source for every retouch done on the scratch. Alternate the clone source from either side of the scratch until you have eliminated the defect.

Figure 9.25
Cleaning an image in logical pattern ensures that the entire image has been inspected.

This zipper pattern also is used for repairing larger tears and holes (see Figures 9.26a-c). You should never be satisfied with one clone source. A circle approach to clone repair is also useful. Make several different clone sources and surround a defect rather than trying to clean it with one stroke (see Figures 9.27a-c).

Finally, after the dirt, scratches, and minor tears have been repaired, take a look at your image. It should be relatively clean and look much better than the original. During the retouching process, and definitely at this point, you should save the image. Rather than just saving one version, save different versions at every stage of the repair. Saving as separate files as you work gives you the opportunity to revisit any stage of the retouching process. Name each file with the same project name and with a suffix of .01, .02, .03, and so on, so that when listed in alphabetical order the most recent version of your project will be last on the list.

Many multimedia programs will read in groups of files in order according to the numbers attached to the file names. This is useful when

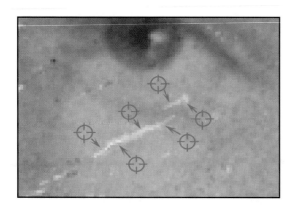

Figure 9.26a
The zipper pattern alternates clone
sources from either side of a scratch.

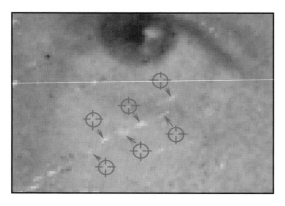

Figure 9.26b
After one part of the zipper is complete,
switch to the other side and complete the
repair.

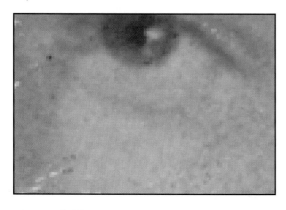

Figure 9.26c
Finished repair.

creating animation sequences. Remember that zero is the first number in any sequence, not the number one. For a sequence of up to 99 images, you must start with .00, .01, .02, .03 and so on to place all the files in order. If you start the file naming with .1, .2, .3 and so on, the files will be placed out of order. Sequences with up to 999 images must start the naming convention with .001, .002 .003, and so on.

Avoid step cloning wherever possible. Step cloning is when you take a clone source and step on top of the previous clone as you repair a large defect. Step cloning only results in a strange regular pattern (see Figure 9.28).

If you need to repair a large area, take as many clone sources as possible and slowly build into the area. Regular patterns are to be avoided at all costs.

At the point that you feel you have completed the retouching, take another zoomed look at the image. Take note of the areas that you have repaired. Place a small dodge and/or burn to darken or lighten areas that may seem too regular. Catch any final dust specks and save your image. If you have the time, step away from the image for an hour or two, and then you can do your final inspector detector routine. Compare the original image to the final retouched image to be sure that the image integrity has not been compromised too much during retouching (see Figures 9.29a-c).

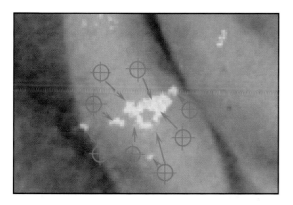

Figure 9.27a
A circle pattern surrounds a defect with clone sources.

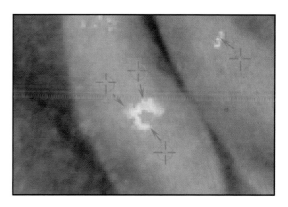

Figure 9.27b
Alternating clone sources ensures balanced amounts of repair material.

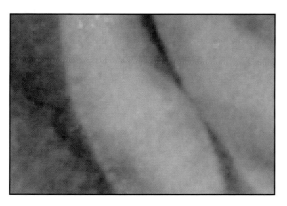

Figure 9.27c
Finished repair.

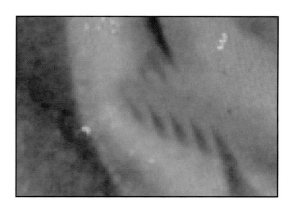

Figure 9.28
An example of step cloning.

Figure 9.29a
The original image before retouching.

Figure 9.29b
An intermediate step during repair.

Figure 9.29c
The image after repair.

Depth of Field

The tendency in digital imagery is to keep everything in sharp focus, which is rarely the case with photographic images. Creating a more realistic depth of field effect lends a better quality and believability to your overall image. The *depth of field* is how far a scene stays in focus in front of and behind the spot where you focus. As you look at objects in nature, you scan back and forth so quickly that everything appears in focus. But when you examine a photographic image, objects in the distance often are out of focus. When you take photographs, images out of focus are the objects outside the depth of field. We understand how photos with images out of focus are at different distances. Our perceptions have been trained to understand that in a two-dimensional system, focus and lack of focus help create a sense of depth (see Figure 9.30).

Figure 9.30
Creating the illusion of depth with focus.

Perspective

Perspective also helps create depth. Perspective is the perception of the spatial relationship of objects relative to one another. Perspective can be achieved with simple awareness of the relationship between objects. For example, in a group of people, the persons in the back of the picture should not be the same size as those in the front. If you are trying to create a realistic crowd scene with different persons, take into account their positions and what their sizes should be in relation to one another (see Figures 9.31a-c).

When collaging images, you should remember the basics of focus and perspective. As in a photograph, you have a depth of field. When trying to create a sense of depth with images, remember that objects at different depths are not always perfectly in focus. Even a light bit of fuzziness for an image that is supposed to be a different depth leans toward a more realistic image.

One of the hardest accomplishments to make in a two-dimensional space is to create a sense of three dimensions. Specific applications, called 3D programs, concentrate on creating realistic three-dimensional objects. These elements can be imported into an image retouching program, but even 3D programs display images in a two-dimensional space and incorporate focus and perspective to create depth.

When creating realistic collaging, always keep in mind anti-aliased edges, depth of field, and perspective.

Figure 9.31a
The original image before adding new
elements.

Figure 9.31b
Adding giant cats won't help make the
scene seem more realistic.

Figure 9.31c
Making the cats appear at a reasonable
size helps create a more believable scene.

Live Picture

A new method of approaching the assembly of digital images is being presented. Developed primarily by Bruno Delean with the assistance of Kai Krause and HSC software, *Live Picture* has introduced a new method of working with digital images. Just as PostScript introduced vector-based graphics to digital line art drawings, now FITS, a French-based company, is introducing mathematics-based manipulation to complex color images.

Vector shapes are resolution independent because a vector is described by a mathematics curve rather than with individual pixels. But in postscript-based graphics, there are no airbrush, cloning, color correction, or smearing capabilities. Live Picture incorporates the concepts of vector drawing into image manipulation. In terms of pure technique, it enables images to be described as mathematics formula. The manipulation of images as formulas is much easier just as Illustrator and Freehand make it easier to create and manipulate shapes and lines.

At the base of Live Picture is FITS technology. FITS provides an interchangeable imaging database and software RIP engine. All the image data in Live Picture is created in a way that enables the RIP engine to provide a mathematical expression of each color at every point of the image. Instead of storing all the pixels of a photo, FITS stores the mathematical expressions of the effect.

What is considered resolution independent is actually effect independent. A pixel-based image is converted into an IVUE format (the word vue is French for "to see" so IVUE means image view or I see), which is the file format used by Live

Picture. But all of the manipulations are stored as math formulas and are resolution independent. Any portion of the image can be represented at any resolution. Formulas can be calculated on all the pixels required to be seen on the screen or rendered to output. When you see the image onscreen, you are literally seeing a ripping process taking place, but for only that part of the image that you are viewing.

The actual pixels are upsampled when you interpolate a bitmap image. The value of the pixels in an image converted into the IVUE format is not interpolated, but the mathematical expressions of the pixels are interpolated. This results in an indirect, and in many cases, a better scale of bitmap images. Similarly, in order to use a large brush in current pixel editing software, a very powerful computer is required to calculate all the brush strokes. In Photoshop, a 50 pixel brush is very slow. Because the airbrush is a mathematical representation, the airbrush with Live Picture and FITS can be 10 or 10,000 pixels in size without any loss of speed.

Live Picture had some very specific features. Although not a complete solution to every situation, Live Picture does provide a giant leap into the future of image creation and manipulation.

All the effects created in Live Picture are resolution independent. Therefore, they can be output at any size without resorting to interpolation of pixels. The effects are mathematically regenerated at the designated output resolution during the output process called FITS RIP.

Because of the mathematical approach, any effect can be progressively modified or undone.

FITS layers can be reordered, deleted, resized, scaled, and so on. Although other programs contain layers or objects, they don't treat brush effects such as painting, lighting, blurring, or color correction as layers. The number of layers is unlimited and does not depend on RAM.

IVUE file format is unique in that it permits both fast viewing and geometric changes. With IVUE you can basically zoom into a 500 MB image in just a few seconds. The other important aspect of IVUE technology is that LP can work directly on JPEG compressed images. It does not have to decompress the entire image before using it. Only the necessary pixels are decompressed. This results in tremendous implications for IVUE use over networks, telecommunication lines, and CD-ROMs.

The LP masking technology is semiautomatic. It easily integrates one image into another. When you have a person on a white background and you want to insert him on a black background, there is typically a white line surrounding him, which needs additional retouching. When the object is silhouetted, LP automatically calculates the difference between the previous and new backgrounds and sets the edge in place. Called Chrominance Compensations, it also works nicely with hair, which is always a difficult chore to mask out effectively.

It is misleading to believe that FITS technology does not work with any pixels. All of the effects within LP are resolution independent. In fact, IVUE is a pixels image format. The quality of the image you start with still is the biggest factor in final reproduction quality. Even with superior interpolation Live Picture is not going to magically create what was not originally there.

You can merge images of varying resolutions much easier because LP works within what is called an imaging space that is resolution independent. There is no fixed resolution until the image is output. The key is that the effects performed on those pixel-based images are all resolution independent.

The FITS file can be used as a method to apply changes to files. For example, when a remote user sends a FITS file to an LP user, all the changes can be made to the high-resolution image from the information found in the FITS file, thus saving the trouble and time of sending an entire finished high-resolution file. You can send back the FITS file and apply it to the original file saved in the IVUE format.

This is unlike a typical proxy method of dealing with large files. In a proxy, a small, easily manageable resolution file represents the larger full resolution file. Image manipulations are performed directly on the proxy. Then after the manipulations are complete, the changes are applied to the larger resolution file. LP works directly with the high-resolution data with no cumulative processing error. The IVUE format not only contains the original image, but a series of reduced resolution subimages. If thought of as a pyramid, the highest resolution would be at the base and the lowest subimage would be at the top. You only see as much data as the screen size allows. This approach allows immediate zooming at whatever level you need.

When you are finished with manipulations, effects are applied to the high-resolution file. Unlike a cumulative method of many recording scripts, LP only processes the information needed to achieve the effects required. In a cumulative method (typical of recording scripts)

every step, including undos, is included when replayed on the high-resolution file. This takes away from the overall effectiveness of the processing.

Think of LP processing as a treasure hunt. You may look all over to find your prize, going over the same territory several times until you find it. But if you are then told to repeat the process, you know to go directly where the treasure is hidden and not waste any time wandering around. In this manner, LP goes directly to the desired effect and eliminates any nonessential steps that do not contribute to the creation of the image.

LP builds or RIPs data as a TIFF file for eventual output to image setter, film recorder, or placement into a layout page. You then designate the desired resolution and size. There are three settings to the RIP: Standard, Fine, and Extra Fine. Any one can be chosen. The standard setting produces an output at least at the same resolution as the original scans. Fine and Extra Fine use oversampling to produce the smooth blends and curves.

LP can import and export TIFF files. Within LP, these files are converted to IVUE format, which itself is a pixel format. Other programs, including Photoshop and Painter, can import and export IVUE files, channels, and masks to resolution independent FITS masks within LP.

Live Picture is a very complex and intriguing program. It offers a wide variety of solutions to image collaging and retouching. Although not a substitute for pixel based programs, Live Picture, and programs like it, will play an important role in image production environments.

Checklist

Before you begin any collaging and repair to an image, you should establish what it is you would like to accomplish, at what level of quality, and in what amount of time.

To ensure that all your goals are achieved, a plan of attack should be sketched out. Do not underestimate the usefulness of doing quick sketches by hand or on the computer in order to flush out your ideas. Print out any preliminary work and use it as a guide or a blueprint.

Approach each element of your project one at a time. Finish each part before moving on to the next. Avoid the tendency to say "I'll fix that later" because usually you won't. If you can, fix it now.

Save multiple files of the work as you finish each aspect of the project. For example, after you have finished creating a mask, save the image and mask as a separate file. Then move on to any collaging you need to do and save another file after the collaging is complete. If later in the project you wish to revisit the image before the collaging, but after the mask was created, you can go directly to that file. Save as many steps as you can during the course of the project.

If you take a little time during the beginning of a project, and carefully plan your steps, you will save more time in the long run and produce the best possible image.

Final Word

The fun thing about collage and retouching is that anyone can sit down and do it right away. It takes only a basic understanding of digital programs to cut and paste images together or to clone a third eye onto a forehead. But when the novelty of being able to merge images together wears off, you may find that good collage and retouching is not as quick and easy as you first thought. When your sights become trained on specific goals, collage and retouching emerges as another craft that requires practice and attention to detail in order to master. It makes no difference if you are creating realistic or unrealistic scenes; taking the time to fine tune even the smallest of details in an image will help ensure that your images are more believable and have more impact regardless of content.

AM dots in most situations
reproduce flat areas of color and
blends much smoother than FM dots
as illustrated in the following
figures. This AM dot is at 150 lpi.

400 dpi FM dot.

300 dpi FM dot.

The sky is 150 lpi AM dot. The rest
of the image is 300 dpi FM dot.

Filter
Effects

10

"You don't get better at something
by knowing less about it."

Marcus Martial

Filters adjust the values of a pixel or group of pixels based on a mathematical formula that can result in visually fantastic effects. When you begin to understand how a filter works, you can develop an effective use of filtering.

Introduction to Filters

The term *filtering* refers to the action of removing unwanted substances by passing them through a porous substance. If you are familiar with sound, you know that filters often are used to remove undesirable noise from a sound wave; filters used with digital images work in a similar way. Passing pixels through a digital filter is similar to using a real filter because the digital filter removes unwanted pixel values.

The distribution of pixel values in an image can be visually described and organized by a histogram. As the name implies, a histogram displays the current history of an image (see Figures 10.1a and b). A histogram displays the number of pixels that fall within a certain value range. The graphic representation of like-valued pixels within a given image can show where tone and colors change within an image. Knowing where tones may shift provides insight as to where correction may be appropriate. A histogram shows the distribution of the values in many different modes. No matter what values the histogram is based on, the corresponding pixel values in the digital image are represented graphically. Used in conjunction with curve correction, a histogram is another useful tool for analyzing an image.

The values of pixels are adjusted easily by color correction methods and painting. Filters simply represent another way of altering pixel values with those value changes based on formulas. Figures 10.2a through 10.4a show a blur filter used several times on the same image. The histogram of each image (Figures 10.2b through 10.4b) demonstrates how the values of the pixels bunch into one range of values. The histogram shows that the image's pixel values are becoming more alike as the effect of blurring increases.

Figures 10.5a through 10.7a show the same image sharpened several times. The histograms of the sharpened images (Figures 10.5b through 10.7b) indicate that the values of the pixels are becoming more spread apart and less alike as sharpening increases. The histogram is simply another method used to monitor change in a digital image.

The math for filters can be complex, but it is not necessary to discuss the specific algorithms in order to understand how a filter works. If you become more interested, there are programs like Convol by HSC software that enable you to create your own filters.

Figure 10.1a
An image and its corresponding histogram.

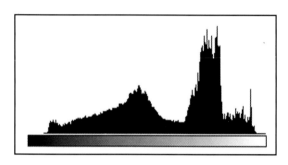

Figure 10.1b
The histogram is a visual representation of the distribution of values in an image.

Figure 10.2a
The image blurred.

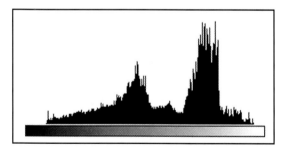

Figure 10.2b
The histogram of the image blurred.

Figure 10.3a
The image blurred more.

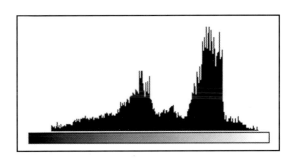

Figure 10.3b
The histogram of the image blurred more.

Figure 10.4a
The image blurred even more.

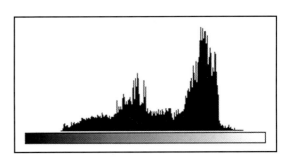

Figure 10.4b
The histogram of the image blurred even more.

Figure 10.5a
The image sharpened.

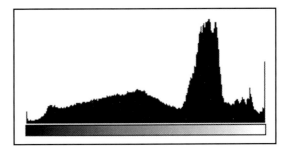

Figure 10.5b
The histogram of the image sharpened.

Figure 10.6a
The image sharpened more.

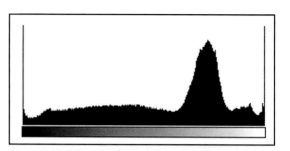

Figure 10.6b
The histogram of the image sharpened more.

Figure 10.7a
The image sharpened even more.

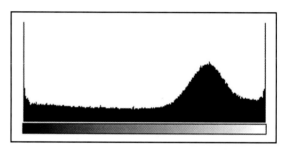

Figure 10.7b
The histogram of the image sharpened even more.

Catch a Wave

Like the surfer who learns the nature of waves and how tides and the time of day affect surf conditions, those of you who ride the pixel waves have more success when you understand the mathematical tides that create the waves of filters. The pattern of waves is predictable, but each wave has its own identity. Similarly, filters are very predictable, but each filter with a new image produces unique results. Understanding what a filter does to your images is important. This understanding intensifies your ride.

Many filters are static, meaning the filter has only one setting. Other filters have adjustable variables that determine the intensity of the filter. Each filter with variables prompts you if variables need to be input. We discuss some of the most widely used filters and their uses later in this chapter.

Most image programs now accept plug-in filters. A plug-in filter is a module written separately from the main program, but it may take advantage of features found in the main program. Some plug-in filters are so elaborate that they appear to be giant applications that simply take advantage of the basic features of the host program. However, they are literally plugged into the program, usually by placing the plug-in module in a specific folder. The plug-in feature of Photoshop filters, which has been adopted by many other programs, is a useful way of incorporating custom filters. Many third-party developers create specialty filters for use with programs that accept plug-in filters (see Figures

10.8a-c). A third-party developer is a company that creates additions to existing programs to enhance the performance of the main program.

Most programs provide methods of creating custom filters within their programs. The variety of filters is incredible, and more are being written every minute. Unique filters are another example of customizing your production environment to suit your needs. Filters can be used to manipulate pixel values. Remember that you are not moving pixels, you are simply reassigning pixel values within a unique bitmap.

Production Filters

Filters are classified into two major types: production filters and creative filters. Production filters are used to specifically improve the reproduction quality of the image. Creative filters are used to create effects that do not necessarily contribute to improving the reproduction quality of the image. A production filter obviously can be used for creative effects, but

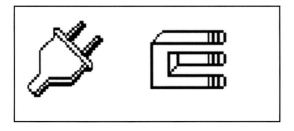

Figure 10.8a
Common icons of plug-in filters.

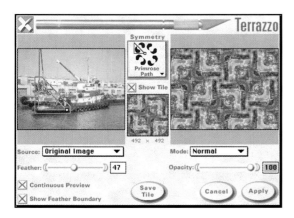

Figure 10.8b
The filter Terrazzo by Xoas is a filter that creates tiles of your image.

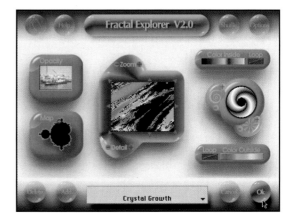

Figure 10.8c
Kai's Power Tools by HSC Software is a plug-in filter that provides hundreds of special effects within a main program.

you should be aware that many filters have specific production uses.

There are "more" filters that basically take a simple filter—for example, blur—and apply it a fixed number of times. For instance, using a "blur more" filter may be equal to using the regular blur three times. When you know that one pass of a filter is not enough, the "more" option works well.

Gaussian Distribution

Many filters offer the option of using a Gaussian distribution curve. A Gaussian curve resembles a bell curve. This mathematical distribution produces an overall higher quality effect for the filter used because the distribution of the effect is based on the distribution of the pixel values. A simple linear distribution is faster, but in many cases, the quality of a complex Gaussian distribution of data is worth the additional processing time (see Figure 10.9).

Blur Filters

Blur filters can average values of a selected area of pixels. The blur filters, which soften an image, are extremely useful when you are trying to create continuity between different images or elements. If you use the blur filter too much, you risk losing texture and depth in an image (see Figures 10.10a-d).

The Gaussian blur filter uses the bell-shaped distribution mentioned earlier. This distribution analyzes the values that exist in the image and decides which pixels to blur by what amount. For example, a pixel near the lower part of the Gaussian bell curve would not be averaged as much as one at the peak of the bell curve.

Motion blur filters create a sense of movement, producing effects much like photographs of a race car in which the car seems in motion because it blurs in one direction. Motion blur filters ask for the direction of movement to produce a sense of motion.

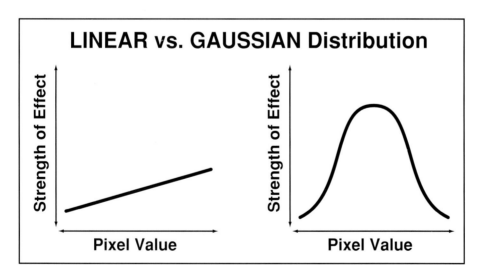

Figure 10.9
The distribution of a linear filter effect vs. a Gaussian filter's distribution.

Figure 10.10a
The original image.

Figure 10.10b
The image with a regular blur.

Figure 10.10.c
The image with a Gaussian blur.

Figure 10.10d
The image with a motion blur.

Sharpen Filters

Sharpen filters increase the contrast between the values of neighboring pixels. In general, sharpen filters should be used only when you want to accentuate the differences between one color area and another (see Figures 10.11a-d). Typically for high-contrast images, these areas involve edges, but you may want to use a sharpen filter to accentuate the grain in wood, the texture in stucco, or similar types of areas. The amount of sharpness is determined by the subject that you sharpen. Subjects with flesh tones or blends of color should be kept smooth and not sharpened too much, whereas subjects with defined edges and elements that need to be distanced from the background can benefit from sharpening. If a sharpen filter is used on a flat tonal area of color, you may produce an undesirable patterned effect.

Some of the most useful sharpen filters include the filters that detect edges and apply the contrast sharpening only to those edges. A sharpen edges filter does this adequately, but the most useful sharpen filter by far is the unsharp masking filter.

Figure 10.11a
An image without sharpening.

Figure 10.11b
The same image with a small amount of sharpening.

Figure 10.11c
The same image with more sharpening.

Figure 10.11d
The same image with a large amount of sharpening.

Unsharp Masking

Unsharp masking (USM) is an unusual name for a filter used to create detail enhancement. The name is borrowed from the older, more traditional process of photographic film separations. When color separations are made photographically, masks are created intentionally "unsharp" (soft), using a frosted glass to enhance the areas of high-contrast edges in an image. Edges indicate a transition between the light and dark areas of an image. The more contrast there is between the lighter and the darker areas of an edge, the sharper or more distinct the edge will visually appear. The masks were made soft not only to exaggerate the areas of contrast but also to create an acceptable transition from the lighter areas of an edge to the darker areas of an edge (see Figure 10.12).

When used properly, the unsharp masking filter produces visually pleasing edges by creating a high-contrast edge while retaining the smooth areas of tone. The sharpening method was incorporated into the first high-end electronic scanners with the name, unsharp masking, following along. If a scanner provides an unsharp masking feature, it is typically better to sharpen while scanning the image, but with filters in modern retouching programs you now can produce a similar unsharp mask effect. Peaking is a term that describes the visual effect sharpening has upon the electronic wave form of an image. The concept of peaking is illustrated in Figure 10.13.

The unsharp filter seeks out and sharpens edges or areas of high contrast depending on the

Figure 10.12
The dark areas and lines indicate where the unsharp masking will have the greatest amount of effect.

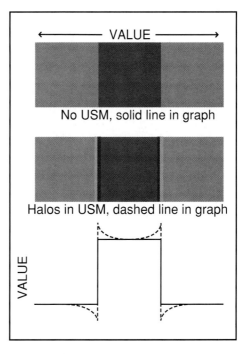

Figure 10.13
The halo used to create sharpness is indicated by the peaks and dips in the dashed line.

control features available in the filter. For example, a subject with both edges and flesh tones can be adjusted to allow for plenty of sharpness in the edges without adversely affecting the flesh tone. Sharpening is more effective on images of normal brightness and tonal contrast. Flat, dark images require more sharpening than normal images.

You should always be conservative when applying unsharp masking. Too much sharpening destroys the realism of a reproduction. Food that looks plastic and eyelashes that look razor sharp are indications of too much sharpening. Also, extreme sharpening creates large halos of black or white around the edges of an image. A halo is an area of contrast surrounded by an area of opposite contrast, such as white around a black edge. Halos make unsharp masking work, and if sharpness is applied correctly, you do not notice them.

Most unsharp masking filters have three primary controls: amount, radius, and threshold. The controls are never the same for every image. Although a standard range can be established, each image requires special attention to achieve the appropriate settings. Determining the settings requires experimentation and experience.

The amount of USM refers to an arbitrary number that determines the effective exaggeration between the dark and light areas of an edge. The amount is simply used as a relative measurement within the filter. An amount of 90 exaggerates the difference more than an amount of 50. The radius controls the width of the halo created. Halos are always present in unsharp masking, but you do not want the halo to be seen easily. Depending on the resolution of an image and its physical size, the radius will vary

slightly. The larger the radius is, the larger the halo. Typically, a one pixel radius is sufficient for small images less than 10"×14", while a radius of two or three may be necessary for images of greater size. The threshold amount controls how much of an image will be considered for sharpening. In an 8-bit system the level ranges from 0 to 255. Zero means that no tone is excluded from the sharpening process, and a value of 255 means that all tone is excluded. As the threshold increases more tone is excluded. This can prove useful when you are trying to sharpen the edges while leaving smooth tones alone. The value is determined by the original image, typically between 1 and 20.

The unsharp masking filter also is useful when used on specific color channels. Perhaps a red image needs the cyan plate sharpened to accent the red detail. Because the black plate of CMYK separation is used for detail enhancement, the black channel is sharpened often to help conceal the halo effects. Most of the detail that the black channel provides is in the midtone to shadow areas. Sharpening the black channel alone limits sharpening to the midtone to shadow areas in an image. If sharpening is required in brighter areas of an image, using the black plate alone may not provide the level of sharpening that you require.

Production filters should be used sparingly and only when the effects are absolutely necessary. You should only apply the unsharp filter (and filters similar to it) once. Applying a filter to an image over and over will degrade the image. Use small areas of an image to determine the appropriate amount of sharpening. Once you have found the amount of the filter you need, you can then apply it to the entire image.

Sharpening a JPEG compressed image is not recommended because the sharpening will accentuate the patterns JPEG uses to achieve the lossy compression. As in all filters, experimentation is necessary to determine the appropriate use of the filter as shown in Figures 10.14a through 10.15d.

Figure 10.14a
The original image before unsharp masking.

Figure 10.14b
The image with some unsharpness.

Figure 10.14c
Too much unsharpness with halos visible.

Figure 10.14d
Far too much unsharpness.

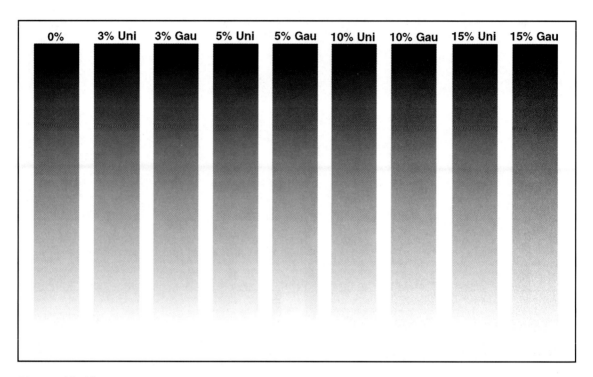

Figure 10.16
Noise added to a grayscale image in noted amounts.

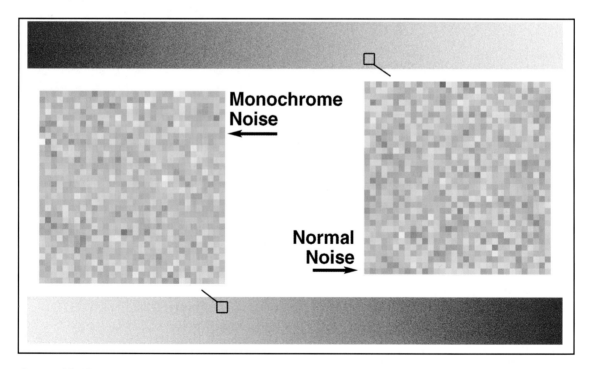

Figure 10.17
A yellow to red blend using regular and monochrome noise. Regular noise
introduces tertiary color to the blend while the monochrome does not.

Figure 10.18a
An image without any noise added.

Figure 10.18b
The image with 5 percent regular noise
accents the finer details of the image.

Figure 10.18c
The image with 5 percent monochrome noise
tends to subdue the fine details of the
image.

Figure 10.18d
The image with 10 percent regular noise.

Figure 10.18e
The image with 10 percent monochrome
noise.

Figure 10.18f
The image with 15 percent noise applied.
Noise over 10 percent is seldom used
except for visual effect.

Final Word

The skill in using filters comes from experimentation. To slightly alter a quote from Steve Martin, "Talking about filters is like dancing about architecture." You need to play with filters to grasp the functions that they perform. With all filters, testing extremes gives you an idea of how the filter actually is manipulating your image. In the case of blur filters, if you use the blur filter on the same image over and over, the filter eventually produces a flat blob of one color. Without a doubt, the most useful exercise is to repeatedly apply the same filter to an image until you have a firm grasp of what the filter is actually doing to the values of pixels—and it actually can be fun to see the resulting effects of filter excesses.

With any digital effect, the more you know about the program's function and its effect on the image, the more you can control the effect for your own purposes. Remember to experiment with the filters on a portion of the image before applying the filters to the entire image. The small selected area takes less time to process than the entire image. This method allows you to try many more variations instead of waiting for the whole image to process one change.

Another useful method for viewing a filter effect is to apply the filter; then immediately use the undo command several times, flipping back and forth to view the filter effect before and after. This method is extremely useful when you are using very subtle effects that you may not immediately see. When you achieve the desired effect, apply the same filter to the entire image. Another powerful method of viewing how a filter works is to zoom in to see the individual pixels and observe how each pixel reacts to the filter effect.

Production filter effects are most effective after you have seen them processed all the way through to final output. Eventually, you will reach a level of comfort where you can confidently predict what the filters will do to your image. The following pages and figures show examples of some filters available in image programs.

Gallery of Filter Effects

CHARCOAL

TWIRL

DARKEN STROKE

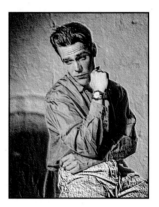

EMBOSS

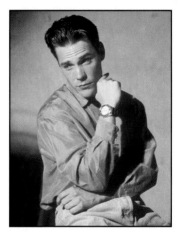

ORIGINAL

MOSAIC

POINTILLIST

GRAIN

WATERCOLOR

RADIAL ZOOM

TRACE EDGES

PIXELATE

TURBULENCE

RIPPLE

FRACTAL TURBULENCE

GRAPHIC PEN

TEXTURE RIPPLE

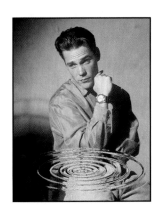

POND RIPPLE

Filter Effects

RECT TO POLAR

POLAR TO RECT

TURBULENCE

SPATTER

ORIGINAL

FIND EDGES

CRYSTALIZE

SPHERIZE

DARK STROKE

RADIAL ZOOM

GRAPHIC PEN

CHARCOAL

EMBOSS

FRACTAL TURBULENCE

GRAIN

WATERCOLOR

TILE

POINTILLIST

CHARCOAL

DARK STROKE

EMBOSS

GRAIN

ORIGINAL

GRAPHIC PEN

RIPPLE

WATERCOLOR

SPATTER

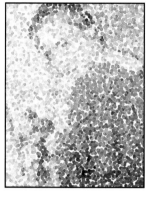

POINTILLIST

PIXELATE

TURBULENCE

FRACTAL TURBULENCE

FIND EDGES

RADIAL ZOOM

TILES

TEXTURE RIPPLE

POOL RIPPLE

Filter Effects   253

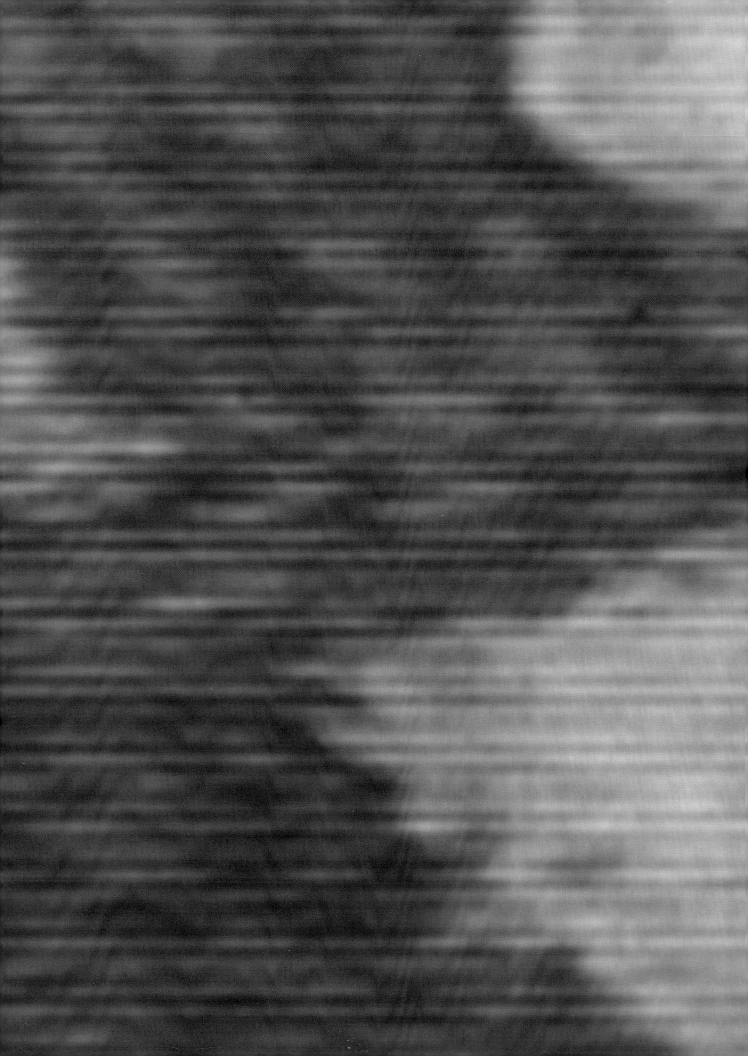

Part

III

Image Reproduction

Targeting
Output

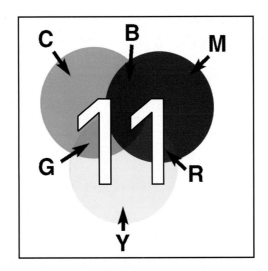

"In the fields of obervation,
chance favors only the prepared."
Louis Pasteur

It's imperative to prepare a course of action before you embark on any journey of color reproduction. You must lay out your travel plans to get to your destination, plan the roads you want to take, and keep a road map with you at all times to ensure that you do not lose your way. You may find that you can reach your destination without a map or plan, but your journey may end somewhere that you had not intended. Travelers who plan a trip by having enough fuel and a knowledge of which roads to take are more likely to succeed in reaching their intended destinations (see Figure 11.1).

Plan Your Trip and Take a Map

When preparing to produce a reproduction, it is always best to plan where you want to go, and then decide how to get there. Reversing your thought process from the end result back to the starting point forces you to be aware of the output requirements. The needs of the output method must be met or the quality of the reproduction will be unacceptable. Knowing your final

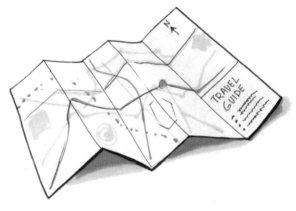

Figure 11.1

destination before you begin allows you to plan the most effective way of producing the output. Preparation of your image file should be done with the end use in mind because only pre-planning will guarantee that the visual result is correct.

The first and most important part of preparing for image output is deciding which type of output you want. You can consider the type of output your destination. During the course of a trip, you may want to visit several destinations, which is like producing different types of output at different sizes. Making these stops is not a problem *if* you decide on all your possible destinations *before* you start your trip.

Take your map and follow it. Guessing often leads to wrong turns and longer trips. You may be tempted to go exploring; that's fine if no one is waiting for you at the destination. Deadlines mean that following your map is imperative. The following sections discuss some of your possible destinations, the fuel you need, and the maps you should follow.

Where Do You Want to Go?

The type of output to produce is the first decision you must make. There is no limit to the kind, size, or amount. Various types of image reproduction (destinations) are possible. Each destination has special considerations that must be addressed. These reproduction possibilities are broken into three main types—luminous, transmissive, and reflective—which include monitors, transparencies, and print mediums.

Luminous Output

The luminous type of output uses colored phosphors, which are illuminated by electrons. These phosphors are packaged on the glass screen of a monitor. Electron guns individually excite either R, G, or B light when they strike the screen. Color from the glowing phosphors radiates from the screen to the viewer's eyes (see Figure 11.2).

The strength of the illuminated image reaching the eye is controlled by the power of the electron guns lighting up the colored phosphors in the device and the ambient light surrounding the monitor. The dimmer the surrounding light outside the monitor, the brighter and more intense the monitor looks. If the surrounding light becomes too bright and distracting, the intensity of the color on the monitor decreases. Conversely, if there is no surrounding light a monitor can look too intense.

The monitor is used to show both static (stationary) and dynamic (moving) images. These images can be color, black-and-white, or any combination of the two. Moving images are called video; the soundtracks played with them

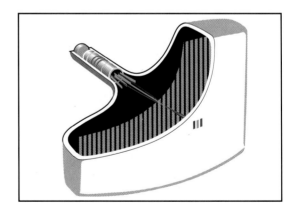

Figure 11.2
The basic workings of a monitor.

Table 11.1   Direct Pixel Output for Luminance Devices

Device to Image File	Result
Number of device elements is greater than the number of pixels in the image file.	Image does not fill the display, all pixels shown.
Number of device elements is equal to the number of pixels in the image file.	Image fills the display, all pixels shown (one to one).
Number of device elements is less than the total number of pixels.	Image fills the display, and not all pixels are shown. File is larger in the image file.

are called audio. A combination of dynamic and static images with audio and text is called multimedia because it combines several types of communication in one visual experience.

Monitors are direct digital output or direct pixel imaging. Direct digital output means each imaging element of the output device requires one pixel of information from the digital image file. This is a one-to-one relationship.

Each display device has a fixed number of imaging elements. The total number of elements from device to device varies with the physical size of the display and the number of display elements per inch (the resolution). For example, 13-inch Apple monitors accommodate a display of 640 by 480 pixels.

Because of the one-to-one digital pixel-to-display element requirement, three scenarios are possible (see Table 11.1).

As with any output device, falling below the basic resolution requirements results in a potential loss of quality. Display devices are no exception to this rule. Visually, the illuminated image quality degrades as pixels start becoming visible and lines become jagged in appearance.

Color Gamuts for luminance devices are based on the RGB color space. Due to the illumination effect, bright saturated colors can be very vivid and intense to the eye. Television color transmission uses one luminance and two chroma channels to describe color, which is the basis of the YCC color gamut used by Kodak's PhotoCD system.

Transmissive Output

Transmissive type images pass light through their material. A color image is observed by viewing light passing through the image from behind. The most common transmissive material is a 35mm slide. Transmissive films are imaged photographically from camera exposure or by digital means using an output device called a film recorder.

As a direct pixel imaging output device, film recorders use digital information to create images on transparency (or negative) film. The exposure unit for a film recorder uses a one-to-one pixel relationship just like monitors. Unlike screens and monitors though, the film recorder requires higher resolution—up to 2,540 pixels per inch.

The film comes in various format sizes from 35mm to 11" × 14" and has been used by photographers since the 1950s. Transparency films are portable and easy to examine for content. These films can be used as a physical image display with back lighting. Also, transparencies can function as image archives. They can be converted back into digital form for output to other mediums. Though film transparencies are the most common type of transmissive substrate, traditional stained glass windows also create transmissive imagery, as shown in Figure 11.3.

Figure 11.3
A stained glass window is an example of transmissive imagery.

Reflective Output

The third type of output available is reflective. Light bounces off these materials and carries the image information to the eye. Reflective materials are imaged by some sort of printing process. Typically, a dye or ink is placed on a receiver substrate (such as paper) using pressure, heat, or a combination of both. The pages of this book are an example of reflected material.

Printing Processes

There are two main types of printing processes possible: direct digital (often called continuous tone) and halftone. The goal of each process is to create a continuous tone appearance. Regardless of how continuous an image may appear, all printing processes use small picture elements to create tone and color.

Continuous Tone

Continuous tone (called CT or contone) printing involves the illusion of smooth contiguous images on a reflective base material. The most common type of continuous tone print is the photographic color print, called the "C" print. C prints are made from photographic dyes processed after exposure from a color negative or transparency.

Digital output devices that print a photographic continuous quality are called CT printers. These continuous tone printers are direct digital output. Continuous tone output devices that create photo-realistic output do not use halftone dots. Each imaging element on the output

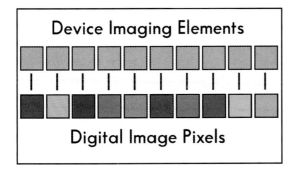

Device Imaging Elements

Digital Image Pixels

Figure 11.4
Direct digital output means that the
digital pixels of an image match up
directly with the imaging elements of an
output device.

device matches with each pixel in the image file to produce a printed picture element, as shown in Figure 11.4.

With direct pixel imaging, 10 digital image pixels will match with 10 imaging elements of the output device. Using dye sublimation, the printing devices that produce these attractive image reproductions create a continuous tone image that looks like a standard photograph.

Dye Sublimation

Dye sublimation printers use the direct digital output method to image the colored CMYK dyes onto reflective receiver paper. Thermal dyes of CMYK are transferred to paper using the heat generated by the imaging element. The amount of heat generated is dependent on the amount of electrical energy sent to the heating elements. Electrical energy varies based on the color values in the digital file. The amount of dye transferred to the paper is proportional to the amount of heat generated by the heating element. In color printing, the paper makes four passes, receiving the dye of each CMYK color. The dyes are

transparent. This transparency enables a mixing of colors to occur to produce the various colors in an image (see Figure 11.5a).

Typically, CT printers have a resolution between 300 and 400 elements per inch (epi); so for every physical inch of output, 300 to 400 pixels are required. For a CT printer with 300 epi and a maximum printing size of 8" × 10", an image file that is 2,400 pixels by 3,000 pixels is required to produce a continuous tone image at 8" × 10".

Dye subprints are popular as comps for ad and design layouts and as color proofs for images and layouts. The unit cost is expensive, and they are slow to produce for large quantity commercial use. There are many dye sub printers that now offer a photographic level of quality. The quality level is sufficient for many people to use as proofs and sometimes as final reproductions.

Wax printers are similar to dye sublimation, but instead of inks, thermal wax prints use a transfer roll of colored wax. Individual control imaging elements are heated to melt pinpoint spots of color onto paper.

Inkjet printers, such as the Iris and Hewlett Packard, propel fine droplets of ink toward the paper surface. Many artists use inkjet technology because the inks soak into the paper and produce a pleasing continuous tone (see Figures 11.5a and b).

Halftone Printing

Traditional halftone printing involves printing with dots of varying size to simulate tone and

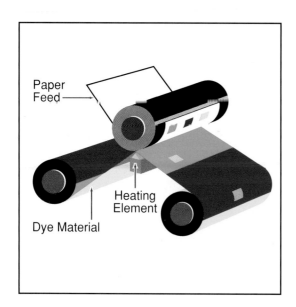

Figure 11.5a
Dye sublimation printers melt color
material onto a receiving substrate to
create color.

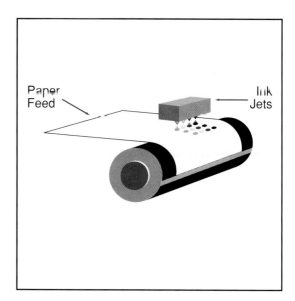

Figure 11.5b
Inkjet printers spray droplets of ink
onto substrates.

color. The resulting reflective print appears, from a distance, to be of continuous tone, not dots. When is a printed image considered to be continuous tone, but is not actually continuous tone? When it is a correctly made halftone, then it looks like a continuous tone.

Halftone printing is the most economical and efficient method of reproducing large quantities of hard copy color images. The per-unit cost on a printing press is pennies compared to the cost on previously mentioned types of output. The low cost helps make halftone printing the most common and widely used method of reproduction in the world. Even if you are not involved directly in the film preparation, but are providing digital files to someone who is preparing the halftone film, understanding the function of halftone reproduction will help you avoid potential quality problems.

The halftone printing process uses a series of various-sized halftone dots to create the illusion of varying tone. These halftone dots are created by a matrix of the imaging elements present in the output device. The number of imaging elements per inch determines the potential quality of the halftone dot. The higher the quality of the halftone dot, the higher the quality of the output (see Figure 11.6).

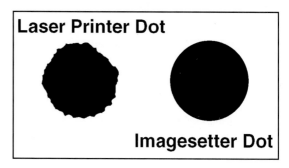

Figure 11.6
The definition of a dot is important to
the quality of the reproduction. The
quality of a laser printer dot is less
than the typical imagesetter dot.

Figure 11.7a
A continuous tone blend.

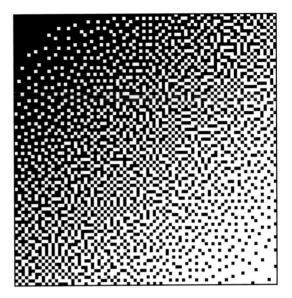

Figure 11.7b
A magnified view of frequency modulated
(FM) dots creating the blend.

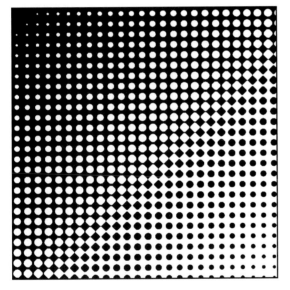

Figure 11.7c
A magnified view of amplitude modulated
(AM) dots creating the blend.

Frequency Modulated Dots

Color produced by printing quantities of
uniformly sized dots is often referred to as
stochastic printing. This approach to reproduction is also called FM halftone printing because
the tones are created by the frequency or
number of dots in an area, not by varying the
physical size of dots, as with AM printing (see
Figures 11.7a-c). Unlike standard halftones, FM
printed images are not prone to moiré patterns
because there are no screen angles used.

The difficulty with FM technology is the retention of the tiny halftone dots. Some presses and
most proofing systems have great difficulty
"holding" or accurately reproducing the minuscule stochastic dots. The result can be a visual
loss of detail and color. Additionally, blends of
color and highlight areas can appear grainy.
Stochastic dot printing is still relatively new in
the industry. The technique of FM printing is
not yet extensively used commercially.

Line Screen

When deciding to create halftone dots, you first must consider the line screen. Line screen is referred to as lines per inch (lpi) and can also describe the number of halftone dots per inch (dpi) in a line of dots. A matrix of imaging elements in an image setter or a plotter creates a halftone dot. Halftone dots are spaced evenly, although the dots themselves are various sizes. If you were to draw lines through the center of the halftones, you would see the distance between each line is uniform regardless of the size of the halftone dot. This number of lines per inch (lpi) is used by printers to indicate the number of lines of halftone dots per inch. Visually, halftone dots at an angle of 45 degrees are seen as smooth because the angle helps conceal the rows. Figure 11.8 shows 10 lines per inch.

You can determine the potential matrix for a halftone dot by dividing the total number of imaging elements per inch (epi) by the planned line screen. The more elements in a matrix, the more continuous the halftone dot. A matrix of 16 by 16 image elements or more is considered a good-quality halftone dot. For example, a

300-dpi printer creating halftone dots with 100 line screen (100 lpi or dpi) has a matrix of 3 by 3 image elements per halftone dot. A 2,400 epi printer creating halftone dots for 150 line screen (150 lpi or dpi) has a matrix of 16 by 16 image elements per halftone dot (see Figure 11.9).

The quality of the halftone dot is determined by the number of dots per inch (line screen) and the number of imaging elements per inch (epi) on the output device.

Understanding that a number of exposing elements make up a single halftone dot, and that the number of elements per inch

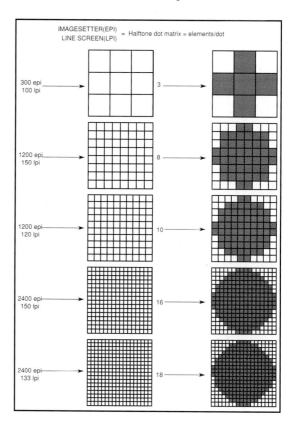

Figure 11.9
The quality of a halftone dot is also determined by the line screen and the resolution of the output device.

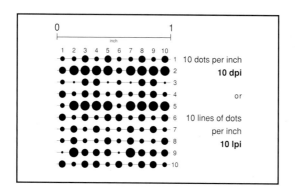

Figure 11.8
The number of lines of halftone dots per inch is called line screen.

determines potential image quality, enables you to produce high-quality, continuous-looking halftone images.

As discussed in Chapter 1, "What are Pixels?", digital images are composed of pixel information. The previous types of direct pixel output required only a one-to-one match of pixels to available image elements. For good quality, halftone dots require more than a one-to-one relationship with pixel information. With halftone printing, the number of pixels required is determined by the line screen used. The most common and simple method to achieve the number of pixels per inch (ppi) required is to double the line screen.

So if you print with a line screen of 150 lpi, you double that number to determine the number of image pixels you need—in this case, 300 pixels per inch (ppi). An image file containing 300 pixels across and 300 pixels down can be reproduced accurately with a 150-line screen, one inch across and one inch down.

Using less than double the line screen does not necessarily mean the quality will be diminished; it only suggests that doubling is near optimum (see Figures 11.10a-c). Many images will not suffer greatly with slightly less pixel information, but the quality of the image will not increase if you have substantially more than double the pixel information. Using more than double the line screen for print output is usually a waste of file space and does not contribute to making the image quality any higher. With large physical output, you may want to consider a ratio less than 2 to 1 to save file space and to keep the quality. See Chapter 16 for more discussion on sampling ratios.

Physical Size

When you choose the number of pixels necessary for an image, the number is predicated on the size at which you ultimately will reproduce this image. The size at which you output an image is the next determination for the amount of information necessary to complete the job properly. As previously mentioned, the need to match the necessary pixel information to the output pixel requirements is important for retaining a high-quality image reproduction. To determine the total number of pixels required, you need to know the final physical output size of your reproduction.

If you do not know what size your final output will be, or if you plan on a number of different sizes, always choose the largest possible size you will output and work from there. For example, if you want to print an image 5" × 6" at a line screen of 150 (lpi or dpi), you need 300 pixels per inch (ppi) and therefore 1,500 pixels across and 1,800 pixels down. If you plan on smaller output or output at different line screens, simply resample the 1,500 by 1,800-pixel file to the desired number of pixels. The following calculations show how the physical size of your output determines the total number of pixels you will need:

Physical size of output × Sampling rate (pixels to halftone dots normally 1.5 or 2.0) × Line screen frequency = total # of pixels required

Or:

(5 inches) × (2.0 × 150 lpi) = 1,500 pixels wide

(6 inches) × (2.0 × 150 lpi) = 1,800 pixels high

Figure 11.10a
The image above has a 2:1 pixel per
halftone dot ratio. The file size is
approximately 3.5 MB.

Figure 11.10b
The image above has a 1.5:1 pixel per
halftone dot ratio. The file size is
approximately 2 MB.

Figure 11.10c
The image above has a 1:1 pixel per
halftone dot ratio. The file size is
approximately 1 MB.

Remember to keep a copy of the original file whenever you perform any type of resampling. This ensures that the best possible source material always is available for you to work with in case resampling is required again. You never should resample an image more than once if you can avoid doing so.

Print Colors

Dyes and inks are the most common methods of creating color in printed output. When reproducing flat areas of color, a wide variety of inks and pigments can be mixed and printed. When reproducing photographic images, we rely on basic cyan, magenta, and yellow pigments called process inks. Though standard process inks produce a wide range of color, there are limitations in their use.

Table 11.2 Total Ink Density

Color	1.	2.	3.	4.
Cyan	100	95	75	68
Magenta	100	87	65	58
Yellow	100	87	65	58
Black	100	80	95	95
Total Ink	400	350	300	280

Additional inks used to overcome the limitations of process inks are called touch plates. Creating touch plates requires a firm knowledge of process color, and adds time and expense to any print run. High-fidelity color is one attempt to standardize the use of touch plates to expand the range of color available in print reproduction.

Process Color

Cyan, magenta, yellow, and black are the basis of most printed complex color images. The combination of the four inks creates the illusion of full color. There are specific issues that need to be addressed when using CMYK. All information regarding printing should be checked out with your printer before converting from RGB to CMYK and before any separations are produced. There are three specific areas that you should always have control of when creating separations: total ink coverage, gray balance, and black generation.

Total Ink Coverage

Total ink coverage is the total amount of ink deposited on the printed page (see Table 11.2).

The maximum is 400 percent (100 percent for each plate of CMYK). The amount depends on the type of press you are using, how fast the press is running, and the type of substrate used. Excessive ink levels cause drying problems, paper sticking together, and ink flying off the cylinders before impression. The range of total ink is usually between 280 percent for fast web presses to 350 percent for slower sheet-fed presses. Table 11.2 shows how the maximums of each ink are added together to show total ink density.

Gray Balance

Gray balance is important to accurately reproduce the tone and color of an image. The relationship of CMY inks to produce gray is called gray balance. Neutral gray is a tone between pure white and black that has no color. A gray that is neutral has no unnatural color bias and does not appear pink, greenish, warm, or cool—just gray. Grays in an image must be reproduced as gray when printed or an unnatural color cast may result. Correct gray balance ensures proper reproduction of color.

In an RGB color space, equal values of RGB produce the neutral gray illustrated in Figure 11.11a. Printing cyan, magenta, and yellow inks at equal values does not produce a neutral gray. Equal amounts of CMY will produce a warm or pink coloring in the lighter tones and brown in the darker tones. Figure 11.11b shows how equal amounts of CMY do not produce a neutral gray, but rather a reddish tone. In order to print a neutral gray, you must print a higher value of cyan and equal amounts of yellow and magenta, as illustrated in Figure 11.11c.

Black Generation

The same ink impurities that prevent cyan, magenta, and yellow from producing neutral gray prevent it from producing a true black. To help create a stronger black, a separate black plate is created. Black values are determined by the tonal range of the CMY values, or in other words, a grayscale of the image. Without this additional black, the CMY inks would produce a muddy brown, and many images would lack the depth and detail required for good reproductions. There are two areas of black generation to address: under color removal (UCR) and gray component replacement (GCR), both of which help set the total ink density of the printed image.

UCR describes the practice of removing quantities of yellow, magenta, and cyan ink from where the black is printing—literally removing color from under the black. This is an advantage on press because the black areas use less ink, but still print just as dark a black. Less ink means better control, faster drying times, and less expense on long runs that use lots of ink. If the proper amount of black is used to replace the amount of yellow, magenta, and cyan that is

Figure 11.11a
Equal amounts of
RGB values
(R:204, G:204,
B:204) creates
gray.

R:204 G:204 B:204

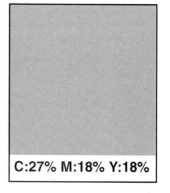

Figure 11.11b
Equal amount of
CMY values
(C:22%, M:22%,
Y:22%) creates
pink.

C:22% M:22% Y:22%

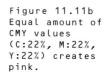

Figure 11.11c
CMY values
altered to a
gray balance
(C:27%, M:18%,
Y:18%) creates a
gray similar to
the tone in
Figure 11.11b.

C:27% M:18% Y:18%

removed, the UCR reproduction should look as good as the same reproduction produced without UCR. Figures 11.12a-c show the UCR effect.

GCR is used to save even more ink than UCR. This function removes yellow, magenta, and cyan ink from where all three inks print together and replaces them with black ink. GCR removes ink from black and colored areas as well. GCR saves ink but still produces a smooth looking image. The black plate carries most of the tone in the reproduction; therefore, neutrals are easier to print. The CMY components are used mostly for making the saturated colors. Though many people think GCR should be used regularly, its main use is for very large quantity, long print runs. GCR is not as commonly used as some people think. Also, color correcting a CMYK image using GCR is not as straightforward as a UCR separated image. Figures 11.13a-c show the GCR effect.

Total ink coverage, gray balance, and black generation values should be verified with your printer before you make your separations. It's not recommended that you mix UCR and GCR separated images on the same printed page because it is impossible to adjust one without adversely effecting the other.

High Fidelity Color

Computer technology has enhanced the color separator's capability to produce standard CMYK separations and additional colored printers called touch plates. Touch plates refer to printing plates on the press. Touch plates add specially desired colors that are not easily made with CMYK ink combinations. Intense red, green, or fluorescent colors are popular touch plate additions. More exotic possibilities available today are violet-blues, orange-reds, or any other combinations made possible by color mixing.

A basic knowledge of CMYK is still necessary because the additional colors are derived from that color space. Hi-fi color is in addition to, not instead of, the standard CMYK inks. You must

Figure 11.12a
Image reproduced with UCR.

Figure 11.12b
UCR image without black plate.

Figure 11.12c
The UCR black plate.

start with properly made CMYK separations to get the full benefit of hi-fi color.

The main advantage of "hi-fi color" is a larger color gamut—from soft pastels to intense brightly saturated hues. What hasn't changed, though, is the high degree of skill required of the pressman to put these multiple layers of ink on the paper in register and at the right densities. Also, prepress proofing for these additional colors may not be available, so the results can be difficult to accurately predict.

Figures 11.14a-e illustrate the creation of hi-fi plates. The actual production of touch plates must take into consideration many issues, including subtraction of appropriate amounts of CMY color replaced by hi-fi colored touch plates.

Substrates

Each kind of paper type changes the way light reflects off the paper and how the inks or dyes used in printing set up or absorb into the substrate (see Figure 11.15). The kind of substrate being printed on will have an effect on the reproduction's appearance. Paper substrates can be coated, noncoated, recycled, and colored. As usual, planning ahead for the effects of the substrate will help you achieve a better printed reproduction.

Coated Paper

The preferred paper stock for high-quality printing is paper that is coated with white clay or plastic during manufacturing. The coating gives the paper a gloss for high reflectance. The white of a coated stock is the whitest possible for paper substrates; because the white is very bright, the darker areas of an image appear

Figure 11.13a
Image reproduced with GCR.

Figure 11.13b
GCR image without black plate.

Figure 11.13c
The GCR black plate.

Figure 11.14a
A CMYK printed image.

Figure 11.14b
The red plate is created by the areas
where yellow and magenta make red.

Figure 11.14c
The green plate is created by the areas
where yellow and cyan make green.

Figure 11.14d
The blue plate is created by the areas
where magenta and cyan make blue.

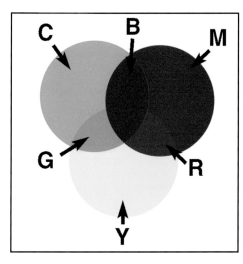

Figure 11.14e
An illustration of how basic hi-fi colors
are derived from the combination of two
CMY inks.

darker. (See the Contrast section in Chapter 13.) Since contrast is perceived by comparing light to dark, coated papers produce the highest image contrast or dynamic range of all printing paper stocks. Also, coated papers are sealed by their coatings so that they do not easily absorb the printing inks or dyes. The more ink or dye on the substrate (instead of in it), the stronger the tones and colors of the printed image will appear to the eye. Absorption of the printing inks will additionally soften the image appearance, causing a slight decrease in visual sharpness.

Noncoated Paper

Applying paper coatings is an extra step during manufacturing. When the price of paper becomes a factor, using noncoated papers can be a way to economize the cost of a printed job.

Noncoated paper stocks are not as bright as coated papers. Therefore, the potential contrast of a reproduction on this type of paper is not as great. These paper types are visibly duller. Additionally, inks and dyes absorb and spread more readily into the fibers of the paper substrate, causing a reduction in potential sharpness and an increase in the size of the halftone dots. The size increase—due to paper absorption—is called dot gain and is mostly concentrated in the middletone dot areas (see Figure 11.15). The pressure of the ink being pressed onto the substrate also contributes to dot gain. Dot gain varies with the absorbency of the paper stock. Typical gain for noncoated stocks is 20-25 percent. Newspaper is one of the most absorbent stocks, with dot gains in the 40 percent range. Knowing that a noncoated stock is to be used, compensation for dot gain and the lower contrast of these stocks during the separation process should be used to achieve optimum printing results (see Chapter 15).

Colored Paper

Sometimes a nonwhite paper is used as a printing substrate. As with all printing substrates, the apparent brightness directly affects the possible contrast that can be reproduced. Brighter colors, such as yellow and green, will not affect contrast very much. Blues, browns, and reds can diminish highlight brightness, thus reducing visual reproduction contrast. In all cases, try to use a pale colored paper, not a heavily colored one. Heavily colored papers are very difficult to use in reproduction because of the diminished highlight brightness caused by the heavy coloring of the paper.

Besides the effect on contrast, the color of the substrate will affect the color of the reproduction—some colors more than others. Colors similar to the color of the substrate will gain color strength and reproduce more saturated and with less value or brightness. Colors that are complementary to the substrate color (see Chapter 2, "Digital Color and Tone") will become darker and less saturated (or dirtier).

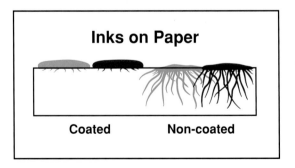

Figure 11.15
Ink absorption on coated paper is typically less than uncoated paper.

For example, a blue colored paper will cause all blues to appear bluer and all yellows and reds to appear darker and less colorful.

Special (Nonpaper) Substrates

Printing is done on any item that can hold an ink or dye. Examples include glass, metal, plastic, wood, and fabrics. Sometimes a base coating material is applied first to help hold the ink or dye pigments on the substrate better and to supply a white base to reflect from.

When supplying digital files for special substrates, separation compensation data should be available from either the ink or substrate supplier or the printer. If this data is not available from the suppliers, try to run a test image to get an idea of how the reproduction must be made for the printing conditions.

Checklist

Each of the three types of output has different requirements for resolution.

Before addressing any of the production concerns, you must have the proper source material. If you do not start with enough pixel information, the likelihood of quality output is diminished.

If you require your image to be used for more than one type of output—for example, print and video—always prepare the file for the output that requires more pixel information first and then resample the file to the output that needs less pixel information. In this case you would meet the requirement of print first, and then video.

Check each of the following steps before starting work on an image:

- Decide on your output device and reproduction process.

- Determine the final size or sizes at which you will reproduce the image.

- Based on the output device's requirements, determine the number of pixels per inch you need.

- If the number of pixels of your source file is less than required, resample the file by no more than 200 percent to retain the highest quality of the image.

When in doubt, use more than enough pixels. A good barber always can cut away more hair if you want your hair shorter, but it's impossible to put the hair back after it has been cut.

Good communication is the key to any successful project; never underestimate its importance!

Final Word

Whether your final destination is luminous, transmissive, or reflective in nature, each type of image reproduction carries its own set of requirements. The best reproductions are achieved by optimizing your files to the output device's tone, color, sharpness, and resolution requirements.

As you can see from reading this chapter, the needs of the different output types are varied and numerous. For a good trip (reproduction), you should plan well at the start by mapping out your destination (output type/device requirements) so that you don't get lost on the way (rejected job) or run out of gas (not enough data). After all, no one likes travel troubles.

As mentioned previously, frequently modulated (FM) dots and amplitude modulated (AM) dots reproduce tone and color in different ways. Experimentation is necessary to find suitable scanning resolution and tone adjustments. Figure a shows a standard 150 lpi AM dot reproduction, and Figure b shows a basic unadjusted 400 dpi FM dot reproduction.

400 dpi FM dot image adjusted minus
20% in the middle tone.

Figure adjusted with minus 5%
shadows.

Figure adjusted with minus 10%
shadows.

Figure adjusted with minus 15%
shadows.

Scanning
Preparation

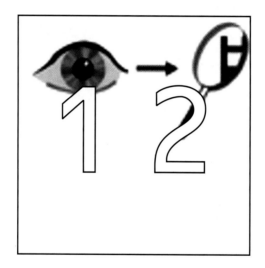

"It usually takes me more than
three weeks to prepare a good
impromptu speech."

Mark Twain

Simply put, scanning is the sampling and digitizing of an image or scene. The scanning process can be a meticulous, methodical analysis and/or a casual, unplanned operation, not requiring much thought. At times scanning is a precise craft, while other times it is more of a push button operation. The choices of control are determined by the type of image reproduction required, the available budget, and the desired image quality.

Because the automatic features of scanning are, well, supposed to be automatic, the procedure of automatic scanning shouldn't need any explanation. Should it? All fun aside, even with auto scanning you should be aware of the more involved, hands-on methods of scanning that are being automated for you. Take a look at the methodical, meticulous craft of scanning and then observe how push-button color is made. Chapters 13 through 15 go into specific detail on color separation theory and analysis. At this point, we simply want to discuss in an orderly, complete way how to approach scanning and color reproduction using any kind of original material.

In the Beginning . . .

Standard procedures on high-end scanners may include up to 30 separate steps to produce a good color separation as a digital file or direct film output. To scan effectively, an operator must closely examine the original image for various clues as to how it should be scanned and reproduced. Once the original is placed in a scanner, and the scanner is set to standard operating conditions, the original image is digitally analyzed for its color characteristics.

After the color separation settings are entered and the proper output specs are set, scanning is initialized. After the image is converted to a digital RGB color space, the information is saved as a file and is available for a variety of uses including video, transparency, or print output. For print output, a conversion to CMYK is available by using either scanner software or an image program. Converting to print involves relating the color of the original image to the values available in the output.

Sounds pretty complicated, doesn't it? There are many steps in the scanning procedure; few shortcuts are available without addressing your basic needs first. Digital color separation has been done for over thirty years, and until recently, it has not been a "fast food trip." Each part of the operation is critical in order to obtain a good quality scan; any weak link in the chain can seriously affect reproduction quality. Let's take a broad look at each part of the operation of scanning closely and discuss some of the "how's and why's."

Prescan Evaluating

As in most things in life, preparation is your first step. Thorough preparation before scanning prevents many potential problems later. Preparing the original images for scanning should be done with great care. Time should be set aside to create a game plan for scanning each image.

Just like the old saying, "an ounce of prevention is worth a pound of cure," good scanner preparation will eliminate re-scans and prevent time-consuming, postscan color correction and retouching.

To make a color scan, three pieces of information *must* be supplied: physical size (and cropping), resolution (ppi), and output conditions. If any one of these pieces of information is missing, every effort should be made to get it. You can determine the resolution from the physical size and type of output. The type of output also determines how you address color conversion. Educated guessing will work, but if all or none of this information is supplied, the quality of your reproduction may suffer (see Figure 12.1).

If you must scan without knowing the physical size, scan using the largest physical size possible. For example, if you are using an image (such as a cover to a magazine) which is 9"×12", you are probably not going to exceed the maximum of 9"×12". The same magazine cover probably does not print halftone dots greater than 150 or 175 line screen. If enough memory space is available, use a resolution that is appropriate for the maximum quality of output. If any adjustments are necessary once the size and resolution information becomes available, you can easily throw away any extra pixel information without sacrificing much image quality. Conversely, if you have fewer than half the amount of pixels required, you may consider the option to scan again (if you can). Digital images with insufficient resolution need to upsample the pixel information; this often means that you have a less than optimum image.

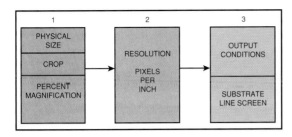

Figure 12.1
The three pieces of critical information
that must be supplied with every scan.

Cropping information is very valuable because portions of the image may not be needed at all. In any production environment, memory space is usually at a premium; cropping information helps you to preserve storage, not to mention processing time. Unfortunately, cropping information often is not available until after the scanning step so you must scan the entire image and crop it later.

The more information about output and printing conditions you can get, the better. Find out what kind of paper stock—coated or uncoated—is being used and the type of printing press—either web, sheetfed, or direct digital printer. The printing substrate and device used to print will affect the final appearance of the image reproduction. Continuous roll printing, called *web printing*, and single sheet printing will print distinctly different results as will a dye sublimation or ink jet printer.

Compensation during the separation stage adjusts for the visual effects caused by the substrate and printing process. Figure 12.2 illustrates the process of compensation. (We discuss these compensations in Chapter 14). Your prepress proof may or may not simulate the effects of the printing conditions. If no printing condition data is available, usually a sheetfed, coated stock condition is assumed.

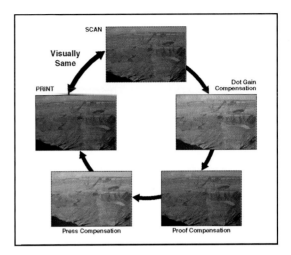

Figure 12.2
Compensation for output conditions follows
a set method.

The line screen characteristic (lpi) also can be a clue as to the printing conditions. Coarser line screens such as 85, 100, and 133 lpi indicate a web printing press with noncoated, high ink, absorbent type paper. Finer line screens such as 150, 175, and 200 are usually used with sheetfed printing on coated stock (less ink absorbent). Having accurate printing condition information prior to scanning will ensure a better final result.

Inspecting Supplied Material

Take a close look at the subjects being scanned. If you are provided with an RGB file, take a look at the image on your monitor. Are the images in good condition? Some original submissions are not good enough to be used for reproduction. If you notice any tears or scratches, make a note of them or contact a customer service representative. Be aware that some customers do not closely examine their originals so that when they get the material back with a damaged original, they may assume that you did the damage. Photographic prints can have spots and dust marks printed with the image. Transparencies can have emulsion hairs, specks, and scratches. Art can have tears and flaws, and preprinted subjects can be smudged, scratched, and out of register. All these imperfections are candidates for electronic retouching corrections that are billable to the customer and make for a better result. Sometimes the customer may have another original from the same photo shoot that does not have the same flaws as the first one submitted.

You should inspect an RGB file in the same way that you inspect a physical original (see Figure 12.3). Many RGB files may have been scanned from poor originals, scanned from lesser quality scanners, or scanned at the wrong resolution and size. You should always inspect provided material to ensure that the material meets the needs of your output. You are responsible for the output production. If clients supply incorrect information, they should be told before you begin the production.

Check the overall focus of the image. If a soft appearance was not done for artistic reasons, the original may be unsuitable for reproduction. Product shot reproduction is a good example of

this situation. Usually, the product being sold must be crisp and sharp looking. The scanner can enhance the apparent sharpness of an image, but there are limits to sharpening before realism suffers.

Next, look at the image for its reproductive aspects: contrast, end setting points, gray, color, and sharp/smooth condition. Be sure to use standardized lighting when viewing an original. Rate the photographic quality of the original. Is the exposure correct or off? (Photographers use f-stops to rate exposure.) Too dark or washed out? High key or low key? Where are the diffuse and specular highlights? Are there true shadow areas? Examine whites and neutrals. Any obvious color casts? How real do the colors look? For example, are the skies blue? Is the image sharp or soft? Smooth or grainy for the magnification being used?

Data for the color value parameters of separation is obtained visually and by reading the color densities of particular areas of the original image with colorimeters or hardware in the scanner. RGB files are checked using the onscreen densitometer as shown in Figure 12.4. While as few as two or three readings can supply enough information, as many as 20 or more

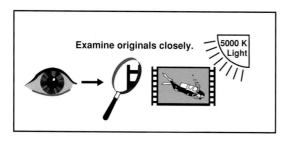

Figure 12.3
Carefully examine all originals, especially 35mm transparencies.

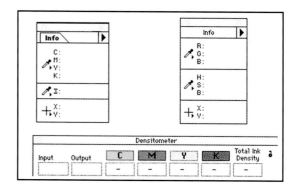

Figure 12.4
Densitometers measure relative densities and dot percentages.

readings may be required for you to figure out the proper separation settings to achieve a good, printable reproduction. Practice and experience will improve your ability to recognize and find these reading points and rate the original's quality.

During the prescan and preseparation evaluation, the original should be placed in a viewing booth with the lighting conditions that will be used to compare and rate the reproduction of that original after the scan. Analysis at this point is easier than when the original is mounted on the scanner. Accurate appraisal of a mounted image is usually less than optimum. This is especially true with small originals like 35mm transparencies. Originals should be categorized as either high-key (bright), low-key (dark), or normal exposures (see Figures 12.5a-c).

End use of the scanned image and/or RGB file will dictate the amount of time and effort spent analyzing and setting up each image to be scanned. For example, scans used for monitor screen displays or comps will require less attention than scans used for high quality print or film recorder output.

Figure 12.5b
An example of a low-key image.

Figure 12.5c
An example of a normal image.

Figure 12.5a
An example of a high-key image.

Experienced separators spend time on prescan examinations because they gain valuable information that gives better results and fewer unwelcome surprises later on in the reproduction process. The benefits from the prescan analysis manifest themselves in the end result: a good, useful scan that requires little or no further adjustments.

Mounting

Whether using a drum scanner or a flatbed design, the most important aspect of mounting is to keep everything clean. Scanners are designed to reproduce every fine bit of detail in an image. Because the scanner is designed to reproduce all tiny details and shades of tone and colors in an image, dust and dirt are included as fine detail too. The scanner cannot tell the difference between a dirt speck on a transparency or the fine detail in an image. Excessive rubbing may also damage an original and should be done with a lintless wipe and film cleaner.

The infamous Newton Ring is a hazard of drum scanner mounting. The smooth Plexiglas cylinders of drum scanners and the smooth surface of transparency originals generate colored patterned circles called Newton rings when pressed together. A law of physics states that two smooth surfaces pressed together cause a visual colored interference pattern called Newton rings (see Figure 12.6). Special powders, sprays, and/or oils are used to keep a gap between the surfaces of originals and drums,

thus eliminating Newton rings. The oils used actually can help conceal minor scratches on a transparency.

The Newton rings are not a problem with reflective copy unless a clear overlay is used to fasten the copy to the drum. The smooth overlay material may then cause rings if the reflective original is smooth enough. Scanners that have flat glass mount chases use a special pebble-finished glass that reduces contact with the original to defeat Newton ring problems. Most basic flatbed CCD scanners don't press the original against clear glass hard enough to cause Newton rings.

Be careful with originals that are bent, kinked, and not flat. Some scanner mounts aren't capable of holding images flat. Warped and bent originals also can be difficult to tape down flat on a drum. Scanners have a very small depth of focus (area above and below the point of focus that stays in focus). Nonflat areas that are not flush against the drum or glass may reproduce out of focus or as dark spots (see Figure 12.7).

Scanner Setup

Every scanner has a standard basic operating position for all controls and settings. The input controls are set for the type of original being scanned (reflective or transparent). Settings are accomplished either mechanically with knobs, switches, and buttons, by software settings, or a combination of both. Color and gray controls

Figure 12.6
Newton Rings are typically located in
light areas of an image.

Figure 12.7
With contrast added the image accentuates
the Newton rings indicated by arrows.

are set for the type of original being separated, as well as its light absorbing and reflecting characteristics. For instance, emulsion type should be set for transmissive subjects (Kodachrome, Ektachrome, Fujichrome, and so on) and reflective subjects (color prints, paintings, rescreens, and so on). Sharpness controls are set according to scan magnification. Light sources are zeroed out or balanced to a neutral area so that the light source is at the same intensity and color balance for each scan. (Paper white is used as a zero point for reflective scans; clear cylinder is used for transparencies.) The scanner must start from the same condition each time to ensure consistent results.

The scanner needs to be set for the three important criteria mentioned earlier: size (and crop), resolution, and printing condition concerns. Some desktop model scanners only scan at 100 percent, so size is achieved by adjusting the pixel per inch input resolution to obtain enough pixels for the final size required. (Refer to scanner resolution in Chapter 3). Other scanners require a magnification or reduction percentage and resolution setting. Adjustment of the scanner's sampling rate also is called scan pitch. The manufacturer normally provides instructions on the scan pitches that are available and which scan pitches are used for the type of output, resolution, and quality desired. Many scanners set the scan pitch automatically according to magnification, size of original, and resolution desired. For example, a 35mm slide may be sampled at 2,000 scan lines per inch while a 4"×5" original would get a 500 scan line per inch sampling. Printing condition specs are adjusted by using midtone adjustment, UCR, or GCR settings. The printer can supply the proper specs for setting these controls.

Once the crop, resolution, and printing specs have been established, readings of the original image's color can be taken. On many high-end drum scanners, the readings are taken by placing the scanner's analyzing beam in the area where the reading is desired. Most CCD scanners perform a low-resolution prescan to take a quick look at the color values of an image. Readouts on the scanner's panel or software come up as density, RGB, or CMYK values. Because the scanner scans in RGB, the CMYK values represent what will be there after the image is scanned and separated. The observations of the prescan analysis become valuable at this point because you know which areas on the image to analyze with the software reading.

The readings provide values and determine how the image should be set and balanced for separation. Currently, the most popular way of obtaining readings for setting separation parameters is by making a quick low-resolution scan of the original. The low-resolution data is then displayed on a monitor. Using your mouse, place a cursor in the areas that you want to analyze. RGB and/or CMYK values are read from an onscreen densitometer. Even though the prescan is low resolution, the color readings obtained should be very accurate. It is from these readings that color adjustments can be made before scanning.

Endpoint selection (highlight and shadow points) can take place before or after the scanning takes place, depending on the type of scanning system you use. The diffuse highlight area is set for approximately 240-250 units RG & B (3-10 percent CMY). Diffuse highlights are the brightest areas containing tone or detail. Shadow density should be around 10-20 units RG & B (90-95 percent CMY). Shadow areas are

places of maximum darkness—the blackest black reproducible by the type of original being scanned. (If the image is without a true shadow, use a grayscale shadow step). If your calibration data gives you a middletone position for a grayscale, look for a value here of 124-130 units RG & B (50 percent CMY).

After the endpoints and contrast have been established, any known neutrals can be adjusted to equal RGB values. (Remember, equal parts of RGB make neutral). If you are not sure that an image area is really neutral, leave it alone. Curves and sliders can be used to establish neutrality if the controls are available as prescan adjustments. Most image programs provide for adjustment of RGB files after the image has been scanned.

Selection of separation parameters involves knowledge of the nature of the original being separated and the end use of the scanned reproduction. Making adjustments to match output conditions is where the craft and experience of color separation is most important. We are converting the photographic (or art, preprinted, and so on) originals to another medium and are expecting them to look similar or even better. With the knowledge of color theory and digital image concerns, you are able to make correct settings of the separation parameters for scanning. An automatic feature cannot conceivably contain all possibilities.

There are some other organizational concerns to confirm before scanning. Check the intended destination of the scan. Is there enough memory space to receive it? Also, check for any special naming conventions required by the customer or your own in-house standard way of labeling image files. It is important to be able to locate each image among many selections. A

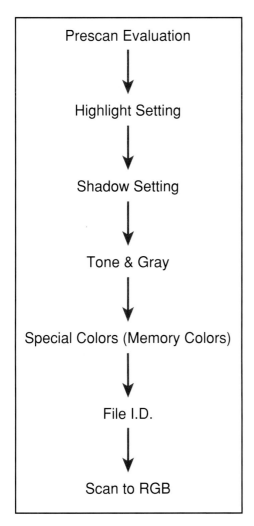

Prescan Evaluation

↓

Highlight Setting

↓

Shadow Setting

↓

Tone & Gray

↓

Special Colors (Memory Colors)

↓

File I.D.

↓

Scan to RGB

Figure 12.8
Flow chart of the scanning setup process.

good label or naming convention helps to accomplish this. Don't forget to incorporate a way to label first, second, or third scans if you require a few go-rounds to get to the final desired color.

Before the scan, do a quick review of your setup parameters. Double check size, resolution, crop (if valid), and any other special settings. Initiate the high resolution scan. Be sure not to disturb the unit while it is scanning. Jolts or outside

vibrations will affect final quality. Keep the scanner away from excessive heat and light. Let the scanner perform its complete cycle. If anything disturbs this cycle or the process stops, reset and start the scan again. Otherwise, you may obtain what looks like a good scan at an initial glance, but later on you may find out the result is not usable. Anything that retards the smooth movement of the analyze optics during the scanning process will cause an unwanted density shift in the reproduction. This density shift can be subtle or intense—in wide bands or as sharp lines. Either way, the scan will not be acceptable. Every scan should be smooth and trouble free.

CMYK Conversion

If you are working with a high-end scanner or desktop unit with 32-bit software conversion, you may be able to scan directly to a CMYK 32-bit file. Otherwise, with most desktop scanners, a 24-bit RGB image file is received (8 bits for each R, G, & B). If the image is going to print, the 24-bit RGB image must be converted to CMYK. The CMYK conversion must be done as a separate postscan procedure. If you receive RGB files from outside sources, you must still analyze the values as if you had produced the scan. At this time, any UCR or GCR adjustments for black generation must be preprogrammed into the conversion software. Also, for accuracy, any gray balance and color correction calibration information should be programmed into the conversion software if possible. Conversion software may have little or no gray balance and color correction calibration possibilities. You may need to develop your own and make corrections to the RGB file before conversion.

Initiate the conversion. Remember that your file size will increase by one third, (from 24 bit to 32 bit). Double check all aim points: highlight, shadow, grays, colors, and any UCR or GCR. Did you get what you wanted during the setup? Adjust as needed. Check resolution and physical size. Adjust the cropping if necessary.

Check the sharpness of the reproduction. Look for a natural appearance. Now that your contrast has been set, sharpness adjustments are most effective. Sharpness is weak at low contrasts and harsh at excessively high contrasts. The image is now ready for output to a device or a page layout program.

Automated Color

After walking through the previous description of how to produce a proper scan, you can see that the entire procedure is not necessarily a "fast food" trip. The craft of color separation at the highest level involves precise checking and adjustments. On a high-end drum scanner designed for generating large quantities of film separations, up to 30 separate steps in the procedure is not uncommon.

But what if your end use of the image reproduction makes high-end scans a budgetary nightmare or a quality overkill? Say that all you need is an image for a screen display or a low-resolution image for a dye sublimation output to place on your comp (for an ad concept in the initial design stage). Is a high-end, hands-on, fully controllable scanner really needed?

The 1990s brought in the era of scanning for the masses. Previously, scanning was done on machines costing more than $100,000 by operators who spent three to four years as apprentices before they were considered experts or craftspeople. Now the price (and size) of scanners has come down so that almost anyone can afford to purchase one for a home or office.

With the cheaper, more compact, basic hardware has come simpler, software-driven operating systems. These operating systems are designed to help the novice users obtain usable reproductions from their scanners in the form of digital images. Claims are being made that expert operators are no longer needed and that high end scanners are now financial overkill. People are looking at how much they spend buying out scans versus the cost of setting up an in-house operation.

As we stated before, be wary of software that claims to "do it all" for you. How much control over the end product are you giving up? Is manual override available, and how often do you have to use the override to get acceptable results on a regular basis?

For some people, the automated color approach will satisfy a majority of scanning needs. The convenience of in-house scanning will save time and money. If the color quality is acceptable to the customer's needs and expectations, then push button color is truly the way to go. With practice and experience, the quality level of the reproductions will get better. Systems like the PhotoCD offer solutions for cheap, quick scans of film but can only be as good as the original image. Color corrections are still needed before separations are made to CMYK. Chapters 3 and 6 discuss PhotoCDs in greater detail.

In other cases, automated in-house scanning only works for certain situations: for use onscreen, for comps, or for lower-quality publications. Images needed for high-quality print applications still require the precision of experienced operators and the quality of high-end units.

Depending on work flow needs, a high-end scanner can provide an image that is already sharpened, color corrected, sized, and converted to CMYK. A desktop scanner needs all the image adjustments performed in an image program like Photoshop. The additional steps required for a desktop scan can impede the work flow.

Knowing what you want, quality-wise and budget-wise, from your scanned reproductions will help you decide if in-house, automated scanning is right for you. What are you spending on scans now? Are you always waiting for your separated images to arrive back from the scanner house? Look at the end uses of your reproductions and think about what you or your customers expect and what you are used to seeing. Be aware that high-quality craftsmanship is not learned overnight and can't be purchased in a box either.

Checklist

■ Establish your goals before you begin scanning.

■ The type of output you will produce is the first decision you must make. Print, film transparency, and video display are the three most common types of output.

■ Determine the size, resolution, and conditions of output.

■ Establish a neutral equilibrium of the scanner and conversion procedures.

■ Keep the scanner as clean as possible.

■ Clean any images with compressed air to reduce the amount of rubbing and physical contact of the original.

■ Keep in constant communication with all people involved in the production process.

Final Word

The printing press is very unforgiving when it comes to high-quality image reproduction. The ink goes on the paper, and the bandwidth of adjustment is narrow. You can only put so much ink down before press and drying problems significantly impair the product. If you or your customers require a close match to a good original or want color that has maximum visual impact, then a scan using all the proper repro techniques and rules of color for print must be followed. The extra effort will show in the final quality.

If your color repro sights are not so high and your budget says, "We can make due with less than the best," then the ease of automated, push-button type scanning can produce a fruitful supply of images. These lower-priced, simplified systems make black-and-white and color images available to more people than ever before.

Expect the best from the best systems. Because of technological advances, expensive, high-end scanners are better than ever. Experienced color craftspeople specialize in making the finest image reproductions on these machines. But, if a Ford will get you there just as well as a Ferrari, the alternative is there for you today in the world of color scanning, too.

Tones reproduced using FM dots may appear different than the standard AM dots. Experimentation is necessary to find suitable scanning resolution and tone adjustments. Figure a shows a standard 150 lpi AM dot reproduction and Figure b shows a basic unadjusted 400 dpi FM dot reproduction.

400 dpi FM dot adjusted minus 15% in
the midtone.

400 dpi FM dot adjusted minus 30% in
the midtone.

300 dpi FM dot adjusted minus 15% in
the midtone.

300 dpi FM dot adjusted minus 30% in
the midtone.

composed of pixels appear to be continuous tone images on the color monitor. The screened image on the separation film is called a *halftone* because it is not a whole, continuous tone. Halftones are actually optical illusions; they appear to be continuous but upon close examination are not.

You may wonder how distance plays a role in viewing a continuous tone using halftone dots. Most everything we read or look at in our hands is viewed no more than an arm's length away. The average person holds an image about 24 inches from his eyes. At that distance you cannot easily distinguish individual dots spaced 1/120th to 1/200th of an inch apart. The dots mush together into a continuous tone. As the viewing distance increases, the size and the distance separating the dots can increase while

keeping a continuous tone appearance. Images on billboards and large displays use dots spaced up to 1/20th of an inch apart to create a continuous tone (see Figure 13.1b)

Dot Size and Tone

As previously mentioned, halftone separation films are high contrast, black or white, dot or no dot, with no tones in between. Yet these high contrast elements can produce an image that is not only black and white, but also one that has shades in between, such as gray (see Figures 13.2a-b). The size or amplitude of the halftone dots create the illusion of continuous tone even though the dots themselves are just black spots on white paper (base substrate). Therefore, the size of the halftone dots determines the weight

Figure 13.1a
An image with 150 lpi.

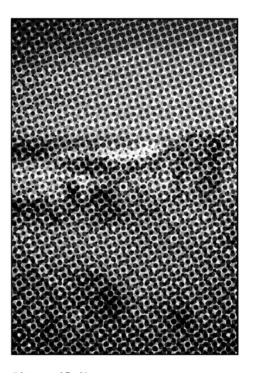

Figure 13.1b
An image with a low lpi will look the same as Figure 13.1a if viewed at a distance.

Figure 13.2a
The blend is created by halftone dots.
Viewed at an appropriate distance, the dot
appears continuous.

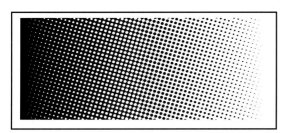

Figure 13.2b
An enlarged view of halftone dots shows
how the changing dot size creates the
illusion of tone.

Figure 13.3a
A 7% dot creates a light tone.
A 7% magenta is light pink

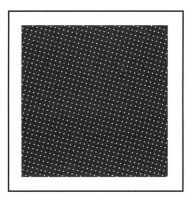

Figure 13.3b
A 95% dot creates a dark tone.
A 95% magenta is a saturated color.

of the tones in the image and the amount of each colored ink in the colors. For example, a 7% magenta dot looks like a very slight pink cast on a white paper, while a 95% magenta dot appears as a strong saturated color (see Figures 13.3a-b).

The size of the halftone dots creates the different tones that you see. The larger the dots are, the darker the tone. The maximum dot is the darkest tone; the minimum dot is the lightest tone. The percentage of the maximum dot size is how you relate tone with halftone dots.

In print reproduction, the smallest halftone dots are called highlights. Highlight dots print typically from 3 to 9% of the maximum dot size and create tone and detail in the brightest areas of the image. When no dots are printing,

there is no detail or tone because only the pure white paper is showing. An image area with no dots is called a *specular highlight.* The specular highlight is the brightest possible tone if the printing is done on a white substrate, such as paper. Reflections on water, metal, and glass are examples of specular highlights.

Dot sizes are referred to by the amount of ink they print. The quarter tone dot prints 25% ink; the middletone dot prints 50% ink (half way between 0 and 100%); and the three-quarter tone dot prints 75% ink. Ink levels beyond 99% are called solids.

You can see by looking at Figures 13.2a-b that as the halftone dot size increases, so does the apparent visual tone or density of that area. The larger the dots are, the darker the image area looks. The smaller the dots are, the brighter the image area looks.

Dot Frequency

Not only is the size of the halftone dots important in amplitude modulated halftones, but the number of potential dots possible in a measured area affects the image appearance, printing process, and substrate printed upon. This measurement, called the *line screen ruling*, the *line screen frequency*, or the *line screen requirement*, is given in *lpi* (lines of dots per inch). Fine, intermediate, and coarse line screens are available on most output devices. A fine line screen ruling of 175 lpi can produce 30,625 dots per square inch (175 squared) and effectively reproduces both fine detail and smooth tones. A much lesser ruling, such as 85 lpi, can produce only up to 7,225 dots per square inch and gives a coarser visual appearance when compared to finer screens. Remember the definition of resolution from Chapter 1: the more picture elements per unit measure, the higher the resolution. Keeping with this example, a 200 line screen has twice the resolution of a 100 line screen and will produce a smoother looking image with more apparent detail (see Figures 13.4a-d).

The printing method and substrate on which the printed image is being applied determines the line screen requirement. High-quality offset printing handles finer screens such as 175 and 200; silk-screen and high-speed web presses print only coarser screen rulings from 65 to 133. Coated paper stock works best with fine screens, and noncoated stock, such as newsprint, demands coarse screens because of its ink absorbency characteristics. Having fewer dots per square inch helps to control the dot spreading (or gain) caused by the ink absorption.

Most halftone output devices also produce dots of various shapes and configurations, such as square, round, elliptical, and chain. Square dots are the industry norm, but the other shapes may help produce smoother effects on *vignetting tones* or blends (areas that gradually go from light to dark), such as flesh tones. Talk to your printer about dot shape options.

The printer supplies line screen requirements and special dot shape information to the separator for every image separated (see Figures 13.5a-c). If this information is not given, the result may be a set of separations that are not optimum for the press conditions. Be sure to get line screen requirements immediately when producing separations for halftone printing.

Halftone dot quality is determined by the accuracy of the exposing light source of the film, the quality of the optics and hardware used in the exposing device, the number of scan lines or line pitch used to image each dot, and the number of matrix cells that create each dot. The microscopic-edge quality of the halftone dots has a macroscopic visual effect on the reproduction. An image made with perfectly shaped, well-defined dots holds sharp detail and smoothness in delicate tones. A dot matrix that is poorly shaped or distorted causes tone breaks and looks choppy when compared to an image of well-defined dot quality. Dot quality should always be a criteria when you are purchasing an output device. The dots created on an imagesetter are defined better than the dots of a laser printer (see Figures 13.6a-b).

Figure 13.4a
A grayscale image printed with round dots.

Figure 13.4b
A grayscale image printed with elliptical dots.

Figure 13.4c
A grayscale image printed with square dots.

Figure 13.4d
A grayscale image printed with line pattern.

Figure 13.5a
An example of round halftone dots.

Figure 13.5b
An example of elliptical halftone dots.

Figure 13.5c
An example of square halftone dots.

Figure 13.5d
An example of a line pattern.

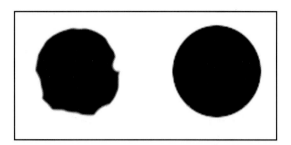

Figure 13.6a
An illustrated difference of a laser dot and an imagesetter dot.

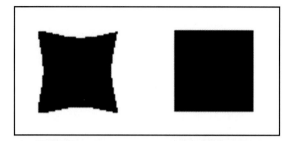

Figure 13.6b
A illustrated difference of a poor square midtone dot vs. a good quality midtone dot.

High resolution does not always mean you will get a high quality dot. How defined a dot the output device can make plays an important role in dot quality and therefore image quality. Note that the HDTV television systems of the future are called High *Definition* (not Resolution) Television.

Film Characteristics

All halftone film consists of two parts: a photosensitive layer called the *emulsion* that is coated on a supporting acetate layer known as the *base*. The film emulsion direction, or image orientation, should be known before you output. To expose the plate properly, the emulsion side of the film must come in direct contact with the printing plate. If the emulsion is not in direct contact with the plate, the light exposing the plate must pass through the acetate base before exposing the plate. Though the distance is infinitesimal, the separation acts like a mini projector, slightly enlarging the dots transferred to the plate. Shine a flashlight a foot from a wall, and you will see a round light. If you move an additional foot away from the wall, the light

becomes larger. The same result happens on a microscopic level when creating printing plates from film.

Emulsion direction is expressed as either RRED, right reading emulsion down, or RREU, image right reading emulsion up. Right reading means that the image is viewed normally, not reversed from right to left. RRED means that you can read the text as you look at the film—while the emulsion is facing down away from you. RREU films are used primarily to make duplicate films. RRED film is the most commonly used film to make printing plates.

The other most important characteristic of film is whether it is negative or positive. The kind of printing plate that the printer uses (negative acting or positive acting) will determine whether you need positive or negative films to create plates. Negative or positive acting printing plates are selected according to the printing process used by the printer and vary from country to country. In general, most North American printers use negative films; most European and Asian printers use positive films, although each printer has his individual needs. Film emulsion direction and positive or negative information should be supplied to the separator by the printer.

Rosette and Moiré Patterns

Working with noncontinuous tone images requires special considerations in order to achieve a reproduction of a continuous tone appearance. The difficulties involved are further compounded when using four or more colors of ink to make a full-color reproduction.

The intricacies of the halftone dot reproduction involve dot angles, rosette patterns, and the problem of the dreaded moiré pattern. Let's look at each of these ingredients for a four-color reproduction.

Rosette Patterns and Screen Angles

To print the halftone screens of each CMYK color and achieve a full-color effect, each halftone screen must be placed at different angles from each other. (See Figures 13.7 to 13.9.) When the CMYK halftone dots of each screen are printed over one another properly, they form an interference pattern called a *rosette pattern*. If one or more screens are angled improperly or if there is excessive misregistration during printing, the rosette may become more visible (see Figure 13.10).

If you use the correct angles for each ink color's dots, the rosette dot pattern is nearly invisible (continuous) to the naked eye. Commonly used angles are cyan (105 degrees), magenta (45 degrees), yellow (90 degrees), and black (75 degrees) because they most often create an invisible rosette for many printing applications. These angles *can* change to match a particular

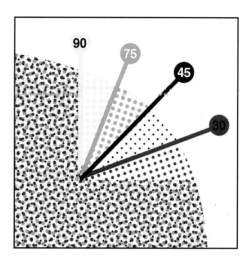

Figure 13.7
Standard angles used to place cyan, magenta, yellow, and black for four-color halftone printing.

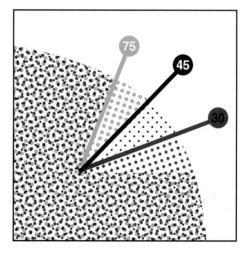

Figure 13.8
Standard angles used for three-color halftone printing

output device's characteristics. It is important to use a combination of screen angles that maintain a continuous tone appearance or the image will appear fake and hard to view.

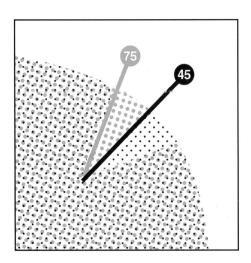

Figure 13.9
Standard angles used for two-color
halftone printing.

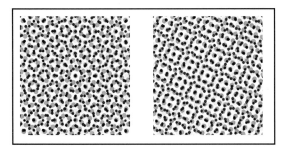

Figure 13.10
The rosette on the right is less pleasing
than the rosette on the left.

Moiré Patterns

The proper angle and placement of dots create the interference pattern called a rosette. The rosette pattern should be invisible. But when you begin to see the dot patterns as an uneven color, the effect is called a *moiré pattern* (pronounced more-ray). An undesirable moiré effect is one of a color separator's biggest headaches. Moiré patterns are caused not only when halftone screens are misaligned, but also when a photographic original introduces another pattern that does not mesh well with the standard halftone dot angles. Fabrics in clothes,

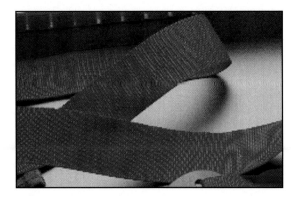

Figure 13.11
A moiré pattern is caused by the texture
in the red fabric.

heavy textures such as a burlap material, and dot and line patterns from grills on computers or machinery are examples of patterns in an original image that cause moirés. (See Figure 13.11). You actually can see "moving" moiré on television when the camera moves on a lined pattern such as a striped tie or mini blinds over a window.

Halftone dot moiré patterns are not visible on the monitor. Moiré will only become apparent when you proof your halftone film. One of the difficulties with continuous tone proofing systems is that they don't show if you have a moiré problem. Anticipating moiré can be difficult if your proofing system does not use halftone dots.

You can subdue moiré patterns by swapping the angles of the CMYK printers (try swapping cyan and magenta first), or scanning the original at a different angle to change how it meshes with the screen angles. If swapping the colors does not subdue or remove the moiré patterns, then blurring the image out of focus with a filter and resharpening the image with an unsharp masking filter will soften the unwanted pattern. The amount of blurring and sharpening is

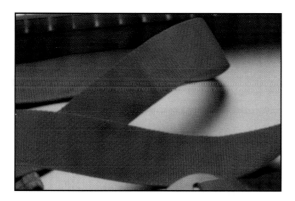

Figure 13.12
Blurring and then sharpening can help
subdue a moiré pattern, but you may lose
fine detail and texture.

found by experimentation and the experience of the operator (see Figure 13.12). Unfortunately, all fine detail in the scanned image is softened by this global technique. With image masking, the moiré area can be localized with a mask and softened with a blurring tool or filter, but this may cause other elements of the image to appear out of place. If the dot pattern (rosette) becomes visible in most normal work, consult the manufacturer of the output device about the best screen angles to use for CMYK.

After the color separation data has been digitized and set up for the halftone requirements and type of printing, there are two routes available to get to the final printed product: film or direct to plate (filmless).

Separation Films and Printing Plates

Images on traditional printing presses are contained on printing plates. The printing plate or plates carry the halftone dot pattern for each color of ink to be printed. A substrate (like paper) is passed through the press and either contacted directly to the plate or to a rubber blanket cylinder. The rubber blanket cylinder has the image offset upon it from contacting the printing plate. Each color of ink has its own plate, and each plate makes a single impression on the same exact place on the paper. Upon exit from the press, the substrate now has a full color halftone image on it.

Printing plates are made of metals, rubber, or paper and are laminated with a photosensitive coating. The plates are imaged by photographically exposing halftone separation films to the printing plates. As mentioned before, the separation films carry the separated color data from the original image.

Digital files that contain all the graphic images, text, and tints are processed together into a single file and then output from a film exposure device called an imagesetter. The digital file data is translated to imagesetter language—usually PostScript—which then flashes a laser light creating the halftone dot pattern on the photo sensitive films. The light sensitive films are developed and produce separation or plate ready films. The separation films can go to the pressroom for printing, or they may be preproofed for content and color fidelity.

Filmless Printing

A longtime goal of digital imaging is the production of printed images digitally from workstation to press, called *direct-to-press* printing. Since all color data is in digital form throughout, there is no need for separation films. Filmless printing has begun to be implemented in the 90s. Most implementation is not completely direct to press, but it is direct to plate. Instead of an imagesetter exposing photographic film, the imagesetter exposes plates that are used on press. The quality of these plates does not provide long printing runs and wears out more quickly than traditional plates, but filmless printing is now being done on a commercial basis.

Digital files are assembled and processed as if films are to be made. Prepress proofs are made using digital printers without films so that the page contents and color quality can be examined and approved before printing. Digital printing presses take image and page file data in digital form and create the printing halftone image directly upon the press cylinder's surface area. No films are needed to expose the halftone image on the plates. Imaging can even happen between each revolution of the press so that a different page or image can be printed consecutively. This means that full-color multiple page books or magazines can be printed completely without stopping the press to change plates for a new set of images. This is truly an incredible innovation to the labor intensive task of multiple page printing.

New Printing Techniques

Just as the digital revolution has affected the previously used analog techniques of separating and manipulating color, today's technologies have changed the way printing is done.

Stochastic Screening

Printing with stochastic or frequency modulated (FM) printing dots eliminates one of an operator's biggest headaches—moiré patterns. Color is produced by printing quantities of tiny, same-sized halftone dots (approx. 1-2% of conventional dot size), resulting in a smoother, more continuous looking reproduction. This approach to printing is called FM halftone printing because printed tones are created by the frequency, or number, of halftone dots in an area, not by the physical size of the dots as in AM halftone printing. With stochastic dot printing, detail is enhanced for lower line screens. Registration is not as big a problem so presses run faster and additional spot colors are easily added.

A problem with FM screening is the retention of the tiny halftone dots. Some presses and most proofing systems have great difficulty "holding," or accurately reproducing, the minuscule stochastic dots. The result can be a visual loss of detail and color. Also, some highlight detail and blends of color can appear grainy to some people. Random dot printing is relatively new to the industry. Although not extensively used commercially, FM printing will find its uses as quality issues are addressed.

High Fidelity Color

Computer technology has enhanced the color separator's ability to produce standard CMYK separations along with additional colored plates—traditionally called touch plates. Touch plates refer to printing plates on the press that add specially desired colors not easily made with CMYK ink combinations. Intense red, brown, or fluorescent colors are popular touch plate additions. Hi-fi color hopes to introduce standard ink additions like violet-blue, orange-reds, and greens, which are difficult to produce with CMYK mixing. The base colors of CMYK are still used in Hi-fi color. In fact, the colors used are based on CMY color theory.

The main advantage of Hi-fi color is a larger color gamut from soft pastels to intense, brightly saturated hues. What hasn't changed is the high degree of skill required of the pressman to put these multiple layers of ink on the paper in register and at the right densities. Also, accurate proofing for these additional colors is not easily available.

Waterless Printing

Offset printing has been done with ink and water since its inception. Achieving and maintaining an optimum ink-water balance during printing has always been a challenge for every press operator. If the balance is off, the printed density of the ink will be incorrect and color fidelity will suffer. The battle to maintain the precarious ink-water relationship continues throughout an entire press run.

With new plate and ink technology, the water component has been eliminated. Using a special waterless printing plate technology, the ink-water balance problem of offset printing is no longer a factor. Additional advantages of waterless printing are finer screen printing capabilities, heavier, more consistent color, greater printing contrast, and faster press make-ready results. You can expect to see more waterless printing as more work is done with FM screening and additional color plates.

The Goals of Color Reproduction

Now that the basic color separation to print process has been described, our next concern is developing procedures to produce color separations for print. You should know which aspects of tone and color that you need to visually achieve a good color-separated reproduction. You also should be able to tell if your results are correct. The remaining text and chapters go into detail regarding the color separation process. You may find that repeated readings of this information will help solidify the processes described.

If the final reproduction is weak in any of the areas listed below, the chances are good that the customer will reject it. To make a good-looking, sellable reproduction, you must satisfy four main criteria:

- Tone reproduction
- Gray balance
- Memory and special colors
- Sharpness

Tone Reproduction

To determine whether a prepress proof is good, the first characteristic to look for (even before seeing the original) is a three-dimensional appearance. For example, if you are looking at a reproduction of a fruit basket on a table, it should look as though you could reach into the scene and pull out a piece of fruit. A believable appearance demonstrates good tone reproduction.

Proper tone reproduction means that for each part of the conversion process—from original to final image—the resulting reproduction looks realistic from a dimensional standpoint. This dimensional realism is accomplished by maintaining all the tonal steps, from light to dark. *Steps* is a key word here. A tonal step is the visual difference between two tones or densities. A density is the light stopping or reflecting capability of a substance. For example, if you look at a checkerboard, the white and black squares are tonally very different. Because one is very bright and the other is very dark, the tonal difference between the two is extreme. You could say that the tonal step between them is great. Some tonal steps are very minimal—such as the tonal difference between a light vein in your arm and the surrounding flesh. When two neighboring tones become visually the same value, no tonal step exists. They become indistinguishable from each other.

All the tonal steps (in the original) being reproduced must be represented in the reproduction, otherwise the tones of the original and the reproduction will not visually match. The goal of tone reproduction is to match the tonal relationships of the original image in the reproduction (see Figure 13.13).

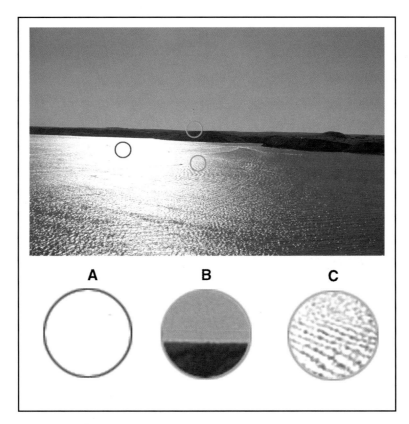

Figure 13.13
The circled areas show different tonal steps. (a) There is no tonal step or detail in areas where there are no dots. (b) There is a large step between the tone of the horizon and sky. (c) Small tonal steps create the shape in the waves.

A poor reproduction does not have enough dot percentage difference between the tonal steps when compared to the original. If the tonal range of the reproduction is too high, the tonal steps in the reproduction are diminished, and the steps between subtle tones can start to disappear. Figure 13.14a shows how the inside square starts to disappear into the outside square. If the tonal step is diminished enough, the eye is not able to differentiate between the two tones. Most people cannot see between two tones when the difference is less than 3% dot value.

Conversely, if the tonal range of a reproduction is too low, all tonal steps in the reproduction are exaggerated. The light areas when compared to each other become too bright, and the dark

Figure 13.14a
The tonal step is less than 3% between the card and table.

Figure 13.14b
The tonal step is 6% between the card and table.

Figure 13.14c
The tonal step is 9% between the card and table.

Figure 13.14d
The tonal step is 12% between the card and table.

areas become too dark. Notice how the inside square in Figures 13.14c and d is darker than the inside square of the normal contrast in Figure 13.14b. The figures illustrate the reproduction of a light gray card on a white table.

The term *contrast* often is used in association with tone reproduction. *Contrast* is the difference between all tone steps, from light to dark. In printed form, the tonal range is the density difference from the density of the base substrate (0.0 density) to the density of the largest ink dots (approximately 2.0 density). The tonal range of printed matter is typically 1.5 to 2.0 density from the lightest possible tone in the image to the darkest. Contrast is a simpler term used to describe tonal range. The contrast of the reproduction must match the contrast of the original, or their appearances will differ. Figures

13.15a-c illustrate how compressing the tonal range of the original will affect reproduction contrast.

The tonal range of your original image is determined by subtracting the highlight density from the shadow density (Dmax). If you take the tonal range and divide into 100, the difference in dot percentage between each tonal step in the reproduction results. As contrast increases in the original, the dot percent difference between the tonal steps in the reproduction increases. Although all tonal steps in the reproduction will be easier to see as the dot percentage difference rises, shadow detail will start to disappear (see Figures 13.15a-c).

Contrast in a reproduction has three possibilities: normal, low, or high. Normal contrast

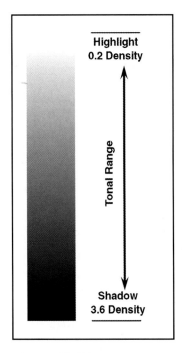

Figure 13.15a
A tonal range of 3.4 density. The difference between each tonal step in print reproduction is 2.9%.

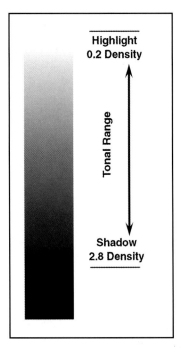

Figure 13.15b
A tonal range of 2.6 density. The difference between each tonal step in print reproduction is 3.8%.

306

Chapter 13

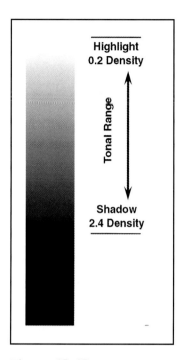

Highlight
0.2 Density

Tonal Range

Shadow
2.4 Density

Figure 13.15c
A tonal range of 2.2 density. The
difference between each tonal step
in print reproduction is 4.5%.

Figure 13.16a
Low contrast.

Figure 13.16b
Normal contrast.

Figure 13.16c
Excessive contrast.

yields a perfect reproduction of all tonal steps in
the original—no visual difference from tone to
tone.

The best way to train your eye to recognize
contrast and tonal steps is by reproducing black-
and-white originals. The eye can easily see the
differences between each tone because there are
no colors to get in the way. After you become
good at adjusting the tones of black-and-white
subjects, colored originals become easier to
analyze for contrast (see Figures 13.16a-c).

As the tonal range decreases, the contrast
increases. Altering the tonal range makes the
light areas appear lighter by making dark areas
darker.

Figure 13.17a.
The image appears flat because the tonal
range is long.

Figure 13.17b.
Normal contrast is achieved by shortening
the tonal range by 10%.

Figure13.17c.
Shortening the tonal range by 20% creating
excessive contrast and loss of shadow
detail.

Figure 13.18a
Low contrast.
Notice the lack
of details in the
flower.

Low contrast or insufficient contrast reduces the difference between tonal steps. Tones can merge together, causing a loss of detail. Also, the darker areas may not be as dark as possible, causing a reduction in visual contrast. Low contrast reproductions also are referred to as flat, weak, and lacking snap or pop. Colors in flat reproductions appear weak and undersaturated (see Figure 13.17a).

Figure 13.18b
Normal contrast
provides good
detail
reproduction.

Figure 13.18c
High contrast
exaggerates tonal
steps.

High contrast means that the differences between the tonal steps are more intense. The lighter areas appear brighter, and the darker areas appear darker. Detail in the brightest and darkest areas of the image may be gone or overexaggerated. Smooth tones that go from light to dark, called *vignettes*, may start to break up into separate bands of density. Colors will look oversaturated, or too intense (see Figure 13.17c).

A deep, red flower is an example of tonal steps in a color image. Proper tone reproduction shows every detail in each petal. Flat tone reproduction makes the image appear dull and causes the steps between details in the petals to disappear. A reproduction with too much contrast oversaturates the color, and the flower appears too dark and heavy. Detail in the

darkest areas goes into the shadows and disappears (see Figures 13.18a-c).

Tone reproduction is controlled on the scanner hardware or software by the highlight and shadow density point selections. These selections set the range of tones that are represented by dots. All tones of the original outside this range are either paper white or solid ink. Control of the interior part of the tonal curve exists with adjustments like the middletone. Selection techniques for these tones, or densities, are discussed in the next chapter on highlight, shadow, and interior curve movement.

If the tonal steps of the original are not represented properly in the reproduction, no amount of adjustment to the colors of the reproduction may help. Correct contrast in your color separations is a must. Bad tone reproduction almost surely results in a rejected proof every time.

Gray Balance

Color craftspeople often refer to gray or neutral when they analyze color. Neutrality represents an important factor of a reproduction. *Neutral* means that something has no bias—does not take sides on an issue. In this case, the issue is color. So a color that is neutral has no un-natural color bias, such as warm or cool. The neutral color is a pure hue, such as sky blue or apple red. Neutral colors look normal, as you expect to see them. Gray, as explained in Chapter 2, "Digital Color and Tone," is a tone between white and black that has no color bias. A neutral gray has no color bias: it doesn't look pink, greenish, warm, or cold—just gray.

A grayscale is a tonal scale that runs from light white to dark black with intermediate shades of gray in between. The scale is used as a guide for color systems to ensure proper calibration and unbiased color balance settings (see Figure 13.19).

The color separation process is in-between the photography stage and the ink-on-paper stage of the entire reproduction conversion process. This in-between position dictates that the color separator must be concerned with the neutrality of the photographic original and the neutral balance of the ink set used on the printing press. For example, if the original image to be scanned appears neutral, the separations should be made with a neutral ink balance. If the image to be reproduced has an undesirable color cast, the balance of the printing inks can be adjusted to defeat, or neutralize, the cast (see Figures 13.20a-b).

A good reproduction contains no obvious color casts: whites appear as whites; gray tones are gray; flesh tones are natural; and no colors have a bias toward a certain color direction.

Each type of photographic emulsion dye has its own color balance and gamut, which the scanner does not always recognize as neutral. Also, the scanner does not see color like the human eye because the eye is an organic system of vision, and the scanner uses a mechanical photoelectric system (see Chapter 2). Because of this difference in vision and color sensitivity, the scanner usually detects color casts that are too subtle for the eye to see.

A transparency may look neutral in the viewing booth, but the readouts on the scanner indicate that the original has a color cast. How do you know when the reproduction is going to be neutral by looking at a four-color dot percent readout on the scanner? Novice operators must learn to read and determine printing ink

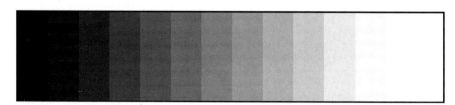

Figure 13.19
A grayscale used to calibrate color systems.

Figure 13.20a
A yellow casted image.

Figure 13.20b
Image neutralized toward a more normal
appearance.

neutrality along with additive and subtractive color relationships. Knowing what is neutral on the press and being able to determine the neutrality of the original that you scan are necessary skills for anyone who wants to produce quality color separations.

Dot Values to Make Gray

Table 13.1 lists the gray balance values needed to reproduce a neutral grayscale as neutral on a prepress proof made by a specific manufacturer. The dot percent difference between the cyan printer and the yellow/magenta printer is

important to notice. The cyan printer must print heavier than yellow and magenta printers to achieve a neutral gray with ink on press. This cyan, magenta, and yellow imbalance is necessary because inks are not pure and do not subtract one-third of the visible spectrum, as they theoretically should. (Pure inks are too expensive for most printing jobs.) Notice that the gray difference changes as you go from highlight to shadow (see Figure 13.21). The difference between the three subtractive color printers that make a printed neutral is called *gray balance*. Proper gray balance reproduces a neutral gray scale as a neutral gray.

Table 13.1 Gray Balance Differences

Density	Cyan Percent	Y/M Percent	Black Percent	Difference
.20	4	2	-	2-3 % highlight
.30	10	6	-	
.43	20	13	-	
.60	30	21	-	7-10 % quarter tone

continues

Table 13.1 Gray Balance Differences Continued

Density	Cyan Percent	Y/M Percent	Black Percent	Difference
.78	40	29	1	
.98	50	37	5	12-15 % middletone
1.25	60	46	14	
1.58	70	57	25	
2.10	80	71	42	8-12 % three-quarter tone
2.68	90	82	62	
2.80	95	87	75	7-10 % shadow

Note: The magenta and yellow values are equal for the type of proofing to which this chart is calibrated. This is not necessarily true of all proof or press conditions. One ink may need to be higher or lower than the other at certain parts of the tonal scale.

Starting at the beginning of the tonal curve, notice the highlight step where the halftone

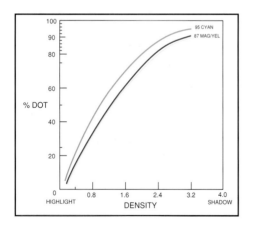

Figure 13.21
Table 13.1 represented as a curve.

dots start to print. The highlight step is the brightest area of the tonal scale because it is closest to paper white. The highlight also is the easiest area for the eye to detect a color cast in because it is so bright. The recommended dot percent difference here involves the cyan printing 2-3 percent more than the magenta and yellow. This dot percent difference yields a neutral tone in which the dots have highlight values. Because the dots are small, the percentages appear to be white. Again, the highlight is the easiest area for the eye to detect a cast in, so you must use the gray balance difference of 2-3 percent.

Printing the cyan, magenta, and yellow ink at equal values does not print *neutral* (see Figure 13.22). Equal values of CMY in the highlight appear warm, not white Shadows print brown. This undesirable result becomes evident immediately.

Ascending the tonal scale, you notice that at the 25% area, called quarter tone, the gray balance

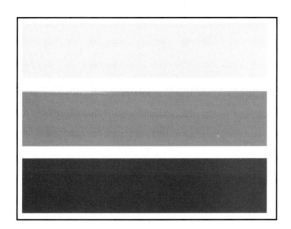

Figure 13.22
Equal CMY dot percentages of 6%, 50%, and
90% do not print as neutrals.

difference increases to 7-10%. This area produces a neutral tone a couple steps darker than the highlight white. The next important tonal area for gray balance is middletone—the 50% dot area in the center of the tonal curve. Gray balance difference is greatest at 12-15%. Now the tonal scale moves toward the dark side—the three-quarter tone's 75% dot area. The gray balance difference decreases to 8-12% to make a neutral tone in the 75% area. This area on the tonal scale carries the last of the shadow detail. Tonal areas with dots larger than three-quarter tone percentages cannot draw shapes and detail visible to the eye. At the top of the scale is the shadow point—the area of the largest printing dots. Here, the gray balance difference is 7-10%.

Using the Gray Balance Chart

The scanner detects color casts in photographic originals by comparing the original to scanner neutral (the scanner's standard operating position), which is set to the neutral condition of the press inks or of the prepress proof. While set to neutral, the scanner has no color bias in its readouts. If the readouts of the scanner say "no cast," the printing inks on the press will not add cast. This relationship between scanner and press is critical for achieving good color.

You will find that almost all transparencies are not completely neutral. The color casts can be different at different areas of the tonal scale, too. It is not unusual to find that a highlight has a green cast, or a shadow reads a blue cast. Reproducing the cast may or may not yield a matching reproduction. (See Chapter 14 on handling transparency color casts.) Reflective copy, on the other hand, is usually neutral or reproduced with any cast it contains. Because reflective subjects and prepress proofs are both reflective images, all color casts of the original should be in the reproduction to achieve a visual match.

The gray balance chart should be memorized by every scanner operator and color separator. By using additive/subtractive color relationships, you can discover which inks should be added or subtracted to neutralize a cast. Using a gray balance chart helps you recognize and neutralize color casts. With the knowledge and understanding of additive/subtractive color and gray balance differences, you can use the four-color readouts of dot percentage from the scanner or separation software to see tone and color without the use of a monitor. Gray and color theory will tell you what any RGB or CMYK color combination will yield visually in regard to tone and neutrality (see Figure 13.23).

A. The original image scanned as a transparency match. The customer required a product match of the computer and mouse which are neutral gray. Because the keyboard and mouse did not photograph as neutrals, they must be corrected to reproduce as gray.

B. An average reading in the mouse shows a cyan/blue balance of 22%C, 11%M, and 5%Y. Using curves or sliders functions, a subtraction of cyan and magenta is made with a slight increase in yellow to obtain a balance of 12%C, 8%M, and 7%Y. The mouse will now reproduce neutral and brighter due to the subtraction of cyan and magenta ink.

C:30 M:18 Y:17

Figure 13.23
Examples of cast and gray balance adjustments.

C. The keyboard is analyzed in the lightest and darkest areas due to its uneven lighting. Original readouts of 25%C, 10%M, 9%Y in the light area of the keyboard and 36%C, 18%M, and a 19%Y, in the dark areas are changed to 20% C, 10%M, 10%Y, in the light area and 30%C, 18%M, 17%Y in the darker areas. Care is taken not to disturb the highlight balance of the mouse and lighter keyboard areas otherwise localized masking must be used. The final result is gray mouse and keyboard.

To develop an eye for color correction, novices are recommended to obtain a set of CC filters used by color lab technicians to color balance C-prints. During the printing of color negatives, color casts are neutralized using the filter pack in the color enlarger. The technicians place the filters over the test prints to determine which filtrations will make a neutral print. The filters are graduated in units of 5, 10, 20, and so on, and in primary and secondary colors. CC filters help the technician choose the right color correction for each image situation.

Gray balance is the second most important factor (after tone reproduction) in producing a sellable reproduction. A proof or print with an obvious color cast is unacceptable even if the scanner is just reproducing what was in the original. The reproduction must appear realistic, and a color cast is not what the eye sees in the real world.

Memory Colors

Memory colors, or psychological reference colors, are colors in a reproduction that everyone knows without having to compare to an original. You do not need to compare a proof of a hand holding an apple to the original subject to know whether the colors look real: everyone remembers in their mind what an apple and the color of flesh looks like. The color of food, blue sky, flesh tones, and white are typical examples of memory colors. (This information comes from Miles F. Southworth's book *Color Separation Techniques*.)

If a reproduction has a memory color that does not look real, the customer is certain to reject it. The automatic response to poor memory colors is that something looks "fake." The tone reproduction and gray balance can be excellent, but customers do not buy orange flesh tones or pink skies!

White is one of the most often seen memory colors. A reproduction of a person in a white shirt that is reproducing as pink never will sell. The gray balance table from the previous section shows you how to determine optimum dot percent readouts for a satisfactory white. Even though white can be called a memory color, its appearance is dictated by the rules of gray balance (see Figures 13.24a-b).

Special colors are colors that the customer wants to match in the reproduction, regardless of their appearance in the photographic copy. Special colors are specifically requested and carefully examined when the prepress proof is delivered for approval—they are just as important as memory colors.

Special colors are usually product colors or spot colors. The customer gives the scanner operator a color matching system number, paint chip, color swatch, or brings in the actual product. Then the original image is scanned to RGB color space and converted as usual to CMYK. After the initial color separation into CMYK, all special color areas need to be checked to see if the requested colors will be reproduced on the prepress proof. To accomplish this, call up the digital file on a monitor in a program that offers CMYK densitometer readouts. Be sure that the

Figure 13.24a
Casting in the white of an image.

Figure 13.24b
Correcting cast to create white.

sampling area size for the densitometer is at least 3 × 3 pixels or 5 × 5 pixels to get a good average readout of the color in the image. (Smaller sample reading areas, such as point samples, are easily affected by grain and textures in the image.) Then take a reading in the special color areas. If the customer requested specific values of CMYK, make sure they are there. If you are matching a supplied sample, check the values in the readouts with a color chart or swatch book. Make any corrections as needed to get the desired special color. If the desired color cannot be found in the chart or swatch book, it may be out of the gamut for the ink set you are using. The customer will have to either select a reproducible color in the gamut or print with an extra touch plate color to get what she wants.

As a color separator, working with the RGB and CMYK color spaces should require developing a color memory for the colors that you use most often. Pay attention to the readouts of the densitometer. Try to visualize color by numbers instead of trying to rely on a monitor that has a

different gamut of color and grays than printing inks do. When it comes to reproducing color for printing, the densitometer is your link to the realities of the printing process.

Sharpness

After you reproduce the tonal steps, solve cast problems, and check memory colors, the last hurdle to creating a sellable reproduction is sharpness. Sharpness added during the reproduction sequence ensures that the scene appears in focus. If the sharpness in a reproduction has been selected properly on the scanner, it should not be noticeable.

The sharpness control on the scanner has a wide range of control and applications. The novice operator easily can get in trouble by overdoing the sharpness settings. Having too much sharpness creates a fake appearance on the reproduction. Not enough sharpness enhancement produces a soft or out-of-focus result (see Figures 13.25a-c).

Figure 13.25a
Too little sharpening.

Figure 13.25b
Appropriate amount of sharpening.

Figure 13.25c
Excessive sharpening.

Contrast has an effect on sharpness too. Good tone reproduction goes hand-in-hand with sharpness to create a natural, three-dimensional look. Sharpness filters and controls operate at their best when contrast is good. Poor tone reproduction has an effect on the perceived sharpness of the reproduction. A flat contrast range hinders sharpness because the tonal steps are not as distinct. A reproduction with excessive contrast exaggerates the tonal steps, and the sharpness circuitry puts abnormally higher sharpness in the reproduction. This exaggeration comes about because sharpness circuitry has its strongest effect on the highest contrast areas. If you refer back to Figures 13.17a-c, they offer good examples of contrast versus sharpness. Notice how the low-contrast reproduction in Figure 13.17a appears softer than Figure 13.17c, even though all three figures are reproduced with the same sharpness settings.

The sharpness settings are the most delicate controls on the scanner. Holding sharp details and keeping flesh and vignetting tones smooth in the same reproduction takes experience and careful adjustment. You should remember that good sharpness is not always noticed, but it certainly is missed if absent.

Judging Color

Accurate appraisal of an image's color characteristics requires both practice and theoretical knowledge of color and the printing process. You must be able to see beyond the general appearance of an image's color and determine the positive and negative aspects of a reproduction.

The Viewing Environment

To ensure proper analysis of color, the viewing conditions must be considered. As previously mentioned, there are physical and psychological variables to color judging; adding another variable, such as lighting, makes a difficult job even harder. Lighting conditions directly affect how the eye perceives color. For example, viewing color in a room with red walls gives everything a warm look and viewing color under dim light makes everything look dull. Standardizing lighting conditions for color appraisal removes a possible variable to color comprehension.

The viewing environment can be controlled by use of a booth to isolate the viewing area from its surroundings. Uncontrolled light is kept out, and the interior lighting and surrounding color in the viewing area are kept constant. Gray is the best booth color because a neutral color contains no bias toward any particular hue. Viewing booths come in large stand-alone units and in portable briefcase versions.

Inside the booth, the lighting is supplied by bulbs of a specific wavelength characteristic. The bulbs are rated by color temperature and color rendering index. Daylight is considered the best for color viewing and sunlight has a color temperature of approximately 5,000 degrees Kelvin (also called D5000). The D5000 lighting temperature is a standard in the printing industry and is used throughout trade shops from the scanner room to the pressroom. Additionally, transparency viewers are loaded with D5000 bulbs for standardized viewing of transmissive subjects.

How to Analyze a Reproduction

Now that everyone is viewing color under the same conditions, judging the merits of the reproduction can be more objective. The color separator produces a reproduction with certain aim points in mind to generate pleasing color. Understanding what the scanner operator is trying to accomplish enables you to accurately evaluate the quality of the color reproduction.

In the following sections we look at the color objectives of tone reproduction, contrast, neutrality, color, and sharpness. Recognizing these important components of a color reproduction allows you to properly judge color for any kind of output.

Tone and Contrast

The first variables of reproduction quality to judge are tone and contrast. Lay the original next to the proof. Look at the lightness and darkness of the two. Do they match? Contrast differences are easy to see, and they can be discerned quickly. If the contrast does not match, the reason is usually because the brightest areas do not match, the darkest areas do not match, or a combination of both.

Reproduction proofs of reflective originals are easier to analyze than proofs of transmissive originals. Proofs and reflective originals both have a shadow density of approximately 1.5 to 2.0. Because printed matter is reflective in nature, comparing reflective originals to prepress proofs requires less interpretation.

A dull base substrate or a colored paper stock will reduce highlight contrast in a reproduction. Maximum ink density limits (UCR or GCR) will subtract shadow contrast. Non digital proofs will have a hard time maintaining weight in the shadow end if large amounts of ink are being removed to compensate for press gain. Be sure to note if UCR or GCR total ink limits go below 300 percent (see Chapter 16).

It is important to understand that printed reproductions of transmissive subjects will not perfectly match a reflective proof because of their tonal density differences. Transparency images typically have measurable density ranges from 0.1-0.4 in the highlights to 2.8-3.4 in the shadows. The back lighting of transmissive images also enhances their perceived density range, making reflective images look dull and flat in comparison.

You should have an 8"×10" photographic color print made from an 8"×10" transparency and compare the two images side by side. Even though the images are of the same scene, the transmissive reproduction and the reflective reproduction will never match perfectly in appearance. Additionally, the longer contrast range of transparencies yields a larger color gamut; so there are some colors in transmissive subjects that reflective prints cannot reproduce.

Another variable that causes perception difficulties during color judging is format size. Ideally,

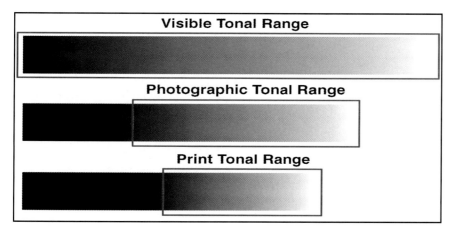

Figure 13.26
The relative tonal range of reproduction methods.

the original image should be approximately the same size as the reproduction for optimum comparison. Images gain visual contrast as they are reduced in size and lose contrast as they are enlarged. This contrast change is due to the light flare caused by the base substrate.

As the image gains size, more substrate is seen, and the substrate color influences the eye more. Most substrates are bright white (including transparencies, even though they are backlit); therefore, visual flare by the substrate over-whelms the colored areas, diminishing their intensity. This substrate influence will introduce a variable in contrast perception. Adjustments need to be made to achieve a visual match between originals and reproductions of signifi-cantly different sizes.

The most common original reproduction format is the 35mm transparency. Measuring 15/16"× 1.25", the small size of this format can cause both perception and comparison problems. Since 35mm originals (also called slides) are so small, they must be magnified somewhat to be properly evaluated. Looking at them unmag-nified does not give you a good appraisal of their content, yet many people submit slides for reproduction without examining them under some kind of magnification. Everyone has some idea of what the reproduction ideally should look like, but those responsible for reproducing the original must know whether they are trying to match the original or the customer's desires—even if unspoken.

The scanner captures and faithfully reproduces everything from the original subject as it is designed to do. When the scanner operator hears the customer criticize a good reproduction

Figure 13.27
Always examine your original images as closely as possible.

of a 35mm transparency, the best reply is to hand the customer a magnifier and ask him to take a *close* look at his original. The customer can then recognize that what he sees in the proof is indeed contained in the 35mm original. We cannot stress enough the importance of closely examining the original subject before and after reproduction (see Figure 13.17).

Color Casts and Neutrality

Next, look closely at the whites and neutrals to detect any overall color casts. White casts are especially easy to see because the eye is more sensitive to highlight areas than shadows. If you notice a cast in the proof, look carefully at your original in the viewing booth. The lighting or processing that was reproduced by the scanner may have caused a color cast in the original. (Remember that unless instructed otherwise, scanner operators reproduce images "as is.") Gray balance casts can be overall in the high-lights, midtones, and shadows, or just in the lighter areas of the image where they are easier to detect. Both neutrals and colors are affected by color casts—sort of like looking at the image through colored glasses. See Figures 13.28a-c for cast removal examples.

Properly separated, the image should have all neutrals reproduced as neutral. If there are no apparent color casts, most colors will fall into place and should match. Without proper gray balance, everything has an overall cast and will not match the original.

Memory and Special Colors

If the gray balance and contrast are acceptable, then individual colors should be examined next. Without looking at the original, the memory colors should be examined for realism. If the memory colors are not correct in a reproduction, you can tell right away that something is wrong. An example of a color that is not a memory color would be brown leather. You could not tell if the shade of brown in a reproduction realistically matches the original until you actually see the original. The key to recognizing memory colors is knowing if the color is a realistic match without seeing the original. Reject any proofs if the realism of colors is not correct to your eye (and feelings) (see Figures 13.29a-b).

If any special colors have been noted for reproduction, view the results on the proof. Special colors are product colors and spot colors especially designated before scanning. An actual sample, such as a paint chip or the entire product, may have been supplied as a color reference. Sometimes a specific dot percentage of inks may be made for a special color area. Check to see if the color requirements have been met and matched.

If the special colors do not match, find out what dot percentages of color are in that area. The

Figure 13.29a
The sky in the image looks unnatural.

Figure 13.29b
Removing some yellow makes the sky look
more believable.

easiest way to do this is to put the image on-screen and get a densitometer readout at that spot. Color professionals also use a magnifying loop to read the dot percentages on the proof or from the halftone films that made the proof. After noting the existing dot percentages in the special colors, obtain a color chart or swatch book and try to figure out what adjustments need to be made to get the color you require. If the first try was very far off, be aware that your requested special color may not be in the color gamut of the ink set being used. A compromise may be needed: an extra printer or touch plate may be required to match that color.

Image Sharpness

After all the tones and colors have been examined for fidelity to the original, clear your mind of them and look at the proof for sharpness. As mentioned previously, if you don't notice the sharpness of the reproduction, then it is probably correct. A natural appearance is best. Oversharpening will cause a fake appearance, and undersharpening will have a soft look. Be sure to notice the sharpness condition of your

original too. Photographic originals are never oversharp, but they can be out of focus. Soft images can be sharpened during reproduction and oversharp reproductions must be reseparated to naturalize the image. Additionally, with electronic masking, sharpness also can be enhanced or reduced locally.

If the overall sharpness is acceptable, look closely for halos—those white and black lines around high contrast areas. Objectionable halos should be removed electronically using cloning tools. Also, look for evidence of pixelization or jagged lines (the jaggies) (see Figure 13.30). An adjustment in resolution will be necessary to cure these effects. (See Chapter 3, "Obtaining Pixels.")

Just like producing color separations, analyzing the printed results requires patience and practice. In the trade, we like to call the learning process "developing an eye for color." If you do not understand the basics of what is involved with creating a color separation, you cannot become a good judge of the final result. Understanding the color reproduction process helps

you not only to judge a color reproduction's appearance but also to effectively communicate your opinions of the result to others.

Prepress Proofs

The prepress proof is made to show what the text, linework, and images will look like when printed on the press. Proofs are used to judge color fidelity of images, accuracy of the placement of the elements on a page, and the overall aesthetic look and design of the printed piece.

There are several different types of proofs used in the industry, and they are made by a variety of manufacturers. Some proofs accurately predict the printed results, while others are only an approximation. We will discuss the six general categories of prepress proofs available today.

Acetate Proofs

Acetate proofs are the cheapest and quickest proofs to make. They consist of an acetate material that is exposed to each separation printer. An acetate yellow is contacted to the yellow separation film, magenta acetate to the magenta film, cyan acetate to the cyan film, and black acetate to the black film. All four acetates reproduce the halftone dots of the separation films. The acetate proof colors are registered on top of each other. In the same sequence, the inks are being printed on top of each other onto the paper stock. Any paper stock can be used. The result is a four-color halftone proof over paper. There are several types of CMY acetates available to simulate different types of ink sets. Some additional colors besides CMYK are available also, but the selection is very limited. Acetate proofs are consistent from proof to proof as long as exposure calibration standards are observed.

The disadvantage of acetate proofs is that the four acetate layers dull the visual brightness of the base substrate or paper. The dulling of the brightness of the highlight areas causes a reduction in overall contrast making a match of a printed sheet impossible. Therefore, acetate proofs are, at best, an approximation of a press sheet. Also, the color gamut of acetate proofs is smaller than ink on paper. Deep reds are usually on the orange side.

Non-halftone Proofs

This category of proofs includes all methods that do not produce halftone dots to simulate the color of a printed piece. The main kinds of devices used here are ink jet and dye sublimation type proofs. These devices produce color images for layout comps and presentations, but they are sometimes used for color approval prior to printing.

Ink jet proofs consist of CMYK splotches of ink that are not true halftone dots. Only certain paper stocks and substrates can be used to receive the ink. Color gamut approximates CMYK ink sets quite well; consistency of proofs has improved over the last few years to become acceptable for use as a prepress proof.

The disadvantages of ink jet proofs as prepress proofs are the limited type of substrates that they can be made on and the fact that they do not reproduce halftone dots as a printed piece.

Dye sublimation printers work as RGB printers that place continuous tones of dye on a receiver sheet. The resulting proofs are great to look at but do not have the same gamut of CMYK ink sets. Dye sub prints are mainly useful for comps and proofs to check the layout and design of complex designs and page layouts. Proper printer maintenance guarantees good proof consistency.

The disadvantages of dye sublimation printers as prepress proofs are the limited stocks that they are able to print on and the fact that they make continuous tone prints instead of halftone dots as do printed pieces.

Toner Proofs

Toner proofs are made with specially formulated powders that simulate CMYK inks and any special touch plate colors being used in the printing process. The separation films are exposed onto a receiver lamination material and coated with the proper color powder. The

receiver lamination is adhered to the paper stock, one on top of another. After each of the CMYK layers has been exposed and toned with the colored powders, the gloss of the proof is then adjusted to a matte or glossy finish to simulate a coated or noncoated paper appearance. The result is a laminated proof that simulates the printed result quite faithfully. The halftone dot pattern of the separations is usually quite good, but temperature and humidity in the proofing area require strict monitoring to maintain accurate dot rendering (especially in the highlight areas) and consistency from proof to proof. Toner type proofs have the widest and most accurate available color gamut for prepress proofing.

The downside of toner type proofs is consistency. Proofers must be very diligent about the proofing environment, and the process must be closely monitored. Otherwise, inaccurate proofs may be delivered which will result in needless color corrections. Sometimes proofing the same set of films over and over will yield different results (such as slight shifts in gray balance and contrast).

Laminated Proofs

Laminated proofs use acetate colors similar to the acetate proofs, but they are laminated to the receiver stock. Laminating eliminates the brightness dulling effect of the acetate layers. Separation films are contacted to each corresponding color laminate until a CMYK proof is made. These proofs will accurately reproduce the halftone dots of the separation films consistently. Color gamut is approximate to CMYK inks with different hues available to match various ink sets and a limited amount of

Color separations have been made for many years, albeit with different technology—from hand to photographic to mechanical scanning. But the basic nature of color separations hasn't changed. Halftone dots of CMYK inks on paper still require the same values for reproduction, no matter how the separations were produced. The values, or aim-points, as they are commonly called, must somehow relate from the original image to the printed reproduction. How these aim-points are identified and adjusted for print reproduction is examined in this chapter.

An RGB scan must have proper tone reproduction, gray balance, memory colors, and sharpness—whether done on a $200,000 or a $2,000 scanner. If any of these reproduction parameters is lacking on a high-end scanner's CMYK separations, the same image properly scanned and separated on a less-expensive scanner will look much better.

If four-color process separations are the final destination, it is critical to have knowledge of CMYK values for a good reproduction (even though most digital images start as RGB files). Using the goals of color reproduction discussed in the preceding chapter, this chapter explains how to set the proper CMYK values in an image to obtain great color results, no matter which kind of scanner is used to digitize the original.

Attention, Attenzione, Achtung

Before we discuss the details of how to approach color reproduction, we need to lay some ground rules that will make understanding this complicated subject less daunting.

The Color Separation Process

Think of the RGB color space as the top of a pyramid (see Figure 14.1). When you are at the top, the RGB color space can see all possible destinations of reproduction. With an RGB file, you can go anywhere.

Let's say, for example, that you don't know if you are printing with Best Printing down the street or Greatest Printing across town. Best Printing prefers to have a total ink density of 340% with UCR and a dot gain of 15%; Greatest

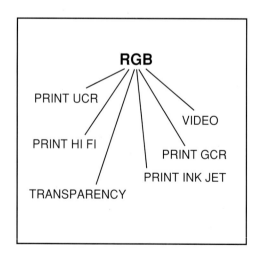

Figure 14.1
From the RGB color space many different types of color separations can be made.

Printing prefers to have a total ink density of 320% with 40% GCR and a dot gain of 20%. (These terms and values will mean more to you later.) So what do you do? Do you create a separation for Best or Greatest? What if you don't even know the desired printing conditions, but you need to start preparing files?

All RGB files must be converted to CMYK for printing. The large color space of RGB is where you should do all color corrections with an eye toward the CMYK color space. You cannot correct RGB files without knowing the CMYK values into which they will be converted. All scanners scan RGB, and then perform a conversion to CMYK. The only difference today is that we bring the RGB data onto our workstations for conversions to CMYK. The techniques discussed in this chapter work with scanners that go directly to CMYK and with scanners that place RGB files on a workstation. The only difference is where you do the conversion to CMYK.

Just as important to understand is that black is created from the values of CMY. The black printer has a critical supporting role in making the tone and contrast in a printed reproduction. Start with good CMY values and the resulting black printer will be optimum. If your CMY values are poor, then the black printer is flawed and the reproduction may suffer.

The key is that you can prepare your RGB files destined for print while they are still RGB files. By referring to the predicted values of CMYK in your image program, the RGB image can be adjusted to work for every possible printing condition. What's that, you say? Every print condition? Correct.

There is a specific path to making good color reproductions. Whether you are a traditional camera separator or are using advanced digital software systems, the path is the same. The steps you take to travel this path must be taken in a specific order to reach your destination. If you wander too far off the path, you may find yourself in the land of poor color, or worse, unpredictable color.

The following chapters provide a map of how to reach your color reproduction goals. The journey is just as important as getting there. If you learn the basic concepts of color reproduction you can go anywhere you wish by following the map. As long as you turn off any post separation functions like UCR or GCR, the values discussed in the following chapters will enable you to prepare any RGB file for any print reproduction possibility.

Arbitrarily using UCR and GCR functions can severely limit your choices. Additionally, using dot gain compensation as a method of lightening or darkening your images defeats the purpose of creating accurate CMYK values.

You will find many popular programs— including Photoshop—do not allow you a direct method of turning off the UCR or GCR functions. In order to receive values that will follow the methods discussed in the following chapters, you must create the following setting in Photoshop or any other program that does not allow an option of turning a post separation function off (see Figure 14.2).

Choose UCR, set the maximum black at 80%, and set the total ink density at 350%, which is the practical ink limit most printing presses can handle. A total ink density of more than 350%

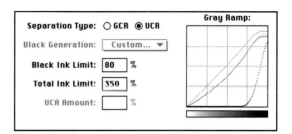

Figure 14.2
The values that you enter so that color is evaluated properly before separations are created in Photoshop.

can cause severe press problems. This setup will not introduce any GCR (and effectively no UCR) into the predicted CMYK values while working with an RGB image. These settings allow corrections to be made in an RGB image before conversion. After an RGB file is properly adjusted, many different types of CMYK separations can be prepared for a variety of printing conditions.

When you correct your RGB image while in the above setup, the predicted CMYK values you will read from the onscreen densitometer will follow the techniques we discuss. After the RGB color adjustments have been made, the color separations are performed with the settings your printer requires of UCR, GCR, and dot gain. Once you have established the actual conditions required by your printer, you will change the separation setup to the appropriate values and convert the RGB image to CMYK.

Therefore, the adjusted RGB file can be separated for any number of printing conditions. Since the RGB image holds the largest number of colors, all your corrections can be made while in RGB. You can wait until you find out which separation you need to make, whether you will be printing at Best or Greatest Printing. You should always keep a copy of your RGB file in case printing conditions change or if more radical color adjustments or retouching is required.

Any additional fine-tuning of color can be made while in CMYK. But after an image is separated into the CMYK color space, the readings will reflect any post operation functions—like UCR or GCR—that you have added to the settings. Any adjustments to the CMYK file should be made relative to the results you see on a proof or based on specific color values. The numeric values of a CMYK file onscreen should match what you get in output.

Some people may encourage you to make all corrections after the CMYK separations have been made. If so, remember that you have already lost a great deal of data after you have converted to CMYK. Details may no longer be available or adjustable when you take the approach of making corrections only in CMYK. Logically, you should work with the largest possible color space until you are sure that you have the desired results.

To create an accurate color separation, you should rely on a very precise method of checking the values in an image's specific tonal points. The value's accuracy depends on the color separation having no post operation function to influence the values. The UCR and GCR options must be turned off to properly analyze an image.

Many color separation programs are beginning to provide as much flexibility and control over the color separation process as do most high-end scanners which scan directly to CMYK. It is our hope that in the future all separation programs will enable the very simple process of turning off UCR and GCR functions.

We actually use the methods we discuss on a daily basis and this approach does work—and it works very well. Some automation experts may say it is not worth getting into this level of detail. Fine. If automation is so complete, by all means, use it. But if you'd like to know a little more about the craft of color, then without further ado, let's get to it.

The Densitometer

The tool that you need to analyze and achieve good color is the densitometer. An onscreen densitometer reads the RGB and/or CMYK densities or dot values of any particular area where the cursor is placed in a digitally displayed image. When you are in RGB mode, some programs will display a densitometer that shows both RGB and CMYK values of the areas being read. Other programs, like Kolorist, also display a relative density, as do many high-end scanners. The CMYK readouts are predictions of the dot percentages created by the program when the file is converted from RGB to CMYK.

If you are using a different program for RGB to CMYK conversion, only the program performing the conversion will give accurate CMYK predictions. Some programs have control panels that enable you to select which effects will be shown in the densitometer readouts.

Figure 14.3 shows a densitometer with the sample size menu. The accuracy of the densitometer readout is critical. The job of the densitometer is to predict the dot percent values that will be on the separation films, as well as analyze the balance and color of the original. The reading area of the densitometer can be adjusted to various sizes—from a single point to several pixels wide. Detail, grain, and texture in an image will cause the dot percent readouts of the densitometer to be jumpy and erratic. If an image is enlarged greatly, the grain structure can cause readout movement of as much as plus or minus 10 percent. To reduce the effects of grain and texture on the densitometer's readings, a wide sampling area of 3 by 3 or 5 by 5 pixels is recommended. Always check the reading area upon opening an image program because many densitometers default to point source readouts and may cause less accurate dot percent predictions.

The CMYK predictions of the densitometer allow accurate adjustment of image files in the initial RGB color space. After the CMYK conversion is made, little or no adjustment should be needed. Additionally, a better conversion is

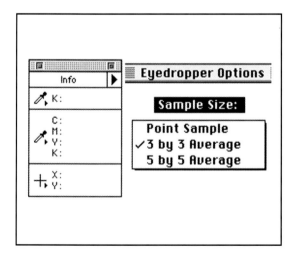

Figure 14.3
A typical onscreen densitometer with sample size menu.

made from a file that is set up near optimum than a file that needs a lot of adjustment after conversion is done.

Precorrecting the image files in RGB will help you get the best reproduction possible. The densitometer is your link to the reality of the printing press. With the help of the densitometer and information contained in this chapter, great color scans are just waiting to be created.

Setting the Tone

First, you should review the information from Chapter 12 on the prescan evaluation. All mechanical adjustments to the scanner and all prescan preparations should be done *before* starting the color setting part of the color separation process. It is easy to forget about the various noncolor parameters that need to be set when you get involved with the setting of the color separation parameters and image readouts. A scan with great color will be of no use if it was done at the wrong size or if the basic color correction was set for the wrong type of original.

The color separation process is complex; it involves many steps to obtain a good color reproduction. Establishing an operating sequence will help ensure consistent results and reduce mistakes. Do it the same way each time. Avoid shortcuts until you are absolutely comfortable with the entire procedure.

The highlight point and shadow point determine where detail and tone will print in a halftone reproduction. Between the highlight and shadow points are halftone printing dots (ranging from 3 to 99%) that create tone, color, and detail. All densities above and below these aim-points are either paper white (no ink) or solid ink.

The tonal range of a photographic original runs from the lightest density to the darkest density. Density is the measurement of a material's light-stopping ability. The goal of tone reproduction is to set the range of printing dots from highlight to shadow. In order to accomplish print reproduction of original images, the tonal range of the originals is compressed into the tonal range of print (see Figure 14.4a).

Highlight and shadow point settings match up the halftone dot printing range to the density range of the original (see Figure 14.4b). The density difference between highlight and shadow also sets the contrast of the reproduction. The following sections show you how to find the proper highlight and shadow points for four-color printing. Having the correct setting of

these endpoints will ensure a good-looking printed reproduction.

The Highlight Point

In all color separation procedures, highlight selection (highlight point) is the first parameter to select because it affects all other steps that follow it. Any readjustment to the highlight after other parameters have been set will result in a shifting of all parameters. If you must reset the highlight point, repeat the rest of the setup to ensure that all parameters are still where you want them to be.

The highlight point of a separation is where the smallest (3-5%) printing dot value of yellow, magenta, or cyan is visible and starts to print. The highlight setting point is found in whites or

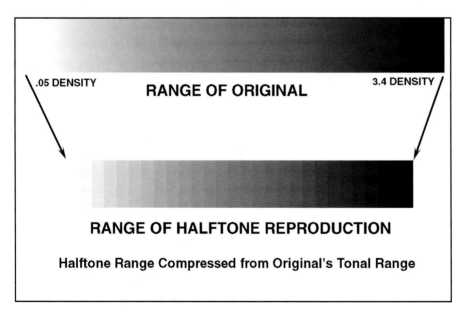

Figure 14.4a
The tonal density range is compressed into the dot percent range.

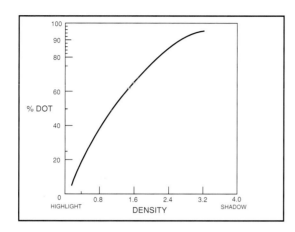

Figure 14.4b
Density vs. dot percentage curve.

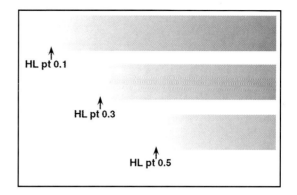

Figure 14.5
The halftone dots begin where the highlight density of the original is located. There are no dots below the highlight density point.

colors. Highlight selection is crucial for a good reproduction because it controls the appearance of the brightest part of the scene and any details in these bright areas. Because the human eye can see the most detail in bright areas (the highlight areas), the selection of the highlight point is the single most important step in the entire color separation process.

Assigning the location of the highlight point on a scanner or color separation program involves selecting a point or points in the original image at which the smallest dots will start printing. Normally, these dots are from 3-5% in value and can be cyan, magenta, and/or yellow depending on the color of the area selected. Figure 14.5 shows how the dot sizes start at a selected density and enlarge as the density of the original increases.

Figures 14.6a-d show how the setting of the highlight point controls the detail in the bright areas of an image. The density numbers of 0.10, 0.20, 0.30, and 0.40 represent the densities of

the original image. Figure 14.6b has the correct highlight selection at a density of 0.20. All important tone and detail are represented, such as the texture of the wallpaper and the fine detail of the fresco on the wall. These very fine details and bright tones are called highlight detail because they are shaped or drawn by tiny highlight dots.

Figure 14.6a has a highlight point selected at too low a density. Since the dot sizes increase as the density of the original increases, a dark-looking result is obtained. Even though all the highlight detail of the image is reproduced, the bright areas are too dark because the highlight dots are too large. The larger the dot, the less white paper shows and the denser the area looks to the eye. These dense highlights are described as being "too full."

Figures 14.6 c and d have a highlight point selected at too high a density. All densities less than the highlight point will be paper white. There are no dots to draw any tones, textures, or details. Notice that the texture of the wallpaper is gone and the fresco has disappeared into the wall. The reproductions are bright, but they are missing the fine highlight details. These examples are described as having a highlight that is "too clean."

Specular and Diffuse Highlights

The key to selecting the best highlight point is knowing where the smallest dots of cyan, magenta, or yellow will start to print. If you can locate this starting density, the resulting reproduction will have the necessary pop and sparkle in the brightest areas of the image. The starting point for the highlight dots to print is also called the *diffuse highlight*. To accurately locate the highlight point, you need to understand where *not* to put a highlight dot.

Locating the Specular Highlight

As mentioned earlier, densities that are less than the highlight point hold no dots and are paper white. *Specular highlights* are areas that *should not* carry tone or dots. Examples of speculars are reflections in metal, glass, and water. They are so bright in nature that they must be reproduced at maximum brightness to look correct in the reproduction. Maximum possible brightness in a printed reproduction is paper white and holds no dots. Specular highlights are not highlight setting points. Their density is normally well below the image's diffuse highlight density. Placing a dot in a specular density results in abnormally dark highlight areas. Also, the further away the specular

density is from the diffuse density, the darker the diffuse highlight point becomes.

Refer back to Figure 14.6a. Notice how it illustrates the pitfalls of setting a highlight in a specular. Compare it to Figure 14.6b, the correct highlight setting. Find the speculars in the image (reflections on the metal goblets). If you place a magnifying glass over the speculars of Figure 14.6b, they will be paper white and carry no dots. Now look in the same spot in Figure 14.6a. The dots you see there cause the speculars to be duller than they would be if they were paper white.

The reason that specular highlights are so important to a good printed reproduction is because of the way the human eye perceives contrast. Contrast is the difference between the brightest and darkest areas of a scene or image. Figures 14.6a-d all have the same shadow density. Their dark areas are equally as dark, yet Figure 14.6d appears to have much more contrast than the other figures. That is because the highlights of Figures 14.6c and d are brighter, showing more paper white than the other images. The greater the range of tone or density between the light and dark areas, the higher the contrast.

If the specular highlight areas in an image are at maximum brightness (which is paper white), then the eye can perceive maximum contrast from the reproduction. Since there is no tone, detail, or texture in a specular white, there is no need for a dot to be there. Putting it bluntly, don't plug up your speculars! (See Figures 14.7a and b.)

For those who prefer the ease of automatic scanning software, be aware that this form of

Figure 14.6a
The highlight point set at 0.10 density.

Figure 14.6b
The highlight point set at 0.20 density.

Figure 14.6c
The highlight point set at 0.30 density.

Figure 14.6d
The highlight point set at 0.40 density.

Color Separation Endpoints

Figure 14.7a
Plugging the speculars decreases highlight
contrast, causing the reproduction to look
dark.

Figure 14.7b
Placing the proper highlight point keeps
speculars open.

scanning has no capability to recognize specular highlights. This scanning software sees images as histograms of densities in which they locate the lowest part. After it locates the lowest density of the image, a tiny highlight dot is placed in that spot. You have the choice of adjusting for the speculars afterwards or trying to override the program.

When performing the prescan analysis of your images, make a note of any apparent specular highlights. Check with your onscreen densitometer and adjust as needed so that no dot percent values in these areas exceed 2%. Otherwise, they will carry a dot and diminish the overall contrast of the reproduction.

Locating Diffuse Highlights

After you have identified the areas of specular highlight, the diffuse highlight can be located. The capability of a color separator to find the diffuse highlight is a big factor in the resulting quality of the reproduction. Refer back to Figure 14.6b. If Figure 14.6b is a match to the original image, will you accept a scan that looks like any of the other figures? The difference between correct and unacceptable in this example is the location of the diffuse highlight. Figures 14.8a and b are other examples of proper highlight selections and plugged specular reproductions.

Understand that some images can still look acceptable if the wrong highlight density is selected (fudge factor), while others will not look good unless the perfect highlight is chosen. The farther away the specular density is from the diffuse highlight density, the less fudge factor you have. Transparency separations are more "highlight critical" than reflective originals because of their greater tonal range. Your best bet in all cases is to strive for the most accurate highlight point selection for every reproduction. Even if a highlight point placement is the only adjustment that you make, you will improve the quality of the image reproduction.

The simplest and most widely practiced method of setting a highlight involves finding the brightest white that has tone or detail and

Figure 14.8a
An image with a properly set highlight
point of 0.25 density.

Figure 14.8b
Highlight point is set too low at 0.15
density and has dots in the speculars.

adjusting (or placing) a 3-5% cyan dot in that area. This method is successful if the white is not a specular. Bright whites with tone in them are usually at or near the diffuse highlight density.

Folds or seams in a white shirt are great aim-points for highlight dots. Without dots, there is no detail; therefore, to reproduce folds and seams in the shirt a printing dot must be present.

Minimum printing dot values should be 3 to 4% for coated paper, 5% for uncoated paper, and 7% for newsprint. Dots under this size do not hold consistently in the printing process; they revert to speculars.

How White Is White?

The next logical question after locating a bright white with tone is "How white do you make it?"

There are three ways to create a true white in a color halftone reproduction. The first method is to use the specular paper white, as already mentioned. A second method is to use a small 2-3% cyan dot. The eye assimilates this light, cool tone into the white paper, and the area appears white. The cyan dot should be less than 8% or the white shifts to a blue tone. Magenta alone does not work (it appears pink), and yellow alone also creates a cast (see Figure 14.9).

Have you ever used laundry detergent that has magical blue flecks in the powder? The blue flecks do not provide any additional cleaning power. They only provide a visual effect that makes the white powder look cleaner. Those manufacturers that use green flecks in their detergent have yet to understand how a small cyan dot provides a cool, bright white.

The third way to achieve a white is to print all CMY in gray balance: 7% C, 4% Y, and 4% M, or 6% C, 4% Y, and 4% M. Both white balances carry the full detail of an image with all three colors printing. These dots are minimums, so the resulting tone is bright because the tone is mostly paper white with a minimum of ink (see Figure 14.10). Of the three methods to get white, the brightest possible diffuse white is the

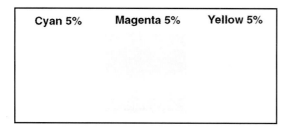

Figure 14.9
A 5 percent cyan dot maintains white better than a 5 percent dot of magenta or yellow.

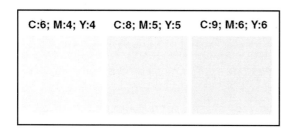

Figure 14.10
Cyan, magenta, and yellow can print together when combined in a neutral balance to create white.

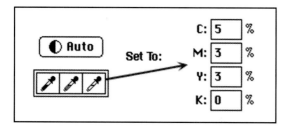

Figure 14.11
Some programs offer specific tools to set a highlight point in an image at whatever CMY balance you require.

cyan dot only. Do not make diffuse areas into speculars because there will be missing detail caused by setting the density to a higher than normal value, as shown back in Figures 14.6c and d.

For highlight setting, the balance of CMY should not be disturbed at first. While the densitometer cursor is in the highlight area, adjust the CMY values equally together (whether it is using curves or sliders) until at least one color reads correctly. Then after tone correction, if you consider the highlight to hold a color cast, make any adjustments needed to handle the cast and to correct towards neutral white.

Most software programs have what is called a "set to value" control (see Figure 14.11). You can adjust a highlight point to any desired values of CMY. The "set to" control corrects the image to match the preset CMY values and is a quick way to pick your highlight point and also shadow point values.

The spot where the cursor resides alters the curve (which adjusts the image) to reflect the desired CMY values. Usually adjusted in RGB before separation, "set to" controls also should work in CMYK. The CMY values you use depend on the effect you wish to achieve. The next section goes into further detail about how to adjust the white highlights to specific values.

Making White Appear White

Because most transparencies have some color bias or casting in the highlights, you must make a decision about color casts when whites are involved. Remember, white is a memory color, so it must be neutral or nearly neutral. Judging the whiteness of whites is how the eye detects color casts in highlight areas.

Since color scanners do not see like the human eye does, they tend to exaggerate color casts. Also, when viewing originals in a viewing booth, the human eye tends to ignore some of the cast it sees. Even if the viewing lights are 5000 Kelvin daylight balanced, some casts tend to be less noticeable to the eye than to the scanner.

The values read from the software densitometer tell you whether white will be white. If the dot percent readouts in an area of an image that is supposed to be white is in a nonneutral balance (as referred to the gray balance), then there is a color cast. (See Chapter 13 on gray balance.) There are three methods to deal with a color cast in white highlights: leave the cast as is, neutralize the cast, or cut the cast in half (see Figures 14.12a-c).

Full Neutralize Casts

Neutralizing a color cast is the most common method of correcting to white. For example, say that you have a transparency of a model in a white dress. Looking at the image in the viewing booth, it seems to be white (not pinkish or greenish white, just white). While separating the transparency, you adjust the overall tone curve at the highlight end to get a 5% cyan dot reading in the brightest part of the dress where you can see detail in the fabric. After this tone adjustment, the onscreen densitometer reads 5% cyan, 1% magenta, and 6% yellow. The entire CMY balance is 5% C, 1% M, 6% Y. Subtractive color theory tells you these values will make a green tone instead of white.

Figure 14.12a
The image as scanned to scanner neutral has a yellow cast in the highlight.

Figure 14.12b
The image with half of the yellow cast in the highlight removed.

Figure 14.12c
The image with the highlight fully neutralized.

The rules of gray balance in highlights require the magenta and yellow dot values to be 2-3% less than the cyan value to make a neutral white. By individually moving the magenta and yellow curves at the highlight, you can adjust until a reading of 6%, 3%, 3% CMY comes up. This balance of CMY value will reproduce the dress as white, and the cast is considered fully neutralized.

You also can accomplish a full neutralize highlight point result when a "set to value" control is available. By activating the "set to value" control, the spot where the cursor resides automatically changes to the neutral CMY values that you have entered.

Next it is very important to take some additional readings in other areas of the image, specifically in the whites. Check several spots to ensure that the entire cast has been neutralized. Be sure that you have not reversed the cast. Reverse casts occur when neutralizing one area of an image causes another area—which should be neutral—to develop a cast. Sometimes color casts can be corrected locally, but localized corrections can create an unbalanced visual effect. If you find reverse casts in an apparently even-looking color area, start over and reduce the amount of neutralizing you apply or use a half-cast method. Refer back to Figure 14.12c for an example of neutralizing a casted white.

Half-Cast

The previous example describes how to balance a casted white so that it reproduces as a neutral white. Another frequently used method of handling color casts in reproductions is the half-cast correction.

Half-cast removal subdues color casts without drastically changing the image's perceived appearance (see Figure 14.12b). Completely neutralizing an image's color cast can cause the reproduction to look too clean or different than the original. This situation is especially true in originals with moderate to heavy casts that extend up into the middletone areas, affecting many tones and colors. Also, not having perfectly neutralized whites reduces the risk of overcorrecting a highlight cast, which may reverse the cast and is not visually pleasing. Laying a proof next to an original that has an opposite color cast is a sure rejection because opposite color casts are easy to see. Also, by removing half the cast, the scanner's tendency to exaggerate casts is reduced.

Determining a half-cast correction involves subtracting what would be the full neutralized value from the original casted value. Then half the difference is added to the smaller of the two values. The resulting CMY values are used to adjust the image as a half-cast correction.

For example, to find the half-cast correction in the last row of values in Table 14.2, first establish what the values are for full neutral. Next, simply go halfway between the values for each color: halfway between the cyan of the casted original and the full neutralize is rounded to 5% C; halfway between the magenta of the casted original and the full neutralize is rounded to 6% M; halfway between the magenta of the casted original and the full neutralize is rounded to 5% Y. The resulting values are a half-cast correction between the original cast values and full neutralize. Use curves or the "set to" control to adjust the image to these values and the cast will effectively be cut in half. The half-cast method is highly recommended for many cast correction situations where full neutralize is not appropriate.

You should consider some additional points when correcting white highlights. If there is only one main white in a scene, such as a close-up of a person in a white shirt, it is best to neutralize any cast present. Remember, white is a memory color, and no customer likes pink or green whites. Select the brightest area of the white that carries all three printer's dots and adjust the area to a neutral balance.

When there are several whites in the same scene, analyze each white for its color balance to see whether it reproduces as a white. If each white is of a similar balance, it is best to neutralize the white with the least amount of cast. This method makes the lightest casts white and the heavier casts closer to neutral. Neutralizing the heaviest white overcorrects the lighter color cast whites, causing them to go beyond white balance and reverse their cast.

Beware of whites in the same image that are being lit differently; they may contain different types of color casts. Having two opposite casts in the same scene is called a cross curve. Cross curves cannot be globally (overall correction)

neutralized because reducing one cast increases the other. Whites in the same scene with different casts should be left as is, or if some corrections are needed, they should be adjusted using a half-cast method or individually using localized masking techniques.

Neutral Comparisons

The third method of dealing with whites is not so much a correction as a method of comparison. Scanners are set up to a neutral basic operating position designed to reproduce a neutral subject as a neutral, with a basic setup of highlight and shadow setting only. This relationship for reproduction is critical because if a neutral gray is reproduced with a color cast, then everything scanned will have a bias towards that cast. So, ideally, a properly calibrated scanner will reproduce a grayscale (without any special adjustments) as a matching gray from the standard operating settings.

Including a grayscale with your image while scanning will provide a useful guide to ensure that the scanner is scanning neutral and not introducing any casts during scanning. If the original being scanned has a color cast, the scanner will reproduce that cast as compared to

Table 14.2 Half-Cast

Casted Original Values	Full Neutral Correction	Half-Cast Correction
12% C, 5% M, 5% Y	8% C, 5% M, 5% Y	10% C, 5% M, 5% Y
9% C, 2% M, 9% Y	9% C, 6% M, 6% Y	9% C, 4% M, 7% Y
3% C, 3% M, 10% Y	5% C, 3% M, 3% Y	4% C, 3% M, 6% Y
4% C, 8% M, 6% Y	7% C, 4% M, 4% Y	5% C, 6% M, 5% Y

neutral so the reproduced cast should match the cast in the original. This method is called separating to scanner neutral and basically means that the scan will match the original image, including casts. Again, the operator can determine what is casted and what is neutral by the densitometer readouts and the rules of gray balance.

Because of the variety of software and hardware that perform color manipulations, you should familiarize yourself with all the controls to adjust highlight density and cast balancing within your software packages. If in doubt about how to handle a cast, separate to the standard scanner neutral (without any corrections) and analyze the color on the prepress proof.

Brightening with Highlight

A customer may submit a dark, low-key original to scan, saying, "It's all I have—can you help it?" Photographically speaking, the image may be several stops underexposed or dark. Stops are a photographer's way of describing tonal steps. Highlight density selection helps normalize dark originals. A good way to normalize dark originals is to make any apparent whites in the scene bright whites (even if they didn't photograph that way).

For example, a dark shot of a white car in a showroom may look muddy, and the highlight density reads a heavy .55 density. If you were actually in the showroom, you would know the car appears bright. A properly exposed original of this white car should read around a .30 density. Find the lowest reading point on the white car and adjust to a bright white dot percentage of 7% C, 5% M, and 5% Y. This adjustment makes the dull white of the original

reproduce as a bright white. Figures 14.13a and b demonstrate this lightening effect. Making an imagined white into a white will cause a drastic change in the reproduction. Be careful not to go too far. Work on the area of the lowest density to avoid creating any speculars. Brightening with highlight can improve a reproduction, but depending on the severity of the exposure problem, this technique may not completely normalize the reproduction.

Balancing for Surrounding Color

Viewing conditions can influence the eye to perceive a casted white as a neutral, as discussed in Chapter 13, "The Basics of Color Separations." In addition to viewing conditions, the colors that surround a white in a scene can also influence its appearance. When montaging—cutting out a part of one image for insertion somewhere else—take readings of the balances from the whites in the cutout area and the scene it is being pasted into. The white balance of each image should be neutral or at least of a similar balance. If the two pieces have opposite kinds of cast (like green and pink), a fake look will result as the eye is drawn to the cross curve casts of the two different whites (see Figure 14.14). Correcting for one white alters the other so that any neutralizing of white should be done before any collaging.

No White Highlights

Many novice color separators get off to a great start when handling highlights, only to run into problems when encountering a subject with no whites or bright areas, as shown in Figures 14.15a and b.

Figure 14.13a
The original image is dark in the highlights.

Figure 14.14
Often images collaged together have different casts in the neutral whites. You should white balance individually so that collaging will look more natural.

Figure 14.15a
An image with no whites cannot have a white highlight point.

Figure 14.13b
The dark image can be brightened by adjusting the lowest density to a bright white.

Figure 14.15b
If you try to create a white highlight point, the image will not reproduce properly.

During the prescan analysis, you should organize originals by exposure categories of high key, low key, or normally exposed. This procedure is handy for highlight selection, whether or not the transparency has a white. The viewing booth enables the operator to make the best possible analysis of an original's exposure quality because of its controlled lighting. Table 14.3 supplies approximate highlight densities for the three exposure categories. Use Table 14.3 to approximate a highlight density value if the original copy to be scanned has no white highlight or light tones. As the table shows, the majority of transparencies have a highlight density between .20 and .40.

If your separation program does not read out in density (most do not), you can purchase a dye or silver grayscale for transmissive subjects from a graphic arts supplier. Read each step of the grayscale with a standard graphic arts transmission densitometer and note the densities. Place the highlight portion (from 0.0 to.60) next to the subject being scanned and make a scan.

Table 14.3 Highlight Density Table for Transmissive Subjects

Density	Classification
.01 to .20	Specular highlight, high key, or overexposed transparency
.20 to .40	Standard highlight range for most normally exposed transparencies
.40 to .55	Low key, underexposed transparency

Using the suggested densities in Table 14.3, set your highlight in the appropriate grayscale step carrying the target density and separate. After the separation is done, crop out the grayscale leaving the desired image area. This grayscale highlight setting technique has been used with color scanners since they first came on the market. Using the grayscale to make an educated guess of the highlight density can be very effective for originals without whites. Refer back to Figures 14.6a-d to see how highlight density step selection works.

Setting up all scans for a .18-.20 highlight density and a shadow point at the last step of the grayscale is a technique for rapid scanning with minimum adjustment. While the scans are being done, the specular highlights of the finished scans can be trimmed to paper white using curves, histograms, or slider controls at a separate workstation. Because almost all specular highlights are below .20 density, setting the scanner at .18-.20 density will guarantee that all diffuse highlight detail has been captured. (The shadows also can be reset as needed with the guidelines discussed in the following section on shadow point in this chapter.)

Using this standard density scanning technique can speed up production of separations. A relatively inexperienced operator can make the scans while a person more trained in color can make adjustments at the off-line workstation. Software with automatic highlight and shadow selection also can be used for this production method because it will automatically search out the highest and lowest densities of the original.

Remember the highlight point does not always mean white. You can also find highlight points in areas of color, and you should be aware of how density and highlight dot percentages relate.

Vignetting Tone Method

A vignette, also known as a gradated tone, is a smooth tone that goes from light to dark. When these tones start from specular white, they can be used as guides to set the highlight point. The trick is to locate the spot where the highlight area goes from specular (no tone) to diffuse (light tone). If your original image contains a vignetted tone, take a reading in the spot where the color is just starting to become visible from specular white. Choose the proper C, M, or Y channel and adjust the highlight dot percent until the readout is 3 or 4%. That is the exact highlight density point at which the color starts to come in from the specular area. For an example of this technique, examine Figure 14.16. Figure 14.16 shows a close-up, black-and-white version of a vignette. Notice where the highlight dots start printing.

This vignetting tone technique also can be applied to colors. Secondary and tertiary colors can be used as highlight setting points. (See the section on color correction in this chapter.) A highlight setting point can be anywhere that small highlight-sized dots of cyan, magenta, or yellow are required. Setting a highlight in a color is an advanced technique that requires knowledge of CMYK color makeup and practice. Common colors used as highlight set points are magenta and cyan (in yellow colors), magenta (in green colors), and cyan (in red colors and fleshtones). The sunset in Figures 14.17a-d is an example of how secondary and tertiary colors as vignetting tones can be used as diffuse highlight points.

Pastels

Pastels, or light colors, are useful as highlight points if the operator knows their dot percentages. Pastels are made of dots in the 5-15 percent range—perfect for highlight setting. Beige, which is 5% C, 5% M, and 8-9% Y, is a handy pastel for a highlight setting. You can set the cursor or eyedropper in the beige color and adjust the highlight dot percentage until a 5% cyan and magenta and a 9% yellow appear on the readouts.

Drawing or Unwanted Color

Another highlight setting technique is to use the unwanted, or complementary, color. The complement is the opposing cast of a color. If the complement is added, the result is a darker, less pure (dirtier) color. For this reason, the complementary color also is called the unwanted color. Table 14.4 lists colors and their complements.

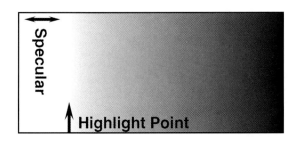

Figure 14.16
Where the tone emerges from a specular is the diffuse highlight.

Figure 14.17a
A sunset is a classic example of how to
set a highlight point in colored areas of
an image.

Figure 14.17b
The yellow channel is the primary color
and contains no highlight values.

Figure 14.17c
The magenta channel emerges from a
specular as a vignetting tone. The diffuse
highlight can be set at this point.

Figure 14.17d
The cyan channel emerges (further out than
the magenta) from a specular as a
vignetting tone. The diffuse highlight can
also be set at this point.

Even though the complement is called an unwanted color, unless a color is pure with no detail, there must be a complementary color to create shape and tone in the color. The unwanted color adds shading and detail to the object made of that color. The detail or texture that the complementary color adds to a color is called *drawing*. Additionally, as mentioned in the vignetting tone section of this chapter, the unwanted color can create light to dark shading in a color.

For example, a ripe orange typically is made of 80 to 100% yellow and 40 to 50% magenta with a minimum of cyan to make the detail in the skin of the fruit (see Figures 14.18a-c). The yellow printer is near solid and the magenta

Table 14.4   Colors and Their Complements

Color in Original	Complementary Color
Red	Cyan
Green	Magenta
Blue	Yellow
Yellow	Blue
Magenta	Green
Cyan	Red
Orange	Cyan
Brown	Cyan
Purple	Yellow

dots are too large to draw the fine texture on the fruit. The third color, the complement, has to make or draw the detail. In this case, the unwanted color—cyan—is a group of tiny dots around 5% in value. Because the drawing color's dots usually are very small, they can be used as highlight points. Magenta in green plants, magenta and cyan in yellows, cyan in gold, cyan in flesh, and magenta in sky horizons are possibilities of highlight setting points in color areas.

Missing details are an indication that the highlight setting values are too clean. An incorrect highlight setting causes the tertiary colors that draw details not to print. You should always be on the lookout for lack of fine detail or textures and understand that their appearance or disappearance is due to the highlight density selection.

Figure 14.18a
CMYK image.

Figure 14.18b
MYK image of oranges with no tertiary color (cyan). Notice lack of texture and drawing.

Figure 14.18c
The cyan plate provides texture and drawing in the oranges.

The Shadow Point

After selecting the starting density of the printable detail at the highlight point, you need to select the maximum density or the shadow density point to set the complete tonal range of the reproduction. This is the range of tones in the original to be printed on the press. The length of the tonal range set by the highlight and shadow points determines the contrast of the reproduction and should match the contrast of the original. Shadow point location is set by placing the 95% cyan dot in the original copy or a grayscale using the shadow end curves, sliders, or a density setting dial. The magenta and yellow values should move with the cyan movements and retain the color cast in the shadow.

Locating the Shadow Point

To find the shadow point, analyze the original for the area of maximum density. This is the darkest looking part in the scene. Shadow point density setting also is called black point because the area of maximum density is usually black. In a densitometer readout, this would be the area of lowest RGB or the highest CMYK percentage.

After taking several readings, select the highest density spot in the copy and adjust the entire CMY shadow dot percentage until a 95% cyan dot comes up on the readouts; let the magenta and yellow values fall. You are basically adjusting all the values of CMY but using cyan as the indicator of how far to make the adjustments. The density of the original, where the 95% cyan dot is set, is the shadow point.

Figures 14.19a-c were scanned with the same highlight points but with different shadow points. Figure 14.19b was scanned with normal contrast, setting a 95% cyan in the black point. Figure 14.19c was scanned with a 10% increase in contrast by setting 105% cyan, and Figure 14.19a was scanned with a 10% decrease in contrast by setting 85%. Notice that a shadow point which reads 100% or more appears to be too contrasted, and a shadow point in the 80% range appears to be too flat. Contrast is changed by adjusting the shadow point dot percentage. Each figure has the same highlight setting.

Along with setting the overall contrast of the reproduction, the shadow point represents the total ink density of the image. Total ink density is an important measurement for every separation that dictates print capability in regard to the printing conditions. Every type of printing/substrate combination has a maximum ink density limit so that the separations can print properly without drying or press problems. The total ink density for high-quality sheetfed printing is 350% total ink density (95% Cyan, 87% Magenta and Yellow, and 80% Black). When initially setting up an image for separation, the shadow point should be set for a 350% total ink density. After the basic setup is complete, any adjustments to the total ink density for printing/substrate conditions should be made at the end—right before separation or scanning. Techniques for this adjustment using UCR, GCR, and dot gain compensation are discussed in Chapter 15.

It is important to understand that the separation contrast should first be set up for optimum printing conditions. After the setup is complete,

Figure 14.19a
Minus 10 percent contrast.

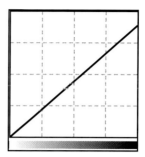

Figure 14.19aa
Curve of minus 10
percent shadow
point.

Figure 14.19b
Normal contrast.

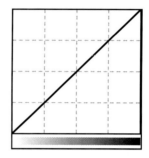

Figure 14.19bb
Curve of no change
in shadow point.

Figure 14.19c
Plus 10 percent contrast.

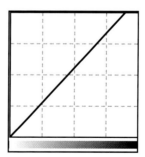

Figure 14.19cc
Curve of plus 10
percent shadow
point.

any adjustments for printing conditions are added at the end before scanning or separations. This way, the press conditions reverse the compensations (if done correctly), and the result is a separation with optimum contrast.

The Shadow Point and Color Saturation

The shadow point is set with the tonal range and resulting contrast in mind, but the strength of the heavy, saturated colors also depends on the setting of the last printing density. (Be aware that an inaccurate standard color calibration program also can cause incorrect color saturation.) Colors such as wine red, apple red, dark violet, and lemon yellow need at least one of the three CMY printers in the high 90% range or solid to faithfully reproduce that color. These are colors of high saturation—which means color strength.

After setting your shadow point, check any highly saturated colors that look like they may

need solid primary components. If none of the heavy saturated colors in the image exceed 95%, the shadow point setting is probably too low and incorrect. This method of checking your shadow with color saturation works well with transmissive originals (see Figures 14.20a and b).

Shadow Point Compensation

To help compensate for high-key, washed-out copy with no shadow point in the image area, increase the dot percentage set in the border. (For example, set 100% cyan rather than 95% cyan.) This procedure adds weight and contrast to the overall reproduction. Check any saturated colors to see if they have reached proper color strength as discussed in the preceding paragraph.

Shadow Points in Reflective Art

Reproducing watercolor or wash art and drawings can be tricky if the colors are not very saturated. Always scan them with a reflective

Figure 14.20a
Contrast is flat, which causes colors to be undersaturated.

Figure 14.20b
Normal shadow point; colors are properly saturated.

grayscale on the side to have a standard for adjusting your shadow point. Setting up on the last step of the reflective grayscale works well for color prints, but drawings have less range and saturation. You must select a shadow density to yield a contrast in the reproduction that matches the contrast of the drawing.

One way to find the shadow point density is to adjust the density setting to match a known color. Choose a color in the drawing that has the most saturation and find a match for it in a color chart. (Note the four-color dot percentages necessary to produce it.) For example, say an aqua color is made of 80% C, 5% M, and 30% Y. Enter the aqua color and adjust your CMY shadow point until the cyan value reads around 80%, the desired value for that color. Then go to the grayscale and find the step that reads 95% cyan and make sure that you have a neutral CMY balance (95%, 87%, 87%, 80% CMYK). Take several readings to be sure that you are not getting readings from an unusually grainy or textured spot in the art. (The texture of drawings can cause the readouts to vary wildly.) Next, go up the grayscale, and locate and note the step that contains the cyan middletone value (45-55%). Separate and proof the scan. If the color saturation is too strong or weak, adjust the shadow point. (If saturation is too high, decrease shadow dot%; if saturation is too low, increase shadow dot percentage.) If the art colors are saturated enough but somewhat heavy or weak in appearance, increase or decrease the middletone values to compensate.

Handling Shadow Casts

The standard program in a scanner compares the original copy to neutral. Because the color separation program is calibrated to reproduce a grayscale accurately, the original and any color casts are compared to neutral and reproduced as is. The balance of the shadow point affects the reproduction from the shadow down to the middletone areas. Unlike highlight areas, shadow casts are not as easy to see and do not need to be compensated for as much. Many times neutralizing out a shadow cast will shift the reproduction away from the look of the original. For shadow point reproduction, most scans should be done using the compare to scanner neutral method. This method has a very high rate of success because the color relationships of the original are not radically changed. Standard dot percentages for neutral comparison are cyan at 95%, yellow and magenta at 87%, and black between 70-80%. The location of the cyan at 95% sets the point of the shadow setting.

Figure 14.21a looks extremely colorful. The oranges are very orange and appealing compared to Figure 14.21b. Without seeing the original transparency, most people like Figure 14.21a. A trained color separator, however, notices the intense redness of 14.21a from the balance of the four-color readouts. The border of the transparency reads 94% C, 96% M, and 92% Y—hardly a neutral balance. The oranges read magenta in the 60% range, which, compared to their appearance in the original, seems over-saturated.

Using that information, we decided to neutralize the border of the transparency to 95% C, 88% M, and 88% Y. The result is 14.21b, which is not as colorful as 14.21a, but it matches the original transparency. Determining shadow casts and how to handle them takes experience. When in doubt about a shadow cast, neutralize it and wait for the proof.

Some originals contain overall casts that extend into the shadow areas. When the shadow point is set, you must choose to separate the original as the scanner sees it or to neutralize the shadow to negate any color casts in the original. Taking readouts of colors in this tonal area will reveal if the color casts in the shadow are needed for a reproduction match or if the cast

Figure 14.21a
Image of oranges, separated compared to neutral. The shadow cast of the original is unchanged.

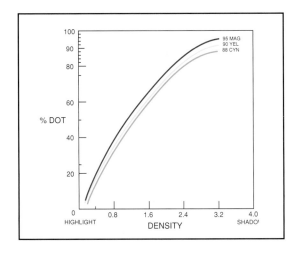

Figure 14.21aa
Curve of image color balance shows a red cast.

Figure 14.21b
Image of oranges with the shadow neutralized.

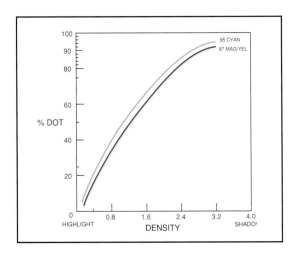

Figure 14.21bb
Curve corrections show shadows neutralized.

will be a problem (see Figures 14.22a-bb). Knowledge of CMYK color makeup is needed to determine which way to go. Half-cast correction is not usually effective. If you cannot decide whether to scan with or without the shadow cast, set up to scanner neutral and take what the calibration to gray gives you. If the reproduction has a definite color cast (not a highlight cast), like the one in the shadow, then neutralizing the shadow cast should yield a better reproduction.

If neutralizing makes a big change in the shadow dot percentages, be careful. Some colors may change and not match. Colors such as chocolate and deep, yellowish wood tones need 95-100% yellow; neutralizing the yellow back in a shadow may prevent matching these colors. Read known colors in the image to determine whether they match as is (non-neutralized) or whether they should be rebalanced by shadow-point neutralization.

Figure 14.22a
Red wagon image, separated compared to neutral.

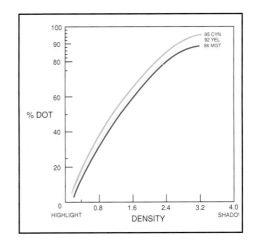

Figure 14.22aa
Curve for above; notice the nonneutral shadow.

Figure 14.22b
Red wagon image neutralized. This image looks more colorful but does not match the original.

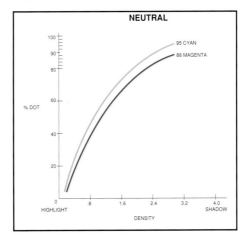

Figure 14.22bb
Curve for b.

Copy without a Shadow Point

Not all images contain a usable shadow point. The subject matter may not have a dark black object or heavily shaded area. Many washed-out, overexposed subjects lack a good black shadow. As with nonwhite highlights, a grayscale can be used in place of a reading area inside the image. The Dmax (density maximum) and tonal ranges are standard with reflective copy such as C prints, so setting a shadow point in the last step of a reflective grayscale usually yields a reproduction of matching contrast. (Typical C print densities are 2.2-2.5 density.) For transparency originals, the density ranges vary widely depending on the format (35 mm, 4" × 5", etc.) and photographic processing effects. If a good, dense, black shadow is not part of the image's subject matter, an alternative shadow setting point is the black border of the transparency. Because the border is unexposed film, it is the maximum achievable density that film can produce because exposure to light reduces density in a transmissive original. Adjusting to get a 95% cyan dot in the border usually will yield a reproduction of acceptable contrast.

Checklist

1. Remember to turn off any UCR or GCR functions to analyze the densitometer values of CMYK from RGB files.

2. Set your onscreen densitometer sampling setting to 3 by 3 or 5 by 5 pixels.

3. Perform color separation techniques in the same sequence each time.

4. The diffuse highlight (which is where tone begins) should have at least 3-5% dot.

5. The shadow point is the maximum density of the tonal range.

6. Be alert for specular highlights in the image and be sure they are paper white.

7. Check all whites for gray balance.

8. When in doubt about color casts, separate using neutral comparison (standard program) and examine a proof.

9. Select a highlight or shadow point from a grayscale if there are no obvious highlights or shadows in the original.

Final Word

Setting the highlight and shadow points is the most important decision when making a color separation. If you become proficient at locating these important densities, the majority of your reproductions will be acceptable without the need for any complicated color corrections.

The key to achieving a good reproduction from just endpoint selection is having a good standard calibration. The color separation system should be programmed to accurately reproduce the tone, gray, and color of a normal type of original by setting only the highlight and shadow points. This simple setup technique then will give you a good-looking reproduction of most originals with a minimum of effort. Chapter 17 discusses the importance of a calibration standards for color outputs.

Setting the highlight and shadow points is the most important decision when making a color separation. If you become proficient at locating these important densities, the majority of your work will be sellable.

Tone and Color Adjustments

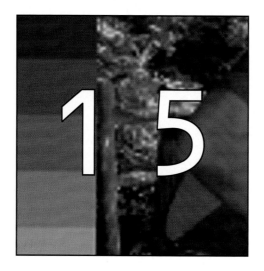

15

"Colorless green ideas
sleep furiously."

Noam Chomsky,
20th Century Linguist

In Chapter 14 we looked at the ways of setting endpoints to match image appearance. The next color separation techniques to be discussed are how to work with the interior areas of tonal range between the endpoints and the individual colors in the image. Adjusting between the endpoints of highlight and shadow is usually done to enhance and correct images of poor appearance. Three of these adjustment methods are called tone, cast, and selective color correction. After all color and tone adjustments have been made, proper reproduction must also address the issues surrounding proper sharpness.

During the prescan evaluation, as outlined in Chapter 12, you should sort your originals by quality of exposure and cast. The main concern is to figure out which scans are normally exposed and which need special handling. Subjects that are exposed normally, with no apparent tone or cast problems, usually reproduce best with a simple setup of highlight and shadow settings. If your color system is calibrated to faithfully reproduce normal originals, endpoint setup is all that is usually needed.

If the originals need improvement in areas of color and tone, then you should adjust your standard scanning method to correct the image at the scanning stage.

Correcting Tone

If you are going to reproduce an original image of poor quality, adjustments must be made to end up with a reproduction of normal appearance. As mentioned in Chapter 14, the highlight point is set to capture the fine tone, textures, and details of the bright areas of the image. The shadow point is set to create the weight and density of the darkest areas of the reproduction. Usually neither the highlight nor the shadow point setting alone is enough to improve the image adequately.

When separating images that are too light or dark, setting only the highlight and shadow endpoints will create a reproduction that matches the original. But since the original needs to be corrected for an improper contrast, the goal is not to reproduce a copy of the original—the goal is to adjust the reproduction so that it has the proper contrast. This goal is achieved by compensating between the endpoints of highlight and shadow.

Software for color separation is equipped with controls to modify the contrast of a subject by increasing or decreasing the amount of ink used in reproduction. You can compensate for abnormally dark subjects by printing a lesser amount of ink in the areas of the image that are too dense. Conversely, weak or washed-out subjects can be compensated for by printing an extra amount of ink in the areas that are lacking in color and weight. Because the endpoints are set for the brightest and darkest areas only, correcting over- or underexposed originals involves adjusting between the endpoints called middletones. The controls that make this compensation are called tone or gradation controls.

Gradation controls work in the area between 10 and 90 dot percent. As discussed in Chapter 6, curves can be used to adjust tones from highlight to shadow. Traditional analog drum scanners segregate controls into highlight, shadow, and gradation. Software-based curve controls are divided into quadrants of 25% to aid in color adjustment (see Figure 15.1).

The tonal scale is broken into 4 main quadrants that are marked by 5 points: highlight to quarter tone, quarter tone to middletone tone (sometimes called midtone), middletone to three-quarter tone, and three-quarter tone to shadow. Be aware that on high-end scanners and many software programs that the quarter tone can be called the highlights control and the three-quarter tone can be called the shadow control. Confusing isn't it? The only explanation given for naming the control that adjusts quarter tones a highlight control is that the terms were borrowed from old-model, high-end

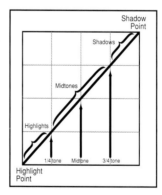

Figure 15.1
The standard software curve is divided into quadrants to aid in image analysis and adjustment.

scanners. Unfortunately, the mixing of tonal terms only promotes confusion. Be very aware of the tonal area that each control is designed to adjust. Do not use a quarter tone control to adjust the highlight point. Similarly, do not use the three-quarter tone control to adjust the shadow point.

One advantage of using curve controls is that you can grab the part of the curve you need with the cursor, thus helping eliminate mistakes in dot percentage adjustment. The visual nature of curves for adjusting tone and casts eliminates the potential for error that knob-type controls have.

With gradation controls, there are two main functions that can be accomplished: tone changes and casts changes. It is important that you understand the difference between these two types of adjustments. Each function has a specific visual effect selected according to the desired adjustment of the reproduction.

Using gradation controls to adjust tone makes the reproduction appear lighter or darker. Gradation controls affect the tonal strength of the reproduction in between the highlight and shadow points. In the tone change mode, cyan, magenta, and yellow are adjusted *together* to create a shift in the visual density of the reproduction. Since the adjustment is equal for each, no change in gray balance is caused, just a shift in lightness or darkness. The areas of the tonal scale that are adjusted and the amount of the movement determine the tone change's effect upon the reproduction. Now we will look at some typical tone changes.

Middletone

The center of the tonal scale is the middletone or midtone. The middletone is the 50% dot percentage, and the midtone control operates primarily between the 35% to 65% dot areas. Since the tonal adjustment is done on a smooth curve, moving the midtone can affect dot sizes beyond the 50% value, but the amount of the effect will drop off gradually as you get further away (see Figures 15.2a-f). Because of its location in the center of the tonal range, the midtone creates a physical increase or decrease of ink printing in the reproduction. Also, because it is in the middle, the midtone does not disturb the diffuse highlight settings or the maximum ink density of the shadow point.

The location of the midtone is established after the original's tonal range is set by the endpoint selection. The endpoints set the tonal range and the midtone falls between them at a specific density. The midtone is located where you find the 50% cyan dot in a neutral grayscale.

Locate the midtone's density position and compute the density difference from the highlight to midtone. Transmissive HL to MT range is between the standard midtone density and a .30 highlight density. Typical transmission midtones are located between .90 and 1.20 density. For reflective copy, highlight density is 0.0. Reflective HL to MT range is between the standard midtone density and a 0.0 highlight density. With reflective copy, the midtone is typically between .90 and 1.1 density.

Figure 15.2a
Standard image with no corrections.

Figure 15.2b
Standard image with plus 5% midtone correction.

Figure 15.2c
Standard image with plus 10% midtone
correction.

Figure 15.2d
Standard image with minus 5% midtone correction.

Figure 15.2e
Standard image with minus 10% midtone
correction.

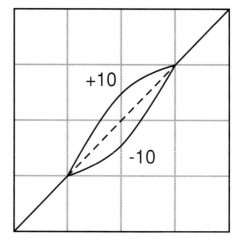

Figure 15.2f

Chapter 15

For example, if your color system can match standard transparencies with the midtone at 1.00 density, then the highlight-to-mid density range is .70. (1.0 midtone minus .30 highlight.) For all normally exposed transparencies with highlights up to .30 density, the midtone position will give a reproduction match of the original. If the original's highlight density exceeds .30 density, add the excess tone difference to the midtone position. Continuing the example with the 1.0 standard midtone, if the highlight of the original is .40 density, then the midtone should be set at 1.10 density (see Figure 15.3).

Setting the highlight-to-midtone range may be complicated, but this adjustment guarantees a reproduction of proper contrast. All efforts to include midtone placement in your image will avoid a reproduction where the overall appearance is too weak or too heavy.

This is a technique used by high-end scanner operators who consistently monitor their midtone positions using grayscales. Locating a midtone in an image without a grayscale is very difficult. The grayscale helps simplify the procedure. If you attempt to use this technique with desktop scanners you need to always scan a grayscale with your image, but many people may not feel the need to be so exact with their reproductions. Good endpoint settings are usually enough to produce a midtone at or close to the proper position.

Midtone Neutrality

The relationship of the highlight-to-midtone area is very important because the human eye is more sensitive to the brighter half of an image than to the darker half. When setting the highlight, a neutral highlight and shadow setup will produce a neutral midtone balance at the midtone density. Setting neutral endpoints and midtone is called the neutral comparison method. If there is a highlight cast in the original and the highlight balance is adjusted to compensate for it, the balance of the midtone will shift as well.

When checking the midtone density position, notice whether the gray balance is set for neutral or whether it represents a cast correction in the highlight or shadow. You have the choice to set the midtone to a neutral balance or leave it in a cast-correction balance. This decision is made depending on how far the casts in the original extend from the endpoints. Usually, it is recommended to initially separate with a neutral midtone, unless you can definitely detect a midtone cast by the dot percent readouts in the image.

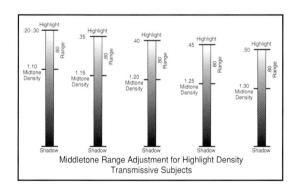

Figure 15.3
Same highlight-to-midtone range, different highlight points, and different midtone position.

For a standard neutral midtone, the cyan value is 12-15% over the magenta/yellow dot percents for transmission copy. There is a slightly smaller gray difference for reflective copy, usually 10-13%. Following the previous discussion on midtone setting (see Figure 15.3), an original with a highlight of .30 would have a midtone of 50% cyan, 38% magenta, and 38% yellow, each set at 1.0 density.

Adjusting the midtone changes the overall visual lightness or darkness of the reproduction. The amount of dot percentage change in a tone adjustment determines the amount of visual change in the reproduction. A rule of thumb for tone change is that a 5% tone move causes a good visual density step change. (Density step is referring to the change in density between the steps of a gray scale.)

Using the previous example, setting 55%, 43%, and 43% CMY instead of 50%, 38%, and 38% CMY would be a plus 5% midtone move. So if you want to darken or lighten a reproduction by one step, apply a 5% change. A 10% change would double the effect (see Figure 15.2). For extremely dark or washed out originals, midtone movements more than 10% may be required.

Quarter Tone

The quarter tone brightens or darkens the medium-to-light areas in an image. Quarter tone corrections center on the 25% tone and work primarily from the 15-35% portion of the tonal curve (see Figures 15.4a-f).

Quarter tone adjustment can be used to create a change in the reproduction by making the highlight-to-midtone area print more or less ink. Because the light areas print lighter, they will cause the darker areas to appear darker, thus increasing overall contrast. Conversely, increasing quarter tone values usually works well for compensating bright outdoor shots that are washed out or are weak in color. Excessive quarter tone changes may affect the diffuse highlight settings, so be sure to check and readjust the highlight areas if they are changed by a quarter tone adjustment.

Three-Quarter Tone

The three-quarter tone brightens or darkens the shadow areas of an image. Three-quarter tone adjustments center on the 75% tone and work primarily between the 65% to 85% portion of the tonal curve (see Figures 15.5a-f).

Three-quarter tone adjustment can be used to create a change in the reproduction by making the midtone-to-shadow area print more or less ink. Decreasing the three-quarter tone control reduces the amount of ink printed in the dark areas and brings out detail that is not easily visible in the original. Decreasing three-quarter tone values is also called opening up the shadows. Conversely, increasing three-quarter tone dot values will cause the dark areas of the reproduction to appear darker, which helps compensate for images that are below normal density. Excessive movement of the three-quarter tone control may affect the total ink

Figure 15.4a
Standard image with no corrections.

Figure 15.4b
Standard image with plus 5% quarter tone correction.

Figure 15.4c
Standard image with plus 10% quarter
tone correction.

Figure 15.4d
Standard image with minus 5% quarter
tone correction.

Figure 15.4e
Standard image with minus 10%
quarter tone correction.

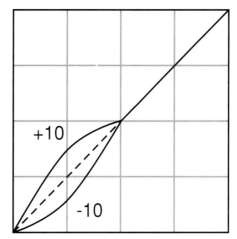

Figure 15.4f

365

Tone and Color Adjustments

Figure 15.5a
Standard image with no corrections.

Figure 15.5b
Standard image with plus 5% three-quarter
tone correction.

Figure 15.5c
Standard image with plus 10% three-
quarter tone correction.

Figure 15.5d
Standard image with minus 5% three-
quarter tone correction.

Figure 15.5e
Standard image with minus 10% three-
quarter tone correction.

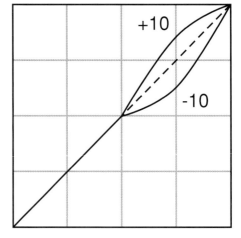

Figure 15.5f

366

Chapter 15

printing of the shadow point. Be sure to readjust any changes to the shadow point caused by the three-quarter tone control.

There is some dispute about how to establish the position of the three-quarter tone in an image. Specifically, the three-quarter tone point is the last visible detail before tone reaches black. Some believe that the three-quarter tone point is set by adjusting the shadow endpoint control. Others set the shadow point density in the darkest areas of the image and use the three-quarter tone controls to maintain visible shadow details.

In order to produce a good visual move, adjustments to both the quarter tone and three-quarter tone controls should be made in 5% increments. A good rule of thumb is to check the nearest endpoint (highlight or shadow) for movement if you make a tone move that is more than 5%. Make sure the gradation moves you make don't affect your endpoint settings unless you are sure of what you are doing. Additionally, do not make any gradation moves unless the endpoints are set correctly.

Correcting for Poor Copy

Because the endpoints are locked into reproducing highlight detail and total ink density, normalizing originals that are unusually light or dark should be done by using the tone controls. (Do this in combination with customizing the black printer, as explained in Chapter 16). Reducing the midtone and three-quarter tone

dot percents will open up dark copy. Increasing quarter tone and midtone values will strengthen a weak, washed out, high-key original.

When correcting images for poor reproduction tonal ranges, check the dot percent values of the areas that seem to be incorrect. Use the tone controls that operate in that tonal neighborhood to adjust lighter or darker. Five and ten percent moves will give definite results. If in doubt about which control to use, try the middletone first. The middletone is close to all areas between the highlight and shadow needing adjustment for correction. The quarter and three-quarter tone controls are more specialized gradation controls for working in a smaller bandwidth of the tonal range. Be sure you use the right controls for the situation.

Try to spot images with poor tone during the prescan analysis. Eventually, you should be able to correct poor originals with a tone adjustment before seeing the first proof. Software that holds separation setups in templates can be loaded with a tone correction for the very first separation. Your first proof may then be the only one needed.

Cast Correction

After the endpoints and tone reproduction are properly set, the separation software is parked in a neutral balance condition, which is the same neutral balance of the colorants of the output device for which the original is being separated. To determine whether an original has a color cast, the separator must know the CMY gray balance numbers for all areas of the tonal scale.

(2-3% more cyan in the highlights, 12-15% more cyan in the midtones, etc. See Table 15.1.) The known neutrals in the original are then examined for this particular CMY balance. Whites are the easiest neutrals to examine and check for gray balance in this way. If the whites look white in the original, take readings to ensure they will still be white upon output.

Adjusting the diffuse highlight balance will remove any casts in the brightest areas of the image, especially whites. Usually, this adjustment is all that you will need for cast correction because the eye detects casts mainly in the highlights. Cast-correcting the shadows will also shift the midtones and three-quarter tones from their standard balance. Either leave the shadows alone or go all the way and neutralize them. The endpoints of highlight and shadow can subdue color casts throughout the tonal range, but when even more control is needed, the quarter tone, midtone, and three-quarter tone dots of the individual CMY printers can be individually adjusted.

Tone adjustments change the tone reproduction of the original without upsetting the neutral balance of the scanner. Individual adjustment of the CMY endpoints and gradation controls change the neutral balance of the separation

Table 15.1 Standard Gray Balance Table

Density	Cyan Percent	Y/M Percent	Black Percent	Difference
.20	4	2	-	2-3% highlight
.30	10	6	-	
.43	20	13	-	
.60	30	21	-	7-10% quarter tone
.78	40	29	1	
.98	50	37	5	12-15% midtone
1.25	60	46	14	
1.58	70	57	25	
2.10	80	71	42	8-12% three-quarter tone
2.68	90	82	62	
2.80	95	87	75	7-10% shadow

software, which imposes a color bias to the reproduction. The color bias can act as an "anti-cast" that will normalize the gray balance of the original.

Making individual adjustments to the CMY printers (taking them out of neutral balance) is called a cast change. Like tone changes, cast changes lighten or darken the reproduction because they add and subtract ink. Cast changes add and subtract ink by moving the C, M, or Y printers individually, not together as a unit (like a tone move), so you must carefully examine the correction to determine if the amounts of ink added or removed will affect the weight of the final reproduction. Also, like tone changes, any cast adjustment will change the appearance of reproduction's neutrals and colors. Tone makes grays and colors lighter or darker. Cast changes may or may not change the weight of grays and neutrals. What cast will do, in all cases, is change the color balance of all neutrals and colors.

To compensate for an unwanted cast in an original, an opposite cast is used to negate, or neutralize, it. To determine which color balances negate casts, use the additive/subtractive colors arranged in a star pattern, as shown in Figure 15.6. The colors that are complements are on opposite sides of the star. (For example, yellow neutralizes a blue cast.) The highlight, shadow, quarter tone, middletone, or three-quarter tone controls are used to adjust a neutral balance. Which controls you use depends upon the area of the tonal curve that has the cast. Also, remember that gradation

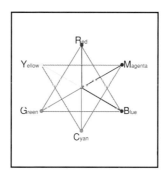

Figure 15.6
The color triangle shows the relationship of RGB and CMY.

controls should be used only after the endpoint adjustments are correctly balanced.

Let's perform a sample cast change to illustrate the cast change effect (see Figure 15.7). The image of a computer and keyboard has a full range of tone from light to dark. The endpoints are set up and the software is at standard neutral balance for the prepress proofing system. First, check the balance in the whites. Take several readings to get an average (make sure the densitometer is 3×3 or 5×5 pixel sampling). For this example, the readout was 6% cyan, 1% magenta and 5% yellow. There is a nonwhite balance and a green cast. At this point, the highlight can be corrected and balanced to a neutral such as 6% cyan, 4% magenta, and 4% yellow using the diffuse highlight controls. The correction is +3% magenta and -1% yellow in the highlight (magenta corrects a green cast).

A. The original image scanned as a transparency match. The customer required a product match of the computer and mouse which are neutral gray. Because the keyboard and mouse did not photograph as neutrals, they must be corrected to reproduce as gray.

B. An average reading in the mouse shows a cyan/blue balance of 22%C, 11%M, and 5%Y. Using curves or sliders functions, a subtraction of cyan and magenta is made with a slight increase in yellow to obtain a balance of 12%C, 8%M, and 7%Y. The mouse will now reproduce neutral and brighter due to the subtraction of cyan and magenta ink.

C. The keyboard is analyzed in the lightest and darkest areas due to its uneven lighting. Original readouts of 25%C, 10%M, 9%Y in the light area of the keyboard and 36%C, 18%M, and a 19%Y, in the dark areas are changed to 20% C, 10%M, 10%Y, in the light area and 30%C, 18%M, 17%Y in the darker areas. Care is taken not to disturb the highlight balance of the mouse and lighter keyboard areas otherwise localized masking must be used. The final result is gray mouse and keyboard.

Figure 15.7
Examples of cast and gray balance adjustments.

At this point, the midtone of the setup can be readjusted to neutral (from the highlight adjustment) or left alone. For those using gray scales with the setup, go to the midtone area and reset the gray balance. If you are using curves, but have no gray scale to use for a reference, then midtone readjustment is not an option.

After the whites are adjusted, check the balance of the gray computer in the scene. Average readouts yield 45% cyan, 40% magenta, and 40% yellow. Checking the gray balance chart shows this is not a neutral balance, but a red cast. The computer looks gray upon examination in a viewer, so the red cast must be neutralized. Also notice the weight of the area you are adjusting. Should you add ink, subtract ink, or add and subtract ink to correct the cast? (See Table 15.2.)

Table 15.2 Ink Adjustment for Cast Correction

Condition in Original	Correction
Casted and heavy for color	Subtract ink
Casted and weak for color	Add ink
Casted and normal weight	Add and subtract ink

For this example, the weight of the computer looked normal, so to correct the red cast, add and subtract ink to maintain that weight. The computer is then corrected to 50% cyan, 38% magenta and 38% yellow. The correction is +5%

cyan, -2% magenta, and -2% yellow, a correction of plus cyan (which is minus red) and minus magenta and yellow (which is minus red). Now the gray balance spread between the cyan and magenta/yellow is 12%, a neutral balance. The computer will reproduce as gray.

Care must be taken to not get neutralizing crazy. Not everything read by the densitometer that appears gray in an image will be perfectly neutral. Some whites may have different or opposite casts (a cross-curve). An object that appears neutral may read out neutral in one area and be casted in another area nearby. If you jump around from area to area neutralizing every spot as you go (putting one spot in balance at a time), you may be taking other areas out of balance. You could spend hours going around from point to point trying to make every reading point reproduce as a gray.

If you seem to be making excessive cast corrections to an image that looks fairly neutral in the viewer, just separate it with your standard program and compare it to scanner neutral. Make a proof and see if any unwanted casts are visible, note where they are, and reseparate them after making the appropriate cast corrections.

Determining and correcting color casts is one of the most difficult parts of color separating. Most transmission-type originals are naturally casted. Sometimes removing all the cast is visually pleasing, an improvement over the original. Other times a complete cast removal will change the appearance of the image too much, especially if a perfect match is required.

Sometimes a middle-of-the-road, half-cast removal approach will yield the best results. For reflective copy, most people want exactly what is shown. Reflective copy is normally neutral and reproduced as such. Figures 15.8a-f illustrate how midtone changes in the magenta affect the cast and neutrality of an image.

As a color separator, you must know the gray balance of the output device colorants being used before you can find out if a color cast exists in the original. A white-gray balance of 2-3% more cyan works in most cases (except newsprint). After a cast is determined, the decision must be made to keep it, subdue it, or completely remove it. Experience and knowing CMYK color values help to make this decision. If the cast is to be adjusted, the adjustment must be done without upsetting the tonal weight of the reproduction. Among all the steps involved with producing good, color separated reproductions, cast correction is the most difficult.

Building Color in CMYK

Professional color separators, such as scanner operators, are adept at working with additive and subtractive colors. Because they are converting photographic originals, printed matter, and art into the RGB and CMYK color spaces, a color memory for commonly used color combinations is developed. (See Chapter 16, "Commonly Used Memory Colors.")

Color combinations in RGB color space are difficult to envision and remember. How many people can visualize that a medium-weight gold color is 239, 217, and 79 in RGB color space? This is not a very descriptive way to have color described to you, unless you are a monitor or a film recorder.

The same gold color in CMYK color space is 6% cyan, 8% magenta, and 80% yellow. Put another way, the primary color of this gold is yellow at 80%, the secondary is magenta at 8%, and the tertiary color is cyan at 6%. If you work with color separation on a regular basis, and someone asked you for a CMYK callout of a light- to medium-weight gold color, chances are that a callout similar to the one mentioned would be made. CMYK color descriptions can be constructed in your "mind's eye," if you are familiar with how they are built. Now let's look at how this is done.

The primary color (in CMYK color space now, not RGB) of a CMYK color combination is the printer of the highest dot percentage. For example, the primary color of a deep red would be the magenta printer, which would be at or near 100%. The amount of the primary helps determine the hue and strength of a color.

Secondary colors add weight and shape to the primary component, and can also shift the hue of the overall color. For example, adding a small dot percentage of magenta to 100% yellow makes tone appear in the color and strengthens the yellow color (see Figure 15.8). As the level of magenta goes from 40% to 60% in dot size, the resulting color is orange. When the magenta dot percentage reaches 90-100%,

Figure 15.8a
Standard image with
no corrections.

Figure 15.8b
Standard image with
plus 5% magenta midtone
correction.

Figure 15.08c
Standard image with plus
10% magenta midtone
correction.

Figure 15.8d
Standard image with
minus 5% magenta midtone
correction.

Figure 15.8e
Standard image with
minus 10% magenta
midtone correction.

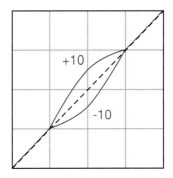

Figure 15.8f

Tone and Color Adjustments

the resulting color is orange-red. Here, the secondary color added tone and weight to the yellow primary, and as the ratio of the secondary to the primary increased, the hue of the color combination changed from yellow to orange to orange-red (see Figure 15.9).

Tertiary colors add additional weight and detail to two-color combinations. Also called the complementary color, the tertiary has two important effects upon the now three-color combination.

First, the tertiary color is a graying component. Combinations of cyan, magenta, and yellow make gray. If a color has all three printers in it, there is a gray component present (see GCR and black generation, Chapter 16). Any graying done to a color darkens it, so that adding a tertiary color will darken or "dirty up" a color. The amount of the tertiary determines the color's purity. The addition of the tertiary graying component (also called unwanted color or complementary color) reduces the purity of a color (see Figure 15.10). Because CMYK inks are not pure, the addition of the tertiary printer moves the color towards reddish-brown. If a reproduction is criticized for being too dirty, that means that the levels of the tertiary must be diminished.

The opposite critique is that the reproduction is too clean, which means there is a lack of tertiaries and the pure colors are too bright and clean. The visual look of clean, bright, tertiary-free color is called "cartoon color." This clean-looking version of color is desired for some types of work, but not for reproductions demanding realism and exact color matching.

In addition, tertiary colors add tone and fine detail to the color combination. Also called drawing, the tertiary color dots are normally small and are used to make fine detail, such as textures in colors with strong primaries and secondaries (see Figures 15.11a-e). Notice that in the image of the flower, the yellow and magenta plates print with large dots. The drawing of detail (texture) in the flower is accomplished by the small dots of the tertiary color, the cyan printer.

The presence of the complementary color is related to the calibration of the color program and the density selection of the diffuse highlight. If the color-correction levels of the basic program setup are too clean, some tertiary colors may be missing from areas that need drawing. A cartoon color condition may exist when it is not desired. If the calibration program is too liberal with the amount of

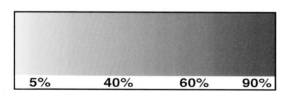

5%   **40%**   **60%**   **90%**

Figure 15.9
The secondary color (magenta) adds tone in the highlights and shifts hue as the amount of magenta added to yellow increases. Yellow is 100% throughout.

5%   **30%**   **60%**

Figure 15.10
The tertiary color (cyan) adds weight to the red color. Yellow and magenta are 100% throughout.

Figure 15.11a
Original image of a flower.

Figure 15.11b
The Yellow plate
of figure 'a.'

Figure 15.11c
The magenta plate
of figure 'a.'

Figure 15.11d
The cyan plate
of figure 'a.'
Notice the cyan
drawing in the
texture of the
flower.

Figure 15.11e
The magenta and
yellow plates
only. Notice the
missing texture
provide by the
cyan plate.

tertiary colors at standard program, then the reproductions may tend to look dirty in the clean colors. Drawing or detail will be fine, but the bright colors will not sparkle in the reproductions. Also, if the diffuse highlight setting is wrong, the complementary colors will be missing or too large. Remember that tertiary colors can be used as highlight setting points in some situations (see Chapter 14, highlight section-drawing or unwanted colors).

The black printer is added to colors for the same reason it is added to the reproduction: to add weight and richness to dark areas. If black is printing with a three-color combination, it is helping the tertiary color create shading and drawing. If your reproduction appears dirty, trim back the black highlight control 5% or more (see Figures 15.12a and b). Selective color correction can also be used to take black out of colors that are too dirty, or help put weight in colors that need black.

Adding black to make a particular color hue is only done as a matter of taste. Some color separators do not use black in food reproductions; instead, some prefer to use complementary or tertiary colors for shading. Some proofing systems reproduce certain colors better by using black as a tertiary instead of the colored complement. An example of this formula would be deep violet. Using black instead of yellow (as a tertiary for a violet color) yields a richer, darker violet color. Having yellow as a complement creates a greenish cast on the violet color.

Black ink makes the violet appear more neutral. For dark reds, using cyan, black, or cyan and black as the complement is another matter of taste and preference. The topic of complements in reds will cause a good argument among color separators.

If you plan to get serious with color separating, or just want to make some decent scans, the more you know about CMYK the better. Practice looking at colors and guessing their CMYK equivalents. Check your assumption with a

Figure 15.12a
The original image where there is black in the reds.

Figure 15.12b
The reds are brightened by removing the black.

color chart. Estimate by strength of primaries, secondaries, and tertiaries. With practice, you will be able to know the approximate CMYK breakdown of the colors you are reproducing, and you will gain confidence as a color separator.

Selective Color Correction

Some models of scanners and some color separation software brands have the ability to control the CMYK values of certain colors in an image. This type of control is called color-selective color correction. (Not to be confused with color correction, which is using any means to adjust color.) The colors of the original that can be adjusted are cyan, magenta, yellow, red/orange, and blue/violet. Using the selective color correction controls, the amount of yellow, magenta, cyan, and black ink can be increased or decreased to globally adjust the appearance of that color. A global correction is one that affects the whole image; a local correction is one that affects just one specific area (see Figures 15.13a-b).

The strength of the color correction control depends upon the design of the control. If the control is preset for color selectivity, colors with the highest saturation or strength will be the easiest to adjust. If a single component of the color is around 100%, then the selective controls will easily affect it. Colors with low saturation, such as pastels or fleshtones, will not be easily affected by color-selective color correction. Be aware that if you color-correct a

Figure 15.13a
The original uncorrected image.

Figure 15.13b
A global color correction affects the entire image.

color of low saturation, any higher saturated colors of a similar hue will be corrected even more, as illustrated in Figures 15.14a-b. Subtracting magenta and yellow to make the fleshtone less warm de-saturates the deep red colors of the jacket.

Be aware that selective color correction of black may not be very effective in some software. Since the black component is created by the presence of CMY in a color (to get good control of the black in a color) some tertiary component must usually be present. Otherwise, for example, trying to add black to a deep violet (100% cyan and 80% magenta) that has no tertiary yellow may not be possible. Since there is no tertiary component to create gray, the program will not produce any black. We have found that the ability to add black with little or no tertiary color varies from program to program. To get control of the black, sometimes you must add some tertiary color also.

Selective color correction only affects the colors in the bandwidth of the particular control. For example, the cyan control affects cyan colors and some of the violet colors. The difference between cyans and violets is the amount of magenta printing with the cyan. As the ratio of magenta to cyan approaches 40%, the color becomes more of a blue(violet) than a cyan. At this point, both the cyan and blue(violet) color-correction channels can have an effect on the color.

A similar sharing of color happens with the red and magenta color-correction channels. As the ratio of yellow to magenta approaches 40%, the magenta color starts to become red/orange.

Both color-correction channels will have an effect on the color.

Although it seems unlikely, the yellow and green color-correction channels also have a bandwidth crossing. As the amount of cyan in yellow approaches 40%, the color starts to become green and can be adjusted with either the yellow or green controls.

Cross-bandwidth color-correction effects can be troublesome. They require going back and forth between colors in each channel that needs and does not need corrections. Fortunately, situations that require corrections to multiple colors that cross channels are rare. If there are large amounts of similar colors needing selective correction, then localized masking is best (if you want to avoid changing colors you do not wish to change with global controls). Consider localized masking in situations where you have fleshtones and reds or orange colors needing adjustment, as in Figure 15.14 a-b.

Standard color-selective, color-correction controls only work on the colors in the image for which their bandwidths are tuned. These controls do not affect grays or the tone reproduction of the image. Because the tone and cast controls affect both tones and colors, they should be adjusted before any selective color corrections are done. Otherwise, overcorrecting of colors will result.

More advanced, selective color-correction controls have variable bandwidths, which can increase or decrease the scope of global correction. Variable bandwidths prevent the cross-channel correction problems previously mentioned.

Figure 15.14a
An original image without corrections.

Figure 15.14b
Correcting low-saturated fleshtones
affects higher saturated red colors.

A very handy and powerful selective color-correction control feature is the ability to create your own color-correction channel. By placing a cursor or the scanner analyze beam in a colored area and then activating a color-selection control, the CMYK balance of the color becomes the target color for correction. Coupled with this type of selective color-correction is an adjustable bandwidth control. The range of correction from the selected color in the image is determined by the bandwidth control. For example, the color-correction effect can be at a tight band within a few percent of the selected color or at a wide band of 20-30%. There is no limit to the corrections that can be made with this type of control. Special product colors can

be easily isolated and adjusted to match the colors of the actual product. Fleshtones can be normalized, even if the person in the image is wearing a red shirt. Cross-bandwidth problems are no longer a problem. You can even isolate a single step out of a gray scale using this type of control. Having a selectable color-channel control reduces the need for a mask in many color-correction situations.

Sharpness

As mentioned in Chapter 13, the sharpness of a reproduction is good if it is not noticeable. Reproductions that are too soft, grainy, or oversharp (appears fake) must be reseparated and resharpened. (Murphy's law of scanning states that the reproductions that have sharpness problems are the ones in which the color is perfect on the first scan.) Sharpness has little to do with tone reproduction, gray balance, or color. But if this parameter is not properly set, your eye-popping color proof will end up rejected.

Amount of Sharpness

The main consideration for sharpness is realism. Oversharpening destroys realism; this occurs when the electronic sharpness enhancement becomes visible to the eye. Your perception of an oversharp reproduction can be simply a feeling of an image being "too crisp looking," or a more specific feeling, such as white lines around tree branches, black lines over exaggerating a person's eyelashes, excessive grain in a pale sky, or plastic-looking lettuce.

Visible sharpness effects come in the form of white lines around dark areas and black lines around light areas. These lines are called halos (see Figures 15.15a-c). Halos are the effects of the sharpness-circuitry working.

On the microscopic level, the edges of the halftone dots are shaped to create these white and black surround lines called halos. On the macroscopic level, any edges or lines appear sharper and bolder (notice the line edges in Figure 15.15c).

When the sharpness halo sizes are optimal, they are not visible to the eye, only to the mind. We see them, but we don't comprehend them as being an unnatural part of the image.

When the halos become visible to the eye and the reproduction loses its realism, the sharpness amount control will reduce the size of the halo. Therefore, the most important control to the realism of the sharpness (in a reproduction) is the volume or amount control.

Sharpness works from contrast. The separation software analyzes the contrast between neighboring pixels. To enhance apparent visual sharpness, the software circuitry exaggerates the difference between contrasting areas. To accomplish this, the sharpness software puts a barely visible dark line around light areas, which enhances visual contrast and a barely visible white line around dark areas.

If an image is lacking contrast, the sharpening effect will be diminished. As the contrast of image increases, the effect of sharpening increases. Figures 15.16a-b illustrate the effect of contrast on sharpness. Both images have the same amount of sharpening applied but the image with greater contrast looks sharper.

Be sure to view your image at 1:1 on your monitor when making any sharpness adjustments. Viewing at a lower magnification does not give an accurate preview of the results because the displayed image does not display all the important pixel data.

Figure 15.15a
Normal sharpening.

Figure 15.15b
More sharpening.

Smooth and Grain

Some sharpening software brands supply smoothing controls and sharpness volume controls. While the volume controls work on the areas of heavy tones and high contrast, the smooth controls work in the areas of smooth tones and low contrast. Also called the grain control, smoothing defeats any sharpening enhancement in areas that should reproduce smooth—such as vignettes, skies, and fleshtones (see Figures 15.17a-b).

Figure 15.15c
Oversharpening.

Figure 15.16a
A flat image does not show sharpness well.
Contrast affects sharpness.

Figure 15.16b
This image has the same sharpness setting
but the increase in contrast makes it
appear much sharper.

Figure 15.17b
Applying
smoothing to
sharpness
adjustment helps
fleshtones.

Smoothing should be separately adjusted, according to magnification and condition of the original. Enlargements past 1,000% and large sizes of high-speed films need smoothing. Smoothing also helps in enlarged color prints, as they tend to break up past 250% magnifications.

Threshold

Another handy sharpness control is the threshold adjustment. Much like the bandwidth control, threshold determines the scope or areas in which sharpness volume and smooth controls operate.

Ideally, sharpness should enhance the areas of high contrast and smooth should work in the areas of low contrast. The threshold control sets where the smooth control works in regard to contrast. If the threshold were open to maximum, the smoothness would operate in the high contrast areas with the sharpening enhancement. The result would be the smoothing effect negating some of the sharpening effect. Threshold at minimum would put smoothing into only the areas of the lowest contrast.

The best way to use the threshold control is to first adjust the sharpness enhancement with threshold off. Then adjust the smoothness volume and threshold amount to subdue grain and keep low contrast areas unsharpened (see Figures 15.18a-c).

Size vs. Sharpness

The amount of sharpening used is proportional to the magnification or reduction of the original being reproduced. Manufacturers of high-end scanners give recommended sharpness settings for every increment of magnification. Extensive tests are done to yield scans that are both sharp and smooth.

As part of the calibration process, you should test for the amount of sharpness versus the amount of magnification. Run the volume control high enough to go over-sharp and then back it down until you find the optimum position. (Going over-sharp gives your eye a reference to how far you can go.) You should need less sharpness for big enlargements because the halos and details are enlarged. After finding your base settings, take a 35mm transparency and enlarge it 200%, 500%, and 1,000% (more if possible). Crop the larger sizes down a bit if you wish. Output and make proofs. Does the apparent sharpness of each enlargement

Figure 15.18a
Original image.

Figure 15.18b
A good threshold setting allows sharpness to sharpen the tower without affecting the sky.

Figure 15.18c
A poor threshold setting allows sharpness to affect the sky and the tower.

Tone and Color Adjustments

match? If not, make adjustments to the volume controls and smooth for graininess. Repeat until the large images look as sharp and smooth as the smaller images. Of course with the biggest enlargements, grain appearance versus sharpness is relative, and you may have to make some compromises in quality. Testing sharpness versus magnification will show you the limitations of your color reproduction system in regard to sizing range. Discover your system's limitations by pushing the limits and examining the results.

Eventually, you should have a sharpness setting menu for the types of originals you separate. Have separate sharpness settings for transmissive and reflective originals, too. This is the starting point for all the separating you do. Be alert for exceptions: some originals are sharpness "sponges" and still appear soft at standard settings; others may oversharpen easily. Do not modify your standards unless a majority of images have problems at that setting.

Sharpness can make or break a color reproduction. Find the best type of software for sharpening the types of images you typically reproduce. Take the time to experiment and test because applying the right amount of sharpness is an art, as well as a science.

Postscan Analysis

Before you output files, double-check them for the aim points you used while making them. If you followed the rules of making good color, you should receive a great looking reproduction, and the densitometer will verify that. However, results may not always be optimal.

Upon examination of the separated reproduction, you may decide to start over from scratch. Sometimes one adjustment that was made negated or overcorrected another. When making complex corrections and color adjustments, you may have chosen the wrong direction and ended up with unexpected results.

The postscan analysis is the time to examine your work before going to the output stage. At this point, the quality of your reproduction should be systematically checked to determine if a proof or other type of output should be made. While the image can be viewed on the screen, the densitometer will ultimately answer the questions involving the quality of the reproduction. You should take the time to perform this quality control operation for every image reproduction you do.

Postscan Analysis on Screen

The reproductions should be viewed the same way each time on the screen—from the same distance with the same background or room lighting. This brings some continuity into the viewing situation. You should get accustomed to these conditions, so it is a good idea to keep the conditions the same. The original images should be nearby for reference, ideally in a properly lighted viewing area.

First, analyze the image for dirt, scratches, bubbles, and moiré patterns. These defects are more difficult to see onscreen than in film. Using the magnifying glass tool, zoom up to a

1:1 viewing mode. Traverse the entire image. Dirt can be easily cloned out. Moirés can be softened using blur or smudge, but you must know that the moirés were there to begin with. If the image was scanned in oil on a drum scanner, look for bubbles. They will look like black rings of various sizes. Bubbles may be single or in clusters. Look for bubbles especially near the image's edges.

While zoomed in, look for sharpness halos and grain texture. (Remember that halos appear between the areas of highest contrast.) If either is excessive, you must rescan with lower sharpness settings. If the reproduction looks smooth, but halos exist, you may decide to remove them by pixel copying.

Next, zoom back until the image fills the screen; stand back five feet and look at the contrast of the scan. After you work with the same screen and viewing conditions for a while, you become a very good judge of whether the contrast of the scan is acceptable. If the reproduction appears too dark or washed out, get some densitometer readings of your shadow point and saturated colors to see if they are above the 90% dot range. If the shadows and saturated colors are reading less or more than the 90% to solid range, reseparate it and repair the separation contrast.

Use the densitometer and check the highlights for proper dot percentage. Are any specular areas paper-white? If they hold a printable dot, you will have to trim it out. Read the diffuse highlight areas you selected when separating. Do they hold the correct dot sizes? If the highlights are too full, you can trim them back

a few percentage points with curves or any other diffuse highlight controls available.

If your highlights are too clean and missing detail, you must rescan at a lower density selection. Adding dot percentage with curves (to put dots into a missing diffuse highlight) will not bring back the missing detail that the scanner did not pick up.

Check the neutrality of the highlight, especially any white areas. Make any necessary adjustments to the individual cyan, magenta, or yellow channels. Check the neutrality of any known grays. A cast adjustment may be necessary.

Examine the black printer's setup. Is the shadow point between 70 and 80%? Is there black printing in the midtone neutral areas? Are the pure colors clean or dirty with black?

Check the dot percentage of any memory or special colors. Do not expect the screen to tell you whether a red apple is red enough. Use the densitometer and a color chart to verify if the CMYK color readouts will yield a color match.

You must decide from the postscan analysis information whether to rescan the original with adjustments, keep the scan as is, or keep the scan and do some correcting to solve any problems you have found.

Producing a sellable set of color separations takes skill, patience, and knowledge of color and the printing process. You should not expect to hit a winner the first time every time, but if you use the techniques outlined in this chapter, your results will be good from the start. As in all situations, practice makes perfect.

Take the time to examine your results carefully and learn from your mistakes. Make every mistake possible and don't repeat it. Patience and practice reward you with color reproductions of excellent quality and beauty.

Checking the Separation Films

If you have access to the imagesetter part of the reproduction step, you can see your images in black and white form. A careful examination of the separation films offers the last chance to detect any reproduction errors before making the prepress proof or printing plates. This examination is much more difficult than a screen examination, but the goals are the same. Instead of a densitometer readout, you use a magnifier to physically examine the halftone dot sizes on the separation films. View the separation films on a light table that is large enough to hold a full sheet of film so that you can look at them from a macroscopic viewpoint.

When you view the films from a distance, you first should look for dirt, moiré patterns, scratches, or bubbles in the reproduction. This is especially true for original copy that has been greatly enlarged during scanning. These problems have nothing to do with color, but always result in electronic retouching to remove them. If there is too much dirt or moiré, a rescan will be warranted.

Even if the films are rejected because of dirt or moiré patterns, you should continue to judge the color of the reproduction. This way, you know whether the color setup for that original is acceptable or if adjustments are needed during the rescan. Remember that a blown out diffuse highlight that is too clean must be rescanned to capture the diffuse highlight detail.

Using a magnifier loop, or glass, examine the dot sizes in the highlights and shadows for proper values. Check any specular highlights. Look for the position of the shadow point, the 95% cyan dot. Examine the saturated colors to see if they are near solid in the proper printers.

Each separation film should have a good range of contrast whether it is in negative or positive form. However, this does depend on the color and contrast of the original subject; but a colorful, normally exposed image should produce four separation films with cyan, magenta, yellow, and black printers that exhibit good contrast from light to dark. If two or more printers appear flat, the shadow point may be incorrect or there may be an overall color cast. Take a good look at the original and determine whether this might be a problem. With positive films, if the overall contrast is good, the cyan printer should look like a good black and white halftone.

Next, look for gray balance. With negatives, the cyan film should appear lighter than the magenta and yellow films in neutral areas. This difference is for proper gray balance, with the cyan printer should be printing more than the magenta and yellow. In a negative-type film, more ink prints in the lighter areas. With positive films, the cyan will appear heavier than the magenta and yellow in gray areas. Be sure you examine any neutral areas in the image.

The black printer should be of good contrast, even for high-key images. Use a magnifying loop and check the darkest shadow for a black dot between 70 and 80%. Notice also where the black highlight comes into the image.

Look at all four films for relative sharpness (from a distance and up close). Check for white and black halos. Is the grain too visible? Is any detail missing? Are the flesh tones and vignettes smooth?

Through careful examination of the separation films, you can decide whether the color reproduction is ready to proof or needs some adjustment or another scan. Examining separation films is a quality control step that can save expensive remakes at the printing press. Take the time to look at your films whenever possible if you wish to develop this valuable skill.

Checklist

Before you perform any tone or cast corrections you should make sure that you have some basic issues addressed such as the following.

- Classify images as high key, low key, or normal to determine if tone changes are needed.

- Make sure proper highlight and shadow point have been selected before performing any tone and cast adjustments.

- Perform tone and cast adjustments before any selective color correction.

- After making any tone and cast adjustments make sure the highlight and shadow points have not moved from their original setting. If necessary, reset the endpoints.

- If in doubt about color casts, separate using neutral comparison (standard program) and examine a proof.

- If important detail has disappeared into the shadows, reduce the three-quarter tone.

- Set your on screen densitometer sampling setting to 3×3 or 5×5 pixels.

- When making gradation changes, read from your on-screen densitometer what area of the tonal curve you need to affect to correct the image.

- Make tone moves in 5% increments.

- Memorize the gray balance table.

- Classify CMYK colors as primary, secondary, and tertiary components.

- Test sharpness settings for various magnifications. Watch for halos.

- When cast-correcting, be aware of how much ink you are adding or subtracting and adjust the overall tone accordingly.

Final Word

From a scanner operator's perspective, tone and cast correction controls are there to help improve poor originals, not fix bad scans of normal originals. The prescan analysis will tell which images need precorrecting of tone and cast. Don't use tone and cast corrections when setting proper endpoints will do the job. If for some reason you can not properly scan the original, manipulating the tonal curve of the image will enable you to normalize the image if you follow the basics of endpoint selection and tone and cast adjustment.

Remember, most programs allow you to make adjustments to the predicted CMYK values while you are in RGB.

Working with tone and cast adjustments takes practice as well as attention to details, and having a knowledge of CMYK values and gray balance values. You have to do a lot of analysis of correction results to develop an eye for tone and color. Use the proof analysis techniques outlined in Chapter 12. With time you will find that color analysis becomes second nature. The alternative is guessing at your color corrections rather than *knowing* how to make them.

Fine Tuning
Separations

16

"Shape without form,
shade without color;
Paralyzed force,
gestures without motion."

T.S. Eliot

The basis for good printed color rests in tone, neutrality, color, and detail. These parameters have been covered in previous chapters, which you should read before this chapter. You should especially read the beginning of Chapter 14 in which the separations setup in Photoshop is discussed.

You can achieve the best results for the printing process by fine tuning your separations. The craft of color involves converting photographic and art originals into color separations that will reproduce properly and easily on a printing press or output device. As with any craft, there are many little nudges and tweaks that a color separator will add to the process to get that little extra out of the final print. Sometimes these extras are based on the operator's intuition or are added merely by chance. Mostly, a separator's bag of tricks is firmly grounded in basic color theory.

In this chapter, you'll find some additional ways to keep your color optimum—adjusting the separations for printing can involve dot gain compensation, tone changes, UCR and GCR functions, and special color corrections. Also, to get the best color, you need to use all the ink available, including the black printer. Getting the most out of the black printer is covered here, too.

The Black
Printer (K)

The purpose of the black printer (for color separation) is to compensate for combinations of cyan, magenta, and yellow, which do not make a very good black. Adding a separate black printer gives additional weight to the shadow areas, and it enables the reproduction to have a more natural-appearing black. Since the dark areas appear darker, the light areas will appear lighter and the printed reproduction's visual contrast will increase. The addition of a black printer on the press increases the Dmax (maximum density possible) from 1.5 with CMY to as much as 2.0 density (in which all four colors print).

The separation software does not analyze the original copy separately for its black component because photographic originals do not have a black dye layer. Instead, the black information is derived from the RGB color input signals. Whenever the three signals are equal—a neutral condition—the black printer information is generated by the separation software. (For a more detailed description of black printer generation, see Gary G. Field's *Color Scanning and Image Systems,* © 1990.)

For the color separator, the black printer presents yet another way to create and enhance tonal steps in addition to using the cyan, magenta, and yellow printers. This section examines the black printer's contributions to the separation process. Even though this printer has a different relationship to the CMY inks and the color separation process, you can't get your best four-color reproduction without an optimized black separation (see Figures 16.1a-c).

The typical black printer operates in the midtone to shadow half of the tonal range. That is why the black separation is also called a "half black." While the CMY printers are busy making tone and color throughout the entire tonal range (from highlight to shadow), the black printer is working hard to enhance all of the tonal steps in the darker half of the reproduction. The black half prints blacker and the light half appears brighter.

The CMY printers are locked in a critical relationship called gray balance. From light to dark, throughout the tonal range, cyan, magenta, and yellow must be in balance to avoid color casting. The black printer is naturally neutral and helps to cover up many of the CMY printers' gray balance errors.

When the total ink density needs adjusting for press conditions, the black printer becomes the most important printer of them all. With GCR or UCR, CM&Y are subdued and the black printer carries the tone and gray responsibility of the entire reproduction. Face it, CM&Y look pretty attractive together, but when you want vivid, eye-popping color, you are nowhere without the black printer.

Is black a color or an absence of all colors? When you are dealing with color separations, the answer is both.

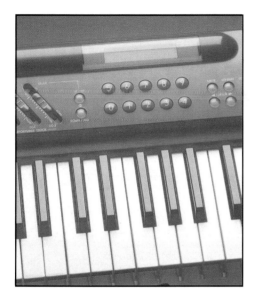

Figure 16.1a
An image without the black printer.

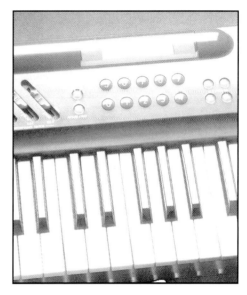

Figure 16.1b
The black printer.

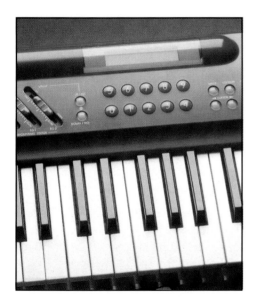

Figure 16.1c
The black printer adds weight and
detail to the image.

Setting the Black
Printer's Contrast

Just as the highlight and shadow density
settings of the cyan, magenta, and yellow
printers affect the visual density of the reproduction, the density endpoints of the black
printer affect its own contrast. A low-contrast
black printer is undesirable because the black
ink does not optimize the tonal steps of the
image. The following section has some guidelines to set up your separation for a good black
printer.

Black Highlight Point

After the CMY printers have been set up for
their highlight and shadow values, the black
printer's end densities must be set. Unlike the

CMY printers, the black printer does not start in the usual highlight densities because it would seriously subdue the bright areas of the reproduction, causing a loss of contrast. To avoid contaminating the highlight areas, the black printer starts to print in the image's midtone range.

The tonal density is measured by the cyan printer's dot size. Because of the cyan printer's larger size (due to gray balance), cyan dot percentages are typically used to determine which part of the tonal scale you are in. (For example a light gray reading 20% cyan, 12% magenta, and 12% yellow is called a quarter-tone area.) For setting the start point of the black printer, also called setting the black highlight, select a value of cyan printing on a gray scale. The black highlight typically starts in a range between 35-50% cyan. Start with 50% if you have no preferences. Many prefer the 50% start point because it keeps the black from contaminating certain colors too soon. Some separators prefer an earlier starting density, like the 35% cyan level, so the black can enhance light shadows in an image or textures. At the 50% start point, the black highlight may seem "too clean" for some, while the 35% level might be "too dirty" for others. Be aware of this control option and find what is right for you.

A dot percent value of 5% works fine as a black highlight. Some brands of software have a separate black start-point control that allows you to enter a number relating to the cyan dot percentage. For example, enter 50% and you get a 5% black dot at the same density on the gray scale as the cyan 50% dot. This start point type of control is easy to use and very effective for

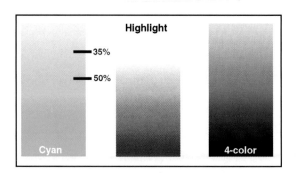

Figure 16.2
The black highlight point for normal images begins where the cyan is between 35 to 50% on a grayscale.

complete control of the black separation highlight (see Figure 16.2).

Beware of black highlight controls that do not take into account the half-black nature of the black separation. If you use a curve or plus-minus type volume control to subtract black highlight, the black highlight dots diminish in size. But, if you try to add to the size of the black highlight dots, suddenly you will find a black highlight dot alongside the CMY highlight dots, way up in the CMY highlight densities. The black dot in the diffuse highlight causes instant contamination of image highlight brightness. We have been particularly surprised to find this problem on software supplied by companies that have been producing high-end printing equipment for many years. Again, this problem is caused by incorrect software design, so it is important for you to set your black highlight starting point with care. Make sure that the black starts in the midtones. (The only exception to this rule is when using large amounts of GCR as discussed later in this chapter.)

Shadow Point

Because of the wide variety of originals that are possible to color separate (35mm and 70mm trans, C prints, etc.), you will experience a wide range of Dmax values at the blackest black shadow points. Because the black separation signal is derived from the three-color CMY signal, the amount of black that the scanner places at the shadow point changes with each subject. Transparency Dmax may read anywhere from 2.2 to 3.4 density routinely. Transparency formats vary in maximum density. Reflective copy can range from 1.0 to 2.0 density. The maximum black reading that the scanner gives you is influenced by this Dmax value.

The darkest black shadow point of a reproduction should read between 70 and 80 percent black to reproduce a rich, deep black on the press. You should not exceed these values unless you use some method of UCR or GCR, as recommended by the printer. Many times, when the operator reads the dot percentage in the darkest black shadow or border of the original, the black reads below 70 percent. For example, you may experience a typical CMY shadow of 95% cyan, 87% magenta, and 87% yellow and get a black reading of only 58%. The CMY printers will carry good contrast because of their full ranges, but the black printer will be weaker or flatter. If the shadow dot percentage of the black plate is low, the image may print flat.

Examine Figures 16.3a-b and 16.4a-b. Notice how the contrast in Figure 16.4a is flat because the black plate shadow dot percent value is 50%, compared to 80% in Figure 16.3a. The black printers for each figure when viewed alone also show the difference in contrast. Having a black shadow point of less than 70% flattens the contrast of the black printer and therefore the resulting CMYK image.

Always be sure to check the amount of black printing in the heaviest border or shadow point of the original. Use the black shadow endpoint control to adjust the dot readout to a value between 70% and 80% (many aim for the middle, 75%).

Customizing Your Black Printer to the Image

Exposure errors can cause some photographic images to turn out high key or low key. High key images are low in density and have a weak, washed-out color. Low-key images are high density, dark, and muddy looking.

Besides looking poor, these types of images cause problems with black generation. As mentioned before, the separation software computes the black printer from the RGB gray (equality) signal of the image. Stronger colors in the original cause more black to be put in the black printer channel. Shadow readouts for the black printer may be low, such as 40-50%. Conversely, low-key images look very dark and generate an excessive amount of black, which makes them reproduce even darker.

Customizing your black printer for high- and low-key originals will help you achieve a

Figure 16.3a
CMYK image with the black printer
shadow point at 80%.

Figure 16.3b
The black printer of Figure a.

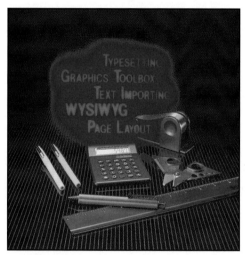

Figure 16.4a
CMYK image with the black printer
shadow point at 50%.

Figure 16.4b
The black printer of Figure a.

Figure 16.5a
A high-key CMYK image with standard black
highlight starting at 50%.

Figure 16.5b
The black printer of Figure a.

Figure 16.6a
An increased black highlight starting at
35%. This helps the high-key image by
adding contrast.

Figure 16.6b
The black printer of Figure a.

normalized image appearance. Since high-key images are weak for color, they tend to generate less black than normal images, compounding the problem of a weak appearance. (See Figures 16.5 and 16.6.) Table 16.1 gives guidelines towards customizing the black printer for poor original copy.

Table 16.1 Black Printer Adjustments for Poor Copy

Type of Original Copy	Black Printer Adjustment
High Key	Highlights start at 35% cyan, shadow at 80%
Extreme High Key	Add 5-10% black midtone to above

continues

Table 16.1 Black Printer
Adjustments for Poor Copy
Continued

Type of Original Copy	Black Printer Adjustment
Low Key	Highlights start at 55% cyan, shadow at 80%
Extreme Low Key	Subtract 10-20% black midtone to above

CMY tone gradation is used to help normalize high- and low-key images. The adjustment process moves the midtone density position of the cyan, magenta, and yellow printers. Since the black printer's highlight start point is set by the cyan midtone position, it moves with the adjustment for the abnormal copy too. This movement of the cyan midtone helps start the black at a better place (in regards to the density of the image). For example, in dark subjects, the cyan midtone may be decreased by 10% and it will start further down the tonal scale. The resulting black highlight starts down the scale, too, thinning out the black printer, which helps open up the dark image instead of "blacking it out."

With poor originals, it is important to remember that the black shadow should still be between 70% and 80% to give weight and contrast to the true black shadows. Setting the black shadow to less than 70% will flatten all the dark areas and diminish the overall contrast unfavorably. To optimize the black printer in extremely dark images or extremely weak images, leave the shadow point percentage between 70% and 80%, and then use the black printer midtone control (if available) to further thin out or strengthen the black in the image.

Remember to check the endpoints of the black printer. Even though many types of software automatically set the black, it is rarely optimized for each image being separated. With CMYK print devices, don't just be concerned with the CMY settings. There are four printers available; use all four to get the best reproduction results.

Press Conditions

Plan for the best; be ready for the worst. Getting quality color on a low quality output is like steering a canoe across a river with a heavy current. You compensate for the current by over-paddling against the stream and aiming further up-river than you want to go. The canoe does not take the direct straight line approach. Eventually, if your compensation is correct, the canoe comes around and you pull into your originally planned destination.

Separations should be set for optimum reproduction first and adjusted for non-optimum reproduction last. Press conditions of dot gain,

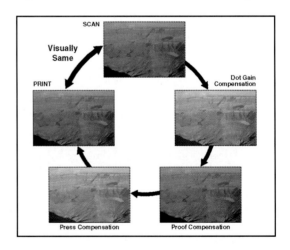

Figure 16.7
An illustration of how compensation works within print reproduction.

type of press, and substrate optical properties will all "de-optimize" your reproduction. Adjustments must be made in the problem areas of the tonal scale; this involves the subtraction of cyan, magenta, and yellow ink, and the addition of black ink. During printing, the compensations are negated by the press/substrate conditions—ideally, you are left with an optimum reproduction (see Figure 16.7).

Dot Gain Compensation

The printing press is aptly named for one main reason, the word "press." Ink is pressed upon a substrate such as paper, transferring a halftone image onto the paper. The pressure used during the process not only transfers the halftone dots upon the paper, but it presses or squeezes them *into* the paper. Because of this violent treatment, the halftone dots have a very difficult time maintaining their original size and shape.

The change in the size of halftone dots during printing is called dot gain. Dot gain is a normal concern in making quality separations for printing, and you must be aware of this effect. You cannot simply ignore it and hope that it goes away. (See Figures 16.8 and 16.9)

Dot gain from press pressure mainly affects the midtone areas of the tonal range. Press speeds and how the paper is fed—sheetfed or web (roll)—will also influence the gain in dot size. A

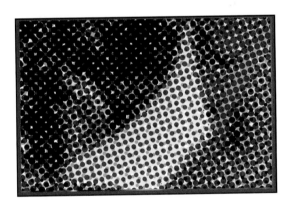

Figure 16.8
Image prints correctly because of dot gain compensation for printing conditions.

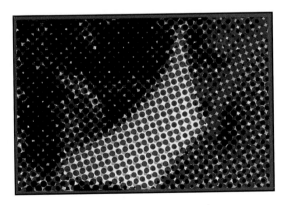

Figure 16.9
Image prints dark because of no dot gain compensation.

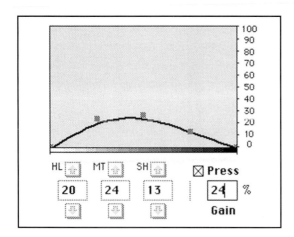

Figure 16.10
A dot gain curve. Notice dot gain peaks in the middle tone areas.

dot gain curve is used to compensate for change in dot size on a printing press (see Figure 16.10). Dot gain is the greatest in the middle tone areas of an image.

To compensate for typical press dot gain, a tone adjustment in the midtone area is most effective. Some brands of software have controls marked "press gain," and you can enter the desired amount. The software subtracts the dot gain percentage from the midtone area of the reproduction. If your software does not have a convenient control for this, go to the tone controls in an image manipulation program and subtract the desired amount from the midtone area.

Total Ink Density

Ink absorption from the substrate can cause problems with sheets sticking to the press and to each other. The shadow areas of the image contain the most ink, and large quantities of ink will cause sticking problems and will take too long to dry. Since there are four (or more) colors

of ink, the total amount of ink that is possible to print is 400%. Solid ink of all four colors will never dry properly.

Using the best coated paper on a sheetfed press at slow speeds, a maximum total ink density of up to 380% could be possible. In this book, we set 350% as an ideal aim point for total ink density. As lower price stocks are used, the total ink density recommended decreases down toward 300% for coated papers. With non-coated papers, the total ink density can be as much as 320% and as little as 240% (for newsprint). (See Table 16.2)

Under Color Removal (UCR)

Both UCR and GCR are designed to be compensations for substrate dot gain in the shadow areas. They reset the total ink density to accommodate dot gain in the shadow areas so that drying and sticking are not problems on the press. Also, these two effects use less ink in a print run. For large print runs, using UCR or GCR can be a significant savings in ink costs. Do not use the functions unless specifically requested by the printer.

UCR removes cyan, magenta, and yellow ink from beneath areas in which black is printed in order to reduce the total ink density. Since UCR removes only ink from beneath areas in which black is printed, this effect only operates from approximately the 50% areas to the shadow point. UCR does not affect color areas and does little to compensate for midtone dot gain. Because UCR removes the CMY component underneath black only, it technically does not change the appearance of the separation, because black still prints as black (see Figures 16.11a-c).

Figure 16.11a
A CMY image with UCR applied. Note that
the dark shadows do not print very strong.

Figure 16.11b
The black plate is strengthened in the
shadow areas to compensate for the removal
of CMY.

Table 16.2 Total Ink Density

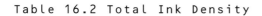

Color	1.	2.	3.	4.
Cyan 100	95	75	68	
Magenta	100	87	65	58
Yellow	100	87	65	58
Black 100	80	95	95	
Total Ink	400	350	300	280

Figure 16.11c
The resulting CMYK image. Notice how the
black adds contrast even in colored areas
where there is no black. Total ink density
is 260%.

Unfortunately, removing large quantities of CMY from the darkest shadows will reduce the apparent weight and richness of the blackest blacks, resulting in a visual loss of contrast. To help reduce this problem, the amount of black ink printed in the shadow is increased to a 95% dot value to keep the color as black as possible and strengthen the entire black printer. (Printers do not like solid blacks in the shadows, so a 95% dot is more acceptable.) The sum of the cyan, magenta, and yellow printing underneath is adjusted according to the amount of UCR required. Typical UCR amounts are described in total ink density: 240%, 260%, 280%, 300%, and 320%. A 95% maximum black in the shadow works well with all UCR programming, from 320% down to 240%.

The black highlight setting for UCR may need to be adjusted for larger UCRs, such as 240% and 260%. As the UCR amount increases, the further up the tonal scale the effect tries to go. Because UCR only removes colors under black, the black highlight may have to be increased 5-10% for the larger UCRs to help cover up what is being removed from the midtone areas. The way to test this potential problem is to take a reading where the black highlight is 5%. Turn the UCR on and off, and notice if there is any subtraction of cyan, magenta, and yellow values. If more than 5% of CMY ink is being subtracted here due to UCR, increase the amount of black highlight printing by 5-10%.

UCA (under color addition) is an extra control for the UCR process that is used to add cyan, magenta, or yellow ink under black to keep the three colors in a neutral balance. Keeping the CMY in a neutral balance ensures that the black areas do not appear casted.

Gray Component Replacement

GCR replaces the gray components in an image with black ink. Since black prints a better gray than combinations of cyan, magenta, and yellow, this effect can work very well. RGB color space gray is equality, therefore, GCR is most easily done while the image is being converted from RGB to CMYK. Wherever an area of the image has equal components of RGB, that part of the color or gray is replaced with black (see Figure 16.12b). The big difference between UCR and GCR is that GCR affects both grays and colors. The black ink carries the contrast of the entire reproduction, and it then replaces part of the secondary and all of the tertiary colors. The only areas in which CMY ink is strong is where they are acting as primary components in highly saturated colors.

Figures 16.12 through 16.16 are composed of a four-color image and series of color chips. The first set of color chips are pure colors composed of one or two colors of ink. A pure color has no tertiary or complementary color component. Since they have no tertiary color, the GCR has no effect upon them. The second set of color chips has a 20 percent tertiary color added to them. This will cause GCR to replace the tertiary component with black. Notice how the tertiary colors are carved out of the colored areas throughout the image and replaced with black. Remember, tertiary colors create texture and detail and that detail is replaced with black when using GCR.

GCR amounts are designated as percentages of gray component removal. Between 40% and 60% is recommended for most normal printing situations. The total ink density must be measured separately.

As mentioned, the black printer is of primary importance in a GCR separation. Since the cyan, magenta, and yellow inks only act as primary and subdued secondary color making components, the weight and contrast of the separation is up to the black. As with the UCR formula, a maximum 95% of black in the darkest shadows is advised. GCR programs have a black generation menu with selections from thin to heavy. As the GCR amount increases from a low of 10% towards a high of 70% or 80%, the black generation must be increased in order to maintain reproduction contrast.

Achromatic black ink is specially formulated for printing GCR separated images. Achromatic black inks print a richer and deeper black than standard process black ink. Because a lot of CMY ink is taken out with GCR, a stronger black ink will maintain the density in the shadows and give you better results. Printers that request GCR normally use achromatic black inks.

You should not mix UCR and GCR separated images on the same printing page. The press operator cannot make ink and color adjustments on the press for one separation without adversely affecting the other separations. Color correcting a GCR image on press will adversely affect the gray balance of a UCR separated image.

Color corrections for GCR are difficult because all the tertiary colors used to control color

balance have been removed by the black. As GCR increases, secondary colors are also partially removed, which adds to the difficulty of color correction. The more GCR added to the image, the harder it becomes to color correct the image. Maximum GCR means minimum color correction possibilities.

Substrate Conditions

The type of material that the reproductions are being printed on has a significant effect on the final printed result. Chapter 11, "Preparing for Targeted Reproduction," discusses the concerns involving paper-type and nonpaper-type substrates. Each type of substrate absorbs some of the printing colorant. Newsprint is the most notorious substrate of all, having typical dot gains of more than 40%.

Substrates can be colored, glossy, or dull. Each of these properties will influence the contrast of the reproduction.

Printing on colored paper

Transparency originals are pigments with white light transmitted through them. Color prints are dyes on white photographic paper. White, white, white… maximum brightness.

Reproducing images on colored substrates is different from printing on white paper. The white paper creates the maximum contrast possible for printed matter. Colored paper is not as bright and reduces the possible contrast in a reproduction. The colored paper also imparts a cast to the reproduction that is impossible to remove.

No black or GCR applied.

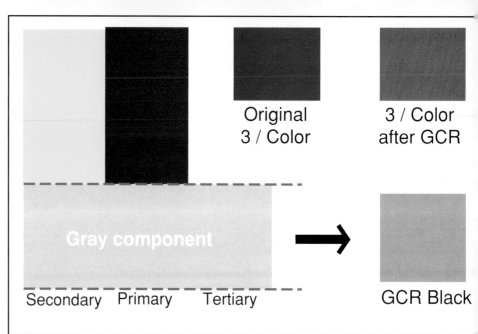

Original
3 / Color

3 / Color
after GCR

Gray component

Secondary   Primary   Tertiary

GCR Black

The diagram indicates how GCR is computed.

CMY after light GCR.

Black from light GCR.

CMYK after light GCR.

CMY after medium GCR.

Black from medium GCR.

CMYK after medium GCR.

after heavy GCR.

Black from heavy GCR.

CMYK after heavy GCR.

after maximum GCR.

Black from maximum GCR.

CMYK after maximum GCR.

after normal UCR.

Black from UCR.

CMYK after UCR.

Colored paper reproductions can look very attractive, or the dulling of the highlights can be cause for rejection. We have seen many colored paper jobs end up being done on white stock after the first round of proofs were delivered. The most impossible task is reproducing an exact match onto a colored stock from an original drawing done on white paper. Table 16.3 gives some suggestions for reducing the effects of colored paper on printed reproductions.

Table 16.3 also gives some possible compensations for separating on colored stock.

Table 16.3 Separating on Color Stock

Color of Paper	Compensation
Yellow	Reduces yellow highlight to 1%, (cyan 5%, magenta 3%); reduces yellow quarter tone 3%.
Pink	Reduces magenta highlight to 1%, (cyan 5%, yellow 1%); reduces magenta quarter tone 3%.
Green	Reduces cyan and yellow highlights to minimums (5% cyan, 4% magenta, 3% yellow). Plus magenta quarter tone 3%.
Blue	Reduces cyan and magenta highlights to minimums (4% cyan, 2% magenta, 3% yellow) Plus yellow quarter tone 3%.

Talk to Your Printer

Information about press conditions should come from the printer. Substrate printing requirement data can be received from the printer or the manufacturer of the substrate. Either way, unless you are using the ideal situation (in which the press is sheetfed, run at slow speed, and the paper is coated), getting press and substrate information is critical for getting a quality reproduction.

UCR and GCR requirements should be obtained from the printer. Arbitrarily using UCR or GCR may cause problems during the pressrun. If an image that is separated with GCR is on the same press sheet as a non-GCR image, problems can arise if one of them is adjusted on the press. Also, special achromatic (richer in color and density) black inks are typically used for GCR-required pressruns to get the best results.

Every printer has specific requirements. One example of high quality commercial printing is the sheetfed press using high gloss coated stock. A 350% total ink density works just fine to produce a dark, rich shadow, and the glossy stock produces a vivid, bright white. If the color was proofed on a standard laminated proofing system (which has about 12% dot gain built in), there should be no problems matching the proof on press.

For high value magazine and book printing, high speed web presses are used. The most common standard for commercial web presses is call SWOP. SWOP (Specifications for Web Printers) standards are used by many publication printers to get separations that they can print. Total ink printing and dot gain specs are given and should be incorporated into your separations (if SWOP requirements are given to you). Do not ignore requests for SWOP standards. The separation films are checked by the printers to ensure that they have been met by the separator.

For as many printers as there are in the world, there are at least that many different ways to approach print reproduction. Don't assume that every printer does things the same way. Always talk to the printer and learn what the specific requirements are before you even make separations. Remember the least amount of control is at the press. Try to give the printer the best separations possible so they can take advantage of what control they do have. Don't underestimate the importance of knowing the needs of your printer. They're people too, you know, and they'd love to talk to you.

Proofing Problems

Accurate prepress proofing can be difficult for files with UCR, GCR, and dot gain compensation. Most laminated type proofs have a visual dot gain of approximately 12 to 24% built into their systems. Additionally, the black pigment, used with most of these proofing systems, has a hard time covering up large amounts of UCR or GCR.

Midtone dot gain compensations may visually weaken the appearance of a proof that does not have the appropriate amount of compensation built into the proofing system. For example, you may need a 240% UCR and 40% dot gain for images printed on newsprint paper. The result on a standard proofing system is an image that

is flat and weak. You have to "imagine" that the press gain will compensate for the visually unattractive proof. If that is true, then what use is the proof? If the customer is not knowledgeable about press conditions, he will surely reject the proof as being too weak in color. If your customer insists on saturating the proof, the result on press may be a very dark, over-saturated image.

One way to avoid a rejected proof is to compare a proof and a printed sample of the same image with the customer to illustrate the effect of press conditions. Though not an ideal situation, it may calm any fears an inexperienced customer may have about accepting a proof that appears weak.

With images requiring compensation for press conditions (such as dot gain), a digital proofing system is a very effective method of predicting what the final reproduction will look like. One advantage to digital proofing is the ability to simulate any press and substrate condition. Compensations can be programmed into the system so that the resulting proof will visually represent the actual result of the press.

Midtone Adjustment for Size

Magnification or reduction of an image will have an effect on the visual appearance of a reproduction's contrast. Reductions gain contrast and enlargements lose contrast. This visual effect is especially important to be aware of if you are reproducing the same image at several sizes in the same publication. You must reset your midtone tone setting to have the images match at different sizes.

The following chart by Ralph Girod[12] suggests a middletone adjustment to compensate for this change in appearance due to size so that the resulting reproductions are similar in contrast (see Table 16.4).

Image Resolution Tips

Digital print production involves the creation and movement of large quantities of pixels. Pixels mean bytes of information and image files mean many megabytes of data requiring processing, transfer, and storage. Any appropriate shortcuts during production saves time and money.

The simple method of determining image resolution is to double the required line screen to get the number of pixels per inch. The doubling action assigns two pixels squared for each halftone dot. As mentioned before in Chapter 3, two pixels per dot yields a good looking reproduction. Exceeding the two pixel per dot ratio will not significantly increase the image quality but will needlessly increase file size. In a production environment, file sizes are kept to a minimum, so having more than two pixels per dot is not an option.

Another option is to use a ratio of less than two pixels per dot. File size decreases as well as any file transfer and processing time. Of course,

there is a downside to shrinking file size using lower resolutions. Pixelization can occur (pixels start to become visible), and lines can become jagged (the jaggies). Both of these effects can be cause for rejection of the final reproduction.

When in a production environment, there are exceptions to many rules in the right circumstances. Resolution and resulting file size can be lowered according to the type of subject matter and magnification of the reproduction. Image files can often be less than the normal two pixels per halftone dot ratio without sacrificing quality.

Images with a lot of fine detail, texture, and lines need plenty of pixel information reproduced correctly. If the amount of pixel information being put into the halftone dots is not

Table 16.4 Middletone Adjustment for Size

% Size	% Middletone Change
20	-15
40	-10
60	-5
80	-3
100	0
600	+5
1000	+7
1500	+9
2000	+10

Figure 16.18a
A 2:1 pixel to halftone dot ratio.
File size is 3.6 megabytes.

Figure 16.18b
A 1.5:1 pixel to halftone dot
ratio. File size is 2.0 megabytes.

Figure 16.18c
A 1:1 pixel to halftone dot ratio.
File size is 900 KB.

enough, the fine detail and texture starts to disappear into the background. Any straight lines (especially diagonal ones) become jagged. Images of this type usually require a resolution of two pixels per dot. See the lines in the keyboard in Figures 16.18a-c.

Images composed of mostly smooth tones and soft details do not require as much pixel information as images with textures and fine detail. Wash drawings, ocean scenes, and sunset scenes are examples of image types that may not require higher resolutions. Using a 1.5 pixel per dot or one pixel per dot ratio can suffice when reproducing these images. See the image of clouds in Figures 16.19a-c.

The 1.5 pixel per dot resolution usually does not significantly reduce the quality of most images. File size is reduced and processing is faster because of less information. The pixel to halftone ratio of 1.5:1 is a medium resolution that can be used often if the reproduction quality is acceptable.

Working in the low resolution of one pixel per dot saves even more file space than the two to one ratio. Be aware that this resolution does not work well with many images and is very susceptible to the jaggies.

The image magnification can be a factor in selecting file resolution. Images being reproduced at reductions or at the same size should use a high (2 to 1) or medium (1.5 to 1) pixel to halftone ratio to maintain detail and sharp lines. Images being enlarged, on the other hand, can use high, medium, or low ratios depending on the degree of magnification and image subject type. High magnification allows lower resolutions because the fine details and textures of the image are enlarged and easier to see (see Figures 16.20a-b).

Some people recommend a low pixel to halftone ratio for coarse lines screens below 120 lpi. Even with coarse lines screens you should use at least a 2 to 1 pixel per dot ratio, which provides more information per dot. Because there are fewer halftone dots in a low line screen, any additional pixel information will help avoid jaggies and make any lines as smooth as possible.

When reproducing large quantities of images, you can consider using lower resolutions to streamline production. Any file space saved can be very significant not only for storage but also for speed of image processing and output. The key is to keep a close eye on quality because not all image types respond well to low resolutions.

Color Correction Tips

No matter how well you set the endpoints, tone, and cast of a separation, some images will need to have certain colors adjusted for proper reproduction. Memory colors are colors that everyone knows without seeing the original. Even if the memory colors are incorrect in the original supplied for separation, these critical colors must be correct in the final reproduction.

This section discusses actual corrections to common memory colors. We also review the technique of working with CMYK color as primary, secondary, and tertiary components.

Working with CMYK color combinations involves one, two, or three subtractive secondary colors (CMY), plus a black printer. When composing a color, the main color is called the primary or base color. The next most abundant color is called the secondary color. If a third color is present, that color is called the tertiary color. Any black component is noted separately.

When analyzing CMYK color combinations, observing the quantity and ratios of the primaries to secondaries to tertiaries to each other gives a better understanding of how the ink combination is made up and adjusted.

Following are some four-color formulas to help you to reproduce the commonly seen colors of blue sky, flesh tones, orange, and red.

Figure 16.19a
A 2:1 pixel to halftone dot ratio. File size is 2.9 megabytes.

Figure 16.19b
A 1.5:1 pixel to halftone dot ratio. File size is 1.6 megabytes.

Figure 16.19c
A 1:1 pixel to halftone dot ratio. File size is 747 Kilobytes.

Figure 16.20a
An image scanned at a magnification of 100% and a 1:1 pixel to halftone ratio.

Figure 16.20b
The same image in Figure 16.20a scanned at 250% with a 1:1 pixel to halftone dot ratio. Notice the detail quality is better.

Blue Sky

Violet, or blue, consists mostly of cyan and magenta ink. A bright blue sky may be composed of only cyan. The sky starts to gain depth and the tone starts to get darker when you add the magenta ink. The increase in magenta ink, as well as the cyan, causes the sky to darken away from the horizon area.

The ratio of cyan ink to magenta tells what kind of blue you have. If the magenta ink is less than a 40% ratio to the amount of cyan—for example, cyan 30%, magenta 8%—the blue appears cool. When the ratio of magenta to cyan is around 50%, the sky appears neutral blue. If the magenta-to-cyan ratio is 60-75% of the cyan value, the blue appears warm. When the magenta-to-cyan ratio exceeds 75%, such as cyan 98% and magenta 88%, the blue shifts to an undesirable purple color (see Figures 16.21a-c).

Pink skies result when the magenta-to-cyan ratio exceeds 60% in the lighter parts of the sky.

Sky blue's complementary color, yellow, contaminates, or "dirties," the sky's appearance. Yellow also tends to make a blue color look greenish instead of darkening the color toward black. (We recommend examining a color chart to see this phenomenon. Compare the 100% C, 50% M, 20% Y patch to the 100% C, 50% M, 20% K patch in the chart.) If depth of color is necessary in the sky, use black ink to give it a deeper, richer blue. Try to keep yellow out of your skies as much as possible (see Figure 16.22).

A good ratio to make a deep violet color on most proofing systems is 100% C, 75% M, 25% K, and a minimum amount of yellow.

Flesh Tones

Flesh tones are very important memory colors, especially if you are scanning a lot of work using human models. Customers do not buy scans of people who look orange, sunburned, or jaundiced.

Figure 16.21a.
Cool blue/cyan
60%, magenta 15%.

Figure 16.21b.
Neutral blue/cyan
60%, magenta 30%.

Figure 16.21c.
Warm blue/cyan
60%, magenta 45%.

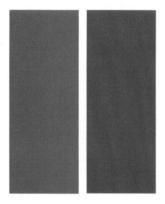

Figure 16.22
Yellow and black as
tertiary colors in
blue. Adding black to
blue produces a darker
neutral blue than
adding yellow.

Examine Figure 16.23a. The flesh of the original transparency looks warm from the effect of the morning sun's light.

Use the color correction control in the orange/red channel to adjust the flesh to the result of Figure 16.23b. Notice that all reds in the scene were also changed because of the selective color correction's global effect (see Chapter 15).

Every time a scan is done with a flesh tone, the operator should take several readings to determine the appearance of the flesh. Take readings in normally lighted areas. Avoid taking dot percent readings in shadowed areas or hot spots that are too light. Find a spot that is a good average of the overall flesh color.

A good rule of thumb is to make sure the yellow dot percentage is equal to, or does not exceed by 10%, the value of the magenta dot percent, in order to avoid yellowish Caucasian flesh. For example, if the magenta is 55%, the yellow should not exceed 65%. This is a very typical correction that yields an acceptable flesh tone most of the time.

The cyan dot value should be between one-third and one-half of the magenta value, depending on the warmth and depth of the flesh tone. And because the cyan is Caucasian flesh's complement, it should just contour a normally lighted flesh tone. Values of more than 30% cyan should be only in the darker, heavier areas of the flesh. Sunlit, bright areas of flesh should carry a minimum of cyan or no cyan.

Novices first should check the yellow-to-magenta relationship and then should wait to see a proof before making further adjustments. Write down the four-color readouts of the flesh tones you take and notice how they look on the proof. Comparing four-color readouts to corresponding areas on a proof is the best way to learn important memory colors.

Figure 16.23a.
Normal scan produces warm flesh.

Figure 16.23b.
Flesh color corrected, minus 20% magenta and yellow.

Oranges and Reds

Orange colors are made mainly of yellow ink, with magenta ink determining how warm, neutral, or cool the colors look. If the magenta-to-yellow ratio is between 30 and 40%, the orange is cool, or to the green side. A magenta-to-yellow ratio around 50% yields a neutral-looking orange, or an "orange-orange." A 60-75% magenta-to-yellow ratio gives a warm-looking orange. When the magenta-to-yellow ratio exceeds 75%, the orange becomes an orangish red (see Figures 16.24a-c).

Creating a rich, deep red is always a special challenge for scanner operators. The type of prepress proofing system you use is important, because each seems to produce different reds with various color gamuts. Scanner operators should try different combinations of CMYK to create red on their proofing systems. Many operators prefer to make red with cyan as the only contaminant. Others prefer to use black, and still others swear by a ratio of cyan and black.

The first thing you need in order to create a deep red is lots of magenta, 95% to solid. Then add yellow in the 80-90% range. When the yellow nears the magenta value, the red becomes orange-red. So to make a deep red, you need to keep the yellow at least a 10 to 20% dot value away from the magenta percent.

Next, add the cyan and black values. Once again, you should view the resulting color on your proofing system to find the best ratios. Create red tints with various values of cyan and

black. You may need to adjust the yellow further to get a cooler red. Keep these proofs and color ratios by the scanner. Reds are strong colors, and many customers have special preferences about how they should look. Operators also should research gold, foliage (green), and wood (brown) memory colors.

Figure 16.24a.
Cool orange: 80% Y and 27% M.

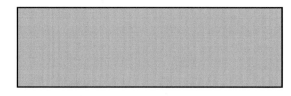

Figure 16.24b.
Neutral orange:80% Y and 40% M.

Figure 16.24c.
Warm orange: 80% Y and 60% M.

Checklist

Here is a quick review of the additional color separation techniques discussed in this chapter.

- Turn off the UCR/GCR controls until all color settings have been done.

- Make sure the black shadow percentage is between 70 and 80% (unless using UCR or GCR).

- Make adjustments to midtone to compensate for loss in contrast due to enlargement.

- Pay attention to ratios of color in CMY combinations, and check color charts.

- Adjust the black printer for high key and low key originals.

- Do not arbitrarily use UCR and GCR unless required by the printer. If you have to decide between UCR and GCR, choose UCR. It is the most common black compensation used by printers.

- When using pixel to halftone dot ratios below 2:1, carefully examine reproductions for missing detail and jaggies.

- Be aware that the tertiary color creates texture and detail.

Final Word

Color separation can be done simply with color management software or step by step using a scanner and image manipulation software. Whichever way you choose to do it, making quality color reproductions takes patience, knowledge, and practice.

The techniques discussed in this chapter, and previous chapters, are all important parts of the color reproduction process. As your experience grows, your ability to use these techniques will increase. The whole process of gaining skill as a separator involves the reproduction of many images to increase your skill at matching color. We like to say that it takes 1,000 images reproduced to finish your freshman year as a color separator.

[12] Girod, Ralph, Change in Contrast in Great Enlargements and Reductions, Hell Topics No. 1, 1984, page 3.

Part IV

Production Environment

Profiles and Calibration

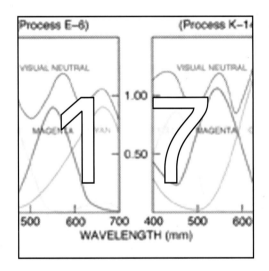

"Computers are useless;
they can only give you answers."

Pablo Picasso,
20th Century Painter

So much has been written about color management systems that it is sometimes very difficult to understand what a color management system actually does. It may take you quite a while to understand how profiles and calibration work with one another unless you understand the difference between profiles and calibration.

Profiles reveal standards of each device, and calibration links the devices together. Profiles are the personality of devices; calibration allows interpersonal relationships between devices. If you could hear a profile talk, it would say, "This is my personality and how I typically perform my function." Calibration provides the different profile personalities with a method of working together.

Profile

A standardizing procedure is always established for a device, whether you form the standard yourself or buy a generic electronic management system. You develop a profile or description of the best condition to operate a device. You profile scanners, proofing systems, imagesetters, and presses. A profile of a device tells you if a device is operating properly. So how does one go about establishing a profile of a device?

First, you find out from the manufacturer the recommended operating conditions. When you calibrate a device for a client, the first thing you need to establish is the proper operating conditions for that device. You have to be sure that the device will operate the same way each time the client uses it. If you cannot rely on the device being consistent, then none of the other input or output devices in the color system will be consistent either, whether calibrated or not.

Calibration

The most basic type of calibration is called prediction. Does the information that you read on the screen densitometer translate to the physical output? If you read 25 percent on your digital file, you should measure 25 percent on your physical output. The accuracy of prediction should be established first because if you cannot rely on your onscreen densitometer, then you cannot rely on the color and tone that you are producing.

After you have established a profile (standard operating condition) of each device in the reproduction chain, you now need to link all the systems together. Figure 17.1 illustrates the relationship between profiles and calibration. System calibration is the linking of reproduction devices in an entire system. How the devices

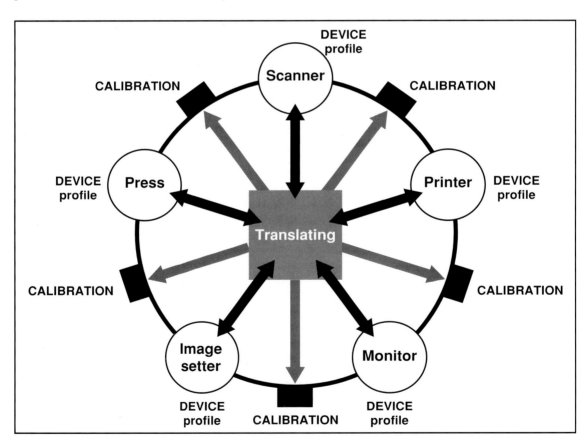

Figure 17.1
The system of profiles and calibration and how they work with one another.

relate and transfer information to one another is just as important as a profile of each individual device. Profiles monitor stability; calibration connects all the devices together. You cannot separate calibration and profiles—they complement one another.

You cannot calibrate devices if the stability has not been established. And even if the stability of each device has been established, the proper transfer of information must be determined. Calibration sets up a color system to obtain the results you desire. Calibration involves relating values from unlike devices. Profiles relate to a single device, and calibration relates to the entire system of devices as a whole. You cannot have one without the other.

Calibration Tools

The two most important tools used in calibration are the densitometer and a test image. To ensure that these devices work properly, your skill at judging color must be developed with practice and experience. No single tool can replace your final judgment of color results. All the tools may say green, but if you don't see green, then you must make the final decision to change things. Relying only on the tools may get you poor results if the tools are not working properly.

The densitometer measures the density of tone. Primarily used for measuring the dot percentage of separation film, the densitometer also is used to measure the density of transmissive and reflective materials. The densitometer provides values as logarithmic density and dot percentage (negative or positive). Some densitometers also provide a colorimeter option.

A colorimeter measures color numerically as CIE values: either x,y,z Lab or Luv. A colorimeter enables you to measure the difference between two colors. The colorimeter is used only when attempting to match a very specific color value. In some cases, the colorimeter can measure a difference when, visually, you may perceive no difference. The colorimeter is most useful when trying to quantify colors relative to each other. The colorimeter also is used in some programs to measure the CIE x,y,z values of ink combinations in order to create custom separation tables for those specific ink sets.

Test Subjects

A test subject is an image or images that you use to establish the working condition of an input or output device. A test subject need not be complex and can be as simple as a grayscale. Specific test subjects are used for both input and output and are also used to maintain quality control. One of the largest providers of test subjects of all kinds is the Graphic Arts Technical Foundation (GATF), located in Pittsburgh. GATF has been a leader in establishing standards for the graphic arts and printing community for more than 30 years.

A good test image has a wide variety of reproduction issues relating to color, gray balance, highlight, and shadow detail—all in one image. Seldom does a single image provide all of the reproduction issues that an input and output device must address, so a group of three or four images is used to ensure that any calibration works well for a variety of situations. At least one high-key and one low-key image should be used when analyzing a device's performance. Figures 17.2a-c show a few test subjects available from GATF.

Figure 17.2a
A high-key image from GATF helps establish
how the device performs with bright tones.
It will be difficult to reproduce the
highlight details of the photo while
retaining the overall feel of the scene.

Figure 17.2b
A low-key image helps analyze the device's
performance with dark tones and shadow
details. It's also a good image when
testing GCR effects.

Figure 17.2c
Good test subjects have a variety of flesh
tones in the same image. The dark clothing
is difficult to hold detail, and the
textured clothing can cause objectionable
moiré patterns.

Transparency test subjects are the most common and useful test subjects for scanners. Prints can be made from the transparencies in order to provide reflective versions of the test subjects. Regardless of the test subjects that you choose to work with, you must have some kind of standard that you can measure against.

Stepped Scale

The most basic calibration measurement is the stepped scale shown in Figure 17.3. The scale helps establish tone reproduction. You can buy a scale for scanning and also create a digital scale for output. The values of a digital scale output to a printer are measured by your densitometer and any difference from the predicted values can be used to compensate. A transfer curve is used before output to provide an accurate scale. Many imagesetters provide an

Figure 17.3
The stepped grayscale is the most
fundamental test subject and should play a
part in all analyses of tone reproduction.

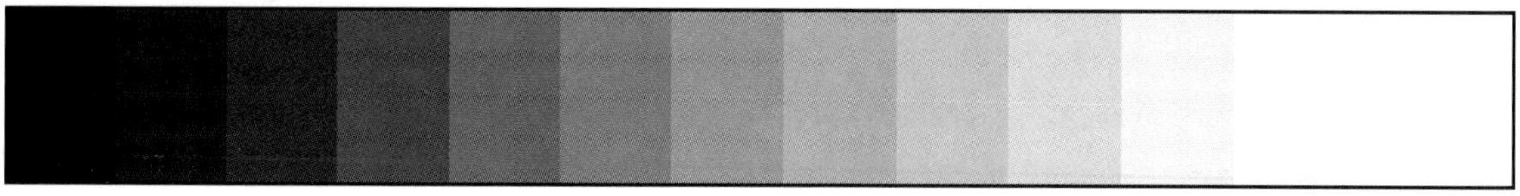

internal method of compensating for any scale differences, and the transfer curve may be unnecessary.

Gray Balance Grid

You can use a gray balance grid to establish the CMY combination that creates a neutral gray (see Figure 17.4). Different combinations of CMY are placed on a grid; the cyan stays constant, and the magenta and yellow vary typically in two percent increments. The magenta values change along the vertical axis, and the yellow values change along the horizontal axis. By viewing each individual square, you can determine the CMY values that create a neutral gray. A colorimeter also can be used to measure precisely which combination of CMY is creating a neutral. If your program provides for the adjustment of gray balance information, a gray balance grid will establish the input values for you.

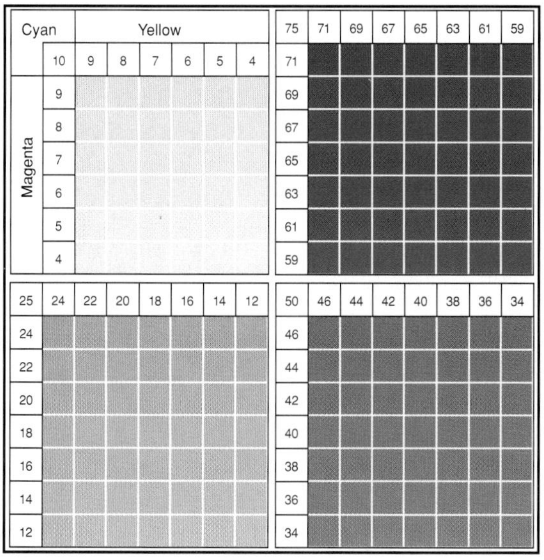

Stepped Color

A stepped color chart is used to establish the color correction controls and also helps with the saturation of color. The chart in Figure 17.5 shows values of color—from solids to pastels. Overcorrecting the saturated solid colors will cause problems with the lower saturated colors. The chart helps to prevent this problem.

The stepped color chart can also help establish a dot gain curve for each ink. A densitometer reading of each percentage will establish the gain of each particular ink when printed. Although perhaps slight, each ink reacts differently when printed on paper, and the dot gains are not necessarily the same for each ink.

Figure 17.4
This gray balance grid provided by GATF helps determine the CMY combinations needed to reproduce neutral at four tonal values (10%, 25%, 50%, and 75%). The individual chips should be viewed while covering any surrounding chips with a neutral piece of paper to eliminate any biases.

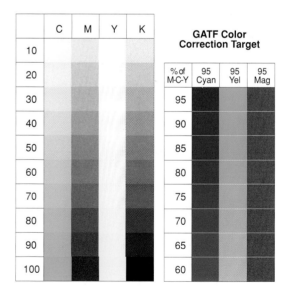

Figure 17.5
A six-color quality control target consists of tints of the CMY inks plus overprints of two colors. The scale helps maintain color standards from job to job as well as dot gain information.

Multiple Color Chips

A quality control target of various color chips should cover all major hues (see Figure 17.6). Various color chips should be viewed individually using a viewer that only enables you to see one color at a time, so that the surrounding hues do not influence your perception. The numbering convention on the chart provides an easy method to relate specific color values from one device to another.

Figure 17.7
This test subject from Fuji provides a wide range of highlight-to-shadow tones.

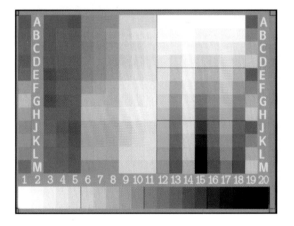

Figure 17.6
A color chip target allows precise analysis of individual color values that may be difficult to identify in a complex scene.

Complex Scenes

Complex scenes provide a real-world check of blended color as it moves in and out of shadows. Color charts with flat color do not tell the whole story of tone and color reproduction. If you rely only on matching color chips, you cannot be assured of reproducing photographic images accurately.

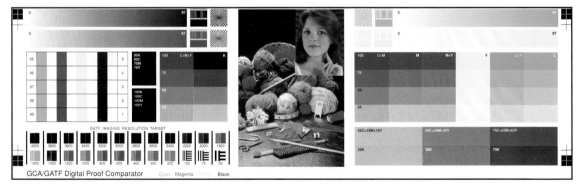

Figure 17.8
The Proof Comparator offered by GCA/GATF.

Quality Control Targets

One of the major problems in digital imaging is confidence that the proof of a digital file is an accurate representation of the information on the file. The large number of digital proofing and imaging technologies has created a need for a reference digital file to compare different systems. Using a standard image from system to system helps evaluate the consistency of each system.

The GATF Proof Comparator is one method used to evaluate the accuracy of digital proofing and imaging systems. In addition to being used as a measure of consistency, the proof comparator is also used to measure key attributes of an imaging system.

The following elements are featured in the Proof Comparator shown in Figure 17.8.

■ A photograph with a wide variety of color and textures is intended for visual evaluation.

■ Three-color gray balance tints are used to visually assess gray balance.

■ Black tints are placed near the gray balance as a neutral reference to judge the gray.

■ Color tint patches are used to measure dot gain, print contrast, and trapping.

■ Blends from 3% to 97% are used to assess the smoothness of the tonal transitions.

■ Star targets indicate resolution of the output device.

■ Density patches of 400% and 300% show the maximum density obtainable from the proofing system.

■ Highlight and shadow patches from 1% to 5% and from 95% to 99% for each process color are used to identify the smallest and largest reproducible dots.

■ A black Imaging Resolution Target measures the resolution of the raster image processing that is used on the digital file prior to output.

■ Smaller resolution blocks for each process color are also included to confirm that the resolution of the raster image processing is consistent from color to color.

To maintain quality assurance, the output and proofing device should periodically undergo some kind of testing. If the targets do not reproduce sharp, well-defined, and with good color reproduction on your output device, then your regular images will not be reproduced well either.

Creating Profiles

Before you begin a calibration and profile of a device, read all of the manufacturer recommended conditions: warm up time, voltage, environmental conditions, type of bulb for the light source, and any other special considerations outlined in the manual. Some of these initial conditions may seem trivial, but establishing consistent operating conditions helps identify variables during operation, not to mention a production routine. If the device suddenly does not operate properly, a routine provides a daily report card from which you can isolate and evaluate any problems.

Each device should have a test image run each time the device is turned on in order to check the reliability of the device. Many devices also have an internal test that they perform when turned on. The test should be checked against an established standard as well as previous results to ensure that the device is operating properly.

Remember, a profile simply establishes the standard operating conditions of a device.

Scanner Profile

An unprofiled scanner is an inefficient tool. The scanner should go through a standard operation to see what the unadjusted regular operating results are for this particular device. If you run a standard in the morning, it should be the same at night. You are trying to establish an MO (modus operandi) for the scanner. You want to make sure that it performs the same way each time. Once you have recognized the standard procedure of the scanner, you can use the results as a measure against future results. In essence, a profile is a measuring standard. The profile describes the normal operation of the scanner.

If, for instance, you scan the same image multiple times without any adjustments and the results are different each time, the scanner may not be stable enough for use in a color reproduction system. Consistency is the key for any device used in a color system. Let's say an inexpensive scanner scans far too dark and green. As long as it does this consistently, you can make adjustments to compensate. If it scans too dark one time, too red the second time, and too light the third time, it is too unstable for a color system. The device profile

helps you establish what is considered stable for the device.

A very simple description of device profile has been provided here. You should continually check the profile to make sure nothing has changed over a period of time. You must understand that every device is unique. If you use a generic profile that is supposed to represent every unit manufactured, you assume that scanner number 232 is the same as scanner number 728. The realities of manufacturing precludes an exact replica. The operating difference between the same model scanner may be slight and barely noticeable, or it may be vastly different. A standard profile cannot assume all of the potential manufacturing differences.

Some profiling systems utilize a direct feedback technique in which the output results of the device (reproducing a standard test target) are fed back into the operating software. The information from the output is used to set the standard operating condition of the device to a manufacturer's norms. This form of profiling eliminates the assumption that every machine was made exactly the same, but instead takes into account the uniqueness of each individual unit.

Output Profiles

An imagesetter is a halftone film output device. An imagesetter is also sometimes referred to as a plotter that uses a laser light source to expose film with a halftone dot pattern. The film is used to create printing plates that are used in offset printing.

To create a profile of an imagesetter, most manufacturers provide an internal program. An example of an internal program is an imagesetter that provides standard output at various exposures. Each specific area of the film output is measured for density. The density values are fed back into the software, and new film is output at the chosen exposure. Dot percentages are then checked to verify that the output is accurate. Measurements are fed back into the software until the dot percentages are correct.

An imagesetter should be checked every shift and recalibrated when chemicals are changed and new film is loaded into the machine. Figure 17.9 illustrates the basic method of profiling and calibrating halftone output. After a grayscale is output, measurements are taken of each patch and numbers recorded. The differences between the standard and the measured percentages are used to adjust the imagesetter or the digital file, and the grayscale is output again. Measurements again are taken and the differences from the standard are

noted and used to adjust the imagesetter or file. This process repeats until the differences between the standard and the measured output are no more than 1% to 2%. Any more than a 2% difference may cause inconsistencies with the color reproduction.

The best way to check a color output is to print the various charts mentioned above to establish its standard operating condition. Catalogue the CMYK equivalents of the various color patches on the charts to use as references when color correcting.

Like imagesetters, some manufacturers provide an internal standard output image from which to take measurements. Density and color values are fed back into the software to insure reliability.

Film Profiles

After the base gray balance settings for the scanner are established, color charts and originals of the Ektachrome and Fujichrome families should be scanned. These two emulsions separate alike and account for a large majority of the transparencies brought in for scanning. Carefully analyze these scans and adjust their color gamut characteristics into the scanner using the yellow, magenta, cyan, orange/red, violet, and green selective color correction controls for each of the four printers. Knowledge of color combinations and correction is necessary to perform this operation correctly.

After you record a program for the Ektachrome and Fujichrome emulsions, start a new calibration procedure for Kodachrome emulsions.

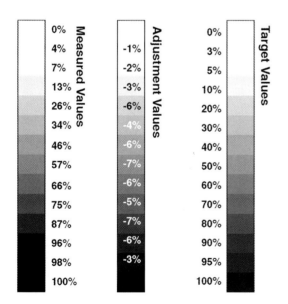

Figure 17.9
The grayscale is the most common control
target used with film output.

The importance of calibration is demonstrated in Figures 17.10a and b. Figure 17.10a is an Ektachrome original and 17.10b is a Fujichrome original. Both images were taken of the same scene, one after the other. Both should look alike. Not having been at the photo shoot, we cannot say which is the closest match to the original scene, but what is important to note here is that the two images do not match. The reason for their different appearance is their film emulsions and the processing of those emulsions. Therefore, a special setup for tone, cast, and color should be made for each type of film emulsion to achieve an image match. Separating different films with the same setup will yield different results. Figure 17.10c illustrates the different spectral responses of two different film emulsions.

Monitor Profiles

Monitors are not a stable source of color. Monitor colors drift over a period of time. Magnetic fields, fading phosphors, and a number of other issues preclude using a monitor as a reliable proofing device. Checking values with an onscreen densitometer, in addition to viewing the color, is required to accurately judge color on a monitor. We applaud those who feel they are able to visually proof color from their monitor. We simply feel the accuracy of monitors has yet to be established as a reliable proofing device.

Monitor manufacturers have given a lot of attention to screen calibrators. These devices optimize and standardize the color and contrast of the viewing monitor. Unfortunately, some people believe that because their screen is calibrated by one of these units, the color on the screen will match the color on the printed output.

Figure 17.10a
A scene photographed with Ektachrome film.

Figure 17.10b
The same scene photographed with Fuji film.

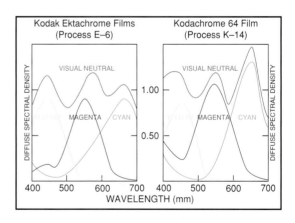

Figure 17.10c
Spectral curves show the different emulsion characteristics of Ektachrome and Kodachrome films.

Monitor calibration devices *are* useful. A calibrated screen does promote a consistent appearance of the images on the monitor. Consistent tones and colors give you a visual feel for the image's appearance on the monitor versus the printed result. But, an *exact* match of the monitor image and press sheet image is not possible. The range of colors, or gamut, of these two color systems is extremely different, so it is unrealistic to expect a monitor screen image to match a press sheet's contrast and color.

The most frustrating exercise is trying to adjust a monitor to the printed colors. It is literally painful to see someone run around in this hopeless maze. However, the calibrating devices many manufacturers offer can keep your monitor's color appearance stable and consistent. And although consistency is the key to keeping a monitor close to reproduction color, the real test is to measure important values with an onscreen densitometer against what you actually get in output.

A densitometer is a color separator's link to the realities of printed output. That is the only way to be absolutely sure of color fidelity. Irradiated phosphorous is different from illuminated printing inks and transparency dyes. They are two different items. You can get them close, but that is all. Do not waste time trying to calibrate a monitor to "exactly" match your printed output.

Checklist

Before you use more complicated methods, you should get a feel for the process of calibrating. The simplest and most straightforward calibration is visual. You probably have already practiced some form of visual calibration if you have altered images in retouching programs.

1. Scan an image with the grayscale.

2. Bring the image into an imaging program.

3. Print the image to your output device.

4. Compare the printed image and grayscale to the original.

5. Make adjustments to the image using curves.

6. Save the curve used to adjust the image and print again.

7. Repeat steps 4, 5, and 6 until you get a result you can accept.

8. Save the curve as Calibration.01.

At this point you have a simple calibration between your scanner and output device. After you scan an image, you need to correct it using the Calibration.01 curve. Unfortunately, you have only established that it will work for this particular image, with this particular scanner, and with this particular output device. You must repeat the process to confirm that this curve will work for other images. You may find that, depending on the type of image, you may need to establish other curves.

Also, it was assumed that you had no control during the scanning process. Many scanners now have the capability to adjust an image while scanning. If this is the case, you can simply print the image after scanning and make any adjustment during the scanning process. If the scanner does not enable you to save the curves or settings, keep a notebook at hand and record the settings for future use.

You also may want to adjust the monitor to match the color of output. After you have established an acceptable print reproduction, display the image on your monitor—adjusting the monitor to match the printed images as you see fit. Using the physical control is one method, but using Software such as Gamma by Knoll Software is more precise. Gamma is shipped with Photoshop and allows you to adjust your monitor display by changing the overall balance, black-and-white points, and gamma settings of the display. The software also allows you to save settings. When the image on the monitor is to your liking, you now have a visual calibration among your scanner, monitor, and printer.

Remember, the colors will not match exactly because each reproduction system does not necessarily contain all colors. You are only trying to achieve an acceptable and predictable relationship among all the colors. For more precise calibrations, you should not only follow the above steps, but include densitometer readings of the grayscale to establish a more numeric relationship to output.

Special areas you should consider when calibrating a system include the following:

- During the color separation procedure, CMYK readings of the dye densities in the photographic originals are compared to neutral standards to determine which kind of color balance the originals contain. The calibration to neutral standards that is used for comparison must be calculated carefully to achieve the best possible standards.

- A well-calibrated system means that setting a proper highlight and shadow point produces a reproduction that is a very close match to most normally exposed originals. Complicated adjustments are not necessary to get good color if the system is calibrated for normal subjects of a particular type of original. Originals with exposure and cast problems always take more work, but normally exposed subjects should come off with a minimum of adjustments.

- Customers who have quantities of art with special pigments should supply the separator with a color gamut and gray chart that uses their pigments so the separator can calibrate to those pigments' color conditions. You can get a closer match to the customer's originals with this new calibration.

- For scanners located in press houses, each press in the pressroom can have a calibration program made for its particular printing conditions.

- Newly installed scanners and color separation software are set up to factory default values. You must feed these color separation devices the proper data for the color conditions of the proofing material or press for which the scans are made. The manufacturer's supplied settings are just starting points for producing color, so calibrating to your color system is your responsibility.

Follow the manufacturer's instructions for linearizing the scanner or software and output device to the film processor. When you complete this procedure, output grayscales from 5% to 95%, check them visually and with the densitometer, and record the dot percentages. If the values are off by more than 2 percent, start again. You must be confident that the readouts on the scanner or computer screen densitometer are giving you the same dot percentages on output.

- Be sure any film processors are operating properly with fresh chemistry. Run several control strips, record their values, and write down the development time and developer temperature.

- After consistency is achieved, the next step in calibrating is to set the tone and gray balance by reproducing a neutral subject tone-for-tone that is completely cast-free on your proofing system. The resulting dot percentages are the base gray balance settings from which all other calibrations are set.

- The best neutral test subject to use for calibrating is a gray scale made of dyes. The available silver scales are cheaper, but these scales have a light-scattering side effect called Callier's Q Factor, which reduces the accuracy of the scanner's readouts. Check the scale's neutrality on the scanner or a densitometer by looking for equal densities of yellow, magenta, and cyan in each step. On a monitor densitometer, look for equal values of RGB in the gray-scale steps, which indicate neutral. Ask your film supplier about obtaining one of these scales.

- To determine gray balance, make a scan of the gray scale, and then separate and proof. Compare the proofs to the original gray scale for neutrality and weight

throughout the tonal area. Make adjustments as necessary and rescan. Note middle tone densities of both reflective and transmissive originals. When you achieve a match, record the values of CMYK and enter them in the separation device's software.

- Try to see as many proofs as possible during the calibration procedure. Work closely with the proofer and be certain that the proofing conditions are to the manufacturer's specifications. A bad proof invalidates your settings.

- After the transmissive subjects are calibrated, switch reflective subjects and run a reflective gray scale. Proof the results and compare. Because both mediums are reflective, the comparison should be easier. You will find that the reflective gray standards may differ from the transmissive gray standards. Reflective copy has a shorter density range, so the gray settings are lower than the transmissive values.

- When you have completed these steps, record all settings and keep a log book to track any correction trends you notice during the daily work. If you constantly make a certain correction over a period of time, make it a permanent part of your calibration standard. Calibration is an ongoing process that takes many scans to perfect.

- At the minimum, you should store a calibration for each proofing system that can be used, with a separate calibration for three types of originals: C prints, E-6 transparencies, and Fujichrome transparencies.

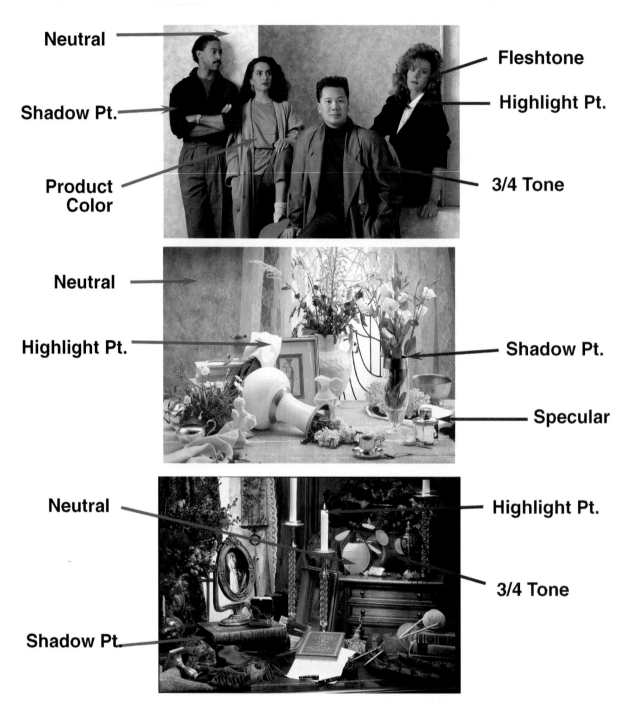

Neutral

Fleshtone

Shadow Pt.

Highlight Pt.

Product
Color

3/4 Tone

Neutral

Highlight Pt.

Shadow Pt.

Specular

Neutral

Highlight Pt.

3/4 Tone

Shadow Pt.

Figure 17.11
You use aim-points as calibration data.
Images courtesy of GATF.

Final Word

Predictability and reliability are the most important parts of color reproduction. If you cannot rely on the devices working properly, every production is a shot in the dark. Sometimes you'll hit the target, but most of the time you'll miss. Calibration requires an attention to detail and an understanding that the whole color process is fluid—it changes from day to day and job to job. Keeping everything consistent at least enables you the ability to know where adjustments need to be made to ensure the quality you need.

Page
Layout

"If one of you decides to build a
tower sitteth down first, and
counteth the cost, to see you have
sufficient means to finish it."

Luke 14:28

The placement of text, graphics, and images together in one cohesive form is called page layout. The page goes beyond just printed output; it is also extended to multimedia productions. The electronic page organizes the different elements in a language that output devices can understand. The page description language is simply a way of relating the positions of bitmaps, vectors, and type to eventual physical output. The page is a director of sorts—it may not contain the actual elements, but it knows where they all belong. The PostScript page language is the most commonly used language.

Life of a Page

There are many different programs and applications that perform page layout, and it would be difficult to mention them all. The specifics of each program may vary, but laying out pages is essentially the function of a layout program. Every page layout system has the capability to place text and images on a designated area that represents eventual output.

Most layout programs can edit as well as place text information, which makes them similar to word processing programs. In fact, the difference between a page layout program and a word processor is blurring. Most word processing programs now handle the insertion of images, and most layout programs are capable of inputting and managing text.

Images that are placed into a layout program are low-resolution proxies or representatives of the entire images (see Figure 18.1). When pages are output, the proxy tells the program where it can find the high-resolution image on the hard drive. If the image is not present, the output device will either leave a blank spot where the image should be, or the low-resolution proxy will be used. If a proxy image is used, the result will be a rough pixelated appearance. Most programs will alert you if an image is missing before you output.

A number of systems now offer automatic picture replacement. Automatic picture replacement allows a color shop to send a client the low-resolution proxies. The client can then lay out the images in the appropriate positions and then send the page back to the color shop. At the color shop, the high-resolution images replace the low-resolution proxies. This gives a designer the freedom to lay out images with smaller-sized files and produce rough proofs that are faster to process and output. The smaller file sizes also make the modem transfer of pages more of a reality. One downside to automatic picture replacement is that the proxy should never be resized or distorted. The changes to a proxy usually do not translate to the high-resolution files.

Any changes to a lo-res proxy need to be measured and duplicated on the high-res file. An operator manually makes the changes and replaces the lo-res file with the high-res file before final output.

After all the elements are completed, the page is RIPed to the appropriate output device. The RIP process renders all the complex digital image information into a complete high-resolution bitmap that the output device can understand. If you review Chapter 4 on rendering, you will recall that all imagery requires translation to a pixel-based bitmap. Pages are no exception.

The high-resolution bitmap is sent line by line to the output device and discarded as soon as the device is ready for the next line (see Figure 18.2). If the raster lines were not discarded, the storage required to hold a fully rendered bitmap page could reach 500 megabytes or more depending on the complexity of the graphics, the size of the page, and the resolution of the output device. As desktop computers and software become more sophisticated, the likelihood of editing fully rendered pages is very high. Entire pages can now be saved as EPS page files. This page file can then be placed into other page layout programs, but none of the elements are editable.

The resolution of the output device determines how fast the RIPing process will produce output. The higher the resolution of the output device, the more rendered bitmap pixels are produced

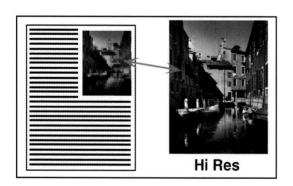

Figure 18.1
A proxy is used in a page layout and is connected to a high resolution file.

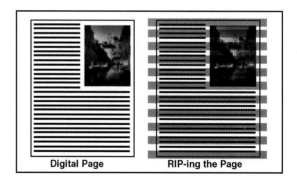

Figure 18.2
A page is processed line by line by the RIP and imaged by the output device.

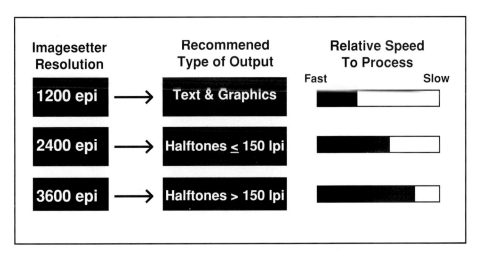

Figure 18.3
The higher-resolution output devices take longer to render and output a page.

from the page. The more pixels in the bitmap, the more information to be processed. The more information to be processed, the greater the time to process the images (see Figure 18.3).

Many imagesetters provide options that use only a certain amount of imaging elements so that pages will process faster. In many cases, the lower device resolution measured in imaging elements per inch (epi) will not decrease the quality. If you are only outputting text or graphics with outline and spot colors, 1200 epi is more than sufficient. If you are producing halftone output up to 150 lines per inch (lpi), 2400 epi is considered the minimum acceptable. Any printing done above 150 lpi should use an imagesetter with at least 3600 epi. Printing text only at 3600 epi only slows down the processing time and does not provide any gains in visual quality.

Production Advice

There are so many different approaches to proper page layout that it is impossible to find a single definitive methodology. There are some very specific guidelines that will make your page layout an easier experience.

NO Scaling

No scaling, rotating, or distortions of bitmap images should be performed by a page layout program. If we could lock out one feature in a page layout program, it would be the resizing of any bitmap image. Page layout programs are not designed for the sophisticated resampling methods that are required by scaling and rotations. The algorithms use simple replication, and if you resize a bitmap it will deteriorate the quality of the image. Also, the rendering process to output will slow considerably if scaling needs to be performed. Scaling vector graphics, such as PostScript, are acceptable because of the nature of vectors, but it is a good habit to prepare all your images to the appropriate size before you begin layout.

Any resizing of a bitmap image should be done in an image program such as Adobe Photoshop. The best plan to follow whenever doing layout is to have all the elements sized properly in their respective image programs before you begin. If you run into a situation in which the image should be resized, go back to the image program and resize the image there. The time you take to perform resizing in the appropriate program will be much less than the time it will take an RIP to complete the resizing, especially if it is a large image. For those of you who say, "I won't know the size until I begin layout," use a low-resolution version of the image, make a note about any scaling, and resize it in an image program. Believe us when we say that the quality will be higher and you will be saving output time.

Image Crop

The page layout program will allow you to crop a placed image or graphic. It is always a good idea to create an image with just a little more imagery than you need. Because many picture windows have borders placed around them, the extra imagery helps ensure a nice, smooth crop with no blank areas showing between the border and the imagery.

You should be aware that the RIP must still manage all the imagery placed in a page, even if it is not going to be output. Do not bring in a large graphic or image only to crop it into a small image, as illustrated in Figure 18.4. The RIP will still have to read and manage the entire file—this slows the entire output process. Crop any excessive imagery in the appropriate image program and then import the image or graphic for placement. Any time that you take to crop before layout will save you more time during output.

Figure 18.4
The RIP must manage the entire image file even if cropped in an page layout program.

Color Separations

Most page layout programs provide basic color separations of spot color. If you are printing with process CMYK inks, make sure that all the colors used in the page layout are created using CMYK values. This also includes any graphics created in PostScript drawing programs. If you should begin a project by identifying colors as pink, red, blue, mauve, blue2, light green, and orange and you output the page to CMYK separations, you will get not only the process color, but all those spot colors as well. Paying for all the additional film produced, plus the time and expense of correcting and producing new film, can be avoided by simply creating special colors with CMYK values. Of course, if you are producing a CMYK job with eight spot colors, you can ignore this suggestion.

Some page layout programs offer features that provide RGB to CMYK conversions of bitmap images. We strongly recommend that you do all color conversions in an image program like Photoshop or Color Access. Color space conversions in page layout programs are unreliable and output processing time is increased substantially. For greater control, color separations should be performed before placement in a page layout program.

Registration Marks

When reproducing color pages, each layer of color needs to be placed precisely in the same position on the printed page. When colors are printed in exactly the same position relative to another, the page is said to be in register. If the colors are misaligned or out-of-register (see Figure 18.5), the resulting imagery will look out of focus. Registration marks are used to visually compose the different colors of a page.

During the printing process, paper is passed through a series of rollers and over cylinders to place ink on paper. The physical realities of printing distort and stretch paper while it passes through the printing press. Registration marks are independent guides that the printer uses to adjust the press and align the colors to one another. Depending on the quality of the paper and the speed of the press, the difference in registration from one color to another should be between 0.01 and 0.001 of an inch.

The slower the press, the easier it is to register the colors. Normal AM halftone dots rely heavily on precise position to create tone and color. The misregistration may not seem like a

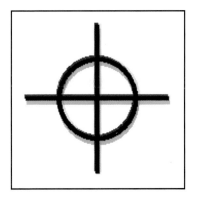

Figure 18.5
When viewed up close, misregistration shows the different colors out of alignment.

large amount, but if you consider the size of halftone dots, poor registration can greatly impact the quality of an image. An advantage to using FM dots (which rely less on position), is that the registration tolerance can be much higher while still producing acceptable tone and color in an image.

Along with the registration marks, crop marks are usually included to indicate where the paper should be trimmed after printing. There are also marks that will indicate where the paper should be folded. Traditionally, registration marks should be placed centered on the top, bottom, and sides of the page. The intersection of lines drawn through the center of properly placed registration marks is a quick way to locate the exact center of the page.

Some of the generic registration and crop marks output with page layout programs are not precise enough for some printers. Many color houses shun the generic marks and create their own custom marks (see Figure 18.6).

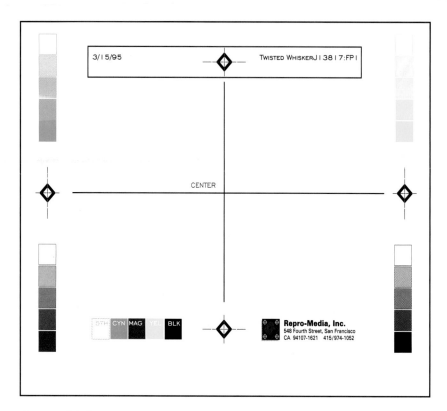

Figure 18.6
An example of custom registration marks.

Trapping

The term *trapping* can mean two entirely different things, depending on the context of the word. If you speak to a press operator, trapping (also called wet trapping) relates first and foremost to the ability of wet ink to transfer to paper. When inks are laid on top of one another during the four-color process of CMYK, the previous ink is still wet. As one wet ink is printed on top of another, they may not mix correctly. The mixing of the wet inks can result in an undesirable color shift.

By adjusting the stickiness, or tack, of the ink, the printer can adjust the trapping of the inks to ensure good color reproduction. Depending on

the type of press used and the speed it runs, too much wet ink can cause trapping problems. This is the reason the total amount of ink is controlled when color separations are created. The ideal situation is to allow each ink enough time to dry before printing the next color. The issue of trapping is a large concern for the idea of hi-fi print, where up to three additional layers of ink are added to the paper. The speed of hi-fi printing may need to be decreased to allow for some drying of each ink before laying down another ink.

The other, and more common, use for trapping is the intentional overlapping of colors along common edges (this is to prevent unprinted paper from showing if there is any misregistration during printing). If registration is perfect all the time, which it rarely is, no overlapping is needed, and any adjacent colors are considered to butt-fit or kiss. Because a butt-fit is very difficult for a press to achieve, most printers want some kind of trap to ensure that slight misregistration will not impact the quality of the reproduction.

Many trap situations involve two solid areas of spot color. But traps are also needed when placing flat areas of color together with images. To approach trapping, you should understand the difference between knockout and overprints.

An overprint is simple. You print one color over another color. Black is an ink that overprints just about everything because the ink underneath only adds to the density of the black. If you are trying to keep them unique, however, other colors are not so easy to overprint. For example, if you print magenta text directly over cyan, the resulting text color is blue (see Figure 18.7a). Overprinting is a useful way to create a third color in a two-color job. But, to keep the magenta text magenta, you need to take away or knock out the cyan where the magenta will go. The knockout allows the magenta text to print directly onto the paper and not mix with the cyan (see Figure 18.7b).

A knockout is a removal of ink from one area to accommodate the printing of another color. The knockout makes it necessary to have a trap. The basic knockout allows the paper to show. If you lay the magenta directly into the space of the knockout, you will have a butt-fit. The movement of paper during the printing process will misalign the magenta and cyan, and paper will show, as illustrated in Figure 18.8a. By either

Figure 18.7a
An example of an overprint.

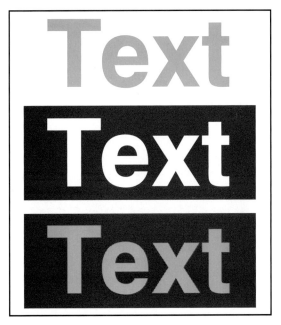

Figure 18.7b
An example of a knockout.

spreading the magenta outward, or choking the cyan inward, you will create an overlap that will prevent any paper from appearing during any misregistration (see Figure 18.8b).

The thin area of overlap created by a trap is called a secondary color. If the trap is too wide, the secondary color will cause more of a distraction to the image than the paper peeking between the cracks of the butt-fit (see Figure 18.8c). It is our experience that printers want at least a little trap, but too much will cause problems. A typical trap is approximately .25 points or .003 of inch or .08 millimeters.

If you want to knock out a process CMYK black to create paper-white text or a paper-white object, you will need to produce a keepaway. A keepaway pushes back the cyan, magenta, and yellow ink from the edge of the black, as illustrated in Figure 18.9. The result is a clean, one-color edge, with black used to define the edge. Any misregistration during printing will not cause the cyan, magenta, or yellow to move into the knocked out area.

If a process-created spot color were laid into the knockout, the colors kept away would be determined by the spot color. For example, if the spot color were red, then only the cyan would be kept away and the black would define the edge with the red (created by magenta and yellow). When a spot color is created with CMY process inks, there is no need for a trap because the process spot color inks link with the process inks in the image and any visible misregistration is minimal.

The need for an individual to trap at all is debatable. Unless you are completely familiar with the intricacies of trapping, which can be many, it is best to leave trapping to the practiced hand. Many service centers offer trapping

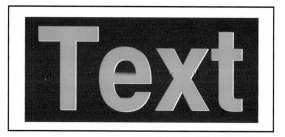

Figure 18.8a
An example of misregistration with no trap.

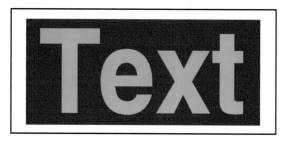

Figure 18.8b
A example of how a little trap will help if there is any misregistration.

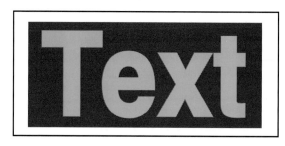

Figure 18.8c
An example of how too much trap creates an undesirable dark line.

during the output process. Programs like TrapWise and Island Trapper are expensive, but effective, tools used by many service bureaus. Scitex systems also offer a very direct route to trapping. Pages rendered through Scitex systems are easily trapped if no trapping has been used on the page. In most cases, it is better to avoid trapping in your drawing programs and allow the service center to apply trapping during output.

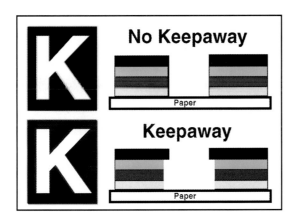

Figure 18.9
An example of how a keepaway is needed
when creating a knockout in a black made
with CMYK process inks.

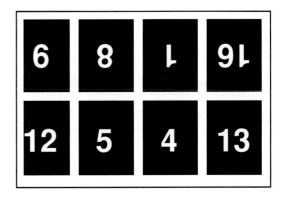

Figure 18.10a
One half of a 16-page signature.

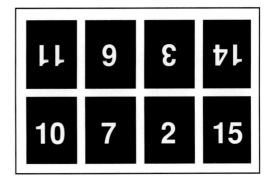

Figure 18.10b
The other side of the 16-page signature.

Imposition of Pages

Pages produced for printing must be arranged in a particular way to accommodate the size of the printing press. Placing pages in the proper position is called imposition. Traditionally, pages are combined or flatted by craftspeople called strippers. The arranged pages are called signatures. The pages are placed in a special order so that when the pages are printed on both sides (backed up) and then folded and trimmed, all 16 numbered pages will be in the correct order. Figures18.10a and b show a 16-page signature.

There are programs now that place pages in position and eliminate the need to physically combine the films. An understanding of the different printing presses is required to correctly position film. Strippers, whether performing imposition electronically or physically, are most qualified to perform this task.

Open Documents

Open documents are the next big move for pages. As mentioned earlier, the compatibility between page files and image and graphic files is very limited. The next step will be efforts directed toward establishing an open document that will be a common format that anyone can read—kind of like a TIFF for documents. There are several open architectures being promoted. The two most talked about are OLE (Object Linking and Embedding) by Microsoft and OpenDoc by Apple. Whether either or both of these systems are adopted, the idea behind them is the same. A document will carry all the fonts, images, and graphics of a page. You will have the ability to view those images without having the program that created the pages. These open documents will be similar to a soft render before physical output. Page layout pages will be rendered to digital documents, rather than directly to physical output. A viewer application will be needed to read the documents.

Using open documents is a movement toward the paperless office. Acrobat by Adobe and Common Ground by No Hands Software are two versions of the open document concept. Open documents allow the user to view and print documents without having to have any of the fonts or the original application used to create the document. Open documents also allow more cross-platform distribution of documents with greater ease and reliability.

Some open documents may provide an opportunity for future editing by users who do not necessarily need to have the original layout program.

Checklist

- Prepare your job ahead of time. Any time taken to prepare images properly before layout will save you time during output.

- The size of choke or traps should be between .25 pts and .40 pts. The faster the press, the larger the potential trap needed. Discuss the requirements with a printer.

- Do NOT scale bitmap images using the page layout program.

- Crop as much of the image as possible in an image or graphic program. Even the portions of the image you don't see on the page must be processed by the RIP.

- Be sure that all the fonts use the image program and that they are available for your output service. Provide a list of the fonts during output.

- Use a TIFF file whenever possible when placing a page layout. TIFF files are the most reliable and straightforward file format. There are some features that require using an ESP file, but TIFF is the way to go.

- Keep it simple. The layout is primarily used for composing elements together. Use the strengths of other image programs to make alterations of the graphics or imagery.

Final Word

Page layout is an important part of the production process. Assembling images and text have always been the domain of the layout artist. There are still postproduction processes like trapping and imposition that are best handled by the output providers. The best approach to page layout is to keep the page as simple as possible, avoiding automatic features that tend to bog down the rendering process. If a feature is not critical to your output, turn it off.

Transparency Output

19

"I think it angers God if you
walk by the color purple in a
field somewhere and don't
notice it."

Alice Walker,
20th Century Writer

on a monitor's color at any time; you should always judge your output according to the values you read with your software and then relate the values to the final output.

Output Concerns

Just as in print, the tonal endpoints of highlight and shadow are the two main areas of concern. First, you should identify your highlight point. In a digital image, pure white is a value of zero RGB. Pure black is a value of 255 RGB. In most transparency outputs, the densest blacks occur between values of 220 and 255 RGB. Any value of RGB above 220 should be watched carefully in the final transparency output to ensure that shadow detail is being reproduced. The detail in transparencies varies depending on the specific film recorder and the type of film that is used. Color-positive transparencies are not the only film type that can be exposed from digital files. Negative and black-and-white film also can be used, and each type of film has special concerns.

Transparencies can capture a wide range of density because of their transmissive nature. Adjusting the contrast of the digital file not only maintains shadow detail, but also brings the tonal range somewhat closer to the tonal range of printed subjects.

The density range of transparency material is very high, and it is more than capable of reproducing 24-bit RGB images with all the desired tonal steps visible in the transparency. Many film recorders have difficulty reaching into the shadow details of a digital image. The result may be a flat black where you expect to see tone and details. The easiest way to bring out the shadow details is to lower the shadow point to somewhere between 220 and 254. By using a curve, you can compensate for the loss of shadow detail.

The highlight and shadow points' positions determine the visual contrast of the transparency that you produce. If you move one end point, the change in tone is greatest at that end of the curve. As you travel along the curve, the difference between the original and revised transparency diminishes to the point where there is no change occurring. If a transparency comes out too heavy overall, you may select lighter densities of the highlight and shadow points. Moving the endpoints of a curve compresses the tonal range of the entire image and should be done sparingly. Figures 19.1a through 19.4b illustrate the compensation of an image using a curve's shadow endpoint.

The best way to compensate for transparency output is to adjust the endpoints using color-correction curves that are found in most programs. Monitors adjusted for viewing print reproduction may result in a darker overall image when output to transparency if compensation corrections are not made. If you use the monitor to judge color, you should make a special calibration to relate the monitor to transparency output, which is different than the calibration needed to compare monitor images to print output.

Correcting for the contrast range bias in a film recorder may make the image appear a bit faded on the screen if the monitor is displayed to

Figure 19.1a
An uncorrected image.

Figure 19.2a
Image with 10% shadow point correction.

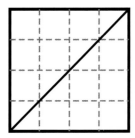

Figure 19.1b
A curve
indicating no
correction.

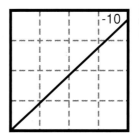

Figure 19.2b
Minus 10% shadow
point.

judge for print. If you take these production concerns into account, however, you should achieve an accurate transparency with no loss of detail in either the highlights or the shadows. Because every film recorder has different amounts of bias, it takes experience to become proficient in compensating for the endpoints. Table 19.1 shows typical situations and possible corrections. Figures 19.5 through 19.10 illustrate how some of the corrections in Table 19.1 correct the tone in an image and grayscale.

Table 19.1 Corrections for Transparency Output

Condition	Correction Method
Highlights too light, shadow (contrast) OK	Increase highlight percentage, reset same shadow
Highlights dark, shadow (contrast) OK	Reset highlights in denser (darker) area, reset same shadow

Figure 19.3a
Image with 15% shadow point correction.

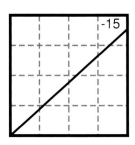

Figure 19.3b
Minus 15% shadow
point.

Highlights OK, contrast heavy	Decrease shadow percentage
Highlights OK, contrast weak	Increase shadow percentage
Highlights heavy, contrast heavy	Lighten highlights, decrease shadow percentage
Highlights weak, shadow weak	Increase highlight percentages, increase shadow percentages

Figure 19.4a
Image with 20% shadow point correction.

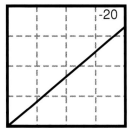

Figure 19.4b
Minus 20% shadow
point.

Always set the highlight point first and then the shadow point, because any subsequent movement of the highlight shifts the position of the shadow. If an incorrect highlight setting has proper contrast, reset the highlight and then readjust the shadow point to the same value as before.

In images such as snow scenes, which have a great degree of white, the more subtle detail could be lost. You may need to increase the first quarter-tone anywhere from 5 to 20 percent to

Figure 19.5a
Original image with highlights dark and shadow (contrast) OK.

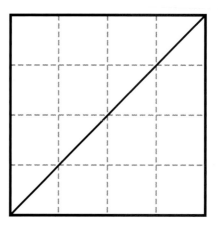

Figure 19.5b
Curve with no correction.

Figure 19.6a
Increase the highlight point to add weight to lighter values.

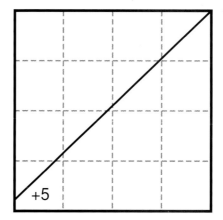

+5

Figure 19.6b
Curve with plus highlight point.

Figure 19.7a
Original image with highlight OK and contrast weak.

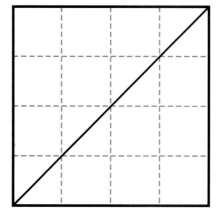

Figure 19.7b
Curve with no correction.

Figure 19.8a
Increase shadow point to add weight to darker values.

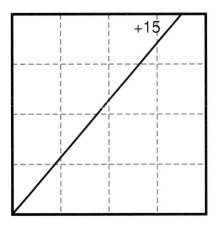

Figure 19.8b
Curve with plus shadow point.

Figure 19.9a
Original image with highlight heavy and contrast heavy.

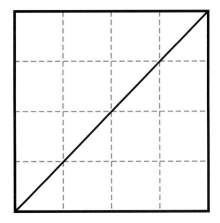

Figure 19.9b
Curve with no correction.

Figure 19.10a
Lightened highlight and decreased shadow percentage.

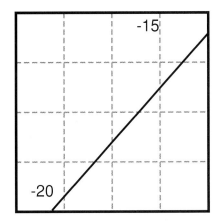

Figure 19.10b
Curve with minus highlight point and minus shadow point.

retain the detail in those white areas. This situation is one of the few exceptions to simply picking endpoints of highlight and shadow.

Film Recorders

Film recording devices actually record pixel information. They are considered direct pixel imaging devices. The elements per inch (epi) that the recorder can produce are directly related to the number of pixels in your image. A film recorder with 1,270 epi exposes 1,270 pixels for every inch of film. This is very different from imagesetters, whose elements create dots. Remember, for film material, you do not have dots, but fine grains of light-sensitive crystals that are exposed by the number of pixels contained in the image.

A high-end film recorder produces 50 pixels per millimeter, or 1,270 pixels per inch. An image with 2,540 pixels across and down results in a 2" × 2" transparency (2,540 divided by 1,270 equals 2).

Because the fine grain in film transparencies requires more information to reproduce a continuous tone image, it results in large file sizes—20 megabytes for the 2-inch-square example. These file sizes can be unmanageable or harder to work with, depending on your quality needs. Upsampling an image 200 percent gives you a greater amount of pixel information and results in a larger potential output size (see Chapter 1, "Pixels"). We recommend that you do not increase the amount of pixel information by more than 200 percent because this may result in a lower image quality (softened edges with interpolation and pixelated edges with replication). In many

circumstances, you may disregard this recommendation if you are not concerned with the highest quality possible.

A typical 8" × 10" transparency needs 10,160 pixels across and 12,700 pixels down. This file size is nearly 387 MB! You seldom see an entire file this size, but as software and hardware begin to accommodate larger files, 387 MB will seem trivial. If large files are a concern, you should use a file with half that amount of information to produce a total size of 90 MB. This file then will be interpolated 200 percent during output; the resulting transparency will still be of high quality.

Text

Combining text with a digital file for output to a transparency is possible in two ways. At very high resolutions, the text does not necessarily need to be anti-aliased. If there is no upsampling of the digital file, aliased text can provide a much cleaner, sharper edge because the resolution of a high-end film recorder is very close to the minimum resolution output required for typesetting.

In most cases where upsampling is taking place, anti-aliased text produces outstanding text in a transparency. "Text," in this case, refers to headlines or display text and not bodies of copy. The reason long galleys of copy are not recommended is because the photographic film reproductions of fine text are not as sharp as standard typesetting procedures. But you can achieve dramatic results with text above 14 points. As mentioned in Chapter 4, you can take a PostScript linework file and render the PostScript into the bitmap. When the edges of the text are properly anti-aliased, you get a fine, pleasing edge and the text is appropriate for film output.

Checklist

- Film output has its own gamut and range of tones or contrast. A special calibration should be made to match the color.

- Sharpness should either not be used or used at a bare minimum because little sharpness is lost with transparency output. Unsharp masking halos are easily visible when used with images destined for transparency output.

- Output of an RGB file means no black printer is needed. Any CMYK files should

be converted to RGB for transparency output. But this is not an ideal situation. If you are going to output transparencies, you should retain an RGB original.

- Try not to scale an Image more than 200 percent before output because the film recorder may also perform an upsampling during output.

- The resolution required depends on the film recorder. A resolution of 1270 ppi (50 ppmm) is the usual maximum. This may result in a very large file depending on the physical size of the output. A resolution of 640 ppi (25 ppmm) is more common and most film recorders upsample an image by 200 percent to achieve the required resolution for output.

Final Word

In most cases, output to transparency offers fewer production concerns than producing an image on film separations. The ability to interpolate 200 percent at the output stage, without loss of quality, enables you to keep images at manageable sizes. Because the artist stays in RGB the entire time, color concerns are fewer and the output is more predictable. In most circumstances, persons trained for CMYK print production would rather make the separation decisions than have an artist guess at the proper figures. This relieves the artist from doing things he or she does not want to do, and keeps the print production expert from correcting mistakes that stem from lack of experience. Because all the desired ad or image information is contained in the transparency, separations of various sizes (and with various printing specifications) can be made easily at the scanner shop. The transparency can be sent to people whose reproduction facilities may not be able to receive digital information. Overall, the options that transparency output can provide make the retouching environment much more flexible.

Video
Output

"Some things are easy only
they are hard to do."

Albert Einstein

The monitor is used to show both static (stationary) and dynamic (moving) images. These images can be color, black and white, or any combination of the two. Moving images are called video; soundtracks played with them are called audio. A combination of dynamic and static images with audio and text is called multimedia because it combines several types of communication in one visual experience.

Video input and output is another method of using digital information to create moving images. Video has different concerns from other types of image reproduction, including flicker and color gamut, and compression. Like all methods of image reproduction, the more you know about the image system, the more control you will have over that system.

Video Data

Video information is made up of continuous analog signals. In order to manipulate the information on your computer, you must convert the analog into digital data. Once converted to digital data, the video images can be stored and manipulated like any other digital imagery.

The analog to digital (A-D) conversion has two steps: sampling the information and quantizing the information. The two steps are very similar (in concept) to the basic visual scanning process discussed in Chapter 3. Like a scanner, the A-D conversion process takes analog information and converts it to digital data. The conversion procession must "look" at the video signal and collect the wave information at a certain sampling rate per second. The sampling rate is analogous to resolution in a scanner. As the sampling rate increases, more samples are taken from the analog signal per second.

Quantizing is a process that reduces the number of colors of the source material to match the number of colors used during output. Quantizing the input color samples is comparable to a 12-bit scanner choosing the best 8-bits of color information for use in a 24-bit color system. Quantizing can be done in several different ways—usually a predefined threshold level compares the original video signal values to the samples that are converted to digital binary values. There are many methods used to quantize color for use in video systems. The type of video system used will determine the method of quantizing used.

A typical analog video signal has several parts that must be separated before using the video in computer graphics. There are several signal formats, including NTSC, PAL, and SECAM. The color spaces that are used in video signals typically use three channels of information: the YUV, YIQ, or YCC models. The Y component of each of the color spaces contains the luminance (or tonal) information, and the two remaining channels carry the chrominance (or color) information. The RGB model used in still images is too complex for transmission of video signals.

Television uses the color space model of one luminance and two chroma values because the chrominance values are easily compressed. Typically, the chrominance data is compressed

using a lossy scheme. The lossy compression makes the entire image file very small and therefore faster to transmit electronically. Remember that the tone of an image carries most of the important image information— color is secondary. Compressing the color information found in the chrominance channels does not substantially degrade the image quality if the luminance values are kept intact. Both the PhotoCD and JPEG file formats employ a lossy compression of the chrominance values to save space on the file.

The two major types of video color spaces are NTSC and PAL. The National Television Systems Committee (NTSC) of the USA established a video color standard adopted by the FCC for general broadcast use in 1953. The Phase Alternation Line (PAL) video color space was adopted by Great Britain and Germany in 1967. The broadcast systems of NTSC and PAL are similar, but the numbers of total picture elements and color gamuts differ slightly (see Figure 20.1).

Colors that are outside the gamut of video will bleed into adjoining areas. This bleeding creates an effect of color smearing, also called *bloom*, which usually is accompanied by undesirable noise interference (see Figure 20.2). Working outside the video color gamut also decreases the sharpness of the image.

Many programs have special color palettes that allow use only of colors within the video gamut. These programs cause the colors on the computer to look duller because they compensate for the limited NTSC gamut. Also available are plug-in production filters that filter out any colors outside the NTSC gamut. A filter that is specific to PAL may be necessary to filter out to the PAL gamut, which differs from the NTSC

Figure 20.1
Color gamuts between NTSC and PAL
differ slightly.

Figure 20.2
An illustration of bloom.

gamut. In both cases, compensation for video's limited color gamut is necessary to ensure the best possible output.

Video Pixels

The pixels of a digital video system are the same as the pixels in a still image, except the pixel values in a video system are constantly changing and are updated over time to create the

illusion of movement. The movement is a sequence of individual still frames that change a minimum of 24 frames per second (fps), which is the standard motion picture frame rate and is considered the minimum frame rate to create a smooth transition of movement.

The PAL system uses 625-line television standards at 25 frames per second, and NTSC uses 525 lines of pixels at 30 frames per second (more precisely 29.97 fps). NTSC video projects alternate horizontal lines (fields) that are one pixel thick. Alternating even and odd fields are displayed onscreen every 1/30 of a second, which refreshes the image every 1/60 of a second. This is called an interlaced mode of display. A computer screen displays a noninterleaved mode, in which the lines are displayed sequentially one directly following another approximately 60 to 80 times per second (see Figure 20.3). This is why you see a band moving down a computer screen when you see one on television. The interlaced and noninterleaved modes are interfering with one another resulting in an interference pattern.

For example, look at the thin lines used to create windows on most graphic user interface windows. The common black-and-white (and also colored) lines are typically one pixel thick. If you were to directly transfer the digital image from your computer screen that has thin one pixel lines in it, the lines would be blinking on and off every 1/30 of second and would seem to jump or flicker on the screen.

A one-pixel-high horizontal line blinks on and off 30 times per second and appears to be flickering more than a two-pixel-high line does, which blinks 60 times per second. (The two-pixel line is refreshed alternately by an even and odd field.) You see continuous motion on a video image when the even and odd fields work

Figure 20.3
Video alternates display the even and odd raster lines. Computer monitors display each raster line one directly following another.

together. If the title bar lines of windows were two pixels thick, there would be no perceptible flicker. When you create or draw images for eventual video output, avoid horizontal or nearly horizontal lines composed of a single pixel. Because video is projected in horizontal lines, vertical lines have no flicker problem.

A kind of video moiré also is created when a person wears a striped shirt on television. The thin horizontal lines in clothing create a flicker that is exacerbated by the movement of the person. So if you ever appear in a video production or television, stay away from thin stripes.

Time Codes

To measure the additional variable of time, the Society of Motion Picture and Television Engineers has developed the SMPTE time code. The time code identifies each frame in a video signal in the form of HOURS:MINUTES:SECONDS:FRAMES. The time coding provides precise editing capabilities and accurate synchronization of audio and video clips. A video sequence with a duration of 00:03:16:15 runs for 3 minutes, 16 seconds, and 15 frames. If the frame rate is 30 fps, the entire sequence plays for 3 minutes and 16.5 seconds.

If you do the math, you can determine the total number of frames in this sequence is 5,895 frames. If the frame rate were 25 fps, the 5,895 frames would run for three minutes and 55.8 seconds, and the time code would read 00:03:55:20. It is very important when you read a time code that you know the frame rate in order to determine the running time of a video sequence (see Figure 20.4).

Without getting too deep into analogies, frame rates are the resolution of motion pictures. Resolution for images is an amount of picture elements over a specific distance. The frame rate is a number of pictures over a specific time.

There are many time code standards used around the world that use different frame rates. You should know the frame rate of the video system used. PAL and SECAM both use a frame of 25 frames per second, which is very close to the common 24 fps used in film motion pictures.

For technical reasons unknown to us, the NTSC standard of 29.97 was adopted as the frame rate. The SMPTE time code assumes a rate of 30 fps, which is 0.1% difference between the time code measurement and the real playing time. To match the SMPTE time code with real time (talk to Stephen Hawkings about this one), two frame counts are ignored every minute, nine out of ten minutes.

This drop-frame time code compensates for the 0.1% discrepancy between the real playing time and the measured playing time. If the time code does not compensate for the difference, it is not considered time-duration accurate. Most video systems do both the drop-frame and nondrop-frame coding methods. You should always be aware of the source material that you are using, and be consistent with time coding during any editing process.

And you thought getting into multimedia would take you away from the complexities of print technology production!

Digital File Size

To get a good idea of why color quantizing and image compression are such critical parts of digital video, take a look at the previous ex-

ample and see how large the videos can be. A video frame with a resolution of 525 by 486 pixels will contain a total of 255,150 pixels. The bit depth of the pixels will determine the size of the image. If the bit depth is 24 bits, the single frame needs 765,450 bytes of storage space. And that's only for one frame—now multiply the total number of frames by 5,895, and you'll get a grand total of 4.2 gigabytes for a little more than 3 minutes of video. Wow! Each second is a whopping 21.9M! No way can you work at this bit depth. An 8-bit color depth will slice the file's size by one third, but this still creates file sizes beyond the manageable level. Hello data compression!

There are many methods to compress video images—most employ some sort of Fourier or Discrete Cosine Transformation similar to the one used by JPEG file formats. The compression reduces the size of the video data by discarding anywhere from 10 to 40 percent of the data in each frame, depending on the quality level

30 fps
00:03:16:15
3 min, 16.5 secs

25 fps
00:03:55:20
3 min, 55.8 secs

Figure 20.4
The time code and frame rate must be included to determine the running time of a motion sequence.

Figure 20.5a
A still background does not change much in
a video sequence.

Figure 20.5b
Only the areas of a scene that change are
saved when using motion compensation
compression schemes.

desired. However, a greater amount of compression can be achieved if the compression scheme looks at the entire sequence of frames.

In many video scenes, only small amounts of data will change from frame to frame. If the compression only concerns itself with the changing data, the amount of storage space required to save a single frame drops considerably. These are called motion compensation schemes, and they only save data that has changed from frame to frame. A background that does not move only needs to be saved once. Only the elements in the scene that change will need to be saved as those elements change or move. If the frames do not change considerably, you can save tremendous amounts of storage space (see Figures 20.5a-b).

Video Output

As mentioned in Chapter 2, "Tone and Color," video boards provide for display, as well as acquisition, and can program for many kinds of output formats. Many video boards can provide

full red, green, and blue (RGB) in-out synchronization for video images. This capability means that you can freely import video images into your computer, as well as export to video, without special encoding needs. Video boards also may supply an 8-bit alpha channel for overlays and *chroma keying*, which is text and title placement in video.

Out to Video (Layoff)

Getting an image from a digital system to videotape is called *layoff*. There are two types of layoff: *analog layoff* and *direct digital layoff*. You achieve analog layoff by recording the animation from your computer into a video tape recorder (VTR), which is an analog format. Typically, in the layoff procedure, sync problems from the computer and tape deck can result in an unwanted duplication of frames. This problem is especially common with 24-bit images because these images cannot be moved fast enough from workstations to keep up with the videotape's frame rate. To solve this problem, a device called a *frame-controller*

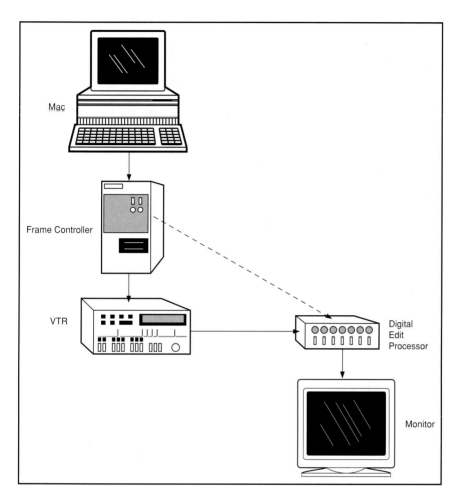

Figure 20.6
A basic setup for video output.

synchronizes the layoff of the image from the computer to the tape. If you plan on using frequent video output, a frame-controller is strongly recommended (see Figure 20.6).

The direct digital layoff directly imports from the digital computer system into the digital edit processor. The advantage of this system is that it maintains a digital-to-digital link. Direct digital layoff involves less loss of image quality because there is no conversion to an analog signal. But the amount of storage required is very high and more expensive than analog tape.

Color Balance

In order to achieve a certain level of color consistency from one system to another, a color chart is often employed to visually match one system to another (see Figure 20.7). The color chart is something that you can create on your own. Any test image should contain not only a stepped grayscale and flat areas of color but also photographic images for comparison. Displaying the standard image on a monitor allows each person to adjust his monitor until all tone and color is represented accurately.

Before you adjust a monitor for color, you should adjust the monitor so that the grayscale displays all tonal steps from light to dark. Next, the grayscale should appear as close to a neutral gray as the monitor will allow. Any color casts will affect the accuracy of all images. After the tone and neutral balance is achieved, any other adjustments should be minor. Unfortunately, adjusting only for tone and cast is usually not enough. The monitor can be very fickle and may not provide all the color you'd like, so fine tuning is always necessary. At the very least, a standard image provides a starting point from which common judgments of color can be made from system to system.

This type of calibration is completely visual and requires no special measurements. Ideally, if spectrophotometer measurements can be made for every display, each color monitor can be adjusted to match more precisely. The time and expense of calibrating each video system with measurements may not justify the increased accuracy.

Gamma

Make sure that the different workstations are all set to the same gamma setting. Programs like Gamma by Knoll software allow adjustments to the monitor's default display. Typically, a setting of 2.2 is preferred for video production, while a setting of 1.8 is typical for print production. See Chapter 2 for more about gamma settings.

Judging color from video systems is no different than any other method of judging color. Consistency is the first consideration. If two companies, Binkus and Bubus, are working on a video project and Binkus is working with a gamma setting of 1.8 and Bubus with a setting of 2.2, the images may not work when viewed together. When the images are viewed on the monitor set at a gamma of 2.2, Binkus' images will look too bright. If the images are viewed on the monitor set at a gamma of 1.8, Bubus' images will look too dark.

One solution is to display the images on a monitor set at 2.0 to split the difference. Another more time-consuming but more effective solution is to correct all the images created on the monitor with a gamma setting of 1.8. Then change the monitor to a setting of 2.2 and correct the image values to match the images on the monitor with a 2.2 gamma setting. The best solution is to have both companies agree on a gamma setting before beginning the project.

During any video production, it is very important that standards are established and followed. Corrections done late in production usually result in lost time and money—if the corrections can be done at all.

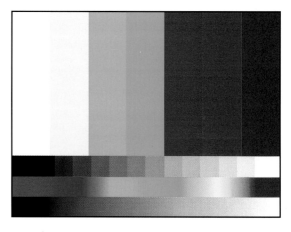

Figure 20.7
A test image is used to provide a standard from which to adjust a monitor.

Final Word

In all color reproductions of digital images, you should always be aware of the conditions and properties of your chosen output. The conditions, demanded by the output which you are using, must be understood and met to achieve the quality level most professionals require. By understanding the properties of your output, you will find it easier to meet the required conditions. Talk to everyone in the loop to make sure that time coding is the same, resolutions match, and color balance is accurate.

Fine Art Reproduction

21

"A work of art must carry in
itself its complete significance
and deliver it to the beholder
even before he can identify the
source or subject."

Henri Matisse—Painter

During the course of this book we have shown you many different images to illustrate production concepts and techniques. We thought it would be nice to show how digital tools are being used by artists. This gallery of images illustrates the different techniques that artists use to explore the craft of digital production. Art means different things to different people, but we hope you'll enjoy the images presented here.

Forest Dream
© Marc Miller 1993 - San Francisco, California

Give Us Bread
© Kent Manske 1994 - Redwood City, California
Visual Artist and Art Educator

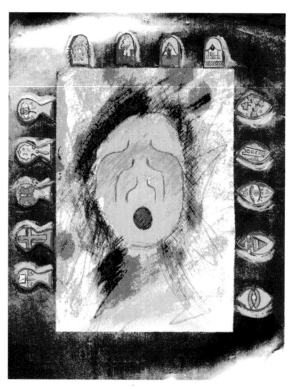

NewScream
© Kent Manske 1994

Scripts
© Kent Manske 1994

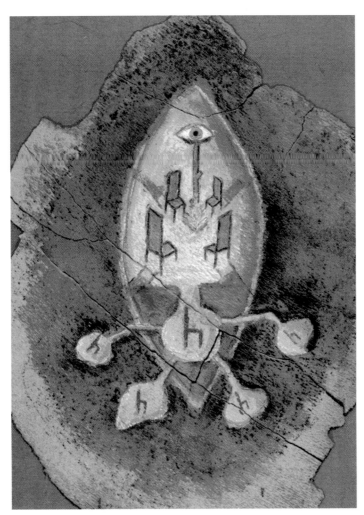

ChairCouncil
© Kent Manske 1994

The Bench
© Tom Donohue 1994 - Philadelphia, Pennsylvania
Photographer and Digital Artist

Fine Art Reproduction

Kushi's Dream
© Hagit Cohen 1994 - San Francisco, California
Digital Artist and Graphic Designer

Real Abuse
© Hagit Cohen 1994

The Forest
© Hagit Cohen 1994

bonoboda
© Jerry Bono 1994 - Minneapolis, Minnesota
illustrator/graphic designer/writer/explorer

Bonoman
© Jerry Bono 1994

Metal War
© Sue Culig 1993 - San Francisco, California
Photographer and Digital Artist

Bodecker Park
© Sue Culig 1993

471

Fine Art Reproduction

Scratch
© John Ritter 1994 - San Francisco, California
Illustrator / Fine Artist

newness
© John Ritter 1994

Light
© John Ritter 1994

Heaven/Hell
© John Ritter 1994

Blue Hawaii
© Ben Barbante 1994
Digital Fine Artist

Pablo Picasso, Painter
© Jeremy Sutton 1994 - San Francisco, Calif.
Digital Painter and Illustrator

Boy's Day Carp
© Corinne Okada 1994 - San Francisco, California
Illustrator / Graphic Designer

Jester
© Jeremy Sutton 1994

Nahaue
Corinne Okada © 1994

Fish Mask
Corinne Okada © 1994

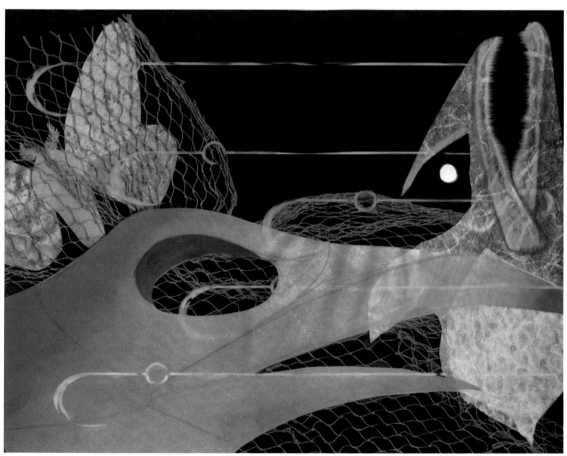

Decay
Corinne Okada © 1994

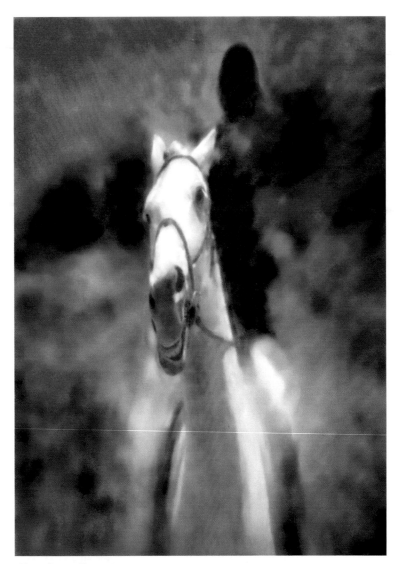

Trojan Horse
© Andrew J. Hathaway 1994 - San Francisco, California
Digital Painter

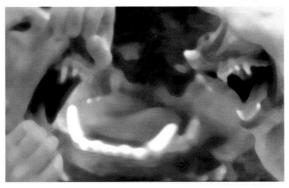

JAWS
© Andrew J. Hathaway 1994

real water
© Marc Miller 1994

Dark Fire
© Marc Miller 1994

Wave Famile
© Marc Miller 1995

Glossary

A/D converter–Generic term for a device that converts analog wave information to binary digital data.

absorption–The ability of an ink to soak into a substrate.

additive colors–Red, green, and blue are the primary additive colors, which when mixed in equal parts, create white or gray. All visible light can be described using various amounts of red, green, and blue light.

alias–An immediate transition from one area of color or tone to another. Describes the edge effect that is possible for various drawing tools.

alpha-channels–Specialized channels of control information for image masking or collaging. Also called mask layers.

analog–Describes a system that records real-world events (visual and audio) using the continuous nature of the original as a basis. Electronic systems, such as video and sound tapes, record analog waves rather than digital binary information.

anamorphic–Unequal scaling in the vertical and horizontal dimensions. Nonproportional scaling.

ANSI–American National Standards Institute is a nongovernmental organization that develops and publishes voluntary standards within the United States.

anti-alias–An averaging or softening of the transition of one color area to another. For jagged lines, anti-aliasing smoothes out the stairstep effect.

application–A generic term used to describe any software program that carries out a specific task.

approval print–A print made for customer viewing to check for proper color, crop, and other special issues relating to a print project. See also proof.

archive–A body of digital information saved for long-term storage and retrieval.

ASCII–Acronym for the American Standard Code for Informational Interchange. Every test and control character has a unique binary number assigned to it.

aspect ratio–The relationship of width information to height information.

banding–A breakup of a smooth blend or vignette into visible blocks or bands of tone or color.

base–The physical support for photographic film and printing plate emulsion typically made of polyester, plastic, acetate, or metal.

baud rate–The measure of speed that digital information can be sent over phone lines. Approximately equal to bits per second.

binary–Digital data system based on 0 and 1.

bin key–Binary code.

bit (or binary digit)–The smallest unit of information available in a binary computer system. A bit is either a 1 or a 0.

bit depth–The measure of the amount of different colors possible in a pixel or display system. Two raised to the number of bit provides the total number of colors possible. 2 to the 4th power is 4-bit color or 16 possible colors.

bitmap–The pixels of an image are assembled in a binary bitmap, or grid, which assigns each pixel a location on the x-y axes and a bit depth of color.

bitmap image–An image described by pixels. Same as raster image.

bits per second (bps)–Measures the speed of the number of bits transferred in a communications system.

black printer–Special additional black used to compensate for the lack of contrast, neutrality, and shadow detail achieved with only cyan, magenta, and yellow printers. Also called key where the letter K is used to designate it.

bleed–Extending an image outside the final trim so that the image goes off the page.

blend–A smooth gradation of tone or color from light to dark, or the smoothing of the demarcation of two neighboring color areas.

blur–The averaging of pixel values.

buffer–A digital storage holding area for temporarily storing digital data until it is ready for use.

byte–A standard unit of digital measurements representing 8 bits of digital data.

C print–A color print, reflective-type subject.

calibration–Adjusting devices so that information is transferred from one system to another in a consistent, predictable, and reliable way.

CCD–Charge Coupled Device, a light-sensitive array of sensors used to sample color data used in scanning devices.

channel–A layer or record of a color image. A 24-bit image has 8 bits of color information in each channel of RGB.

chroma–Hue. Color information in an image.

chrominance–Color of an image or a mixture of hue and saturation.

chroma-key—A video overlay system that allows for special effects and text to be added to video programs.

chrome—A slang term for transparency, a transmissive-type subject.

clipboard—A buffer holding area the Macintosh uses for digital information.

clone—To copy from one source point of pixel values to another area. Cloning also is called pixel copying.

CLUT—Color Look Up Table. Color indexing system used to reference and match specified values of color.

CMYK—Cyan, magenta, yellow, and black—the subtractive secondary colors used in color printing.

coated paper—Smooth and/or glossy paper. Less absorbent than uncoated paper and dot gain is less. Typically more expensive.

color balance—Suggests the overall hue of colors in an image reproduction is acceptable for creating a desired effect or realistic duplication of the original scene.

color casts—An imbalance of color from neutral, "unreal" color appearance.

color correction—Altering the reproduction color of an image.

color curve—A graphic method of color correction using a 45-degree line to gauge change and as a point of reference.

color key—A prepress proofing system manufactured by 3M composed of separate CMYK acetate overlays.

color separation—The breaking up of the visible spectrum of the subtractive colors of cyan, magenta, and yellow into black-and-white film halftone records of the original copy. A black separation is added for extra detail and depth in the darkest areas.

color space—A system used to describe all available colors graphed on a set of axes. RGB, CMYK, and HSV are examples of color spaces.

complementary color—The color that moves (dirties up) a pure color toward gray. Creates the shape in a colored image.

comprehensive drawing—Also called a comp, comprehensive drawing is a close representation or drawing of what a finished job will look like (with all elements to size and exact position) before production begins.

cones—The light sensors clustered near the center of the human retina used to sense chrominance or color values.

contacting—Copying the dot values of one film to another photographically.

continuous tone—An image whose picture elements are not visible and whose tones realistically blend together to create a scene.

contrast—The amount or degree to which tones and colors are separate and distinct from one another. Also the range between the lightest areas and the darkest areas in a reproduction versus an original.

convergence—The focusing of RGB electron signals onto one spot on the surface of a video display screen so that it displays one color.

cool colors—Colors appearing bluish or greenish.

color temperature—Measured in degrees Kelvin and represents the temperature of visible light. 5,000 Kelvin is considered a standard temperature for viewing and evaluating color. Below 5,000 Kelvin tends toward yellow and above 5,000 tends toward blue.

colorimeter—A device used to measure color values.

copy—Items or images to be scanned.

CPU—A central processing unit is the main part of the computer that receives instructions from memory and then executes the instructions.

Cromalin™—A prepress proof made of toner powders representing CMYK and specialty colors that are all laminated into a single sheet.

crop—The area of an image to use in a reproduction.

cropping—Reproducing only the desired portions of a scene and eliminating the surrounding area as needed.

cropping tool—A tool to select and size an area of a digital image.

crop marks—Lines on a comp indicating where the finished page is to be trimmed.

cross curve—Also called crossovers. An original that has two opposing casts in the same scene, such as a magenta cast and a green cast. The color balance is nearly impossible to achieve because as you correct one cast, the other is heightened.

CRT—Cathode-ray tube, which is used to display images on a phosphor coated screen.

CT file format—Continuous tone file such as TIFF, PICT, and Scitex CT.

CT prints—Hard-copy reflective images that are continuous tone photographs.

D/A converter—Digital to analog converter. A device that converts digital data into analog singles. A modem is a D/A converter.

DAT—Digital Audio Tape, which is used for noise-free data storage onto magnetic tape.

DDS—Digital Data Storage. A sequential DAT tape format.

diffuse highlight—The location in an image where dots begin to print and create tone.

densitometer—A device that reads the density of transmissive subjects or the reflective capabilities of reflective-type subjects. Readouts from the densitometer can be in density values or dot percentages.

density—The light-stopping ability of an original subject or film. Density is inversely proportional to the amount of light reflected or transmitted by an image. One photographic f-stop relates to .30 density units.

density range—The gamut or range of tones from the lightest printing tone in a scene to the darkest printing tone in a scene. The range of tones that carry a printing dot. Also the difference in density from the lightest to the darkest portion of an image.

depth of field—The range of focus from the foreground to the background of a scene.

digital—Describes a system based on binary code of base two.

digital proof—An output device that produces a proof of the final image directly from the digital data without creating film or plates.

digital still camera—An image capture device that digitizes a scene as a single frame of digital pixel information.

direct digital layoff—Importing a digital signal directly on an imaging device to a digital video processor.

direct pixel imaging—Outputting one pixel for every pixel in a digital file.

dithering—A randomizing pattern to simulate tones and color by changing the distribution of pixels.

disk array—Combining hard drives to create additional speed and redundancy.

Dmax—The maximum density in an image or material. Black.

Dmin—The minimum density in an image or material. White or clear.

dot gain—An increase in the size of a halftone dot when printed onto paper. The increase in dot size affects the density and therefore the tone and color of a reproduction.

dots per inch (dpi)—The number of halftone dots in an inch. Also used to describe the number of analyzing or exposing elements being used; a device resolution measurement. See epi.

duotone—A full-range black-and-white image combined with a second color of lesser tonal range to create an image of greater tonal depth.

drawing—Creating fine detail using small printing dots.

dye sublimation—The process of printing color images using a thermal dye process in which the amount of heat determines the amount of dye transferred to a carrier sheet.

dynamic effects—Image processing procedures that include sizing, rotating, scaling, flipping, and distortion.

8-bit color—A binary system that assigns 8 bits of information for each pixel in an image, making 256 colors or shades of gray possible.

electro static printer—An output device that uses special paper that can be charged. Toner adheres to charged areas of the paper.

elements per inch (epi)—The number of exposing or analyzing (sampling) elements in one inch. A measurement of device resolution.

EMILY–Specification of a hard drive or a neurotic black cat.

emulsion–The light-sensitive coating on photographic film that creates the photographic image.

endpoint–Relating to the tonal range, the highlight and shadow points set the beginning and ending of the tonal range.

EPS or EPSF–Encapsulated PostScript file, a meta file format used to transfer PostScript information.

equalizing–Distributing all color or tone equally along a density range or at a particular density.

eyedropper–A color sampling or choosing tool.

fiber optics–Thin glass fibers that are used to carry digital data through pulses of light.

file–The name of a grouping of digital data.

file compression–Reducing the amount of space used to store a digital file. See lossy and loss-less types.

file server–A central workstation or hard drive from which people share files through a network.

fill tool–Also known as paintbucket, a tool that replaces selected areas with flat colors, blends, or patterns.

film recorder–An output device that produces digital images in transparency form.

filter–An algorithm that modifies the pixel matrix of an image to create a visual effect.

5000 degrees Kelvin–The recommended color temperature of viewing lights that approximates daylight. A standard designation for fluorescent viewing lamps.

flat–Description of an image that lacks contrast from the highlight to shadow.

flipping–Creating a mirror-image representation of an image.

floating selection–A selected group of pixels that floats above the image until it is deselected and dropped onto the desired position on the image.

focus–The act of adjusting an image to appear as sharply defined as possible.

footprint–The physical area that a machine occupies.

four-color process–The CMYK color system using for printing.

gamma–The slope of the line that represents output value versus input value. Also a description of the contrast of a monitor.

gamut–A range of possibilities, such as the range of colors that a color film can produce.

Gaussian distribution–The bell-shaped curve distribution of pixel value information.

GCR–Gray component removal, replacing the gray components where CMY inks are used in a reproduction with black ink.

gigabyte–One thousand megabytes.

grain–The granular or sand-like appearance in a print or transparency.

gray balance–The balance of cyan, magenta, and yellow ink that will reproduce as a neutral gray.

grayscale–A tonal scale graduated from white to gray to black. Used for calibration and setup of color systems.

grayscale image–A black-and-white image with more than one bit of information in the image. Typically an 8-bit image with 256 levels of tone.

grid–A defined area of vertical and horizontal lines, either visible or mathematic. Specific spots on a grid are identified as x and y coordinates.

half black–The black halftone printer that starts printing at the reproduction's middletone and ends at the shadow point.

half-cast method–Removing half of a color cast from the white areas in a reproduction.

halftone–A reproduced image created with various size dots to create the illusion of tone. The larger the dot, the darker the tone.

halos–Lines of white or black around lines of detail or between contrasting areas. Halos should be felt, not seen.

hard disk–The generic designation of a disk used to store large amounts of digital data.

HDTV–High definition television. A proposed television standard based on digital data transmission. Increases the total amount of pixels transmitted with an image aspect ratio of standard television from 12: to 16:9.

high key–An original subject composed of very bright subject matter. Also an original subject that is improperly exposed so that the color is abnormally weak and washed out.

highlight point–The density in an original subject where the smallest printing dot of cyan, magenta, or yellow starts to print.

histogram–The distribution of pixel value information shown visually in a special type of chart or graph.

HSB–Hue, saturation, and brightness.

HSL–Hue, saturation, and lightness.

HSV–The hue, saturation, and value color space.

hue–The color of something. Hues can be specified by wavelengths of light or CIE coordinates.

image aspect ratio–The horizontal number of pixels versus vertical pixels of an image.

image processing programs–Applications specifically used to manipulate image data, as opposed to image creation programs, which specialize in creating images from scratch.

imagesetter–An output device that produces separation halftones and text on film or paper.

indexed color–A color system using information from a file as a pointer to a look up table of values for specifying color. See CLUT.

interlaced–Describes the display process of raster image on television. Every other line of pixels is redrawn on each pass of digital information.

internegative–Negative film created from an original positive transparency used to create prints.

interpolate–Using the interpolation method of resampling. Often misused to describe all upsampling.

interpolation–A resampling method used to create more pixel information by averaging the existing pixel information.

ink jet–A printing device which sprays inks onto substrates.

jaggies–Digital images that appear staircased or jagged rather than smooth. Often the result of low resolution or a lack of digital information.

JPEG–Joint Photographers Experts Group. A lossy compression-decompression standard for digital files.

juke box–A device that holds multiple hard disks or optical disks and physically moves disks to and from a single hard drive.

kilobyte–One thousand bytes.

landscape–Horizontal orientation of an image, as opposed to portrait orientation, which is vertical.

lasso–A selection tool that allows a free and arbitrary selection of pixels.

layoff–The transferring of digital data to video format.

LED–Light-emitting diode, an exposing element.

lines per inch (lpi)–Refers to the number of lines of halftone dots in an inch. Used as a halftone screen designation such as 150 lpi, which is 22,500 (150 squared) halftone dots per inch (dpi).

local area network (LAN)–Description of computers connected through telecommunication lines over a short distance.

loss-less–Nondestructive file compression. Keeps all original pixel information regardless of how many times it compresses and decompresses the data.

lossy–Destructive file compression. Discards file information to achieve file size storage.

LZW compression–Method of loss-less compression used with various file formats. Developed by Lempel, Zev, and Welch.

magnification–Any increase in physical size of an original during reproduction.

marquee–A tool for creating rectangular selections of pixels to be altered or cropped.

mask–A mask designates an area that is to be changed or protected from change.

Matchprint™–A prepress proofing system by 3M that is made of laminated pigments.

megabytes–One thousand kilobytes.

meta file–A file format that contains bitmap image information and one or both vectors. See EPS.

magnetic–Basis of floppy and hard disk storage technology. It records analog or digital signals onto specially prepared iron oxide material.

magneto optic–Similar to a magnetic disk, except a laser uses aluminum material rather than iron oxide to store digital data (the laser heats the aluminum material).

MIL–One thousandth (1/1000) of an inch. Used to describe paper or film thickness.

middletone–The 50 percent dot printing area. Also called midtone.

moiré–A visible, undesirable dot pattern made from incompatible screen angles or a pattern in the original copy.

modem–Short for modulator-demodulator. Device to send digital signals over analog telephone lines.

monochrome–An image composed of a single color. Most images are black-and-white, although any color can be substituted for black. A one-bit image.

montage–To combine separate images into one image, also called a composite image.

motion blur filters–Filters used to create a sense of movement.

Newton rings–An undesirable interference pattern caused when two smooth surfaces do not meet exactly. Typically found when mounting images to drum scanners.

neutral–An area of no color bias: white, gray, or black.

neutralizing–Changing the existing color balance to a neutral, noncasted balance.

NED–Network Emitting Diode.

node–A point of connection in a network.

noise–Pixels with randomly distributed color values.

opacity–The degree of apparent density, or the amount of background a graphic element shows through itself.

PAL–Phase alternation line. The European video standard.

palette–A selection of colors available in a color system.

Pantone Matching System (PMS)–A color identification and matching system.

pastel–Light colors that contain printing dots in the 5 percent to 15 percent range.

photo-realism–Images that resemble actual photographs.

photomultiplier–A light-sensing, photosensitive device that transforms light intensity to a stream of electrons. The eyes of a color drum scanner.

PICT–The standard Apple file format.

pixel–A word derived from picture element. A discrete unit, having a location and a value.

pixel aspect ratio–The horizontal versus vertical size of a pixel. Square pixels have an aspect ratio of one.

pixelization–A condition of too-low resolution that allows individual picture elements to become visible.

pixels per inch (ppi)–The number of pixels that occupy one inch. A measure of a file's resolution.

plug-in filter–A third-party vendor-developed software that provides an extra function not available in the standard software application.

portrait–A vertical image orientation, as opposed to landscape.

posterize–Limiting the gamut of color values to create an intensified visual result.

PostScript–A page description language by Adobe Systems, Inc., that describes text and graphic elements. Files made with PostScript can be used with any PostScript-compatible output device, regardless of resolution.

print server–A dedicated computer in a network responsible for queuing and sending printer output.

process inks–Cyan, magenta, yellow, and black are process inks or subtractive colors. When they are combined on the printing press, they make a complete printing color gamut or range of colors.

proof–A sample representing the finished result.

peripheral–Any device in addition to the main computer. A printer is a peripheral.

pitch–The distance a mechanical device can move.

pica–Unit of measurement used in topography. One pica equals 12 points.

prepress–Anything having to do with the preparation of printing images.

press proof–A printed sample of how a project will look when printed with similar, if not identical, printing presses and conditions.

proportionality–The horizontal and vertical ratio of an original remains the same, regardless of any scaling. See anamorphic.

quad tone–An image in which a monochrome image is printed with four different density inks to create a greater tonal effect.

quarter tone–The 25 percent dot printing area, a bright area of the reproduction.

QuickDraw–A set of drawing routines for the Macintosh trademarked by Apple.

RAID–Redundant Arrays of Inexpensive, or Independent, Disks. A storage device that uses several hard drives working together to provide increased performance.

RAM–Random access memory.

raster lines–Lines of pixel data used to image bitmap and object data.

RAW–An image of raw pixel data not corresponding to any particular file format type.

real time–A term used to indicate little or no waiting for computer processing to occur.

record–To place information on a storage medium, also the actual storage medium.

register–The exact positioning of a color on top of other colors.

register marks–Marks on a separation that are in the same spot for each of the four colors. When the negatives are assembled, the register marks are positioned on top of each other to ensure accurate positioning of colors.

render–The process of interpreting digital data image information into bitmap image information.

replication–A resampling method used to create more pixel information by duplicating existing pixel information. Also called nearest neighbor.

reproduction–A second generation image based on an original.

resampling–Changing the resolution of an image by adding or discarding pixels. Also known as "res-ing."

rescreen–To reseparate a subject that already has been separated as a halftone.

resing-up (or down)–See resampling.

resolution–The number of discrete elements per unit of measure that make up an image, or the number of imaging or sampling units used in a device.

resolution independent–Describes images, such as vectors, that are not dependent on resolution, so they do not lose edge quality with enlargement. Being resolution independent is desirable for text. Bitmapped images are not resolution independent.

retouching–Techniques that attempt to alter or improve an image without detection.

right reading–The correct orientation of an image as it is to be reproduced.

RISC–Reduced Instruction Set Computing. Computer system with a special microprocessor that functions with fewer instructions and therefore is faster.

RIFF–Raster image file format used by ColorStudio.

RIP–Raster image processing, a device that breaks an image into lines of pixel data. See raster lines.

RLE–Run-length encoding, a type of file compression.

rods–The plentiful tonal light receptors in the human retina that sense value.

rosette–A circular pattern of halftone dots created when the process colors are printed at proper angles and in register—creating a visually pleasing result.

rotating—Turning an image from its original axis.

rubber stamp—The name of a cloning tool. See clone.

sampling—Making a copy of something. Another word for scanning.

sampling rate—The number of samples made in a specified area, such as 200 pixels per inch.

saturation—The strength of a color, or how far a color is from gray. The greater the saturation of a color, the further it is from gray.

scaling—Changing the size of images or graphics.

scan line—The basic unit of sampling used by a color scanner and created by a sampling spot on a rotating drum.

scanner—A device that samples analog images and converts them into digital form.

screen—To describe a continuous tone image using halftone dots.

screen angle—The direction of the lines of dots for each of the process colors. Proper screen angles place the halftone dots next to each other on the printed page to make an invisible rosette pattern and the tone looks continuous to the eye.

SCSI—Small Computer System Interface. An industry standard for connecting peripheral devices to a computer. Pronounced "scuzzy."

selection—An item, location, or group of pixels isolated for manipulation.

shade—A pure color mixed with black.

shadow—The dark areas of an image.

shadow point—The area of greatest density in an original where the 95 percent printing dot is set.

sharpen—To enhance the edge contrast in an image to make the scene appear sharper, more in focus.

skewing—Distorting an image as if it were being italicized.

sliders—Controls that increase or decrease an effect by moving a control bar right to left or up and down.

special colors—Colors that are critical to the customer in a reproduction, such as product colors.

specular highlight—An area of a reproduction that carries no dots, being paper white. These areas include reflections on glass, water, and metal that are extremely bright and carry no color.

spot color—A single ink color applied to a specific area, such as a product color.

spotting—Retouching a scanned image to eliminate tiny white spots or dust caused from a dirty original.

stairstepping—See jaggies.

stat—A low-quality reproduction of an image on a comprehensive drawing that represents an image's position, cropping, and sizes.

subtractive secondary colors–CMY (cyan, magenta, and yellow) when added together, subtract all light and make black. The total absence of CMY creates white.

substrate–Material on which images are reproduced.

super cell–A large halftone cell built from a matrix of halftone cells.

surround color–The color that surrounds a featured color and has an effect on how the featured color is perceived.

terabyte–1024 gigabytes.

TGA–TARGA file format.

three-quarter tone–The 75 percent printing dot area.

threshold–A defined level to determine whether a pixel will be represented as black or white.

TIFF–Tagged image file format, the most common image file format used on many platforms.

tonal range–The range of printed densities in an original or a reproduction.

tone–Any color or neutral that is denser than specular white. Tone creates the shape in an image.

tone reproduction–The reproduction of all the tonal steps from an original that also matches the contrast or dimensionality of the original.

toolbox–The area on the screen in which the working tools are assembled for easy access.

transmissive subjects–Subjects that allow light to pass through them—transparencies. Also called transmission copy.

transparency–A photographic transmissive color subject in various format sizes such as 35mm and 4" × 5".

trap–Making two neighboring colored areas overlap into each other to prevent white gaps caused by slipping and misregistration during printing.

trichromatic color–Color modules that use three color modules to specify color. All trichromatic color is based on RGB.

tri tone–Using three colors of different density with a monochrome image to increase tonal range.

tweening–Creating intermediate steps between objects, with the steps metamorphosing from one to the other.

24-bit color–A binary system that assigns 8 bits of information for red, green, and blue in an image, making more than 16.7 million color possibilities.

UCR–Undercolor removal; subtracting CMY under black areas and replacing the undercolor with additional black as a means of saving ink on long press runs.

uncoated paper–Paper without a glossy finish. Absorbs more ink than colored papers and has a higher dot gain.

undo–A function that takes you back one step or command, erasing the previous command.

unsharp masking (USM)–The circuitry in a scanning device or software that enhances the sharpness of a screened reproduction.

upsampling–Increasing the number of pixels in a file.

value–The degree of lightness or darkness.

vaporware–Hardware and software that is still on the drawing board and in development, but not available. Generally software that is promised by a manufacturer but never released.

video tape recorder (VTR)–A device that samples visual data on videotape for playback to a video display.

vignetting tone method–Locating highlight density by looking for tone coming off a specular area.

vignetting tones–Densities that go from light to dark.

virtual memory–Hard disk memory space allocated for an image being worked on in order to supplement a computer's RAM.

visual spectrum–The range of visual light from 400 to 700 nanometers of light wavelength.

warm colors–Colors that are on the red-orange side.

workstations–Computers set up primarily to perform a group of specified functions with added speed and efficiency.

WORM–Write-once, read many. A CD-ROM.

zoom–To change the size of the viewing area to examine a larger or smaller area in greater detail.

Appendix

Measurement Reference

To determine the file size of digital image files without compression, use the following steps:

1. TOTAL NUMBER OF PIXELS ACROSS **(multiplied by)** TOTAL NUMBER OF PIXELS DOWN **equals** *TOTAL NUMBER OF PIXELS IN AN IMAGE*

2. TOTAL BITS USED IN AN IMAGE **(divided by)** EIGHT **equals** *NUMBER OF BYTES PER PIXEL*
(Note: The total number of bits in an image is determined by adding the number of bits in each channel being saved. In the common 24 bit RGB system each channel is 8 bit. In a 36 bit RGB system each channel is 12 bit.)

3. Line #1 **(times)** Line #2 = *TOTAL NUMBER OF BYTES IN THE DIGITAL FILE*

4. Line #3 **(divided by)** 1024 **equals** the NUMBER OF KILOBYTES

5. Line #4 **(divided by)** 1024 **equals** the NUMBER OF MEGABYTES

For example: A 24bit RGB image with one mask channel, 1200 by 800 pixels works out as follows:

1200 x 800 = **960,000 pixels** x [(24bits + 8 bits) ÷ 8] = 960,000 x **4** = **3,840,000 bytes.**

3,840,000 bytes ÷ 1024 = **3,750 KB** (kilobytes) ÷ 1024 = **3.66 MB** (megabytes)

The same image as CMYK with one mask channel produces the following file size:

1200 x 800 = **960,000 pixels** x [(32bits + 8 bits) ÷ 8] = 960,000 x **5** = **4,800,000 bytes.**

4,800,000 bytes ÷ 1024 = **4,687.5 KB** (kilobytes) ÷ 1024 = **4.58 MB** (megabytes)

Many image systems are based on millimeters. Pixels per millimeter (ppmm) is commonly stated as "RES. . . and the number", as in "RES twelve". To convert from inches to millimeters multiply by 25.4, and to convert from millimeters to inches divide by 25.4.

72 ppi = RES 2.83   300 ppi = RES 11.81

RES 1	25.4	ppi	RES 15	381	ppi
RES 2	50.8	ppi	RES 16	406.4	ppi
RES 3	76.2	ppi	RES 17	431.8	ppi
RES 4	101.6	ppi	RES 18	457.2	ppi
RES 5	127	ppi	RES 19	482.6	ppi
RES 6	152.4	ppi	RES 20	508	ppi
RES 7	177.8	ppi	RES 21	533.4	ppi
RES 8	203.2	ppi	RES 22	558.8	ppi
RES 9	228.6	ppi	RES 23	584.2	ppi
RES 10	254	ppi	RES 24	609.6	ppi
RES 11	279.4	ppi	RES 25	635	ppi
RES 12	304.8	ppi	RES 26	660.4	ppi
RES 13	330.2	ppi	RES 50	1270	ppi
RES 14	355.6	ppi	RES 100	2450	ppi

72 points	**= 1 inch**	**= 25.4 millimeters**	
0.25 pt.	.0035 inches	.08 mm	
0.50 pt.	.007 inches	.18 mm	
0.75 pt.	.011 inches	.26 mm	
1.00 pt.	.014 inches	.35 mm	
1.25 pt.	.017 inches	.44 mm	
1.50 pt.	.020 inches	.53 mm	
2 pt.	.028 inches	.70 mm	
3 pt.	.042 inches	1.06 mm	
4 pt.	.055 inches	1.41 mm	
5 pt.	.070 inches	1.76 mm	
6 pt.	.083 inches	2.11 mm	
7 pt.	.097 inches	2.47 mm	
8 pt.	.111 inches	2.82 mm	
9 pt.	.125 inches	3.175 mm	
10 pt.	.138 inches	3.53 mm	
12 pt.	.166 inches	4.23 mm	
14 pt.	.194 inches	4.94 mm	
16 pt.	.222 inches	5.64 mm	
18 pt.	.250 inches	6.35 mm	
20 pt.	.278 inches	7.05 mm	
22 pt.	.305 inches	7.76 mm	
24 pt.	.333 inches	8.47 mm	
30 pt.	.417 inches	10.58 mm	
36 pt.	.500 inches	12.70 mm	

Decimal Equivalents of Fractions

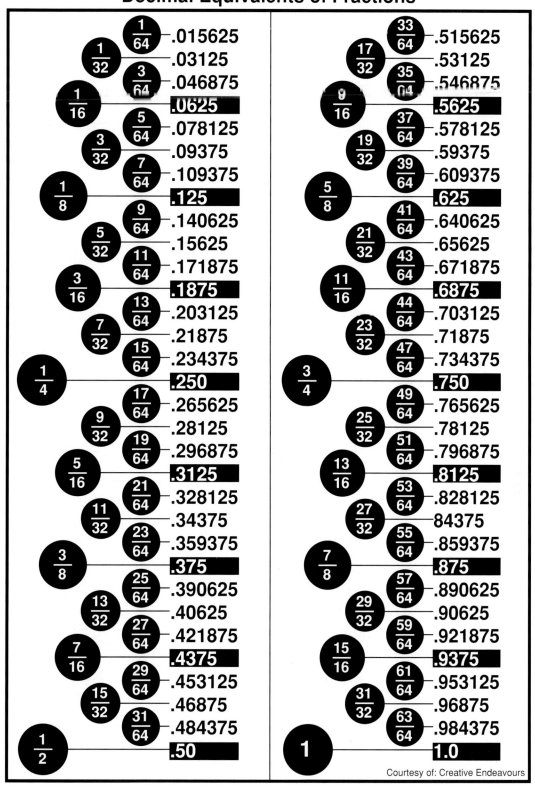

Fraction	Decimal		Fraction	Decimal
1/64	.015625		33/64	.515625
1/32	.03125		17/32	.53125
3/64	.046875		35/64	.546875
1/16	.0625		9/16	.5625
5/64	.078125		37/64	.578125
3/32	.09375		19/32	.59375
7/64	.109375		39/64	.609375
1/8	.125		5/8	.625
9/64	.140625		41/64	.640625
5/32	.15625		21/32	.65625
11/64	.171875		43/64	.671875
3/16	.1875		11/16	.6875
13/64	.203125		44/64	.703125
7/32	.21875		23/32	.71875
15/64	.234375		47/64	.734375
1/4	.250		3/4	.750
17/64	.265625		49/64	.765625
9/32	.28125		25/32	.78125
19/64	.296875		51/64	.796875
5/16	.3125		13/16	.8125
21/64	.328125		53/64	.828125
11/32	.34375		27/32	84375
23/64	.359375		55/64	.859375
3/8	.375		7/8	.875
25/64	.390625		57/64	.890625
13/32	.40625		29/32	.90625
27/64	.421875		59/64	.921875
7/16	.4375		15/16	.9375
29/64	.453125		61/64	.953125
15/32	.46875		31/32	.96875
31/64	.484375		63/64	.984375
1/2	.50		1	1.0

Index